Soli Deo Gloria

Soli Deo Gloria

A Daily Walk Through Romans

MYRON S. AUGSBURGER

Herald Press

Scottdale, Pennsylvania
Waterloo, Ontario

Library of Congress Cataloging-in-Publication Data
Augsburger, Myron S.
  Soli Deo gloria : a daily walk through Romans / Myron S. Augsburger.
    p. cm.
  ISBN 0-8361-9293-1 (hardcover : alk. paper) — ISBN 0-8361-9289-3 (pbk. : alk. paper)
  1. Bible. N.T. Romans—Devotional literature. 2. Devotional calendars—Mennonites. I. Title.
  BS2665.54.A84 2004
  227'.1077—dc22

                          2004017538

SOLI DEO GLORIA
Copyright © 2004 by Herald Press, Scottdale, Pa. 15683
            Published simultaneously in Canada by Herald Press,
            Waterloo, Ont. N2L 6H7. All rights reserved
Library of Congress Control Number: 2004017538
International Standard Book Number: 0-8361-9289-3 (paperback)
                          0-8361-9293-1 (hardback)
Printed in the United States of America
Cover and book design by Sans Serif, Inc.
Cover art by Esther Augsburger

10 09 08 07 06 05 04 10 9 8 7 6 5 4 3 2 1

To order or request information, please call
1-800-759-4447 (individuals); 1-800-245-7894 (trade).
Website: www.heraldpress.com

To
Paul and Esther Kniss,
veteran missionaries of over fifty years
in contextualized partnership
with compassion and grace
under Mennonite Missions
in India and Trinidad

Preface

It dawned upon me one day in my personal devotions that the book of Romans has only a few more verses than there are days in the calendar year. Consequently, I began writing a page each day in devotional journaling. In reading Romans as the story of the gospel of God, one can soon discover the beauty of Paul's conversation about the gospel in the context in which he worked.

The story is rooted in history, the account of how God met the children of Abraham in the past, the full expression in the death and resurrection of Christ. The story expresses the way God has extended this word to reach out to all peoples and the meaning of this gospel in our lives. The presentation of the gospel communicates beyond the ethnic community. It is the amplification of a theology of freedom in Christ as presented also in the Galatians epistle.

The epistle has overlapping stories and general themes such as salvation in chapters 1–3, justification in chapters 4–5, sanctification in chapters 6–8, reconciliation in chapters 9–11, consecration in chapters 12–15, and salutations in chapter 16.

This devotional began from journaling in 1987, a momentous year when Esther and I lived in Washington, DC. I was pastoring a Capitol Hill church and also commuted weekly to Eastern Mennonite University in Viriginia, teaching a seminary course on Romans. But these meditations draw from many life experiences: from my family of origin in Ohio, my father's death during an evangelistic crusade, leadership at Eastern Mennonite University and in Christian higher education, and preaching and teaching missions in many countries around the world.

Many thanks go to my wife, Esther. She has made a very important contribution in the writing and editing of the manuscript.

—Myron S. Augsburger

Our Calling

Paul, a servant of Jesus Christ, called to be an apostle, set apart for the gospel of God. Romans 1:1

Called by God, a marvelous beginning for the new year! Each of us should recognize this calling from God. We are called first to himself and then to his service. Relationship and service are to be held together. Who we are and what we are cannot be separated. To be a servant of Christ, to be a sent one, to be set apart for God's gospel—each express one facet of belonging to the new order which God is creating. There is no greater purpose than the glory of God, no greater service than that which glorifies him.

God's calling for us as believers is universal as to our character, but it is individual in relation to our service. All of us alike are called to respond to God's grace, but each of us individually is gifted to serve in a particular way to the glory of God. The variety of gifts in the "body of Christ" constitute the rich fellowship of the community he is creating.

We need to recognize that discipleship of Christ is our primary vocation. We often use the term *vocation* in a lesser sense to mean occupation. Actually, we have one vocation: that of being his disciples, of walking with him daily. This awareness will give to each day a special sense of meaning, of purpose, and of long-range perspective.

Dr. Ida Scudder was a child of missionary parents in India. At age five she returned to the States. At twenty she visited India, fully determined that she would never work there. But after being exposed to the need there, she returned to America for study, then went back to India as a medical doctor and spent the rest of her ninety years in mission. She developed the outstanding hospital and medical college at Velore, in South India, and served the people of the area with excellence and compassion. And why? It was the calling of God that led and sustained her.

Father God, on this first day of pilgrimage in Romans,
Let my first awareness be my calling in Christ;
Let my greatest joy be in serving my Lord,
And my greatest mission be living in the good news,
Set apart for God's gospel. Amen

January 2

God's Gospel

[The gospel] he promised beforehand through his prophets in the holy scriptures. Romans 1:2

A promise is a PROMISE! Here is a promissory note, good over against the date of its fulfillment. But before that fulfillment, it is as good as the word of the one making the promise. Since the word of grace is God's promise, it is as good and as timeless as God himself. God is as good as his Word; he will always perform what he says.

God's word of grace is not an afterthought. We were in his plan, his mind, his love, and in his purpose for history. Paul speaks here of "the gospel of God, which he promised beforehand through his prophets in the holy scriptures." We are a part of God's history, the actions of God in redemption. Christ wasn't just dropped in "out of the blue." God prepared humanity for his coming. The promise came through his own disclosure in history.

We can rest in his promises (KJV): "Him that cometh to me, I will in no wise cast out." "As many as received him to them gave he the power to become the children of God." "If we confess our sins he is faithful and just to forgive us our sins and to cleanse us from all unrighteousness." "And the peace of God that passes all understanding shall keep your hearts and minds through Christ Jesus." We can claim these promises and many more, such as Psalm 34, each day. One's faith in this is an anchor in life.

By his promises God has bound us to himself in his grace. Whatever the future may hold, this year and every year, for the child of God, our greatest security is the assurance that God will be in it with us.

Years ago, Rowland Hill was a great British preacher. At the age of eighty-four, following the service late one evening, walking among the pews he was heard saying:

> *When I am to die, receive me I'll cry,*
> *For Jesus has loved me, I cannot tell why;*
> *But this I do find, we two are so joined,*
> *He'll not be in heaven, and leave me behind.*

The Gospel of God's Son

The gospel concerning his Son, who was descended from David according to the flesh. Romans 1:3

The good news of the gospel means that we can speak of God in personal terms. Jesus spoke of him as Father and invited us to do the same. These are words by which God ties the human family to himself. As Jesus taught us, so we pray, "Our Father in heaven, hallowed be thy name." We do not speak of God in abstract terms as the "Universal" or the "principle of life" or "the ground of our being." God is our Father and has made himself known to us in his Son.

To hold together the awareness of Jesus as God's Son and recognize his human nature as well, is one of the most outstanding affirmations in history. That God could become human, be incarnate, means that humanness can be made sacred, can be sanctified. This means that humanness and sinfulness are not synonymous. Sinfulness is a perversion of the truly human. It is secularism which is anti-God, which claims falsely that the secular is everything; a position Bishop Pike described as "there-ain't-any-more-ism." But this gospel says that there is more, that the sacred completes the secular.

Salvation includes a re-creating of the truly human, a correcting of the perversion, a re-identification with God from whom humanity has broken away by sin. This new life, announced in God's gospel, is a new belonging as members of the "household of faith."

This Son of God did not suddenly spring onto the human stage, resplendent in dazzling glory, forcing everyone to say, "Wow, this is God's Son!" Rather, he came after years of preparation in which the prophetic word announced that the Messiah would come as David's descendant. And this Son, coming in "human nature," was God-incognito. This disclosure preserves the authenticity of faith. People only see God in Christ when they want to see him. God doesn't dazzle us, but he gives evidence for the thinking mind. Faith is not a blind wish; it is response in clear thinking.

The great preacher Henry Ward Beecher entered the pulpit at Plymouth Church and found a note written to him with one word, "Fool." Addressing the congregation he said, "I have occasionally received a letter from someone who failed to sign his name, but this is the first time that I have received a note with no letter, just the person's name!" The gospel of Christ does seem foolish to the unbeliever.

Resurrection Proof

And was declared to be Son of God with power according to the spirit of holiness by resurrection from the dead, Jesus Christ our Lord. Romans 1:4

That he is risen, that he is Lord, is the heart of the gospel! Jesus is the Christ, our Messiah, the Redeemer, sent by God, the eternal Word. The earliest creed of the Christian church was simply, "Jesus is Lord!" The confession of his disciples, even in the face of emperor worship in the Roman world, which declared that Caesar is lord, in contrast and at the risk of their lives, declared "Jesus is Lord!"

That Christ is the Son of God is not an affirmation based on philosophical conclusions, nor even on stories of his miraculous birth (as true as they are), but the evidence of his deity is his resurrection from the dead. Only God can raise the dead! The fact of his resurrection is God's guarantee that Jesus was who he claimed to be, the one who came from the Father. He is no imposter. God certified his claims by resurrection.

Paul's trinitarian theology is expressed here by his reference to the Spirit of holiness, God's presence acting in the world. The Holy Spirit is God's other name, God's other radiance. An authentic faith acknowledges God as Father, as Redeemer expressed in his Son and by the presence of the Holy Spirit "whom God has given to those who obey him" (Acts 5:32). We do not mean three Gods, but the three-ness of One God, the community of love expressed as Father, Son, and Spirit.

To live in a world where Jesus Christ is risen means that he is Lord, he is our contemporary, he is accessible, and he is inescapable. As E. Stanley Jones has said, "I don't have religion, I have him." And Lesslie Newbigin has said, "Resurrection fits no other worldview." We do not simply have immortal souls that will live on; we will live on as persons of history, sharing life with God. Jesus said, "[God] He is not the God of the dead, but of the living." "Many will come from the east and the west and eat with Abraham, and Isaac and Jacob in the kingdom of heaven."

*Thank you, Father, for sharing yourself
and your life with me.
I commit myself to walk with you in my daily life,
my service, and my love. Amen*

For the Sake of His Name

Through whom we have received grace and apostleship to bring about the obedience of faith among all the Gentiles for the sake of his name. Romans 1:5

Someone has said, "All is of grace and grace is for all." Grace is God's graciousness. It is his gracious involvement of himself in our lives. It is the first aspect of reconciliation with God. He takes the initiative, he moves into our lives.

This grace is expressed in the Son. He calls us to be his, to be disciples, to walk with him. And in this relationship we experience both forgiving grace and transforming grace. In transformation we are made new people in character and in calling. This calling for Paul was to an apostleship, being sent to the nations as an agent of reconciliation.

The gospel is "for obedience to the faith among all nations for his name." God's kingdom is transnational, transcultural, transracial, trans-everything! How do we relate to people other than ourselves— our black neighbors, our white co-workers, Latinos, Muslims, and those of differing expressions of faith? Our common ground is not common ethnicity, nationality, race, or class, but rather the obedience of faith as a new community.

The conclusion of this verse adds, "for his name." There are many religions in the world reaching groping hands toward God, but only the Christian message moves beyond religion to speak of a God who has reached his hand to us. Jesus has come as the "light of the knowledge of the glory of God in the face of Jesus Christ" (2 Cor. 4:6).

G. K. Chesterton said, "It is not that Christianity has been tried and found wanting; but Christianity has been found difficult and not tried."

> *Father God:*
> *Help me to seek you in longing,*
> *and long for You in seeking.*
> *Help me to find you in loving*
> *and love You in finding.*
> *Help me to worship you in joy*
> *and enjoy you in worship! Amen*

Called to Belong

Including yourselves who are called to belong to Jesus Christ. Romans 1:6

Each of us has, above all else, the calling to be in Christ, to belong to him. This is the essential nature of being a disciple. It is not just a matter of being religious, it is belonging to Jesus. But what does it mean to belong to another?

For fifty-three years Esther and I have shared the covenant of marriage. We belong to each other in a covenant of love and freedom. To belong means that I have a common identification with Esther; above all other relationships I belong first to her. I am accountable to her. I am responsible to live in faithfulness to her. At the deepest level it means that here I am loved and trusted, accepted, affirmed, and supported. In turn, I love and live in support, in affirmation, and encouragement.

From this human experience I can project something of what it means to belong to Christ. First, we have a primary identification with him; we have entered a covenant with Christ, which we demonstrate each day of life. Second, it means that we are accountable to him, to live and serve in a manner that honors him. Above all this means that we live in the security of his love, secure in the fact that he owns us, accepts us, and supports us.

Yieldedness is a mark of faith, for we entrust ourselves to him rather than to live by our own self-determination. To belong to another, to God, is to surrender one's self-orientation and to become God-oriented. We go about our work in a covenant partnership with God. As we enjoy our friendship with others, we can enjoy, with the deeper sense of covenant, our relationship with God. Daily decisions are made in dialogue with God.

An old mountaineer once asked Jedediah Johnson of the frontier, "You've come far, pilgrim; was it worth the trouble?" He replied, "What trouble?"

Father, help me to walk today in awareness
that I belong to you.
Make all that I do to be a sacrament of praise,
an expression of the covenant we share.
Remind me that you have called me "in Christ"
to actualize this covenant of belonging. Amen

Called to Be Saints

To all God's beloved in Rome, who are called to be saints: Grace to you and peace from God our Father and the Lord Jesus Christ. Romans 1:7

Salvation is not just being saved *from sin* but it is being saved *to a new life*. We have been obsessed with our guilt, which limits us from seeing the joyous freedom of the new life. We who believe are disciples of Jesus Christ, living in covenant with God.

To the believers living in Rome, Paul emphasizes that their real calling is being saints, persons who belong wholly to God. This is what makes one a saint, not perfection, but belonging to him. And the word "saints," as Paul uses it, is usually in the plural. We are a people who together belong to God.

I recall a day I spent with my eighty-nine-year-old parents, preparing lunch and praying with them, listening to Dad tell, from his keen memory, stories of his boyhood. He talked about his maternal grandparents, the death of his mother when he was a little lad, and the death by tuberculosis of ten others of his mother's eleven siblings. He wept as he thanked God for his own good life and for his family, who were in God's service. God's grace puts meaning into brokenness, healing into pain, and purpose into life that transforms us.

The question is not simply Who am I? It is also *Whose* am I? Do I belong just to myself or to the family of God? Do I not belong also to the congregation where I worship, to the society in which I share, to my nation, and even to the world? Christian faith is personal, but it is never private.

Paul's greeting to this family of God is this: "Grace to you and peace from God our Father and the Lord Jesus Christ." Grace comes first, peace follows. Grace is not an "it," but a spirit of gracious relationship with Christ and with the family of God. Annie Johnson Flint wrote:

> *How thou canst love me and be the God thou art,*
> *Is darkness to my intellect but sunshine to my heart.*

January 8

Letting One's Faith Be Known

First, I thank my God through Jesus Christ for you all, because your faith is proclaimed throughout the world. Romans 1:8

Paul's message in our text is clear, a life-changing faith! The news of a community of Christ's disciples in Rome spread across the Roman world, a witness to the victory of Christ and the power of the gospel, the building of a church in the very presence of Caesar, challenging his claims to divinity, confronting social secularism and Rome's anti-Christ stance. In witness for Christ, the Holy Spirit led the church to move into cities as the centers of power, the nerve centers of the sociopolitical order.

One morning while riding on the train from DC to Philadelphia for a board meeting of the Presbyterian Ministers' Fund, just north of Baltimore, we slowed to a snail's pace as we passed the wreckage of a very serious train accident of the preceding week; a head-on collision at over 100 miles an hour killed fifteen persons and wounded 150. I looked at the people in the car; they had continued their reading, not even noting the signs of the accident. Yesterday passes and in a few days we forget.

Paul's letter and his sense of mission calls us to care for people in the inner city. In the midst of the many varieties of ethnic groups, cultures, races, rapid changes, alienation, and loneliness, they need the message of Christ. This calls us to establish identity with them. To live among them is to say, "We are here because we care." As a pastor I helped lead an urban church seminar each January for which rural and suburban students came to the city for two weeks. More important than the lectures was our sharing on-site exposure to some twenty inner-city programs. When many city churches fled to the suburbs, Gibson Winter in 1961 published *The Suburban Captivity of the Church*. The situation has remained much the same.

A news reporter interviewing Mother Teresa at her work in the large, densely populated city of Calcutta commented to her, "I wouldn't do this for a million dollars." Mother Teresa responded, "Neither would I."

Master, help us to recognize that mission is around us,
that mission is not going somewhere as much as primarily
being here as a presence for Christ. Amen

Specific in Prayer

For God, whom I serve with my spirit by announcing the gospel of his Son, is my witness that without ceasing I remember you always in my prayers. Romans 1:9

Paul is regular in his prayers for the believers in Rome, and here he invokes the witness of God! This is to say, his covenant with God is the ground on which he affirms his covenant with them. Prayer is opening our lives to the will of God. To intercede for others helps engage them in this openness.

Prayer-thoughts for others is one of the ways to "pray without ceasing." But prayer is not simply general thoughts; it is to enter into the situation or need of others with compassion. Intercession is to identify with them before the Lord. Such prayer enriches us in the development of empathy as well as benefiting others by our sharing.

Just as "Christian community" means that we relate to one another through Christ, so it also means that we hold one another before the throne of God in loving, united prayer. The sense of God's mission should be so clear for us that we support one another in prayer, whether we are in full agreement or not. We are on the same team.

During the years of our large tent crusades, we held one in Archbold, Ohio. One day we were invited to the home of a family of twelve children for dinner. As we sat around the table, the children lined up on benches at each side of the table, listening. Their mother kept the conversation going with many important questions about our work. This had an impact on those children, of course, but even more significant, we would regularly receive letters from this mother saying that she and the family were praying for us every day. This prayer support was such an encouragement, and it put us on the same team.

Good news, like electricity, flows best where there is good contact. People touch people, and the witness of transformed lives means that the gospel becomes visible in us as believers. As we walk with Jesus, we pray for others that they will learn of him.

Lord, help me live from day to day
In such a self-forgetful way that,
Even when I kneel to pray,
My prayer shall be for others. Amen

January 10

By the Will of God

Asking that by God's will I may somehow at last succeed in coming to you. For I am longing to see you so that I may share with you some spiritual gift to strengthen you. Romans 1:10-11

Paul describes his prayer in this verse as a request. This is the way in which we come to God, asking that we may receive guidance from him. Paul's interest is to visit the believers in Rome, with a desire to journey to Rome, to the center of power in the world that he knew. His interest was not Rome, but the community of God's people in Rome.

His prayer is submissive to the will of God, to his plan, and to his security. Prayer is not ordering God, but requesting from God. Prayer is not using God, but opening one's life to the work of God. Prayer is not overcoming God's reluctance; it is laying hold on his willingness. Prayer is not manipulating God; it is surrendering to God.

In the Anabaptist movement of the sixteenth century, the word that expressed their piety most fully was the German word *Gelassenheit*, meaning an active yieldedness. This is expressed by Jesus in his prayer in the garden, "Not my will, but yours be done." The disciple of Christ, a follower of our Lord, is actively yielded to his will.

The text further confirms Paul's caring spirit for others to share "some spiritual gift to strengthen you." When we are colleagues in the work of Christ, anything that enhances the strength of our partner enhances our own strength. Too often we express a competitive rather than a cooperative spirit. Thanking God for what he is doing through others shows commitment to God, not to self.

Our vision, like Paul's, calls for the enriching of the church both local and universal. We should support the work of God and pray for people who are not a part of our own circle. The Spirit uses us in any situation, sharing with us in prayer for grace.

In praying, I want to not be selfish;
Not my will but yours.
Take my will and make it yours.
As I commit my way unto you as Lord, mold me.
Put within me the desires of your heart! Amen

Mutually Encouraged

Or rather so that we may be mutually encouraged by each other's faith, both yours and mine. Romans 1:12

Mutuality is a dimension of community too seldom emphasized. In our day of global community with its inequity, a conviction for mutuality will enhance our compassion. We do belong to each other; we receive from each other and are mutually encouraged.

While busy in the pastoral ministry, I have commented to Esther that the strain is the constant expectation to support others, but often with little support in turn. Perhaps this was a surrender to my self-interest.

In this day's text, Paul's statement to the believers in Rome has become very personal to me: "That you and I may be mutually encouraged by each other's faith." In the community of believers the faith experiences of different persons enrich others of us and give evidence of the divine presence and work in our midst. During and after a heart operation in which they placed a stent in a main artery which was nearly closed, I became deeply appreciative of the "community of faith," for the many friends who joined in prayer for me.

God created us in community and for community. Small groups have been very important in our congregational life, for these groups maximize openness, as well as hold one another accountable. And the larger congregation enhances the enrichment of each beyond the small group. We have found that these two, small groups and congregational fellowship, interface to enrich each other.

Representative Sam Rayburn served the House of Representatives for forty-eight years. Asked, "Under how many Presidents did you serve?" he replied, "I served under no President, I served *with* eight." We too share a Spirit-inspired partnership of mutuality.

> *Help me, Father,*
> *to enjoy the community you are providing.*
> *Give me the spirit of sharing with others in and through Christ,*
> *to avoid any tendency to control, coerce, or manipulate*
> *and to allow the Holy Spirit to be sovereign in our relations.*
> *In the name of Christ our Lord. Amen*

Plans That Are Long Range

I want you to know, brothers and sisters, that I have often intended to come to you (but thus far have been prevented), in order that I may reap some harvest among you as I have among the rest of the Gentiles. Romans 1:13

Paul's plans, his dreams of visiting the sisters and brothers in Rome, had been in mind for a long time. It is often in the period of anticipating the execution of a plan that the plan itself is refined. The sincerity of the plan is seen in that he hadn't surrendered it. For Paul, the plan meant sharing the gospel at the very heart of the Roman world.

The primary makeup of the church in Rome included many Gentiles. Paul, a Jewish man, had been involved in cross-cultural evangelism, ministering to the Gentiles. He had worked at what we today call "contextualization," allowing the forms of applying the gospel to be authentic in a given cultural setting. In India I have reminded ministers and seminary students that they must think *post*-Western; not minimizing the contribution of Western missionaries, but moving beyond it to be an Indian church of the twenty-first century.

In our Washington, DC, inner-city church we needed to contextualize by creating a congregation to authentically represent the cultural mix of this setting. We tried to share the faith of Christ as holistically as possible, calling persons to become disciples of Jesus in a community of the reconciled and to be reconcilers in the inner city. As workers, we should be less controlling and more flexible in the freedom to follow the Spirit.

Bernard Joinet, a French Catholic missionary in Tanzania, wrote of his call to be a "stranger in his Father's house," that he needed to learn to serve people the way in which they needed to be served and not in the way he wanted to serve them. This is contextual.

> *Thank you, Father,*
> *that there is one body and one Spirit,*
> *calling us in one hope,*
> *that there is one Lord, one faith, one baptism,*
> *one God and Father of all, who is above all*
> *and through all and in all. Amen*

I Am Obligated

I am debtor both to Greeks and to barbarians, both to the wise and to the foolish. Romans 1:14

This verse expresses the first of a series of three personal affirmations by the apostle Paul articulating his sense of calling: "I am debtor," followed by "I am ready," and "I am not ashamed of the gospel of Jesus Christ." What an amazing expression of his dedication! Having received freely from God's grace makes us debtors to share with God in the mission of extending this grace. Or Paul may mean that in knowing an answer to the human predicament of sinfulness, we "owe" it to others to share this news.

As a part of our urban seminary in Washington, DC, I spent the night taking care of homeless women at St. Peter's Evangelical Lutheran Church. We prepared their evening meal, gave them their medicines, and showed them their bed for the night, then later prepared breakfast in the morning. I was impressed by the different worlds in which we live. I am indebted to these persons.

Esther conducted an after-school art class for inner-city African-American children as a vehicle of love and to give them a sense of value. One day as the children were painting around the tables, they began to rap, then got up and began to dance. So, instead of reprimanding them for this unusual behavior, Esther taped huge sheets of paper on the wall for the children to paint as they rapped and danced. In this she was contextualizing their activity, thereby making their activity meaningful to them.

Theodore Wiedel, a rector in the Episcopal church, borrowed from a renewal movement in France when he affirmed that mission involves *presence, service,* and *communication.* We are a presence for Christ in any setting. We serve in the love of Christ, and thereby we earn the right to be heard. This is a matter of *being* before doing, of *presence* before proclamation. By my definition, evangelism is anything and everything that makes faith in Christ a possibility for a person.

Help me Lord,
  to make my faith in you attractive,
  to make it visible in my life,
  to witness in a way that reflects your joy, and
  to invite, but not pressure, persons to respond.
In your Spirit. Amen

Eager to Preach in Rome

**Hence my eagerness to proclaim the gospel to you also who are in Rome.
Romans 1:15**

"My eagerness" is evidence of Paul's enthusiasm, his worthy ambition, his optimism, and his unabated energy in the work of mission. As an older man Paul has not lost his vision. We need this challenge to avoid becoming routine in our Christian living, to avoid relinquishing the sense of responsibility for God's mission. We may not be on the front line, but we can be supporters of others who carry leadership roles.

His vision to share the gospel kept guiding Paul's travels in a world in which all roads led to Rome. Having a sense of responsibility to share the gospel, Paul affirms his eagerness to carry the gospel to Rome. In another context he wished not to build on another's foundation. But perhaps more significantly, in going to Rome he would be moving into the center of world power, confronting the thought makers and power brokers of the day with the message of Christ.

A close friend and brother in the faith, Dr. Donald Jacobs, has had many years of service in East Africa missions, as well as years of involvement in leadership training on a global scale. His advice to me, at the senior stage of my life, is to be free to work more globally. His vision corresponds with mine, including a responsibility to not only share the gospel, but also to inspire and enable younger persons to follow the path of ministry. Wherever we work, it is God's work and not ours; he has always opened the doors without our pushing on them! We must remember that evangelism is the work of the Holy Spirit and we are only tools in his hands. We are his agents of reconciliation.

Dr. George Glover, minister in England, said, "The early church grew because it out-thought, out-lived, and out-died everybody around."

> *Give us Lord,*
> *a sense of your direction for our future,*
> *your vision for the time you grant us.*
> *Help us to fulfill your calling,*
> *to give ourselves to the work of your kingdom.*
> *For the glory of Christ. Amen*

January 15

The Gospel of the Unashamed

For I am not ashamed of the gospel; it is the power of God for salvation to everyone who has faith, to the Jew first and also to the Greek. Romans 1:16

The hymn writer says, "Ashamed of Jesus? Sooner far let evening blush to own a star." Once we have come to know him, it is inconceivable to be indifferent to others who are missing out on knowing Christ. We want others to know him, for fellowship with him is our greatest focus and joy in relationship and in meaning in life.

For the disciple of Christ the faith walk with Jesus is primary, not secondary. And when it is primary we share the faith unapologetically, boldly, but not dogmatically or belligerently or in triumphalism. Being unashamed is a gentle spirit of commitment, of confidence that Jesus is the most important person with whom we can relate.

Paul's statement, that he is not ashamed of the gospel, is based on his assurance of the power of the gospel. He is confident that the gospel will do what it claims, that it will never embarrass him by failing to achieve its goal of reconciliation. He has seen it work. It is God's *power* unto salvation, reclaiming estranged lives, re-creating the truly human.

We need to share this assurance with the apostle, that the gospel is the one positive word we have to share with our society. This is not being overly confident in our opinions but is being confident in our focus on Christ. In fifty years of evangelistic missions in which I have been privileged to share the power of the gospel, it has been evident that the Spirit has transformed and worked in people's lives. As a pastor in an inner-city church, I have seen the power of the gospel in maturing believers in discipleship of Christ. We have seen the Spirit take people of many backgrounds and create a congregation united as disciples of Christ. Mother Teresa said, "Jesus is the message, and Jesus is the method."

Forgive us, Lord, when offering our opinions rather than your Word,
for sharing good views that too often eclipse the Good News,
for missing people holistically while we minister spiritually,
or for trying to minister to the social and not the whole person.
You love us as persons, and we want your help to reach others
as persons in your love and acceptance. Amen

January 16

The Righteousness of Faith

For in it the righteousness of God is revealed through faith for faith; as it is written, "The one who is righteous will live by faith." Romans 1:17

Righteousness is right relatedness with God and with one another. It is not so much a matter of what we do as it is a matter of relationship. We are brought into right relationship with God by his grace. In Christ the law is no longer the mediator of our relation with God, for Christ is the mediator. "Christ is made the end of the law for righteousness" (10:4), for now we have the better way of right relatedness with God.

In reading our text we must recognize that our theological presuppositions determine how we hear the verse. We may hear it, "The one who is *righteous,* by faith shall live." Or we may hear it, "The one who is righteous by faith *shall live.*" Or we may hear it, "The one who is righteous *by faith* shall live." The first may have been the meaning of Habakkuk, the Old Testament prophet, but the last one is evidently the meaning that Paul sees in the text. It is faith in Christ that is the way to be righteous.

This text is a key to Paul's theology. His emphasis on the righteousness of God is a basic thesis in Romans and the new covenant to which the law could only point. Jesus himself alluded to the law as a provisional reality, saying, "Unless your righteousness exceeds that of the scribes and Pharisees, you will never enter into the kingdom of heaven" (Matt. 5:20). By faith in Jesus we are in God's family, in right relatedness.

Right relatedness with God is our privilege by faith in Christ. This is not an achievement, but is a celebration of reconciliation with God. It is shared, but it is not coerced. Barbara Reynolds of *USA Today* in the late 1980s wrote of a young woman who was valedictorian of her class and who concluded her graduation address by saying, "I want to close with the Lord's Prayer, and if you want to join me, you may do so." All 900 students stood and joined in the prayer. At its conclusion they broke into applause.

Dear Father,
Help us to come to you, not just to be religious.
Let nothing come between us as an end in itself.
Teach us to open our inner self to you
And to commit our outer self to walk with you. Amen

God's Wrath, Yet Grace!

For the wrath of God is revealed from heaven against all ungodliness and wickedness of those who by their wickedness suppress the truth. Romans 1:18

God's wrath and God's love are two sides of the same coin. God's love is seen in his full self-giving concern for us, involving himself with us to the death. God's wrath is God's love granting us freedom to say "no" to him even while his wrath is his strong disapproval of such a decision. Love does not violate another personality, does not manipulate another. Yet love holds another accountable for the best in life, and love gives of one's self to enable fulfillment. Love seeks the well-being of another; wrath exposes.

There is a legitimate and dynamic place for anger in one's life, for anger means that one cares deeply and, in caring, rejects and exposes what is wrong (Eph. 4:26). Wrath is a deep concern when the well-being of a person is being perverted. Love without wrath is not holistic love, but a partial relationship. Love does not minimize problems that will harm one as a person. Love condemns the problem while loving the person.

In this text, wrath is God's opposition to perversion and sin in human life. Sin in its essential nature is a perversion of the good. We were created in the image of God, and sin is any perversion of that image. Sin is first expressed in rebellion against God, of saying "no" to him, but sin is then a perversion of the character of one's life and behavior.

Beyond sin as estrangement from God are the actions of our sins, the expressions of our perversion. This eclipses the reality of what could be. Sin alters our way of thinking about ourselves, about life, about God. Consequently the truth of God is lost to the human mind; life centers in one's self, in one's realm of experience, in one's interests.

The anguish of Nietzsche's life as an atheist is expressed in an early poem: "I must know Thee, unknown One, Thou who searchest out the depth of my soul and blowest like a wind through my life. I must know Thee and even serve Thee."

As we come to you today, our God,
We do so recognizing you to be God;
You are in charge, you are sovereign,
And by faith we will let you be God in our lives. Amen

Natural Theology

For what can be known about God is plain to them, because God has shown it to them. Romans 1:19

There are things to be known *about* God, but this is different than *knowing* God. To know him in intellectual arguments such as "'First Cause" or "the Unmoved Mover," or as "evidence in the creation and design of the universe," or in the "moral consciousness" given to each of us—each are aspects of knowing *about* God. But to know God in fellowship, like we know a person by association, is to know God in relationship.

One only needs to begin to address God in honest prayer and let him in turn address us. God takes the initiative in disclosing himself. The question is not whether there is a God, but do we want God in our lives. This is the crux of the issue.

We were warned in the preceding verse against suppressing the truth. The truth is that we didn't just happen. We are the result of action beyond ourselves. The reality of a thinking mind is itself enough to point one to God. It is inconceivable for a thinking person to assume that, in spite of our intelligence, one of these days it will all be over and there won't be an intelligent mind in the universe that knows we ever happened.

This argument is only from the reality of mind and thought. We could think of the harmony of the physical body, the miracle of life beginning with a single cell at conception to develop into a beautiful, fully equipped human. Or we could contemplate design, the beauty and purpose of the universe, and the divine person and energy.

We cannot prove God, but we have evidence that informs our faith. It is also true that the atheist cannot disprove God for he takes his stance by faith as well, not by intellectual achievement. One cannot prove a negative claim. If I say there is no gold in Virginia, I cannot prove this, for I'd need to dig up every bit of earth and rocks and examine them. If I say there is gold in Virginia, I need only find one nugget.

Two agnostic philosophers, C. M. Jodd and Bertrand Russell, sought to disprove Christianity. In his seventies Jodd wrote, "The one whom I denied all my life I must now embrace." Line one of the Apostles' Creed says:

I believe in God the Father Almighty, maker of heaven and earth.

Without Excuse

Ever since the creation of the world his eternal power and divine nature, invisible though they are, have been understood and seen through the things he has made. So they are without excuse. Romans 1:20

God is fair in that we are each accountable for what we know. Jesus taught that we will be judged according to what we have received and how we respond to the same. This verse is a strong statement of what we call natural theology or general revelation. God's word written is special revelation, while God's world is general revelation. One of my professors at Eastern Mennonite University, Chester K. Lehman, said, "God's Word and God's world, when rightly understood, always agree."

Paul says that the created order speaks of the invisible God. True. It has enough clarity to hold us accountable, but too much mystery to bring us to salvation. But it can bring a person to call on God for a saving grace reaching beyond religious forms. If persons will refuse to idolize their religion and reach to God, he will meet them in grace even though they may not call God by his right name.

From Genesis, chapters 1 and 2, we learn (1) that the Creator is distinct from creation, (2) that he created a good world, (3) that sin is a perversion in the world, and (4) that humanity expresses the image of God in being the highest level of creation. This word says that we have all been created in the image of God. Consequently, we have not only a mind but a conscience, moral accountability, freedom to choose, ability to create, and the aptitude for fellowship with others.

I recall looking into the eyes of a young man in Kenya, in the town of Kusumu, seeing there the dawning of faith. His culture and race was very different from mine, but his mind and spirit had the potential to respond to God and to walk with him. God has created each alike and loves each alike. It is in recognizing the *imago Dei* in all persons whom we meet that we are helped to move beyond the cultural and racial barriers that divide us and to more empathetically share the good news of the gospel with them.

Father, we pray for the millions who don't know Jesus,
That they may, by your Spirit, be stirred to seek You,
That they too may recognize and come to know You,
And participate in the grace we know in Christ. Amen

Futile Thinking

For though they knew God, they did not honor him as God or give thanks to him, but they became futile in their thinking, and their senseless minds were darkened. Romans 1:21

One of the deeper sins is to turn against what is known of the truth. "No one turns his back on the light: what he increases is the darkness in his own soul." Jesus said that the person who blasphemes the Spirit of God has turned off the one divine presence that could bring him or her to repentance. Such are without hope, for noother power can draw them to God. In our text, although they "knew God, they glorified him not as God" (KJV).

Christian commitment is simply to let God be God in one's life. This is what Jesus told the rich young ruler in Mark 10. The young man asked how to know eternal life. Jesus said that he should begin with what he knew, the commandments of God, and he claimed to have kept them from youth. Then Jesus said that he lacked one thing, and added, "Come, follow me." Here is where the young ruler backed off, for he wasn't ready to let the Master call the shots for him, to let the Eternal One be God for him.

A man named Gustav Thieben once said, "No sooner does one expel God from his life then every other part is successively summoned to be god!" Rejecting God does not bring freedom, for every part of the mind becomes engaged in the futile quest of finding an answer for life and its purpose. Rejecting God, one becomes subject to vastly lesser gods. The center of motivation, what the Bible calls "the heart," is thereby darkened.

Malcolm Muggeridge, famous British journalist, testified of his conversion, saying that when he was confined in a cell of darkness, the light of God shone in through one little window of his mind, and he was converted by looking into that light—Jesus!

> *Help us, Lord, to keep looking into the Light;*
> *the Light that lights every one,*
> *the Light which has come into the world,*
> *the Light of Jesus, in whom we see*
> *the glory of God. Amen*

The Foolishness of Idolatry

Claiming to be wise, they became fools; and they exchanged the glory of the immortal God for images resembling a mortal human being or birds or four-footed animals or reptiles. Romans 1:22-23

There is a legend of Abraham, in Ur of the Chaldeans, now Iraq, working in his father's shop and making idols. One evening he stepped out of the door and gazed up into the star-studded heavens. Suddenly it hit him: the object made is never greater than the mind or person who makes it. In this awareness he opened his mind to the God who made the stars. He took off his apron, placed his tools on the workbench, and left the idol shop.

Many persons lack the wisdom to make such a choice. Idolatry remains common in our lives; worshipping things that are, at best, a means to an end rather than to worship the ultimate One himself. Even in our religious observance we may fail to distinguish between the symbol and meaning and give our primary attention to the symbol rather than to what or whom it symbolizes.

When Polycarp, the apostle John's disciple and colleague, was asked to offer the pinch of incense and say "Caesar is Lord," he answered, "Eighty and six years have I served Jesus, and he has done me no wrong. How can I deny my King and my God?" Polycarp was martyred and many believers lost their lives for this same stance of faith. In the twenty-first century our allegiance is not questioned by a call from a Roman Caesar, but often to materialism, to militarism, to secularism, to liberalism, or even to conservatism. No ism can become our ultimate loyalty, for our loyalty is to Christ and his kingdom.

Father, keep us from the idolatry of worshipping visible programs
when we truly want to worship you.
Teach us how to focus our minds and spirits on the transcendent
even while we recognize your eminence. Amen

January 22

God Gave Them Over

Therefore God gave them up in the lusts of their hearts to impurity, to the degrading of their bodies among themselves. Romans 1:24

What troubling words! What a tragic picture. Persons created in the image of God become so self-centered and rebellious that they insist on their own will. But God permits us to say "no" to him, to exercise a freedom to rebel against him. Our depravity affects the totality of our person. Our intellect, our desires, our choices are all oriented around ourselves.

One of the more immediate desires in our lives is sexual. When persons fail to think holistically about themselves and others, they reduce others to sex-objects rather than persons made in God's image. Consequently, sex becomes an obsession and persons become enslaved to their own passions. Once we become God's children by a spiritual birth, the center of life changes and the whole of life is put in proper perspective. We need to recognize that sex can be servant rather than master, and we can enjoy our sexuality in God's order. We should see sex as a gift for the intimacy of covenant love as husband and wife, a bonding in intimacy that involves the whole person.

We should think of both sin and sins. Our basic sin is rebellion against God, and this can be answered in a crisis response to the Holy Spirit's call. But our sins, the expressions of this sinfulness, need the therapy of counsel and further work of God's sanctifying grace. The wonder of salvation is in the liberating freedom we know in Christ.

A poet and an artist were looking at a painting by the French master Nicholas Poussin, depicting the healing of the blind man at Jericho. The artist asked what the poet saw as most remarkable. The poet's reply was that it was the expression of hope in the man's face. The artist pointed to the steps where the man had sat; there lay his cane! Grace liberates.

Dear Lord,
Help us to enjoy relationships that are not based on sex
And to enjoy sex in the relationship that you intend;
The passion between a husband and wife in sanctity,
The total self-giving of intimacy
That calls us to an intimacy with you. Amen

Worship of Creature or Creator?

**Because they changed the truth about God for a lie and worshiped and
served the creature rather than the Creator, who is blessed forever! Amen.
Romans 1:25**

Our worship, authentic worship, is of God, the Creator. He alone is worthy of worship. To give our full
loyalty to anything else is a perversion of thought, of life, of loyalty. We can live this day with a
conscious loyalty to our Lord. A thinking person who is honest cannot be satisfied with less than the quest
to identify with the ultimate reality. Idolatry is turning from the truth of God to the deception of a god
made in our own image. It may be a philosophy, a self-gratifying passion, or a product of human creation.

The biblical picture of creation (Gen. 1–2; John 1:1-12; Heb. 1:1-3) presents a Creator distinct
from and over the creation. Our God is Creator, Redeemer, and Sanctifier—the three-in-one God,
known as Father-Son-Holy Spirit.

If we turn from God, we will give our loyalty to something else. Once we have moved from God, sin
becomes enslaving; it is never satisfied. And the sins of thought, of ego, of passion, of violence are all
extensions of the heart that has said "no" to God and "yes" to anything else. In contrast, Jesus said,
"Blessed are those who hunger and thirst for righteousness, for they shall be satisfied" (Matt. 5:6, RSV).

> *O Lord, our God,*
> > *we long to know you better,*
> > *we live to see your face.*
> *Free us from worship of the creature:*
> > *we would use the world but not abuse it;*
> > *we would enjoy it without surrendering to it.*
> *Give us of your wisdom:*
> > *we would seek to understand your way;*
> > *we would walk in your will.*
> *Help us to worship you:*
> > *We would live our lives with you;*
> > *We would celebrate your grace.*

God Gave Them Up . . . to Vile Affections

For this reason God gave them up to degrading passions. Their women changed natural intercourse for unnatural, and in the same way also the men, giving up natural intercourse with women, were consumed with passion for one another. Men committed shameless acts with men and received in their own persons the due penalty for their error. Romans 1:26-27

When people exclude God from their lives, God gives them up to the perversions which issue from their choices. Here Paul clearly calls homosexual practice a perversion. Of the creation of humanity the writer of Genesis says, "Male and female he created them." Both are alike created in God's image. Paul writes that neither masculinity nor femininity is complete without the other (1 Cor. 11). It takes both the masculine and the feminine to express the full characteristics of the *imago Dei*.

For persons to pursue sexual gratification apart from a covenant of intimacy in heterosexual love is to pervert the wholeness, the unity of persons in God's creation. But the perversion itself is deeper. As gay persons have told me, they do not have a normal sex drive simply focused on a person of the same gender, but they have an abnormal obsession that enslaves them. While being homosexual may not itself be a choice, yet homosexual behavior or practice is a choice. One who is homosexual may live celibate.

As unitary beings we can, by the disciplines of mind and spirit, control the body and its response patterns. Some say, "God made me this way," or again, "My gayness is a gift of God." However, this tendency may be the result of a lack of meaningful same-sex relationship in their developing years, a need which could be met by meaningful relationships without sex. The need of single persons should be met in the fellowship of the church.

Help us, Lord, to seek your will and presence in intimacy,
to enjoy our sexuality without demanding sex,
to engage sex in the covenant of your love,
where we know as husband and wife
the joy of total belonging and intimate sharing.
We would honor you, Lord, in our intimacy. Amen

A Depraved Mind

And since they did not see fit to acknowledge God, God gave them up to a debased mind and to things that should not be done. Romans 1:28

A depraved mind is one that excludes God and will not worship him. In a sophisticated term this is secularism: the orientation of life around humanity as though God didn't exist. As quoted, Bishop Pike described secularism as "this-is-all-there-is-ism," and again, "there-ain't-any-more-ism." The psalmist says that the fool says in his heart there is "no God where I'm concerned." This is a choice some persons make, to exclude God from their lives. The mind closed to the truth of God cannot think with God nor live in the will of God.

The secular life actually becomes a limited life, for all that God can bring into one's life is excluded. As Christian thinkers we need (1) to keep the secular from claiming wholeness for itself, (2) to expose the perversions that make up the secular, and (3) to permeate the secular with a loving witness of the larger meanings that faith in Christ brings into life. The Christian thinker, who integrates a Christian perspective with learning, can have a broader engagement with knowledge than with the secular alone.

We need to be realistic about the fact that many secular people develop their intellectual, cultural, artistic, or rationalistic areas beyond many of their Christian contemporaries. But we must remember (1) that some of the greatest minds of history have been committed Christians; (2) that comparing persons is a limited test, for not all apply themselves to their privileges; (3) that many persons with limitations are better as Christians than they could have been without Christ; and (4) many accomplished persons who are not Christians could be even better by walking with Christ.

The Christian faith enriches the mind, informs the conscience, engages creative thought, and interprets holistically. Christian thought is not to limit intellectual pursuit.

> *Broaden out our lives, Lord,*
> *beyond the narrow confines or our selves.*
> *Show us the larger circle of truth beyond,*
> *and as we grow, humble us by how much more*
> *there is for us to engage. Amen*

Being Godless Results in Sinfulness

They were filled with every kind of wickedness, evil, covetousness, malice. Full of envy, murder, strife, deceit, craftiness, they are gossips, slanderers, God-haters, insolent, haughty, boastful, inventors of evil, rebellious toward parents, foolish, faithless, heartless, ruthless. Romans 1:29-31

All of us alike are sinners, although we are not sinners alike. True, some of us live more disciplined lives than others, yet each alike is sinful, having rebelled against God. When a room has no light, it is filled with darkness, but when even the smallest light is brought into the room, the darkness is dispelled. We should invite God into every room of our lives. John wrote, "If we walk in the light as he himself is in the light, we have fellowship one with another, and the blood of Jesus his Son cleanses us from all sin" (1 John 1:7).

When God is excluded, then potentially every type of sin can be expressed. Paul speaks of wickedness, evil, greed, and depravity as the characteristic of the human fallen state. Having been created good, in God's image, our rebellion has perverted humanity, and each one is born a sinner. Near the equator there is a "diet-deficiency belt." People born and raised there suffer the consequences. Just so we are born with a God-deficiency.

In various Eastern cultures there is not a sense of sin as we think, using terms of what is morally right or wrong. But there is a deep awareness of right and wrong, the wrong being especially unfaithfulness in relationship to one's family, one's parents, one's companion, and to those in authority. Perversion reduces one's life to the mundane; it limits rather than expands life with a vision of glorious fulfillment.

A business tycoon said to Dr. Parker in London, "I'm a self-made man." To this Dr. Parker responded, "You have just lifted a great burden from the shoulders of the Almighty."

> *Thank you, Father God,*
> *that you are no respecter of persons,*
> *that each of us alike can say "yes" to you,*
> *that your gracious mercy calls us,*
> *and your love accepts us. Hallelujah! Amen*

Spitting in God's Face

They know God's decree, that those who practice such things deserve to die—yet they not only do them but even applaud others who practice them. Romans 1:32

The very serious human problem is in being presumptuous. When we know that God's call and provision is to convert and walk with him and yet we defy him, we share the more despicable evil. Paul, in good psychology, first seems to expose the Gentiles, then he addresses the Jews. He refers to persons who know God's claims, yet practice the wrong. This speaks to each to avoid any defiance of God's will.

Good news is that the One we so long rejected, the One we slapped in the face, has continued to reach out his arms of love. He is always ready to embrace us. Like the father of the prodigal son, the forgiving grace of our Father moves beyond the issue to the person. He forgives because he cares more about us than about what we have done. God welcomes us back and says, "Bring the best robe and put it on him," the symbol of relationship restored. He wraps us in his robe of acceptance and love.

A little girl in a Sunday school class told her pastor that when she talks to Jesus, he talks to her. The pastor suggested that impressions in her mind must have been God's speaking. She insisted that Jesus spoke to her. In desperation, he said, "Okay, I have a question for you to ask God, and if he answers it, then I'll believe you. I made a confession to him several weeks ago. You ask him whether he remembers it." "Sure, pastor, I'll ask him." Then he added, "And while you are at it, ask him what I confessed." At the next class meeting he asked the little girl: "Did you talk to Jesus?" "Oh yes, I did." "Did you ask my question?" "Oh yes, I did." "And did he answer you?" "Oh yes indeed." "Well, what did he say?" "When I asked him, he said 'yes' he did remember that you made a confession. When I asked him what you confessed, he said, 'Oh, I forget.'"

> *Father, I thank you for your forgiving grace,*
> *keep your servant from presumptuous sin.*
> *In your keeping we shall be upright,*
> *innocent from the greater transgression.*
> *Help us to walk in your truth,*
> *to enjoy fellowship one with another. Amen*

Without Excuse

Therefore you have no excuse, whoever you are, when you judge others; for in passing judgment on another you condemn yourself, because you, the judge, are doing the very same things. Romans 2:1

Each of us alike stands before the judgment of God. And we are all accountable to him. We are without excuse, for each is responsible to follow the "light" that we have. Our sense of moral accountability itself calls us to responsibility before God. Since life has too much potential to fulfill it in our few years, we even contemplate immortality.

It is easier for us to see the faults of others than to face up to our own. Judging another makes us inexcusable, for the same discernment that critiques another brings judgment on our own behavior. The call to honest confession is the beginning of change in our lives. In the act of confessing we break sin's tyranny, for our judgment upon it places us above it. This is true psychologically and theologically. In the stance of confession we identify with God. Let us pray with the eighteenth-century poet and saint John Donne:

> *Wilt Thou forgive that sin which I have won*
> *Others to sin and made my sin their door?*
> *Wilt Thou forgive that sin which I did shun*
> *A year, or two, but wallowed in a score?*
> *When Thou hast done, Thou hast not done,*
> *For I have more.*

> *I have a sin of fear, that when I have spun*
> *My last thread, I shall perish on the shore;*
> *Swear by Thyself that at my death Thy Son*
> *Shall shine as He shines now, and heretofore;*
> *And having done that, Thou hast done,*
> *I fear no more.*

God's Judgment in Truth

You say, "We know that God's judgment on those who do such things is in accordance with truth." Romans 2:2

If you are like me, you are inclined to rationalization. Psychologists say that there is some value in this in that it helps one process failure or mistakes without carrying undue guilt. On the other hand, it can become a pattern of excusing oneself and, in essence, it is refusing to carry responsibility for one's part in a problem. In-depth cleansing by the Spirit can only happen when there is in-depth honesty.

Paul's focus on God's judgment calls us to accountability before God's truth. To be judged by God is awesome. To know this is to face the awareness that each day, as a human being, I can bring my thoughts and actions under judgment. The good news of grace is that God forgives us when we ask and will not remember our sins against us! The psalmist says that he removes them as far as the east is from the west. "If we confess our sins, he who is faithful and just will forgive us our sins and cleanse us from all unrighteousness" (1 John 1:9). This is not our holiness, but our honesty.

The self-righteous person does not admit being sinful, but emphasizes human goodness. Some quote the psalmist, "I say, you are gods, children of the Most High, all of you." Yet persons stop quoting at that point. But, the passage continues: "nevertheless you shall die like mortals" (Ps. 82:6-7). In the context, God is sitting in the midst of his counsel among the heavenly beings and holding judgment. Jesus quoted this to answer the Jews who thought him presumptuous in his claim to be God's Son (John 10:34).

Of difficult passages, St. Augustine said that we are to interpret the darker passages by the clearer. In the differences between the Testaments, the full revelation in Christ is clearer than the Old Testament. We interpret the Old through the more complete knowledge of God's will in the New Testament. In Jesus's words, "It has been said, . . . but I say unto you."

Bishop Festo Kivengere of Uganda was converted in 1977. In his newfound freedom he rode his bicycle fifty miles to the home of a white man, whom he hated, to ask his forgiveness. In this expression of grace they fell into each other's arms and embraced in forgiving love.

Presumption

Do you imagine, whoever you are, that when you judge those who do such things and yet do them yourself, you will escape the judgment of God? Romans 2:3

Our judgments of others are often projections of our own consciousness of guilt. We are most critical of others for things that have been a problem to us. But love recognizes the problems in ourselves, as well as in others. Love is an affirmation of worth; it sees the life of the other as of ultimate importance, seeing in each person his or her intrinsic worth, and then seeks the fulfillment of that person's potential.

Paul is condemning the lack of integrity in our judgments of others, for we often blame others and excuse ourselves. Gentile and Jew alike as accountable before God. Recognizing the standard of God's righteousness as higher than that of either Jew or Gentile, it is futile for the Jew to brag that his standard is higher than that of the Gentiles. The religious Jew also needs the gift of righteousness.

Jesus taught us moral discernment: "You will know them by their fruits" (Matt. 7:20). But this discernment is not a judgmental spirit. It is, in fact, necessary for true compassion. In the recognition of evil we are enabled to truly care, to give our best in love and prayer for the well-being of another.

Father Elias Chacour of Palestine tells of the time when Israeli soldiers came to the elders of Biram and told them that for their safety the people needed to move out of the town for a few days. A few days later, on their return they found all of their houses occupied. Frustrated, Elias's father, in true Christian spirit, prayed, "Forgive them, O God. Heal their pain, remove their bitterness. Let us show them your peace."

> *Help me, dear Lord, to hear your Word,*
> *to study it with care,*
> *to find in it the lamp to my feet,*
> *to follow it as a light to my pathway.*
> *Help me in your Word to meet you,*
> *to know that you are not other than what you say,*
> *to recognize that you share what you expect,*
> *to hear you in your Word, and obey. Amen*

January 31

God's Kindness

Or do you despise the riches of his kindness and forbearance and patience? Do you not realize that God's kindness is meant to lead you to repentance? Romans 2:4

How wonderful that our God is holy, just, merciful, and loving. He is not a scorekeeper. However, his wholeness means that he justly holds us accountable for the fractured lives and relationships in which we live. It is wonderful that his justice seeks to achieve the correction of our problem rather than to seek revenge. This is the theology that undergirds Paul's reference to the kindness of God.

Many persons seek to use God rather than to yield to him. Simple minds and selfish hearts tend to cry out in their problems and ask, "Where is God to let this happen to me?" As though God owes us more than patience, owes us his service in our selfishness! No, God awaits our turning to him. He calls, but doesn't coerce. He waits for us like the father waited for his prodigal son and didn't ask, "Where have you been, boy? What have you been up to? What did you do with your money?" The father simply said, "Son, it is so good to have you home." In 1 Corinthians 13:4-8, love is the greatest affirmation of worth.

> *Love is*
>> *Patient, it is kind,*
>> *Rejoices in the truth,*
>> *Bears all things, believes all things,*
>> *Hopes all things,*
>> *Endures all things.*
>> *It never ends.*
>
> *Love does not*
>> *Envy, boast,*
>> *Is not arrogant, is not rude,*
>> *Does not insist on its own way,*
>> *Is not irritable, is not resentful,*
>> *Does not rejoice in other's wrongdoing. (altered)*

Storing Up Wrath

But by your hard and impenitent heart you are storing up wrath for yourself on the day of wrath, when God's righteous judgment will be revealed. Romans 2:5

We should each check up on the spirit of our inner self, our attitude toward God. Paul describes our sinfulness as an expression of stubbornness and unrepentant attitudes. And our attitudes determine God's actions toward us. While God is patient, the continued defiance by humanity adds a proportionate disapproval by God. Our indifference or our belligerence makes it impossible for God to transform us.

Persons who think of God in terms of love only, rather than recognizing his holiness, often find it difficult to think of God's wrath. However, love and wrath are not so far apart. The opposite of love is not wrath but indifference. Love means that we are never indifferent to the other; we are always personally open to them.

As noted earlier, wrath is the integrity of God's love disapproving of our acts while at the same time being open to us. Or put another way, God's wrath is his love refusing to approve our perversions because of what they do to *us* and to our relationship with him. Our sin alienates, and his disapproval is his controlled wrath.

God has said "yes" to us, and it is for us to say "yes" to him. This, E. Stanley Jones has called "the eternal yes." God has moved to us in grace; it is our move next. Faith is our "yes" to God, the attitude that permits him to be himself in our lives.

> *Grant us, Lord, integrity of mind and spirit,*
> *   the honesty that will honor you.*
> *Give us freedom to choose for you,*
> *   by opening our minds to your grace.*
> *Grace our lives with your presence, and*
> *   transform us by your completing work.*
> *Help us to grow one step at a time,*
> *   never putting a ceiling on our lives,*
> *But always looking up to your awesome majesty. Amen*

Writing Our Own Sentence

For he will repay according to each one's deeds: to those who by patiently doing good seek for glory and honor and immortality, he will give eternal life. Romans 2:6-7

God gives eternal life to each according to the person's choices and attitudes. That God is just means, among other things, that he treats each of us fairly, and responds to our choices with an integrity that doesn't violate our freedom to decide for or against him. We should regularly stop and think deeply of God's love, and inhale this awareness as though we are taking a deep spiritual breath. We should open ourselves to the emotion of being loved, of knowing love as the first awareness of God brought to us by his word "grace."

God is love, and love does not coerce. Love respects a person's right to make decisions, even the wrong ones. As a God of love, God respects our freedom to respond one way or the other, but he does not approve our wrong choice, and this is his wrath. He cares for us so genuinely that he cannot overlook our sins without thereby hurting us.

We are made to live for the ages, and as I have often said, "Fifty billion years from now I will be a young man living on with God." Eternity with God is joy, but an eternity apart from God is hell. God calls us, but he does not force us to turn from evil. He warns us that evil self-destructs; it is the eternal black hole turning in upon itself.

Each of us knows whether our face is toward God or our back is toward God. In this word picture the prophet Isaiah calls us to face our responsibility. We must choose today to walk with God rather than against him, to share with him in the life that is eternal. This is a *quality* of life before it is *quantity* of life. A young pastor, Doyle Masters, suffering terminal cancer at age forty-eight, wrote in a note to his congregation: "Today is all you have, today is all you need, today is all that you can handle."

> *He gives us immortality.*
> *It is not our intrinsic right.*
> *He promises to share eternity with his own,*
> *Fifty billion years . . . and then some!*

The Consequence of Self-Seeking

While for those who are self-seeking and who obey not the truth but wickedness, there will be wrath and fury. Romans 2:8

It has been our privilege to attend the National Prayer Breakfast held in the Washington, DC, Hilton Hotel numerous times. At the breakfast on February 5, 1987, there was an unusual clarity on the centrality of Christ for daily life. The main address was brought by Elizabeth Dole, Secretary of Transportation at the time, giving a personal testimony of how her commitment to Christ brought order and meaning into her life.

Having attended many of these prayer breakfasts since the late 1950s when Dwight Eisenhower was president, this was one of the more unusual ones by the absence of the usual emphasis on civil religion. The kingdom of Christ is not to be identified with any political system; it is the rule of God in all lives that are open to him.

We have the danger of being corrupted by our privileges. At the level of government the problem is that people of power are too often corrupted by power itself. This is a special danger now for America as a superpower and for the church in America, as it may easily succumb to civil religion. True believers recognize that power seeking and the desire to control are wrong; we avoid seeking to dominate and control.

We tend to divide society between the liberal and the conservative. But this is too simple. We may think of ourselves as progressive or conservative, but either way, we are responsible for truth, justice, equity, human rights, and well-being. These terms are biblical injunctions for all people. We are accountable to God as disciples, to walk in his truth. His will is not captured in any thought system that doesn't recognize the priority of his kingdom.

> *My own will is far too small, too narrow.*
> *It robs me of all that God offers.*
> *His will has the breadth and focus of eternity,*
> *A quality of life, not only extent.*

According to Our Quest

There will be anguish and distress for every one who does evil, the Jew first and also the Greek. Romans 2:9

While God in grace takes the initiative and comes to us, he meets us on the basis of our attitude toward him. God does not impose himself upon us; he comes to identify with us and to share himself with us. God is a God of grace, of mercy, but this does not mean that we can go on sinning, presuming on his grace.

Our text is a note of judgment upon those who decide against letting God actually be God in their lives. The unbeliever may ask, "Can a loving God send a person to hell?" I do not believe that God sends anyone to hell by some divine fiat. God permits our making choices. We can choose to go into eternity apart from him, and that is hell! One could perhaps better ask, "Can a God of love do other than to allow some people to choose hell?" Love does not manipulate persons.

The Scripture enjoins us to seek the Lord. If we want God in our lives, he wants to be there even more, sharing himself with us. If we say "no" to him, we experience the resultant estrangement. If we say "yes" to him, seeking his will, we experience the glory of his presence, the honor of being God's person, and the peace of being in his will.

We are responsible according to the privileges of the heritage in which we stand. Identifying with the Anabaptist people, I am responsible to fulfill the values of this tradition. But a tradition is not the authority. God's Word alone is the authority for faith and life. Yet none of us come to the Scripture neutrally; we are conditioned by our particular perspective. Paul's reference "to the Jew first and also the Greek" is not a statement of partiality, but of responsibility in proportion to the knowledge given them.

As a young student, George Washington Carver prayed, "Lord, show me the secret of the universe." He felt God answer, "George, that is too large for you." So he prayed, "Then, Lord, show me the secret of the peanut." He felt God saying, "That is more your size." He unlocked the resources of the peanut as a huge blessing for society.

> *I sought the Lord, and afterward I knew. . . .*
> *It was not I that found, O Savior true,*
> *No, I was found of Thee.*

February 5

Glory, Honor, and Peace

But glory and honor and peace for everyone who does good, the Jew first and also the Greek. Romans 2:10

What a wonderful affirmation! God blessing those who walk with him by his gifts of glory, of honor, and of peace. I (we) am reminded that it is said of Abraham that he was known as the friend of God. I covet nothing higher than this for myself and, as the Scripture says, we have a Friend that sticks closer than a brother or sister.

This is a *relational* faith that we enjoy, not a legalistic faith that drives us. A legalistic religion focuses on its laws rather than on its Lord. God graciously rewards us for walking in the light that we have. Doing good is set in the context of the knowledge of good as the will of God. This stands in contrast to each one seeking to have his own way.

While in India, talking with some Buddhists, I pointed out that Buddha, who dates before Christ, sought to follow the light as an example for others. It is hardly conceivable that Buddha wanted people to worship him. There is a writing that claims to be a conversation between a Brahman and the Buddha, and the Buddha told him not to follow or worship him but to worship another who was coming to represent God, and that one would be recognized by the marks in his hands. This may be only a legend, but we do have the words of the prophet Isaiah, "He was wounded for our transgressions; . . . upon him was the punishment that made us whole" (Isa. 53:5). Buddha may have read this!

A benediction is a blessing from God, and one of my favorite benedictions to end a worship service is found in the letter to the Hebrews (13:20):

Now *may the God of peace,*
Who brought back from the dead our Lord Jesus,
The great shepherd of the sheep,
By the blood of the eternal covenant,
Make you complete in everything good so that you may do his will,
Working among us that which is pleasing in his sight,
Through Jesus Christ,
To whom be the glory forever and ever. Amen

God Is Not Partial

For God shows no partiality. Romans 2:11

God has no favorites. This is an amazing affirmation. He treats us with the same caring love that can enable each person's fulfillment. His kingdom is global. He loves the persons in countries who are at enmity with our country the same as he loves us. This is a call to peace, for in his global kingdom we cannot be at enmity with one another nor engaged in destroying one another. I must view each person, even an enemy, as a soul for whom Christ died and whom I want to win to be my brother in Christ.

Further, what a marvelous assurance in prayer—that God will hear me in Christ and answer me as well as anyone else! Having just said, "to the Jew first and also to the Greek," he is holding an order of responsibility before us. The phrase "also to the Greek" is an assurance that God is not dealing with a privileged ethnic group, but with all of us.

At times in history, and for particular roles, God calls and uses one people differently than another, but for the good of all. It is when we become selfish in our privilege that we actually turn God's goodness against his purpose. Our privileges as North Americans have often been perverted when we flaunt our affluence and strength rather than to serve God's global community. We too often want to protect what we have for our purposes rather than to seek the same freedom for all people. We tend to use God in a civil religion rather than to recognize our accountability to God with all peoples.

Speaking to Executive Club members in the Chicago suburb of Oak Brook, I shared my theme for my talk with a man in the taxi, "Love, Power, and Freedom." In reaction he said, "They don't fit!" To this I responded, "If you have power and have love, there will be freedom, but if you have power and no love, there will be no freedom, but rather, tyranny." He looked at me a moment and said, "Young man, if you could get that message across, it would change the world."

> *Love is positive in relation to all peoples,*
> *for love takes the initiative.*
> *Love shares in purpose and spirit,*
> *and love makes us partners.*

Judged by What We Know

**All who have sinned apart from the law will also perish apart from the law,
and all who have sinned under the law will be judged by the law. Romans 2:12**

In Genesis 18 we read of Abraham's amazing conversation with God about the destruction of Sodom. In his intercession with God he was asking God to save fifty righteous people. Eventually he asked for just ten righteous people. He may have had reason to expect ten (his nephew Lot, Lot's wife, possibly two married daughters, their spouses, and the two unmarried daughters whom Abraham could have assumed also had spouses). His appeal was: "Will not the judge of all the earth do right?"

Paul's words in our text express this justice in that God holds us accountable for the highest level of our understanding. In education a teacher would not give someone in the eighth grade an examination prepared for college juniors or vice versa. However, God's expectation is not only measured by levels of knowledge or religious works, but by our response in seeking him.

We are called to "obedience of the faith," to obey God as we understand him. And obedience itself is a way of knowing. This is a major insight for discipleship. In a skill course, we learn by *doing*—playing piano, riding a bike, playing tennis. Similarly, in the spiritual life we learn to pray by praying, to witness by witnessing, to worship by worshipping, to sing by joining in singing, to enjoy God by associating with God.

We have a commission to live by love, to love our neighbor as ourselves. As we put this love into practice, we will find that love overcomes evil with good. We sin as we turn against reason, conscience, moral law, or against God's revealed Word. In repentant faith we are called to turn from our own way to God's way. And God meets us, for "anyone who resolves to do the will of God will know whether the teaching is from God" (John 7:17).

Help us, Lord, to live obediently, to begin doing,
that is, doing what we know.
Enable us to live the Word we acknowledge,
to behave by our relation with Christ.

Hearing and Doing

For it is not the hearers of the law who are righteous in God's sight, but the doers of the law who will be justified. Romans 2:13

Charles Wesley, John's gifted brother, prayed, "Lord, unite the two so long disjoined; knowledge and vital piety." Knowing and living in worship are dual aspects of the meaningful life. Knowledge without the wisdom of God is only to know about reality without coming to *the* Reality.

Deed and word must be held together. The deed authenticates the word, and the word articulates the deed. The deed demonstrates the word, and the word interprets the deed. Our standard is not so much what we declare but what we do. An esteemed literary churchman, Paul Erb said: "We are to behave our beliefs." Faith is trust, acting on convictions. It is not simply mental agreement with statements.

The question in our text is not whether we are able to obey the law but rather, whether we have any just claim to being righteous when we don't obey the law. As disciples of Christ we cannot be at peace in only giving mental assent to his principles, but peace is in an attitude of obedience that seeks to do his will as fully as possible.

The Christian life is to walk with the one who lived and taught the will of God. Jesus, in his life, expressed the nature of God and the nature of true humanness. He taught the will of God in life and word and in his self-giving sacrifice and resurrection. He is our model and redeemer. We relate ethics to Christ in the same way we relate salvation to Christ. We are saved in relation with Jesus, and we "behave" our relation with Jesus.

Such faith enables one to achieve. Glenn Cunningham as a lad was so badly burned his doctors thought he would always be an invalid. In 1940 he won the race that marked him in athletics as the fastest runner to date. Motivation became transformation.

> *Dear Father:*
> *We would behave our beliefs,*
> *Practice our profession,*
> *Live the life of grace, and*
> *Enjoy the fellowship of life,*
> *For we wish to be truly a new creation.*

February 9

Conscience Bears Witness

When Gentiles, who do not possess the law, do instinctively what the law requires, these, though not having the law, are a law to themselves. They show that what the law requires is written on their hearts, to which their own conscience also bears witness; and their conflicting thoughts will accuse or perhaps excuse them. Romans 2:14-15

Conscience is not *the* standard; it is to be *standardized* by the Word of God. Conscience is like a computer; it speaks in accordance with the way it has been programmed.

Differences between the consciences of people are evidence that we need to honestly examine the way in which a person's conscience, or our conscience, has, like a computer, been programmed. The differences call us to seek together for the truth. Another person's lack of conviction on some issue means that I need to examine the issue as to whether I have idolized my opinion. My own conviction also means that the other must examine the issue to discover whether he is missing an expression of God's truth.

This examination is in full awareness that, while different consciences speak differently depending on the way in which they have been conditioned, there is one thing that is universally the same. In the function of every person's conscience, the universal is that the conscience casts its vote on the side of what a given person believes to be right. This judgment role is universally the same, whether the issue or conclusion is the same or not. This mental judgment seat calls all persons to be accountable to truth.

Paul sees the function of conscience in our text as the law written on our hearts. Our thoughts either accuse or excuse us. Conscience is thus a witness to all, to those not informed by the divine law, to the Gentiles, that all alike answer to God.

> *Dear Lord, these are not mere words;*
> *You are my Lord; I am your servant.*
> *Help me to understand and live by your standards;*
> *In attitude, relationships, and choices.*

February 10

God's Judgment of Secrets

On the day when, according to my gospel, God, through Jesus Christ, will judge the secret thoughts of all. Romans 2:16

To be alive, to be a human being, to know that I will be in all eternity the very person who has done what I've done today—this is a most awesome reality in life! One could not be at peace with this without finding in God's grace the answer to this awesome confrontation.

Paul speaks of God's judgment as a coming event. Clearly, (1) it is a day of accounting to God, (2) it will expose the secrets or motives of our hearts, (3) it will be an exposure through Jesus Christ, and (4) it will be according to the gospel Paul was preaching. There is a present judgment, for, as we meet God in Jesus, the basic issue is whether I want to share my life fully with this God.

The fact that we are ultimately judged by God is not only that "on that day" we will be judged, but also that already everything we do is under the judgment of God. True, our behavior is judged by family, friends, and social community, but it already stands under the judgment of God. No wonder the Scripture says, "If we would judge ourselves, we would not be judged." It is a call to critique our actions in light of the example of Christ.

Peter writes, God has set forth Jesus as "an example, so that you should follow in his steps." He is our mentor, as well as our Savior. We must accept the whole Jesus, not just the benefit of his being our Savior, and we must be participants with him as our Lord. We know the expression of the will of God in Jesus as we read his life (1 Peter 2:21). He himself is the Word, not just what he said, as important as that is, but in his life as our mentor. To know him is to "walk just as he walked" (1 John 2:6).

We speak of being transparent,
Open and honest before our Lord;
But what a stupendous claim,
When we were born with our fists clenched.

41

Bragging About God

But if you call yourself a Jew and rely on the law and boast of your relation to God.... Romans 2:17

Privilege adds responsibility. Since we stand in a tradition of religious knowledge, we are accountable for that privilege. Paul, in speaking to the church at Rome, has addressed the Gentiles, but now he pointedly addresses the Jew. Here he begins a list of privileges that have led Jewish people to brag about being God's favorites.

Our text reminds us of one of the prophets. Isaiah exposed the religious pride of those who say, "Stand by thyself, . . . for I am holier than thou" (Isa. 65:5, KJV). He condemned the presumption of those who claim to be God's people by ethnic privilege or by identity with God's law. Amos asks those who claimed to know God, "Do two walk together unless they have made an appointment?" (3:3). Belonging to God means walking in the will of God, and this is expressed in Jesus rather than in law.

Here Paul makes clear that when one fails to understand the law fully enough to discover his own need of grace, one fails to come honestly to the Lord. The law points us to God, and it exposes our inability to fulfill that law without him.

For all of our privilege, as evangelical Christians in the Western world, as a part of only 7 percent of the world's population, how do we answer for our role in God's ministry of reconciliation to the other six billion people? As such a small percentage, how do we justify using so much of the world's resources with limited sharing with those in need? These are issues which the mind, set on God, must answer through his Word.

How dare I boast, rest on my own privileges,
Dare to think that I am one of God's favorites
When grace means that God loves all alike,
Has acted to redeem humanity in its need,
Including, . . . yes, including me? Boasting?
Only of such a wonderful redeeming Friend!

Approving What Is Superior

...and know his will and determine what is best because you are instructed in the law, and if you are sure that you are a guide to the blind, a light to those who are in darkness, a corrector of the foolish, a teacher of children, having in the law the embodiment of knowledge and truth. Romans 2:18-20

To know God's will is to know the superior quality of life. God's laws do not rob us of life but simply point us to the higher quality of life. Paul here develops a base for this declaration, in turn, showing that the Jew, as well as the Gentile, stands under God's judgment. In doing so, he affirms the advantages in the Jewish tradition. Life has a better quality because of God's acts of revelation. Any society is better where there is a live and consistent church, a people of God. In noting the privileges of the Jews, Paul's reference to the "truth of the law" expresses a high view of the revelation of God to Moses.

The question is implicit: What are we doing to share this enriching quality of life in our social order? The Christian order of life is a far better lifestyle than life without these qualities. In our educational systems we should study the Judeo-Christian way as we, in our universities, study the Greek way and the Roman way. Studying the Judeo-Christian way may guide persons in allegiance to God. By studying the Greek or Roman way, persons are led to give allegiance to the secular philosophy of these systems.

If we want others to "walk in the light," we ourselves must walk in the light of his presence. One cannot be a guide to others unless they know the way. Jesus said, "If the blind lead the blind, both shall fall into the ditch" (Matt. 15:14, KJV).

> *Peace, what an easy word as it falls from our lips,*
> > *but peace, what a marvelous claim.*
> *Peace does not mean inactivity;*
> > *it is not to live without concern.*
> *Peace can be known in conflict,*
> > *when one is not engrossed in defensiveness.*
> *Peace is not shared at a distance;*
> > *it means looking one another in the eye—with a twinkle!*

February 13

Practicing What We Preach

You, then, that teach others, will you not teach yourself? While you preach against stealing, do you steal? You that forbid adultery, do you commit adultery? You that abhor idols, do you rob temples? Romans 2:21-22

The gospel calls us to relate to God for ourselves, to relate personally. We now know him as our Father; we are his children. We live in the sphere of his influence; we express the family characteristics. If we are God's children, we are to live like it.

The Jews claimed to be the people of God, a people who expressed his calling and will. Paul is calling them to move beyond profession to practice. Intellectual perception is not an end in itself. As Helmut Thielicke, a famous theologian, wrote to young students, "Beware of thinking that when you've read something you have experienced it." The Jews gave ardent intellectual assent to the law, taught it to others, emphasized the ethics of godliness, and yet failed to fulfill the law that they taught.

Paul's conclusion to his arguments comes later, in Romans 3:20, where he states that both, Jew and Gentile, are guilty of sin. His presentation shows that although the Jews looked down at the Gentiles and professed a superior standard in their law, since the gospel of God's grace presents a higher standard yet, both are condemned as sinners.

My Presbyterian professor in graduate studies, Dr. John H. Leith, commented on this text, "We are all alike sinners, but we are not sinners alike." Practices in sin are varied, but sin is more than deeds; it is estrangement from God. In honesty and confession, we come before God "before whom all hearts are open, all desires known."

> *It has been said, when you see some preachers in the pulpit,*
> *you think that they should never come out.*
> *But when you see some preachers outside of the pulpit,*
> *you think that they should never go in!*
> *Yet, really, who is worthy to stand in for the Lord?*
> *It is his Word that is perfect, not we as voices.*
> *With Isaiah, the vision of God will make us very humble;*
> *we too are persons of unclean lips.*

February 14

The Name of God

You that boast in the law, do you dishonor God by breaking the law?
Romans 2:23

Dishonor God? No, we exalt his name, but do so by walking with him. In the book of Acts (5:41) we find Christians described as followers of "the name," a people of the name. In Matthew 28:19 we are told to baptize persons into the name. A name is the identity of the person. Our mission is to make people conscious of the identity of the God we worship. We should live consistently with the name we profess. This is kingdom identity! We are called to walk with Jesus in life.

I recall once driving from Washington, DC, to Messiah College, near Harrisburg, Pennsylvania, to speak in the annual pastor's conference held at the college. The theme given me was, "The Gospel of Reconciliation in an Urban Context." My focus was on God's grace as he takes the initiative in reconciling us as his enemies, and our role is now to be agents of reconciliation extending that grace to others (2 Cor. 5:19-20). Grace, not judgment, reconciles. Judgment exposes the estrangement, but grace brings us together.

Paul is holding the legalistic Jew accountable for obedience to the law that he understands. For one to boast in the law and then to break the law as though it is for him to manipulate, is to dishonor God who gave the law and holds us accountable. We who profess to live by the will of God are responsible to live up to our profession.

When we are a Christian for ten years or more, we have the potential danger of formalizing or in-stitutionalizing our religion. We may be presumptuous in spiritual matters and become routine in religious exercises. We are worshipping the sovereign God, and this calls for a meaningful, awesome reverence and obedience.

I am amazed at Daniel's prayer in chapter 9, for as holy a man as Daniel was, yet he prayed for Israel, saying, "*We* have sinned," taking his place with others. Of our church, of our community, and of our nation we should say together, "We have sinned."

Lord, help us to be honest in confession
and grateful for your forgiveness. Amen

A Cause of Blasphemy

For, as it is written, "The name of God is blasphemed among the Gentiles because of you." Romans 2:24

"Blasphemed because of you." What an insightful judgment. If, as professors of faith, we live inconsistently, the unbelievers around us will continue to reject the God that they should be seeing in us. Paul, in another letter, refers to believers as living letters "known and read by all" (2 Cor. 3:2).

To live in a style inconsistent with the name we profess is to pervert the kingdom identity. Paul quotes Isaiah that the inconsistency of the Jews caused the Gentiles to blaspheme God. What a challenge to each of us, for our lifestyle in the marketplace is to express the identity of our God, the Father of our Lord Christ Jesus.

Once during a speaking engagement at the Mellingers Mennonite Church, Lancaster, Pennsylvania, I visited a man who needed to come to God and wanted to excuse himself. He defended his aloofness by saying to me, "You look at me as a man who needs to be saved, as a man that is lost, don't you?" Upon my attempt at a tactful response that was not judgmental, he moved on to his real point: "I am an atheist, and I bluntly say that there is no God. Tell me, what about those persons in the church who say, 'Yes, there is a God,' but they go and live as though there isn't one?"

A loving response disarmed him as I told him that the reason I was preaching was my concern for such practical atheists, that they might repent and open themselves to God. He did come to the meeting and much later, apart from my presence, he came to God in faith. Unbelief is not simply intellectual, for the question is, Do we want God in our lives?

The Lord has compassion that recognizes the limitations of our minds, as well as our passions. Doubts are not final when viewed as the normal function in which thinking persons seek reality. The Lord will answer the honest heart cry:

> *Lord, I believe! Help thou my unbelief.*
> *(Mark 9:24, KJV)*

Symbol and Meaning

Circumcision indeed is of value if you obey the law; but if you break the law, your circumcision has become uncircumcision. So, if those who are uncircumcised keep the requirements of the law, will not their uncircumcision be regarded as circumcision? Romans 2:25-26

My wife, Esther, is an artist, a sculptor, who has gained a reputation for her creative work. She is also well-known for various conferences for Christians in art, which she has often convened in Asia and Eastern Europe. She speaks of line as "a dot going for a walk." It has more symbolic meaning than physics, where a line is defined as "the shortest path between two points." Both approaches are true, but her use of line in art is so much more expressive.

In Christian faith when we discuss such things as the sacraments, we are involved in distinctions between sign, symbol, and meaning. The different symbols convey the meanings that persons are led to share. Symbol is more than sign, for symbol partakes of the reality which it represents. In old Israel, the rite of circumcision was a sign of being a distinct people of God. The meaning was of being set apart as God's people; the rite was only the sign, as a reminder. Paul uses the phrase "circumcision of the heart," a symbol of the heart belonging to God. Paul's argument is that to carry the mark of belonging to God while living contrary to God's law is to deny the very meaning of the symbol.

Symbol points to reality, but should not be confused as the reality itself. Rites of religion have their place, but they are not to be made absolutes. Sacraments communicate grace, but they are scarcely the mediators of grace. Jesus used symbol, often tying his story to symbols from the Old Testament:

> *I am the Living Water.*
> *I am the Light of the world.*
> *I am the Bread of life.*
> *I am the Door.*
> *I am the Good Shepherd.*
> *I am the true Vine.*
> *I am the Resurrection and the Life.*
> *I am the Way, the Truth, and the Life.*

February 17

Spirit Above Letter

Then those who are physically uncircumcised but keep the law will condemn you that have the written code and circumcision but break the law. Romans 2:27

We have seen that our faith is not in the symbol, but a relationship with God, to whom the symbol points. Throughout Scripture God calls us to an attitudinal relation with him. Through the prophets he said, "I desired mercy, and not sacrifice," (Hos. 6:6 KJV). Actually, in reading his Word, our attitude is to seek the spirit or meaning of the Scripture, not just see the words. In Jesus's Sermon on the Mount he begins with what we call the Beatitudes: *be-attitudes*! In Paul's second letter to the Corinthians he says the Spirit helps us understand the spirit of the Word and not just see or read the letter (2 Cor. 3).

Paul is saying that Gentiles who walk with God as honestly as they can are actually a judgment on the Jews who profess to be the people of God but do not follow his law. This has a definite application to the church and society. In some cases, society's consciousness of righteousness is actually a judgment when the church lacks a social consciousness on racism, war, handgun violence, human suffering, or ecological issues.

Following a lecture at the Evangelical Conference, "Peacemaking in a Nuclear Age," held in Pasadena, California, in 1983, a Christian leader confronted one of the speakers who had been quite nationalistic about his expression of civil religion. He said, "Gandhi was a non-Christian man with a Christian message; you are a Christian man with a non-Christian message." There is a spirit of Scripture that transforms the letter.

This is not just the contrast between the outer and the inner Word. The outer refers to the Word written, the inner refers to the light of the Holy Spirit. Above all we should recognize the Word in Christ, the Word in his person, which is God's full disclosure. The spirit of Scripture expresses its basic intent. It does not ignore the letter, but reads it as symbol, seeking the meaning of communication with God.

Lord, help me to grasp the spirit of meaning,
your vital word for my life today.
I need your Spirit's presence to understand
and to empower me to live your word. Amen

The True Jew

**For a person is not a Jew who is one outwardly, nor is true circumcision
something external and physical. Romans 2:28**

Paul, a Jew, is straightforward with his associates as to who is truly a Jew: one of God's people. The sign that one belongs to God is not outer but inner, not of the flesh but of the heart, not of the letter but of the spirit, not of man's recognition but of God's. What a text for today—exposing a religion of works as the opposite of a religion of grace.

Our part is response, not in order to gain or earn God's favor. He has already extended his love. Rather it is to testify to joining in covenant with our saving God. The focus is always on God. The witness is that this God, in accepting us, will accept all others who respond to him. For any group to imply that God accepts us because we are "special" is to be guilty of opposing God, whose mercy is for all peoples.

The tragedy of ethnic religion is that it is a pragmatic blasphemy. It stands in the way of God's plan for his saving grace. No ethnic group has an edge on the grace of God. His grace is without respect of persons. No denomination has captured the kingdom of God. No national identity or cultural sophistication has an advantage in the realm of faith. "For God so loved the world. . . ."—this gospel is a leveler for all peoples. When Paul says that he shared the gospel to the Jew first and then to the Greek, he was not giving preference, but recognizing priority in accountability.

To hear is to be responsible. In John Bunyan's, *Pilgrim's Progress*, a person at the Interpreters House is called "the man with the strong countenance." Hearing the gospel of grace, he said, "Write my name down, sir, for I have looked this thing in the face and come what may, I mean to be Christ-like and I will be."

To the first Jew, Abraham, God said, "In you all the families of earth shall be blessed." This was the promise and in this the blessing, that from his seed would come the "earth-bless-er," of the seed of Abraham, of the seed of David, incarnate by the Holy Spirit of the virgin Mary. It is to him that we commit ourselves as disciples.

Lord, give me the heart of Abraham,
a faith to pass on
to the many generations to come. Amen

Spiritual, Not Literal

Rather, a person is a Jew who is one inwardly, and real circumcision is a matter of the heart—it is spiritual and not literal. Such a person receives praise not from others but from God. Romans 2:29

We tend to be literalists in our simplicity, yet most of what we hear and interpret is figurative. Our language is filled with word pictures, similes, metaphors. And for God to speak to us in the use of language, in any language, he has to present eternal truth in patterns that we humans can grasp. To the woman at the well, Jesus said, "True worshippers will worship the Father in spirit and in truth, . . . God is spirit" (John 4:23-24).

Paul identifies himself as the seed of Abraham as he speaks of his call by God. He is tying his lineage, not to the flesh, but to Abraham's faith. This is not letter, but the spirit of meaning. We who are a people of faith are the seed of Abraham. God is creating a people for himself, not an ethnic tribe nor a particular race, but a people of faith who belong to God. In our text Paul says that this people of God is not the Jew of the flesh, but rather the inward Jew of faith. This includes all peoples, all races, all nations.

The New Testament language is "whosoever" language. The offer of grace is open to any and all who hear and respond. The real circumcision is internal, the inner directedness of walking with God. This is a work of the Spirit, a circumcision of the heart. Paul wrote an amazing book to the Galatians to make this point clear: our salvation is by the rightness of faith and not by achievement of righteousness by the law. Edwin Hatch wrote:

> *Breath on me, breath of God.*
> *Fill me with life anew,*
> *That I may love what thou dost love,*
> *And do what thou wouldst do.*
>
> *Breath on me, breath of God,*
> *Until my heart is pure,*
> *Until with Thee I will one will,*
> *To do and to endure.*

February 20

What Advantage Has the Jew?

**Then what advantage has the Jew? Or what is the value of circumcision?
Romans 3:1**

Our role in education is to pass on cultural values from one generation to another. Education is to excite the student about learning, to expand the circle of knowledge in a meaningful and responsible way. Education is one of the functions of the church. We are to teach all that our Lord has taught us and to model a spirit of learning the things of God that have been passed on to us. Jesus said, "It is enough for the disciple to be like the teacher" (Matt. 10:25).

In this text, Paul imagines the question in the Jewish mind in his declaration that salvation is not simply in being Jewish or by identifying with the law. What then is the advantage in being part of a strong tradition? Paul answers that heritage should be read as the foundation on which a people build, for it is the testing ground of history. James Baldwin, the writer and a leader during the Civil Rights Movement said, "A people not at peace with their past can have no meaningful future."

In history we have the proof of values, followed or disregarded, and we can read a tradition to find what works or what happens when a people disregard values. But the tradition stays where it is, as our background, and we live in the present and the future. The meaning of a tradition must be claimed again in each generation, and the goal of being a people of God must be found ever new by each generation. We have time-binding power to select from history and can channel it into life through our choices.

That God has done something unique in history through the Hebrew people is the story of the Bible. Even in unbelief, the presence of the Jewish people anywhere in the world is a reminder of Jehovah. He continues to use this people as a sermon to the world. But God's focus is on a people, not a land, for he said, "The land is mine; . . . you are but tenants and aliens" (Lev. 25:23). This understanding could help bring peace in Palestine.

*Privilege carries with it responsibility.
The Spirit gives gifts according to his own will;
he gives them for the good of all.
Consequently, our gifts are to be shared,
our talents put to use for mutual enrichment.*

February 21

The Oracles of God

What advantage has the Jew? Or what is the value in circumcision? Much, in every way. For in the first place the Jews were entrusted with the oracles of God. Romans 3:1-2

Of highest value in Jewish history is the Torah, the law of God. That God has spoken is an awesome reality. The one "wholly other" has come to us in grace, has communicated with us his will. And this oracle, given at Sinai, begins with the word of grace, "I am the LORD your God" (Exod. 20:2). Here God identifies with those he is calling.

It is an advantage, par excellence, to have and to know the oracles of God. Today there is increased biblical illiteracy. If people took God's Word seriously, it would lead to a spiritual renewal. The church would be renewed if we would hear the Word in context, not proof-text to prove our point. John Calvin said that the interpreter is responsible to let the writer say what he wants to say and not to make him say what we want him to say.

The advantage of the Jew is first that he has the knowledge of God's actions in history. This is what Dr. Oscar Cullmann has called *Heilsgeschichte*, salvation history. Through the history of the Jewish people, God has demonstrated his grace and presence. Yet Jesus said to the religious leaders of this people, "You search the scriptures because you think that in them you have eternal life; and it is they that testify on my behalf. Yet you refuse to come to me to have life" (John 5:39-40).

We can read God's disclosure in and through history, but we must also ask what God is saying in current history. Just as he had a people through whom he wanted to speak to the larger world, so today he has a people by which he speaks of his love to the world. A few years ago a communist challenged Christians, saying, "You have the most powerful message in the world. Nevertheless, it is we who will finally beat you—we do not play with what we believe.... We are willing to die for our cause."

The oracles of God are his Word,
His will given to Moses, shared with Israel;
The highest level of morality in human history.
So writes Peter after walking with Jesus,
Who models the person and the will of God!

February 22

What If . . .

What if some were unfaithful? Will their faithlessness nullify the faithfulness of God? Romans 3:3

Where I grew up as a boy, I had a neighbor who was a very fine Christian, practicing his faith in a Christian lifestyle, but he was very parochial and simplistic. He lived into the time of the age of space flights and to my knowledge never believed that persons had traveled into space around the earth or to the moon. But his unbelief did not change the facts of what has been done, from the astronaut John Glenn's first trip to the present.

Similarly Paul says, "If some did not believe," that does not change the fact that God has spoken his word and we are both privileged and accountable. Faith is response to evidence; it is a normal response of the mind when evidence is given. It takes a choice to say no to truth, for one to live in unfaith.

A young man in a university classroom was taken aback by the agnosticism of his professor. Raising his hand, he asked, "Doctor, what percent of the knowledge of the world would you say that you understand?" The professor paused a moment in thought then answered, "Perhaps as much as 3 percent." The student then asked, "Has it ever occurred to you that God just might exist in the other 97 percent?"

John the Baptist sent his disciples to Jesus with the question, "Are you the one who is to come, or are we to wait for another?" (Matt. 11:3). But Jesus went on about his work. Later he told the messengers to go back and tell John what they had seen. In doing this he gave John evidence, but not proof. As thinking persons, we look for evidence as an intelligible basis for faith.

> *God is not an it to be proven;*
> *God is Person.*
> *We come to God as the Thou,*
> *the Thou of the Universe.*
> *An honest approach will be open to God,*
> *and when we listen we will hear.*
> *Jesus said, "Anyone who resolves to do the will of God will know*
> *whether the teaching is from God." (John 7:17)*

53

February 23

Let God Be True

By no means! Although everyone is a liar, let God be proved true, as it is written, "So that you may be justified in your words, and prevail in your judging." Romans 3:4

Our basic problem is elevating self and displacing God. In the encounter between the tempter and Eve in the garden of Eden, the first temptation was to question God—his word, his goodness, and his intent. Paul's declaration in this text is the truthfulness of God and the deceptiveness of humanity. His cry, "Let God be true but every man a liar" is an outburst of assurance! God is the one true foundation on which all else can be built.

Each of us is called to recognize "the truth" as it "is in Jesus" (Eph. 4:21). It is this person of truth in whom we understand most fully the work and word of God. He is the one who is both the fulfillment of Scripture and is the full expression of the meaning of Scripture. The Bible is not a flat book, all on a level. So we do not build our faith on Israel's history unless it is further confirmed in or by Jesus as Lord.

Paul quotes from the prophetic Scripture as God's truth, with clarity for both relationship and judgment with integrity. We stand before a God who can be trusted to function by his word. God is sovereign; he will always act in a manner that is true to himself. He is not capricious. His word is God's commitment to us and the basis for our assurance. This can be universalized, for faith can be experienced in any and every culture, beyond religious expressions, by standing in judgment of idolizing those religious expressions and calling us to reach out to God beyond them.

When asked of my assurance of salvation, while I know of the doctrines of election and predestination, *my* assurance is simply that Jesus is as good as his word! Jesus said, "Anyone who comes to me I will never drive away" (John 6:37), and "Faith is the assurance of things hoped for, the conviction of things not seen" (Heb. 11:1).

Indeed, by faith our ancestors received approval.
By faith we understand.
(Hebrews 11:2-3)

February 24

God's Right of Vengeance

But if our injustice serves to confirm the justice of God, what should we say? That God is unjust to inflict wrath on us? (I speak in a human way.) By no means! For then how could God judge the world? Romans 3:5-6

Is it right to be perturbed, even to be angry about sin? It is often only when we see the destructive consequences of drugs, of alcohol, of pornography, of racism, of violence that we become deeply enough concerned to be angry about the evil and act against it. Only God in his holiness knows the full depth of human perversion in our sin.

Perversion is not only in acts of commission, but in sins of omission as well. Just as a parent may have dreams for a child and may live with the awareness that the dreams are not fulfilled, so God extends grace when we have failed his dream. A parent's dream may be selfish or totally unrealistic, but God's plan is for our good, fitted to our particular gifts, and designed for the very best in our experience. As we fail, God patiently works to correct us. One who stumbles is not down unless he stays down! We should learn to forgive ourselves, to release ourselves by facing our failure honestly.

Paul makes clear that we should not rationalize or excuse ourselves, as though to say, our failure is not so serious because it magnifies God's grace. Wonder of wonders, God's grace is more than enough to match our failures; he doesn't need failures as an excuse to express his grace. God is righteous, extending grace for wholeness.

God's wrath is not the opposite of love.
    The opposite is indifference.
Love includes a refusal to manipulate us.
    Wrath is to deeply disagree.
God's wrath is his exposure of our sin.
    It should lead to a correction.
God is right to express disapproval,
      Yes, and to think that he tempers wrath
        with forgiving love.

Do Evil That Good May Come?

But if through my falsehood God's truthfulness abounds to his glory, why am I still being condemned as a sinner? And why not say (as some people slander us by saying that we say), "Let us do evil so that good may come"? Their condemnation is deserved! Romans 3:7-8

There may be no greater wholeness than honesty with one's self in the presence of God. This honesty means that we are transparent before him. We should refuse to play games with ourselves to thereby avoid being honest with our discipline and growth. Authentic persons are those who own responsibility for their decisions.

Some argue that evil is acceptable as a basis on which good may be built; Paul condemns those who so argue. Yet how often we hear comments that in the fallen state of society we have to cope with evil by using evil? We do so, and then we ask God to be forgiving in the situation. Here Paul says in verse seven that someone may argue that since the ultimate is God's forgiving grace, it is legitimate for us to do evil that his grace be magnified!

Paul also counters the legalistic mind which goes to the other extreme, holding that by doing good one merits God's grace. Such might interpret Paul's stance by saying, "I may as well sin to provide occasion for God to forgive, for thereby my sin glorifies God." Paul is emphatic in saying that freedom in grace does not mean presumption. It is said, "When you work through your sin to the cross, you will never go back easily to it again." How marvelous our deliverance! "If we confess our sins, he who is faithful and just will forgive us our sins and cleanse us from all unrighteousness" (1 John 1:9).

> Can we "sin boldly that God may forgive boldly,
> and his grace be magnified"?
> Be careful; that we sin, yes, and we accept this fact
> with assurance of God's grace to forgive.
> But to justify and excuse ourselves,
> we in no way dare be presumptuous,
> For we are called to follow holiness,
> to belong totally to God.

All Are Under the Power of Sin

**What then? Are we any better off? No, not at all; for we have already charged
that all, both Jews and Greeks, are under the power of sin. Romans 3:9**

There are some sinners I would rather have as neighbors than others. There are different levels of
behavior among us whether we walk with God or not. Having one's back turned to God condemns us,
not the level of life we express in walking away from him.

Emil Brunner, the great European theologian, once wrote that two people taking an examination
may be quite different, one writing with impeccable style and the other with a scribble, but if both give
the wrong answers, both alike fail the exam. So our sophistication is not in itself a means of covering
our failures.

Many persons live by high levels of human achievement, and some unbelievers live more
admirable lives than some believers. There may be persons who are highly educated and sophisticated,
but are not walking with God, while others who may even be illiterate and poor live with God. It is the
latter who know God's grace. Our trust is in God's love, not in the excellence of our lifestyle. Some
limited persons have come a lot farther with what they have than have others who have so much talent
given them.

We will never forget one of the baptisms of two persons in our church in Washington, DC. The first
was a middle-aged man who had been a homeless streetwalker since age fifteen. The other was a
sophisticated young woman who was a violinist in a prominent orchestra in the city. Together they
came to the foot of the cross for baptism! There was hardly a dry eye in the congregation for God's
unlimited grace was awesome!

> *All of us alike come to God*
> *for the foot of the cross is level.*
> *Our differences may reflect our choices,*
> *which attest our accountability.*
> *Grace is God's offer to accept us,*
> *regardless from where we come.*

February 27

None Righteous

As it is written: "There is no one who is righteous, not even one." Romans 3:10

None is righteous . . . that is, not one of us is in right relationship with God. Righteousness is first belonging and then it is behaving. Unrighteousness is the position of independence from God that we have taken, not simply things we have done.

To recognize one's need is the first step toward a change. This is the need of God in our lives, of someone great enough and something good enough on which to build our lives. Only when an alcoholic or an addict will honestly recognize the seriousness of the problem can help be affective. If we are not convinced we are lost, we will keep on driving—making good time but in the wrong direction. I know I have done this. Paul has argued that Jew and Gentile are both on different paths; both alike have disobeyed God. Each has committed the sin of independence from God; thereby both are going down the wrong path.

The words "as it is written" take us back to the authoritative writings on which the Jewish community built its faith and life. We can only come to God because of his goodness, not ours. With this awareness, we place ourselves in his hands as a patient in the care of the doctor. This became especially real to me in trusting the cardiologist when I needed a stent in a clogged artery. Even while I watched the picture of the catheter moving in my heart and trusted the doctor, above all, it was God's grace that I trusted in the treatment. He is the doctor who offers to meet us in our unrighteousness by his loving acceptance.

God, I thank you for your love,
that it means your constant care.
You are there for me and I praise you,
acknowledging you today as my Lord.
You are my God and I worship and adore you
in my limited way but as sincerely as I know how. Amen

None Without Understanding Search

"There is no one who has understanding, there is no one who seeks God."
Romans 3:11

St. Augustine said, "For Thy glory we were and are created, and our hearts are restless until they find their rest in Thee." The longing for God, recognized or unrecognized, keeps us from being fulfilled merely with *things*. We were created for fellowship with God, for participation with God. Less is a compromise of our worth.

Human tendency seeks fulfillment in almost everything in life and makes each thing in turn to be a substitute god. The word of Scripture Paul quotes here declares that "no one understands, no one searches for God." True, God is beyond us, the wholly other, yet our deepest thoughts call us to recognize a sense of meaning, a vision of purpose, a reality that gives us meaning, and we should seek to understand this reality.

And tragedy of tragedies, humanity ignores the evidence that God keeps invading our sinful experiences to call us to himself and to his will. In the perversions of life people continually raise the question, "Where is God?" as though he is to blame. But we should be asking, "What is God telling us through this mess?" And he is telling us that this is what life is like when we shove God out of its center.

It is in reading God's self-disclosure and meeting the full expression in Christ that the honest mind asks, "Why seek some lesser God?" On this day you and I can open ourselves to him and recognize him as present with us in life.

> *Many religions*
> > *reach groping hands*
> > *trying to find God.*
> *The gospel of grace*
> > *tells us that in our reaching*
> > *we suddenly feel them clasped,*
> *from above!*

March 1

All Have Turned Away

All have turned aside, together they have become worthless; there is no one who shows kindness, there is not even one. Romans 3:12

Our problem is in turning away from God. Perversions follow from our turning from him. Alienation is the source for our deeds of evil. The correction of our problem is not simply in confessing certain wrongdoings, but correction happens in turning back to God. This is why the focus of Christian faith is on confessing Christ as Savior.

Jesus is my Savior, not only in the past, but also he saves me today from being what I would be without him. He is the one in whom we experience the righteousness of God, right relatedness with God. He has called us to himself, called us to the Lord.

Again our text is pointing to all having turned away from God. This is Isaiah's definition of sin: "All we like sheep have gone astray; we have all turned to our own way" (53:6). This is the definition of sin—going our own way rather than God's way. This may be in a dignified, sophisticated way of seeking our own fulfillment without God in an expression of pride, or in a sensual way of seeking fulfillment in the things of the more animal self, but at either level all have gone away from God.

Religious sinners need to turn to God just as much as the irreligious. The story of the prodigal son (Luke 15:11-32) shows that the religious son who stayed at home had a difficult time in experiencing grace. The pride of self-seeking has two expressions: the pride of power or position-seeking, and the pride of selfish sensual engagements.

> *Guilt is a servant, just as is pain,*
> *alike they warn us, not again.*
> *But loneliness, emptiness, futility,*
> *this is an even louder voice.*
> *Within each of us there is a God-sized hole,*
> *a vacancy to be filled by God himself.*
> *Made for fellowship with God,*
> *we are restless until fellowship is restored.*

Their Tongues Practice Deceit

Their throats are opened graves; they use their tongues to deceive. The venom of vipers is under their lips. Romans 3:13

A prominent mark of our depravity is the way in which we construe things to our advantage, including manipulation of the truth. And this is true for all of us, in the church and in the world. Each of us try to say things in a way that makes us appear good.

Several years ago I was a participant in the program of the National Association of Evangelicals meeting at Buffalo, New York. In the evening a group of us listened with deep interest to the president of the United States addressing the nation from the oval office concerning the Iran scam. It was evident in our discussion that followed that it is difficult for us to hear and to share the truth.

Years later, the United States became involved in a war in Iraq, a war many of us saw as unwise, unnecessary, and unjust. While caring deeply about the tyranny that has been dominating Iraq, we believed a coalition of containment, involving Arab neighbors, could have been negotiated with patience. Thousands of people suffered, and many problems followed. One deep problem was the attitudes toward the United States by the Arab world. It is difficult to know what to believe and to ever know what could have happened if an alternative had been heard.

The problem of untruth undercuts the possibilities of reconciliation between peoples. A lack of trust results in the lack of a common ground of relationship. In contrast or in contradistinction to human fallen state, God is trustworthy; his faithfulness extends from generation to generation without compromise.

> How futile life would be if no one could be trusted,
>   if words were always a cover-up.
> But the mind and conscience calls us
>   to a higher level of respect.
> With Emmanuel Kant's categorical imperative,
>   reason does speak to us:
> "Behave so that your behavior could be a universal law."

A Mouth of Cursing

Their mouths are full of cursing and bitterness. Romans 3:14

The denunciation of others is an extension of a warped ego, an attempt to climb over others, a strategy of put-downs to gain personal power. What a contrast to the words of Jesus: "Whoever wishes to be great among you must be your servant" (Matt. 20:26). Or again, "You know that the rules of the Gentiles lord it over them. It will not be so among you" (Matt. 20:25).

Our text says cursing is a spirit of denunciation. In a different sense, when I served on the board of directors of the Valley National Bank and was to be sworn in, in respect for my conviction on Jesus's words to not swear, the president instructed the lawyer taking our oath to permit me to affirm. But the problem of cursing is denunciation, although swearing may be trying to bind God to support our wishes. We avoid denunciation of others, as the text specifies, but seek to be supportive. On this matter, my wife, a fine sculptor, has worked in various countries of the world. She is not working in competition with others, not putting others down, but expressing her creative gift.

The arrogance of self-aggression leads us to do put-downs of others. In various ways we curse, we count another as undesirable. Cursing is the ultimate put-down, the verbal way of destroying another. Cursing is an expression of a misplaced ego, a spirit of dominance and supposed superiority. To curse is to act as though we are in control rather than to respect others and the power of God at work in each of us.

Jesus said, "Do not swear" (Matt. 5:34). We are to love, to be persons of positive discipline. When frustrated, the Spirit will enable us to transcend frustrations by creative action. Anger should call us to clarify but not to condemn, condescend, or compete.

> *Curse words are thoughtless speech,*
> *venting one's feelings without regard for others.*
> *Curse words are to elevate one's self*
> *at the expense of others.*
> *Compassion stands in noble contrast,*
> *attitude and action with love.*
> *Caring enough will correct one's relation,*
> *will gender a spirit of grace.*

Destructive Ways

Their feet are swift to shed blood; ruin and misery are in their paths.
Romans 3:15-16

The ultimate extension of self-interest is in the destruction of those who stand in the way. In more primitive patterns, persons just "rub another out," but in our more sophisticated societies there are other, more subtle ways to remove a person who is a threat.

In the Sermon on the Mount Jesus tells us that not only is killing wrong, but anything that leads to killing is wrong. Violence of spirit, as well as violence of deed, is destructive to human personality. The breakup of marriages is often a reflection of violence of spirit. The increase of teenage suicide is often the frustration of being violated or robbed of the sense of worth that one needs.

I was privileged to be a speaker at the National Association of Evangelicals Convention in Buffalo, New York, in a session on capital punishment called "Point-Counterpoint." I stressed the role of government as protecting the innocent and punishing the guilty, but emphasized containment rather than execution, recalling the Old Testament cities of refuge. An important approach is to help people accept a justice that works to correct the problem instead of ending a life and the possibility of repentance.

As disciples of Christ, we can in no way excuse evil and violence. Grace is in contrast to violence. Life imprisonment for a major crime may be as effective a punishment as we can give, and it does give opportunity for some experience of grace. Our penal system could be recrafted and nonviolent criminals engaged in constructive work for society to make retribution. The violent criminal should pay the penalty in appropriate confinement for the safety of others and accountability and reflection. A person is redeemable in grace even while the consequences of behavior are not erased.

> *To love, what a noble injunction of Scripture.*
> *But how counter to human nature.*
> *How embarrassing our violent nature.*
> *Persons without God succumb to violence.*
> *But God's nature is willing to suffer,*
> *To take the sting and pull out the stinger!*

Peace Often Unknown

And the way of peace they have not known. Romans 3:17

Grace and peace go together, not simply as two words in Paul's repeated greeting, but as cause and effect. There is no peace apart from grace. Peace with God is derived from his graciousness. Grace is personified in Christ "for he is our peace" (Eph. 2:14).

But peace is a foreign language to the self-centered humanist, for peace comes to us from God and is expected of us by God. One who does not understand God as a God of grace can neither share nor express his peace. In a world of violence, to present the kingdom of the Prince of Peace is to present another worldview.

God's love seeks to correct those of whom Paul says, "The way of peace they have not known." The prophet Isaiah says, "The effect of righteousness will be peace, and the result of righteousness, quietness and trust forever" (32:17). In Psalm 23 and the scenes in Isaiah, chapters 11 and 55 and others, we are introduced to a God who calls us *in* peace and *to* peace. Of this peace, God has called "you into his own kingdom and glory" (1 Thess. 2:12).

A wonderful statement on this theme is in Ephesians: "He is our peace; in his flesh he has made both groups into one and has broken down the dividing wall, that is, the hostility between us. . . . So he came and proclaimed peace to you who were far off and peace to those who were near; for through him both of us have access in one Spirit to the Father" (Eph. 2:14, 17-18). He made Jew and Gentile to be one new humanity, so making peace. This is a great social change by the evangelical gospel!

> *Lord, help me to know your peace,*
> *to experience peace with you*
> *and peace with others.*
> *My Redeemer, you are the Prince of Peace;*
> *you have made the two one and*
> *created one new humanity.*
> *May your community be my priority,*
> *your peace be my belonging, and*
> *practicing peace mark my behaving. Amen*

March 6

No Fear of God

There is no fear of God before their eyes. Romans 3:18

No fear, no reverence for God. Fear, in relation to God, is a word that means reverence, not terror in its use in Scripture. In Proverbs we read, "The fear of the LORD is the beginning of knowledge" (1:7). Our reverence for God puts everything else in order. The difference between a believer and a nonbeliever is that the believer worships God.

A people of nonfaith is a people with no reverence for God. It is a world in which reverence for God is not seen as a privilege, but is often viewed as an escape from one's own responsibility. The vision of life for the selfish person is determined by the limitations of the self. Our vision is as great as our understanding of God. As St. Augustine prayed, "Enlarge thou the mansion of my soul that you may enter in."

This lack of reverence for God is the concluding judgment in this list of evil. If we would be quality Christians, we must let God actually be our God. The transformation of life matures only in this reverence for God. Our daily worship is our recognition of his worth-ship in our lives. This is the essence of our prayers, our dependence upon God.

To give reverence is to worship, to live with a sense of relationship with God. And this is not simply a function in the assembly of worship, but is a practice of worship day by day. Our daily life is to be set in the context of our faith, of our highest priority. It is unbelief that refuses to worship.

When we join others in a worship service we should gather as a people of God who have walked with him all week in worshipful reverence. Now we meet to offer our praise jointly in the community of faith at worship.

The greatest divisions in our world
are not racial, cultural, or even national,
but are when people do or do not fear God.
Reverence for the Lord determines reverence for life.

All Are Guilty Before God

Now we know that whatever the law says, it speaks to those who are under the law, so that every mouth may be silenced, and the whole world may be held accountable to God. Romans 3:19

God deals with all peoples in grace by equity, and this equity also holds all people equally accountable to God. Those who think themselves righteous have no problem judging others as unrighteous, but our text is showing us that those "under the law" are also judged by the law and exposed as unrighteous. The language is pointed: "that every mouth may be silenced." That is, that no one has a right of argument or self-justification.

Our human nature always seeks to defend itself. A. W. Tozer once said, "We seem to have been born with our fists clenched." This pattern of self-defense is extended to cover the whole of life in self-justification. Before we can enjoy God's forgiveness, we need to confess our need and our failures. It is an admission of our need that can turn us to God.

But being motivated to a higher level as we come to God is not by guilt, for our higher motivation is by his love. God calls us to walk with him, and in fellowship we find new dimensions of life opening before us. True faith does not limit life, it expands life.

During a preaching mission for revival, an attendant at a service station told me, "I don't need this conversion you preach about! God and I are on good terms." I replied, "That is what I'm really concerned about, that people be on good terms with God. Let's pray together. Would you lead us?" He was startled by this and, of course, refused. He wasn't on such good terms with God after all. Our claims are bold until made before the Lord. Washington Gladden wrote:

> *Help me the slow of heart to move,*
> *by some clear, winning word of love;*
> *teach me the wayward feet to stay,*
> *and guide them in the homeward way.*

Consciousness of Sin

For "no human being will be justified in his sight" by deeds prescribed by the law, for through the law comes the knowledge of sin. Romans 3:20

The function of the law is clearly stated in this text. The law wasn't given to save persons; rather, it was given to show our need of a Savior. By it our sins are exposed. A plumb line reveals a leaning wall, and a level shows a slope on an incline. Just so the law exposes our deviations from the will of God. By the law is the consciousness of sin.

At best, we may affirm that the law serves as a guideline for the people of God. It serves as a directive for behavior, but it offers no motivation or power in itself for our behavior. At the deepest level, we must want to live by the will of God. In ethics the big question is not "What do we do?" but "Why do we do what we do?"

Since we cannot fulfill God's law in ourselves and thereby win his approval, we come to him totally dependent on a gracious God who cares more about us than about what we have done. God moves beyond the issue to the person. God accepts us in love and changes us by love. Much like a standard by which test papers are graded in school, its value is to help us grow in knowledge. The test itself will not shape us. God's use of the law will create consciousness of our need of his help.

My wife, Esther, has been a counselor and mentor to a woman since she was in her teens. It was difficult for this woman to truly believe God loves her. As a child, her father used the law as a weapon without love. For example, when she was sixteen years old, she came home one day wearing something against one of his unreasonable laws. In anger, her father bent her over his knee, pulled her pants down, and beat her with a stick. No wonder she had a problem believing that God's laws are in perfect love. No wonder she said she wanted nothing to do with a strict and angry God. Thankfully, she has finally claimed God's grace and love in faith.

A Righteousness Apart from Law

But now, apart from law, the righteousness of God has been disclosed, and is attested by the law and the prophets. Romans 3:21

The bold claim made by Paul is of a different kind of righteousness, a rightness or right relatedness with God that happens through faith rather than through law. In a very real sense this is not setting aside the law, but seeing its limited role and moving beyond it by a faith that reaches to God himself.

The Old Testament Scriptures affirm what Paul is teaching. Samuel said to King Saul, "To obey is better than sacrifice, and to heed than the fat of rams" (1 Sam. 15:22). The prophet Isaiah represents God as saying, "Bringing offerings is futile . . . New moon and sabbath and calling of convocation—I cannot endure" (1:13). Micah interprets God's will, "He has told you, O mortal, what is good; and what does the LORD require of you but to do justice, and to love kindness, and to walk humbly with your God" (6:8).

God calls us to walk with him in life. We should say with David, "I delight to do your will, O my God" (Ps. 40:8), and again, "As a deer longs for flowing streams, so my soul longs for you, O God" (Ps. 42:1). As St. Augustine said in words that are now immortalized, "For Thy glory we were and are created, and our hearts are restless until they rest in Thee."

An Anabaptist, Hans Denck of the sixteenth century, said, "No one can truly know Christ except one who follows him daily in life, and no one can follow Christ without first knowing him." This is the essential nature of discipleship.

There is a way of knowing that is more than ideas; it is knowing another as in friendship, in love, in covenant. This is the way in which we are called to know our Lord. Paul said that his greatest desire was simply, "That I may know him" (Phil. 3:10, KJV).

> *Let me hunger for nothing other than God,*
> *to yearn for his presence and joy;*
> *To know his grace in daily living,*
> *his purpose as my one desire.*

Righteousness Through Faith in Christ

. . . the righteousness of God through faith in Jesus Christ for all who believe. For there is no distinction. Romans 3:22

What a fantastic view; God is seeking to redeem all peoples freely in Christ. The verse reads, "the righteousness of God through faith in Jesus Christ." It is from God himself, he has moved to us to reconcile us to himself. Right relatedness comes by faith, by a response of identifying with God and his will.

To respond to God is not to respond to some impersonal force, some unknown authority, some principle of life, but to respond to a personal God known in the person of Jesus Christ. Jesus said, "Whoever has seen me has seen the Father" (John 14:9). We come to Jesus as God's expression of himself in human experience. We confirm that since Jesus is what God is like, we'd rather walk with him than anything in the world.

Regardless of the experience or degree of our understanding of God's laws, there is a new criterion of deciding for God. We meet him in Jesus.

In one of the artists' conferences in Eastern Europe my wife, Esther, was involved with the curator of a National Museum of Art. She was not a believer but was brought to the conference by some Christian artists. Throughout the week she would go off to the side, smoking, grumbling, and criticizing. On the day before the closing of the conference, she came to Esther and, almost in tears, said, "Esther, I can't come to God! I've committed every kind of sin you can think of. I can't come to God!" Esther responded to her gently, "Rena (not her name), you don't need to come to God. God has already come to you, and all you need to do is say 'yes' to Jesus, and God will do the rest." She quietly responded, "I never heard that before." The next morning, in the last session, Esther opened with giving opportunity for anyone to express what may have happened to them during the week. Immediately, Rena ran to the podium. In tears she said, "I'm coming here to say 'yes' to Jesus!" To know that God has come to us in Jesus is to know God's marvelous grace.

> *God, we thank you that you*
> *came to us in Jesus, your Son.*
> *In him you stooped to us and gave us*
> *enough understanding to guide us in faith. Amen*

March 11

All Have Sinned

Since all have sinned and fall short of the glory of God. Romans 3:23

Paul's argument to this point in his letter to the Romans has been developed to show that all have sinned. It was necessary for him to show that everyone is estranged from God, that we all stand in need of salvation through the grace of God. It is with this awareness that each of us alike must kneel at the foot of the cross; here the depth of our sin is exposed. But now, in this verse, the depth of God's love is expressed.

James wrote that if we offend in one point, we are guilty as though we had broken the whole law. He, with Paul, is exposing the fallacy of pride in limited moral achievements when the actual problem is our disobedience of God and consequent estrangement from him. It is not the extent of our sin that constitutes our lost state, but it is our rebellion against God. The good news, the gospel, is better understood with this groundwork for human accountability.

Today we tend to erase the word "sin" from our vocabulary. Operating as though everything is relative, we negate the moral guidelines of God's Word. The function of God's law, while not to save, is to show us that we need to be saved. God calls us to himself, and in his very call it is implicit that, being away from God, we return to him.

Heavenly Father, we come humbly before you,
confessing our sin and our sins.
Our sin is in turning against you;
then follows the perversions in our lives.
We confess and turn back to you in answer to your call,
and then confess and deal with our perversions.
Thank you for accepting us in Christ our Redeemer;
by your Spirit and counsel free us from evil.
We would follow holiness in our lives
by walking with Jesus in the way. Amen

March 12

Justified Freely

They are now justified by his grace as a gift, through the redemption that is in Christ Jesus. Romans 3:24

What a wonderful God. He is not one who is difficult to approach, but one who has opened himself to us. He not only took the initiative; he personified his grace in Jesus Christ, actualizing divine love even to the death on the cross—a death that redeems us and brings us back to God!

In longing to change persons who have been in rebellion, God moved to us in his love. One reason Jesus had to die is that in loving a person who is in trouble you don't drop out, but you hang in with them in their problem. And Jesus did just that, he hung in with us in our rebellion, even when the antagonism led to his death.

"God so loved the world that he gave his only Son" (John 3:16). And he keeps giving himself, identifying with us. He forgave us, knowing that he would have to forgive again and again. The sacrifice on the cross was once and for all; he tasted death for every person. But the meaning comes again to him and to us each time he forgives.

With this larger meaning of forgiveness, we come to the cross, not to be finished with the cross, but to begin our identification with the cross. Through the power of the cross he keeps on delivering us from our sin. In 1 John 1:7, the present tense verb in the Greek means "keeps on cleansing us." To be justified by grace is to be free in grace to walk with God today and each day. Julia A. Johnston wrote:

> Marvelous grace of our loving Lord,
> Grace that exceeds our sin and our guilt,
> Yonder on Calvary's mount outpoured,
> There where the blood of the Lamb was spilt.
>
> Grace, grace, God's grace,
> Grace that will pardon and cleanse within.
> Grace, grace, God's grace,
> Grace that is greater than all our sin.

God's Amazing Expression

. . . whom God put forward as a sacrifice of atonement by his blood, effective through faith. He did this to show his righteousness, because in his divine forbearance he had passed over the sins previously committed. Romans 3:25

Mercy is an affirmation of worth. The offending person is still more important than the offense. Mercy enables one to forgive even while holding persons accountable for their offense. Mercy tempers justice by working to correct the problem. God sent forth Jesus as his expression of mercy—as his mercy seat, his place of meeting with us.

Early on, God had Moses guide the children of Israel in building the tabernacle as the place for his meeting with them. This was located at the center of their camp. God's presence was to be central for their life together. The symbol of God's presence and guidance was seen in the pillar of cloud over the tabernacle in the day and a pillar which glowed as fire appeared by night. It rested over the most holy place, specifically over the mercy seat. God said to Moses, "There I will meet with you" (Exod. 25:22).

As the sacrifice of atonement symbolized that forgiveness by a cost paid beyond ourselves, so in Christ our forgiveness is an amazing cost to him—his very life. In his blood, in the total giving of his life for us, we have forgiveness: at-one-ment with God.

In 1891, a book of twenty-four handwritten pages entitled *The Daily Sacrifice* was bought at public auction and passed down in the Emerson family. It was a book of prayers by George Washington. He prayed, "Oh blessed Father, let thy Son's blood wash me from all impurities that I may know my sins are forgiven by his death and passion."

How is God just in accepting us?
 Justice is the correction of the problem.
Our problem is one of rebellion, of estrangement.
 In Christ, he calls us back; brings our rebellion to an end.
Hence, God is just in expressing mercy to us who repent.
 For it is in our turning back that he has corrected the problem.

March 14

That He Might Be Just

It was to prove at the present time that he himself is righteous and that he justifies the one who has faith in Jesus. Romans 3:26

All of us are pleased when, in life, mercy tempers justice, whether that is expressed by the parent to a child, by the traffic officer, or by the judge in court. We could ask whether justice, true justice, can be expressed without mercy. We are not dealing with a mathematical equation when we deal with justice; we are dealing with persons in whose lives are the complex convergence of many influences.

God is just in meeting each of us on the basis of our responsibility for our actions. We cannot answer for Adam's mistake and its influence, but we can answer for what we do about it in our lives. In setting forth Jesus as an expression of mercy, God makes it possible for us to deal with the problem that alienates us from him. Therefore God is just in his dealing with us. Justice is a correction of our problem, that is, turning us back to God. We have gone away from God in our own self-interest. He confronts us in Christ and so is just. This is not a simplistic escapism, but an honest correction of the broken relationship.

Justice is not paying back in kind or giving one "his just desert." Full justice is the *correction* of the problem. God in Christ does not treat me on the basis of my sin, but on the basis of his character. This impels him to correct me rather than to destroy me, to turn me back into fellowship with him.

Some problems remain, but we live in his grace. A young boy in Bismarck, North Dakota, born without arms, remained triumphant in his spirit. He said, "I know there are some things I can't do. But I think of all the things I *can* do, and I don't worry so much about the rest of it." Justice? Who can say? But victorious in spirit? Yes!

> *That He might be just*
> *the hosts of heaven celebrate, I'm sure,*
> *and the legions of hell are silenced.*
> *God works in grace to reconcile us to himself;*
> *this is the basis for our justification,*
> *this is the end of rebellion.*
> *God is just in transformation by his mercy!*

The Ground Is Faith

Then what becomes of boasting? It is excluded. By what law? By that of works? No, but by the law of faith. Romans 3:27

When we affirm that we are children of God, saved from rebellion and alienation by his marvelous grace, we are not boasting of our achievements but are witnessing to this gift of God's love. All boasting (of one's heritage, of religious performance, of achievements in good works) is excluded by the recognition that salvation is of God.

This recognition cuts away the nerve of prejudice toward others whom we tend to look at as less spiritual. They may be responding to God as honestly as they know how, and he accepts all who respond to him in faith. We are responding. He is saving.

Assurance of salvation is based on our confidence that Jesus is as good as his word. He has called us and has said, "Him that cometh to me I will in no wise cast out" (John 6:37, KJV). We have come in faith, and we rest in the assurance that Jesus keeps his word. If we seek assurance by keeping the law, we could never be assured that we have kept it well enough to be accepted; we would only have a "hope so" salvation. And one presumes to obey enough to be acceptable, his boast affronts the lesser achiever. But Paul says, no, there is no boasting, for to each alike grace is a gift.

Paul's testimony becomes ours: "May I never boast of anything except the cross of our Lord Jesus Christ, by which the world has been crucified to me, and I to the world" (Gal. 6:14). The cross is the depth of love, the price of forgiveness. It is the sacrifice making possible a new devotion to a self-giving Lord. In the power of the cross we are made to be new creatures. We participate in a new relationship, a new order in Christ.

> *In Christ we comprehend the incomprehensible.*
> *We know the breadth and length and depth and height*
> *of his matchless love beyond our comprehension.*
> *For we know in part and we prophecy in part,*
> *but the perfect will come and the partial will be gone.*
> *We don't understand the depth of his grace,*
> *but we know him in grace and that is enough.*

Is God a God of Ethnicity?

For we hold that a person is justified by faith apart from works prescribed by the law. Romans 3:28

Through nearly fifty years of ecumenical evangelistic ministry, I recognize that no one group has captured the kingdom. There is no Christian culture as such, but Christians in a multitude of cultures and denominations witness to the presence of the kingdom. In any culture, when people come to Christ, their values change and their lives are enriched. However, it is on this very point that we must be careful as Christians, for it is easy to assume that the change will conform the new believers to our culture.

In the past, groups sending missionaries often operated as though converts would move into the missionaries' culture. From the West we tend to Westernize. The developing churches in other cultures should become post-Western; they should move beyond the missionary dominance, for God's grace can meet people in any culture. The Jews had a problem with the Gentiles, accepting them only when they converted to Judaism. The Jerusalem Conference declared that it is God whom we worship, not our cultural patterns (Acts 15).

Paul's affirmation is liberating. God is also the God of the Gentiles. In saying this, he is affirming that Gentiles can come to God through Christ in a direct route and not through the Jewish pattern. That which has placed Jew and Gentile on common ground is the recognition that there is only one way to come to God—by faith in Jesus.

Grace is a great leveler, for none has an edge over the other. He has broken down the middle wall of partition. In the early 1950s, as a pastor in Sarasota, Florida, I knelt to wash the feet of my black brother, and we affirmed the freedom we shared in grace.

> *We are citizens of a global community.*
> *We know that in our modern world,*
> *With six billion persons, which we can't fathom,*
> *We belong to each other and with each other.*
> *God's kingdom is global;,*
> *We know this in our study of the Word.*

Faith Apart from the Law

Or is God the God of Jews only? Is he not the God of Gentiles also? Yes, of Gentiles also. Romans 3:29

Our world of over six billion people is one world. It is so interdependent that it must be seen as one village. The greater spiritual challenge is how to share the good news of Christ in this one world with a variety of cultures and religions.

We should note again the perspective expressed by Mahatma Gandhi to the missionary statesman, E. Stanley Jones, responding to Jones' question whether he should go back to America. Gandhi gave a very helpful guide for missions. He said stay, but (1) live your religion, (2) be clear about what you believe so that we can understand it, (3) make love primary, and (4) be more understanding of other religions.

We too often fall short on understanding other religions. Edmund Perry says that to be missionary to persons of another religion we must study their religion until we understand it so well and see its values so clearly that we could be tempted to join it. Only then can we show them what Jesus has to offer that is greater. We can regard others as sincerely religious rather than as pagan, and then show them what Jesus has to offer that is not in their religion—a firsthand relation with the forgiving God.

A number of years ago we were in Bangkok, Thailand. We saw two Buddhist monks sitting on a bench and reading a New Testament. I asked them what they were reading and what they were finding. Their reply was that Christ teaches forgiveness, something, they said, that their religion does not have.

> *All religions are in a quest to be right with God;*
> *following religious rites and laws in this attempt.*
> *But, these rites and actions are but achievements*
> *and may be other than an attitude that reaches to him.*
> *How subtly we seek our own fulfillment,*
> *rather than engaging the God for whom we yearn.*
> *As we look into the light, let us be sure that we seek him.*

One God

. . . since God is one; and he will justify the circumcised on the ground of faith and the uncircumcised through that same faith. Romans 3:30

God is not capricious, he is consistent with his own person. This is why we can be prophetic. We can project into the future on the basis of the manner in which God has worked in the past. He will be consistent with himself, with the principles that express his holiness, his loving spirit toward all of his creation.

Paul has now concluded that the only way in which the Jewish people can be saved, even as a people who have lived under the law, is by *faith*. Once this is recognized, it follows that Gentiles who come by faith are similarly saved without having lived under the law. All are saved only by the grace of God through faith.

The text says God is one. This profound perception of God, in both the Hebrew *ekhad* (meaning *one*) and the New Testament words, "There is . . . one Lord, one faith, one baptism, one God and Father of all" (Eph. 4:4-6), can scarcely mean a numerical one in either case. God is One as *oneness* rather than a numerical one. God is a person of community, a *perechoric* community of mutual interrelated participation, as John of Damascus interpreted the idea of the Trinity. Beyond our comprehension, this oneness is of Father-Son-Holy Spirit. In God we recognize our Creator, Redeemer, and Sanctifier.

God has redeemed us, and we can accept his grace as the ground of salvation. Each of us is invited in grace to respond by faith. The gospel is God's "yes" to us; now it is our move. Faith is our "yes" to God, inviting him to be himself in us.

> *God says "yes" to us, how wonderful!*
> *We can't ask why without exalting him.*
> *He says "yes" because of who he is.*
> *He, is our Creator, the God of grace and of glory.*
> *He makes himself known, as Jesus said,*
> *"No one knows the Son except the Father,*
> *and no one knows the Father except the Son*
> *and anyone to whom the Son chooses to reveal him." (Matt. 11:27)*

Upholding the Law

Do we then overthrow the law by this faith? By no means! On the contrary, we uphold the law. Romans 3:31

We relate to other persons by the laws of association, expression, and response. This does not mean that we ignore moral laws. We simply recognize that a relationship moves beyond the constraint of law. To be justified by faith is not negating the law, but recognizing that law is not the mediator of our relationship with God. The one mediator is Christ, and by faith in him we are actually relating to God.

Justification by faith (*sola fide*) is one of the four basic principles of the Reformation. The other three are *sola scriptura*, the universal priesthood of the believer, and the sanctity of the common life. As Anabaptists, we would emphasize an overall principle of *sola christus* (only Christ) and his call to discipleship. The law was not given to save us, but to show us we need a Savior. Salvation by faith upholds the law in its role; it does not nullify the law.

The law has been God's pointer for humanity, and it is only that. It doesn't save a person. It points us to the Savior. The law makes us aware of our accountability to God, aware of our being away from God and of our sinfulness, which makes it easier to do the wrong than to do the right. In this awareness, it points us to our need of a Savior.

Again, Jesus is my Savior now; he saves me from being what I would be without him. We should be careful that we recognize this daily, that we avoid any tendency to feel that we don't need him—that we don't need the Doctor!

"For God so loved the world that he gave his only Son, that whoever believes in him should not perish but have eternal life" (John 3:16, RSV). This is our assurance of salvation. Charlotte Elliot found release from her deep bitterness when a guest, the Reverend Caesar Milan, confronted her with the meaning of grace. Charlotte expressed her discovery of this wonderful privilege in a hymn:

> *Just as I am, without one plea,*
> *But that Thy blood was shed for me,*
> *And that Thou bid'st me come to Thee,*
> *O Lamb of God, I come, I come.*

Abraham's Discovery

What then are we to say was gained by Abraham, our ancestor according to the flesh? Romans 4:1

Abraham is spoken of as the father of those who come to God in faith. Tragically, many have professed to be children of Abraham without being children of faith. When Paul calls Abraham "our ancestor," he is addressing Jew and Gentile alike, the one to whom both look as a mentor in faith. Hearing God's call, he responded in obedience, and as he walked with God, the next steps were made clear.

Reading the story of Abraham in Genesis (12–25), we discover the interplay between Abraham's steps of obedience and God's further disclosures. Several times we read the words "*after that*, the Lord appeared to Abraham again." It is the "after that" in the act of obedience that conditions the next phase of the story. For too many of us, there has been a lack of obedient faith—no "after that," and the next steps have not followed.

Abraham's life is not one of perfection, but one of faith. He made his mistakes but, "he looked forward to a city, . . . whose architect and builder is God" (Heb. 11:10). Jesus said, "Abraham rejoiced that he would see my day; he saw it and was glad" (John 8:56). We now have more evidence for Christ has come, has died, and has risen! We rejoice in faith.

Faith for Abraham was to take God at his word. His salvation was in the integrity of faith, not in his perfection. Who of us has not staggered at his faith in offering Isaac, yet believing that if Isaac was to die, God would raise him again to fulfill his promise? (Heb. 11:19). This faith is beyond what many of us know, but note, this is faith in God not faith in faith.

> *What is there about faith that is the avenue to salvation?*
> *Faith honors the person to whom we come.*
> *Faith responds to evidence of his grace, not our achievements.*
> *Faith is active, not passive, for faith commits.*
> *Faith works by love, according to the Scriptures. (Gal.5:6)*
> *We are saved by grace through faith. (Eph. 2:8)*

Not by Works—No Boasting

For if Abraham was justified by works, he has something to boast about, but not before God. Romans 4:2

We are told that God took the faith that Abraham had and credited it to him for the righteousness that he didn't have (Gal. 3:6). Righteousness is right relatedness, and this relatedness with God was lacking in Abraham's life until his faith response. God accepted him in his faith response, and he became known as "the friend of God" (James 2:23).

Of Abraham, Paul says that if his works had gained him access to God, he could then boast. But God called, and he was honest enough to admit his need and humble enough to answer God's invitation. The affirmation of faith is response to a gracious God, who gives us confidence in being chosen by him.

A reporter was once in an Asian country where a man could secure a wife for two cows. If she was quite beautiful, he would need to pay three. However, if she was not so beautiful, he could secure her for one cow. Hearing of an eight-cow bride, the reporter made a long trek through the countryside to see her. As he came to the cottage, a man and his son were working in the garden.

The reporter asked about the eight-cow bride. The man replied, "She is my wife! You may meet her. In fact, she would want you to stay for dinner." He did just that. As the woman served them, he noted that she was not physically beautiful, but he was impressed by her gentle, gracious, beautiful spirit.

After an enjoyable visit, he expressed his thanks and excused himself. The man walked down the path with him and said, "You've seen the eight-cow bride, but you don't understand. When we were young, I fell in love with my wife, but she was not outstanding in beauty. No other had courted her. I could have gotten her for one cow. But how would she feel in life as a one-cow bride? I decided I'd take care of that, and I offered her dad eight cows! Now look at her self-esteem and her beautiful countenance! Do you now understand an eight-cow bride?" God's love elevates our worth. Rowland Hill wrote:

I cannot work my soul to save,
For that my Lord has done;
But then, I'd work like any slave
For love to God's own Son.

March 22

Belief Accredited as Righteousness

For what does the scripture say? "Abraham believed God and it was reckoned to him as righteousness." Romans 4:3

A humble spirit in receiving from another results in receiving what we could not achieve on our own. When one of great position accepts those of us of lesser position, we are "graced," but it should be with a spirit of humility. Our joy in being accepted is to boast of the one receiving us; it is not that we have gained access. What we could not achieve, God has offered us—access to himself.

This brings our religion under God's judgment, for as in the Sermon on the Mount, we are called to more than a simple practice of religion. Jesus said, "Unless your righteousness exceeds that of the scribes and Pharisees, you will never enter the kingdom of heaven" (Matt. 5:20).

To live in faith is to live in fellowship, it is to walk with God. This is the dynamic of transformation. For "Christ . . . became for us wisdom from God, and righteousness and sanctification and redemption" (1 Cor. 1:30). Of these four, the first two, wisdom and right relatedness, are now experienced in the present. Holiness and redemption are to be fulfilled. The form of the Greek word for holiness means in process, and redemption, as a release into the presence of God, is yet to fully come.

As we will read later, God has chosen us and "we are predestined to be conformed to the image of his Son" (Rom. 8:29). The writer of Hebrews encourages us to go on "toward" perfection, that is, to maturity in Christ (Heb. 6:1). To live in faith is to live in fellowship. It is to walk with God. Abraham believed God and walked with him. This is more than an inner peace, it is a presence walking with us and we with him. Washington Gladden wrote:

> *O Master, let me walk with Thee*
> *In lowly paths of service free,*
> *Tell me Thy secret, help me bear*
> *The strain of toil, the fret of care. Amen*

March 23

A Gift, Not Wages

Now to one who works, wages are not reckoned as a gift but as something due. Romans 4:4

What a marvelous understanding of God: that he is gracious to all, giving freely of himself in forgiving, reconciling grace. When we could not earn his approval by works, he moved to us with a mercy that forgives and accepts us so that we can now walk in obedient response.

Our salvation is not wages; it is a gift from God. Having come to the cross in reconciliation, we now work out from the cross in discipleship. A disciple is not working to earn salvation; rather, a disciple identifies with the Master in grace and serves in the spirit of love. We belong to Christ, and we live in a relationship with him as Lord.

A disciple comes to the Scripture with his mind already made up to obey it. We come to God's Word with the prayer that God will show us his will. Ours is a relationship of faith, which means response; it means obedience. Our obedience is an obedience of freedom, not of legalism. Wages? No! For if so, mine would be so paltry as not to accrue. On that score, I'd always have a deficit. But—another has granted me a draft that more than covers the account. In Christ we share the riches of glory. We have all that it takes and more to be accepted in the circle, and we can say, "Abba, Father."

> *O the depth of the riches and wisdom and knowledge of God!*
> *How unsearchable are his judgments and how inscrutable his ways!*
> *"For who has known the mind of the Lord?*
> *Or who has been his counselor?"*
> *"Or who has given a gift to him, to receive a gift in return?"*
> *For from him and through him and to him are all things.*
> *To him be the glory forever. Amen*
> *—Romans 11:33-36*

Faith Counted as Righteousness

But to one who without works trusts him who justifies the ungodly, such faith is reckoned as righteousness. Romans 4:5

God takes the faith which the believer expresses and credits it for righteousness, or "as" righteousness. The basic meaning of righteousness, right relatedness, can also be translated "justice." Since faith is relational, a trust relation, the faith that God accepts as justice/righteousness is the faith that has ceased rebelling. Christ is our righteousness, our right relatedness. This is not a legalism but an existential (personal) relationship.

This concept divides between religions that reach out to find God and salvation by God's reaching to us. If we seek to approach him by religious deeds and ritual, we deny the gospel itself. Faith is "believing and receiving" rather than trying to merit access to God. The world is full of religion, but God only wants response in faith.

Paul opens the door to all people, expressing that God is a God who justifies the wicked, but he narrows the aperture by saying that salvation is for the one who trusts God. His argument is to show how any and all of us can come to God. There is one ground for any and all to come to God: his mercy toward all who believe.

This is the good news, the gospel of the kingdom: all who will come in faith can become children of God. "To all who received him, who believed in his name, he gave power to become children of God" (John 1:12). This is our joy and strength this very day.

> *Dear Lord,*
> *I come in the humility that can only receive,*
> *accepting your grace in forgiveness and love,*
> *returning as the prodigal to receive your welcome,*
> *to be identified as your own grateful child,*
> *receiving the robe of your acceptance,*
> *through Jesus Christ my Lord. Amen*

God Credits Apart from Works

So also David speaks of the blessedness of those to whom God reckons righteousness apart from works. Romans 4:6

That God cares for us so deeply that he forgives and accepts when we cannot bridge the gulf will always remain the wonder of grace. How blessed! God has chosen me! In his mercy he has reached into my life and turned me to himself. And as I respond by faith, he credits my account with a righteous relationship that he made possible.

The fact that God accepts "apart from works" means that the acceptance is totally his decision. This is not denying that the accepted one is accountable for the new covenant of fellowship. This covenant relation is initiated by God but enjoined upon me as response. To ignore the implications of fellowship and fail to walk with God would be to deny the covenant. Righteousness is by this covenant relation.

"Blessed be the God and Father of our Lord Jesus Christ! By his great mercy he has given us a new birth into a living hope through the resurrection of Jesus Christ from the dead, and into an inheritance that is imperishable, undefiled, and unfading, kept in heaven for you, who are being protected by the power of God through faith for a salvation ready to be revealed in the last time" (1 Peter 1:3-5).

Peter's expression "given us a new birth" may be a confessional awareness. It may be a celebration that, having denied his Lord, he has even so been reinstated. Robert Robinson wrote the verse:

> *O to grace, how great a debtor*
> *Daily I'm constrained to be!*
> *Let Thy goodness, like a fetter,*
> *Bind my wand'ring heart to Thee.*
> *Prone to wander, Lord, I feel it,*
> *Prone to leave the God I love;*
> *Here's my heart, O take and seal it,*
> *Seal it for Thy courts above.*

Blessed Are the Forgiven

Blessed are those whose iniquities are forgiven, and whose sins are covered.
Romans 4:7

Forgiveness is not a package that you receive and run away with. Forgiveness is only in relationship. The power of forgiveness is the restoration of relationship with the other. For the forgiven one, our forgiveness is also a release, the freeing of one from being intimidated by failure, of being dominated by guilt.

To be forgiven is to become free, open, able to look up into the face of the forgiving one. Through tears, yes. Through repentance, assuredly. But to look up and to stand up in praise to God. Again, forgiveness means that God cares more about us than about what we have done; he moves beyond the issue to the person.

Until we work through our sins at the cross, we haven't been honest. Honesty calls us to the cross, for only here can we recognize and confess the full intensity of our sin: our rejection of God and his will. Consequently, only at the cross can we experience forgiveness, for only here can we meet God in the pain he bore for us.

God is faithful and gracious in forgiving our sin. No other religion of the world has a message of forgiveness by a personal God. Various leaders in Far Eastern religions have told me that they had to borrow the idea of forgiveness from the Christians, but forgiveness is more than an idea—forgiveness is engagement with a personal Lord.

> *To be forgiven is to be included in fellowship:*
> *It is to be accepted by the Forgiving One.*
> *It is to be delivered from guilt.*
> *It is to be liberated to live in freedom.*
> *It is to be enabled to look up in joy.*
> *It is to be open to walk arm in arm.*
> *To be forgiven is to be redeemed, to belong to him!*

When Sin Is Not Imputed

Blessed is the one against whom the Lord will not reckon sin. Romans 4:8

To know in my soul the meaning of forgiveness is to walk in the freedom of God's company. I well know my sins, but I also know that they are forgiven; they are not on my ledger. Accepted by God, we are forgiven and in this relationship of love. God doesn't throw our sins up to us again. One's memory may do so, but if so, we can turn to the promises of God. John writes that if our heart condemns us, God is greater and he knows all things (1 John 3:20). He speaks assurance of forgiveness. As Corrie ten Boom put it, "God casts them into the sea and puts up a sign, 'No Fishing Allowed!'"

We are blessed with a spirit of joy, of newness, of relationship. Being forgiven means that I have processed my perversions. I can now walk with God, with my head up. The blessedness of the redeemed is the privilege of being in the family of God, of being God's children. "See what love the Father has given us, that we should be called children of God; and that is what we are" (1 John 3:1).

My father-in-law was a saintly man who had invested his life in missions in India, as well as teaching and pastoral service in various settings in the States. As he faced death, the one thing that he wanted to review with me was this truth of assurance. Nothing was so important to him as the assurance of being accepted in grace as a child of God.

Forgiveness means that God releases us in freedom. God affirms the intrinsic worth of the individual and seeks to help us walk in a way that transcends our limitations.

I pray, dear Lord,
Help me today to walk with you,
To live above my self-centered tendencies,
Renouncing all that perverts and limits life,
Engaging the freedom and joy of the Spirit,
Enjoying the liberty of the new creation.
In his grace alone. Amen

The Circumcision Only?

Is this blessedness, then, pronounced only on the circumcised, or also on the uncircumcised? We say, "Faith was reckoned to Abraham as righteousness." Romans 4:9

Who has the right to claim God's blessing? This text asks the question, Do the Jews have an edge on God's blessings? The answer is no. Not on God's mercy or the claim to salvation. But the answer is yes, in having received God's special revelation to understand his offer of grace. This grace of acceptance is offered to all, and the Jew ought to be the first to understand and thereby show others the way.

However, institutionalized religion becomes a hindrance. We can make a form of idolatry of religious insights, which makes concepts an end rather than a means to an end. We do not worship laws but the Lawgiver, not religious rites but the One of whom they witness, not religious values but the One from whom they come. We do not pray to a philosophy, but to a Person.

During a conference for Christians in art, convened by my wife in Bulgaria, it was refreshing to hear young Christians who had been Communists some months before, now saying, "Before I was a *believer*," "Since I am a *believer*," or "Now that I am a *believer*." It was refreshing because in many countries the term "Christian" means a Western religion. To speak of being a believer marked the transition and transformation of life in the grace of Christ. Belief is beyond rites of religion, for they are only signs, pointers to the God for whom religion hungers. Love is never complete until in the embrace of the Lover. In 1950, in revival meetings in Ohio, I sang in a trio with Bishop S. E. Algyer, age 91, and Dr. J. Otis Yoder. I was 21 years of age when we sang these words by F. M. Graham:

> *The old account was large, and growing every day,*
> *For I was always sinning and never tried to pay;*
> *But when I looked ahead and saw such pain and woe*
> *I said that I would settle, and settled long ago!*
> *Long ago, down on my knees, long ago, I settled it all!*
> *Yes, the old account was settled long ago, Hallelujah!*
> *And the record's clear today, for he washed my sin away.*
> *Yes, the old account was settled long ago.*

March 29

How Is It Reckoned to Us?

How then was it reckoned to him? Was it before or after he had been circumcised? It was not after, but before he was circumcised. Romans 4:10

The question of preconditions for God's grace is answered by this text. What do we have to do to qualify for God's grace? The answer is simply *nothing*. God moves to us, to all people, caring for everyone. The decisive aspect is our response to God, the opening of our lives to him in faith, the response that honors God for himself.

Paul's question is focused on Abraham, as to whether God accounted his faith for righteousness before or after circumcision, and the answer is, Before. Rites of religion are only symbols, signs, and affirmations before others of our commitments. If we place our faith in the rites of religion, even in the sacraments, we are, in essence, making God a more distant personage, and we are making salvation more methodical or mechanical.

Again, salvation is partnership with God. God does not want our religion, our works—he wants us. When he has us the rest will follow: our worship, our obedience, and our service. Abiding in Christ means that the center of our lives, our motivation, our affection, and our actions will be in conformity to his person and will.

Let us on this day, and each day, come to God with grateful hearts for his mercy and grace. Our prayer should echo that of the psalmist, "May God be gracious to us and bless us and make his face to shine upon us" (Ps. 67:1). Thomas O. Chisholm wrote:

> *Oh! to be like Thee, blessed Redeemer,*
> *This is my constant longing and prayer;*
> *Gladly I'll forfeit all of earth's treasures,*
> *Jesus, Thy perfect likeness to wear.*

> *Oh! to be like Thee, oh! to be like Thee,*
> *Blessed Redeemer, pure as Thou art.*
> *Come in Thy sweetness, come in Thy fullness,*
> *Stamp Thine own image deep on my heart.*

The Father of All Who Believe

He received the sign of circumcision as a seal of the righteousness that he had by faith while he was still uncircumcised. The purpose was to make him the ancestor of all who believe without being circumcised and who thus have righteousness reckoned to them. Romans 4:11

To those who call themselves "children of Abraham," of these and to these Jesus said, "If you were Abraham's children, you would be doing what Abraham did" (John 8:39). In our text Paul identifies this work of Abraham as believing in God. We who believe are Abraham's seed. The gospel is the good news that all who believe, Jew and Gentile, black or white, Oriental or Caucasian, rich or poor, Democrat or Republican, become children of God, a part of the people of God which he is creating.

The theology here is very important for mission, for our freedom in cross-cultural communication. We need to recognize that while one's faith is lived out in a given culture, it is never to be identified with or synchronized with that culture. We are not marketing a brand of American Christianity, nor white Christianity, nor franchise churches as First McDonalds, Second McDonalds, or Third McDonalds! We are announcing that all people can come to God by a faith response to his call.

God cares about the world. He does not think in terms of nationalities, of superpowers, nor of first-, second-, or third-world distinctions. When close to God, we too will think of the global community, of a network of disciples.

Gandhi said he was not a Christian, because to be Christian meant to be western, and he was Indian. He took Jesus more seriously than many who call themselves Christian. He was, in some degree a disciple; we leave him with God as judge, but we recognize his commitment.

> *Lord, I honor Gandhi's limited response to Jesus.*
> *I am not judge, but I believe that whoever*
> *experiences the grace of God*
> *comes to him only by what we know in Christ.*

March 31

Walking in Steps of Faith

. . . and likewise the ancestor of the circumcised who are not only circumcised but who also follow the example of the faith that our ancestor Abraham had before he was circumcised. Romans 4:12

Abraham, as the father of those who believe, is mentor for both the circumcised and the uncircumcised. That which equalizes both is that they come to God on other grounds than religious rites. All come to God on the ground of faith. Abraham responded to God's call; the rites of religion were an add-on as a sign of his relationship.

There is a significant phrase in this text, a reference to those who walk in the steps of faith. Faith is response to evidence, it is saying "Yes, Lord" to each encounter with the Word and the will of God. The steps of faith are deliberate choices, reasonable responses to the evidence that God is in and at work in one's life and on behalf of that life.

For too many, faith is a blind wish, an uninformed hopefulness, an exercise in trying to convince oneself of a wish-thought. However, faith is a normal intellectual exercise of moving from one indicator to the next, amid contrary elements, catching the glimmer that leads to more light, saying "yes" to each indicator so that one may move on to the next. Saving faith is normal faith, relational faith, placed in the Savior.

*How was Abraham saved? By **faith:***
called before he had done any works,
granted salvation before and without the law!
*And how are we saved? By **faith:***
not by our religious conduct,
not by our ethnicity.
*We like Abraham are saved by **faith***
in the God of grace,
*in **walking with the risen Christ**.*

April 1

The Promise

For the promise that he would inherit the world did not come to Abraham or to his descendants through the law but through the righteousness of faith. Romans 4:13

On April 3, 1987, I flew to Sarasota, Florida, to preach for eight days in a region-wide evangelistic mission. Some seventy-five churches sponsored this venture, held in Roberts Arena, with an ecumenical spirit of sharing. Ken and Betty Masterman, having worked with us as our music team for over thirty years, joined Esther and me for this meeting. The text for today offered me great assurance for this mission. Our faith is built on the promise of God that all people of the world are welcomed in the righteousness of faith, and to this we call people.

God's plan of reconciling people, of saving persons from their perversion, indifference, and unbelief, is the motivating aspect of an evangelistic preaching mission. I go there to offer Jesus! In him we come into right relation with God. In him we are forgiven and restored, reborn and redirected as his disciples, renewed by the indwelling of his Spirit. We become his body, the church, the expression of the risen Christ.

We who are disciples of Christ will, of course, be evangelistic. We know how we came to faith, how we came to walk with Christ, and we can explain this to others. If we know Christ, we want others to share the same privilege.

A few evenings before leaving for this Florida mission, I visited my parents at Harrisonburg, Virginia, spending extra time with my father, who was not well. He was a wonderful layman, a devoted Christian, and was committed to pray for my work in evangelism. Some of his last words on my visit were to wish me God's special blessing in this meeting. I did not know then that I would not see him alive again in this world, but I confess with Philip Paul Bliss:

> *'Tis the promise of God, full salvation to give.*
> *Unto him who on Jesus, His Son, will believe.*
> *Alleluia, 'tis done! I believe on the Son;*
> *I am saved by the blood of the crucified One.*

Faith Is Not Made Void

If it is the adherents of the law who are to be the heirs, faith is null and the promise is void. Romans 4:14

At the ecumenical Gulf Coast Crusade in 1987 over four thousand persons from seventy churches graced the opening service. Preaching from John 14:6, of Jesus as the way to life, I felt God's anointing and rejoiced with those who came forward in the invitation to come to Christ. Christ is the one mediator of life in its larger dimension, life with God. In him we are given assurance of salvation.

The proclamation of the gospel led persons to Christ, for the proclamation was not a voice for the law, but a herald of grace. True, as John Wesley said, "Before I preach grace I must preach law." People need to become aware of their lostness so that they will come to God. But above all, the preaching of the Word is to make clear the gospel, the good news that in Christ we can become children of God.

Law is a spiritual standard. There is nothing wrong with that. But you don't use a yardstick to cause a child to grow. You nurture the child in tender loving care and watch the growth. Similarly, law exposes our need for God, but the gospel nurtures our hunger until we turn to God and identify with him. Salvation is walking with Jesus, opening one's life to him, and living in and by his love.

How can I know God when he is so other.
I can not even think of him correctly,
nor speak of God properly.
Yet, think I must and speak, I am impelled,
though at times incorrectly; it is still faith
reaching out to the one who is other.
This is engaging justification by faith!
Believing the stories that reveal him.
Believing his promise that I can come to him.

The Law Works Wrath

For the law brings wrath; but where there is no law, neither is there violation. Romans 4:15

My message on the second evening of the Gulf Coast Crusade at Sarasota, Florida, was from Genesis 3. I reviewed the nature of the mistake of Adam and Eve, their rebellion against God, and the broken fellowship. I emphasized that, long years prior to the law, sin had brought estrangement. Their problem was what some call a "finitude anxiety." Their basic problem was seeking to have their own way, to find their fulfillment apart from God.

As I said before, "No sooner does one expel God from his life then everything else in life is successively summoned to be god." And so it has been for all humanity. The divine law was given to make us conscious of the nature of our sin. Paul says in our text, "The law brings wrath." Yet, his wrath is not a rejection of us but to expose us and help us to be accountable for our own decisions. He does not box us in.

Where there is no law, Paul says, there is no transgression, that is, no consciousness of disobedience of the law. But ignorance of God's will before the law does not mean that one is right with God. The question is, Do we want God as God in our life? Oh yes, for any other god is much, much too small, reducing life and shrinking it by emptiness. The surrender to God expands, enriches, and enlarges life.

On a visit to the Greek Island of Rhodes, we enjoyed the evening program, "Sights and Sounds," as they enacted the ceremony of knighting those who would serve as Knights of Saint John. When the candidate knelt beneath the sword that was laid on his shoulder, the question was asked, "Do you have the strength to surrender?" What a question! I have long pondered it, for this strength is the recognition that there is more to life than what one controls. Accepting this, one moves beyond self-determination.

> *To surrender to God, this is our greatest privilege,*
> *for in this surrender, God can be God for us.*
> *We can live by his direction, hear his voice,*
> *rejoice in his presence.*

That It Might Be of Grace

For this reason it depends on faith, in order that the promise may rest on grace and be guaranteed to all his descendants, not only to the adherents of the law but also to those who share the faith of Abraham (for he is the father of all of us). Romans 4:16

On the third day of the Gulf Coast Crusade at Sarasota, Florida, I felt led to check on my father's condition. Calling in the morning, I learned that Daddy had died an hour earlier. The word was stunning in its finality. It hit me especially in the words, "He is gone, he has gone home." I had known it was coming. He had talked to each of us about dying soon, having a weakened heart, but we hadn't expected it this quickly. I had to face the grief from miles away, during an evangelistic mission in which I was accountable to seventy churches and to the community of thousands of people.

Almost numb in my grief, I went about my mission that day. I lectured in the School of Evangelism, went to the radio station for an interview, then to a TV interview in which the questions were about TV evangelists who recently had been exposed in moral failings. I responded candidly about the need for integrity on the part of workers for Christ, quoting the words from the play *Murder in the Cathedral*, "They who serve the greater cause have the greater danger of the cause serving them." Finally, I preached in the evening service. Though with inner pain, I felt that I should fulfill my commitments and then go north. As our text says, "It is by grace" that we are enabled to serve.

> *Dad was a patriarch, an Abraham in my history:*
> *An orphan at seven, growing up mostly with an aunt,*
> *Meeting and falling in love with Estella,*
> *Married and father of six children,*
> *A mentor of discipleship for each of us,*
> *Not a perfect man, nor overly pious,*
> *But a wonderful man who walked with God,*
> *Who urged us to do what he didn't get to do.*
> *Thank you, Lord, for Clarence Augsburger,*
> *My Abraham!*

Who Quickens the Dead

As it is written, "I have made you the father of many nations"—in the presence of the God in whom he believed, who gives life to the dead and calls into existence the things that do not exist. Romans 4:17

On the morning after I learned my father had died, Esther and I flew to Washington, DC, rented a car, and drove to Harrisonburg, Virginia. We went first to see Mother and share sorrow and assurance with her. We joined the family at the funeral home to meet scores of friends and were strengthened by their love and faith. What a marvelous text in this verse, especially for this occasion: "God, who gives life to the dead." We affirm our belief in the resurrection and assurance that some day God will raise us together. As we looked into Dad's cold but peaceful face we knew that "his triumph only precedes ours."

God made Abraham a father of many nations, one who passed on to the world the faith of Yahweh. My dad, father of six children, twenty-six grandchildren, and sixteen great-grandchildren, passed his faith from generation to generation. This is a challenge and responsibility for each of us.

Values are taught by example more than by ideas, and I thank God for a dad who lived with us, with whom I worked for significant years, and who was an example of taking God seriously, though not perfectly. This heritage lives on in us as a family, one that will continue to shape our lives and guide us in decisions in a changing world. God's grace is sufficient, his promises sure.

The changes of our times are too close to us to fully understand. We have had more changes since 1935 than in the history of mankind up to that time. I have lived through most of those changes. The one who is dependable and unchanging is ever with us.

In the words of Scripture we can trust our Lord for, Jesus is "the same yesterday and today and forever" (Heb. 13:8). I recall clearly one of the last songs I sang with my dad while I played on the piano. We sang together, "My Jesus, I love Thee, I know Thou art mine." Then at his request we sang, "And when the battle's over, we shall wear a crown." In the words of an old hymn text we rest:

> *God is still on the throne.*
> *He never forsakes his own.*
> *His promise is true, he will not forget you.*
> *God is still on the throne.*

Believing Against Hope

Hoping against hope, he believed that he would become "the father of many nations," according to what was said, "So numerous shall your descendants be." Romans 4:18

We had not lost a family member in our Augsburger clan before my father died. We had said farewell to Lloy Kniss, Esther's father, seven years before this, with the sorrow and faith that accompanied this loss. We have sorely missed him. And now Daddy is gone. My brother Dan and I went up to his house, out to the back lots, where a pair of Canada geese were the last birds of a hobby of swan, and geese, which Dad and I had shared for years. I opened the gate, and we chased them out and over the hill to our farm pond in freedom. It was like closing a chapter, and we wept.

Then we went to worship. The funeral service was truly a worship experience. The music and the spoken word were like a healing balm. How strengthening was the sermon by a family friend, Roy Roth. I wept for Dad's going, but in joy as we sang together, "Jesus has risen, and we shall not die."

In this text, in the context of salvation history, Paul writes that Abraham believed against hope, yet he believed in hope! And this is the way life is; we believe in the hope of what God has promised, in faith that he who has spoken will bring it to pass. Jesus fulfills his promises, and he did for us. Following the funeral, we flew back to Florida to preach that evening. God enabled me to share the word.

> *O eternity, how long art thou?*
> > *Let your ages roll on;*
> > *you can not silver the locks of God,*
> > *nor scar the walls of hell;*
> *O eternity, how long art thou?*
>
> *O eternity, there is a joy in his presence,*
> > *there is no fear;*
> > *perfect love casts out all fear;*
> > *there is only anticipation.*
> *O eternity, we anticipate being.*

April 7

Not Weak in Faith

He did not weaken in faith when he considered his own body, which was already as good as dead (for he was about a hundred years old), or when he considered the barrenness of Sarah's womb. Romans 4:19

Sometimes things seem almost impossible. After returning to Florida for the crusade, we traveled to Dayton, Ohio, the following day and drove to Elida for a second memorial service. Dad's burial was in the old Salem cemetery, a few miles from where he grew up. An orphan at seven from Berne, Indiana, his aunt Mary and uncle Jake Greider had given him a home for work on the farm. Here amid friends, he came to Christ, married Estella Shenk, and they raised their family to serve Christ. I have four brothers and, as dad would say, "Each has a sister," our sister, Anna Mary. My father and mother imparted faith to us through adversities, limited finances, and the Depression. Father did not weaken in faith.

Our text is about Abraham, who can bring meaning into our own lives. Those who have gone before are models. But we have what psychologists call time-binding power. We can reach back into history and select values found in Abraham and others and channel them into life again by our choices and faith. Abraham was looking ahead, believing in God's promise. Jesus said to his disciples, "Abraham rejoiced that he would see my day; he saw it and was glad" (John 8:56). Abraham lived by the vision of God's purpose. In faith he looked for the "city whose builder and maker is God" (Heb. 11:10, KJV).

> *Hope is not wishful thinking;*
> *hope is projection of his promise,*
> *living in anticipation,*
> *secure in his purpose.*
> *Hope is a spirit of certainty,*
> *being assured that he will follow through,*
> *he will perform what he has said;*
> *the future is his arena.*
> *We are saved in hope,*
> *for we are in his family even now!*

He Staggered Not

No distrust made him waver concerning the promise of God, but he grew strong in his faith as he gave glory to God. Romans 4:20

Our last deed of love for dad was my four brothers, my brother-in-law, and I carrying Dad's body from the Salem Church near Elida, Ohio, across the road and through the cemetery to its final resting place until that day when the trumpet of God will sound. It was heavy, both in weight and in the loss of a dad we loved and who loved us. We staggered a little. But as in the text, we did not "waver concerning the promise of God."

Perhaps I am deviating from the primary meaning of this text, but Abraham's faith meant God would fulfill his word and give him a son of promise. Actually, it is faith in his God that makes him strong.

Our assurance is through faith that God is as good as his Word. He will fulfill his promise, and we can rest in that fact. Jesus said, "He that believeth in me, though he were dead, yet shall he live" (John 11:25, KJV). And so we said good-bye to Dad in the language of his Swiss background, simply, "*Auf Wiedersehen—*I'll see you again." And we'll enjoy the next fifty billion years together exploring God's heaven.

We flew back to Sarasota, Florida, in time to preach the evening message and then conclude the series. As God gives me life, I want to continue to preach his wonderful gospel, holding his great commandment and his great commission together.

It is not easy to believe against hope,
when there is not human reason for expectation,
when God's word is our sole basis for trust,
and God's Spirit our only confirmation.
To believe is to act in faith.
It is to honor the Lord by affirmation,
to walk on even in the dark,
looking at the one beckoning light,
that no density of darkness can put out,
always fixed on that Light, the Eternal One.

April 9

He Was Able to Perform

. . . being fully convinced that God was able to do what he had promised.
Romans 4:21

The Gulf Coast Crusade in Florida closed with a good spirit among the participating churches and the thousands who joined in the arena. The fact that a diversity of churches came together in this way for eight nights was a witness in itself. And most important, some one hundred persons made responses to Christ during the eight days. This was the work of the Spirit among us in spite of the disruptions in our schedule. God was faithful in giving me freedom in sharing his Word and the witness of his grace.

The many adjustments which I needed to make were reminders that it was not my meeting, but the work of the Holy Spirit. As in our text, God was able to do what he had promised. And he did so in the various ministries. The gospel is the power unto salvation, not our personalities. What he promises he is able to perform. Paul's statement in this text is an expression of what we note as *Heilsgeschichte*, salvation history. Through the ages God has been at work, unfolding a revelation of himself, saying more and more until he said it most fully in Jesus. God is our redeemer, not simply an idea about a supernatural realm or of life beyond the here and now; he is a personal God who reconciles us to himself right now.

> *The gospel is story,*
> > *the story of God at work in history,*
> > *the story of his self-disclosure in Christ,*
> > *the story of his redeeming love.*
> *We are part of the story,*
> > *written into the thousands of years of his work,*
> > *signed by his own deeds of love.*
> *Our name is written in his book,*
> > *sealed by his promise,*
> > *written there for eternity.*

April 10

Therefore . . .

Therefore his faith "was reckoned to him as righteousness." Romans 4:22

Our faith is our expression of right relations with God. Our friend Tony Campolo says, "Faith is the attitude that permits God to be himself in us." And this is for the daily walk, not just for crisis times. God is righteousness. God is our peace.

Often after a high point in one's service, the next days can be a letdown. After closing the Gulf Coast Crusade meetings in Florida, we returned to Washington, DC, and our work with the church on Capitol Hill. We were back into the demands of a pastorate and increased work from having been away. But faith must be active in daily life. God is our strength and courage.

How fitting is today's text for such life experiences. None of us is perfect, but our faith is credited for righteousness. How wonderful! And, as Paul wrote this of Abraham, each of us can affirm this as true in our lives.

God accepts us in his love, a love that opens his arms intimately to us; we share that love as we open our arms to him. Love is the ultimate ingredient in righteousness. First, God's love expressed and lived out for God keeps us from unrighteous living. We allow God to be our love and righteousness.

This text, actually taken from the Old Testament, is of justification by faith. The theology that is expressed here recognizes God as a gracious self-giving redeeming Lord, with grace as the bridge by which we come to him. To the Ephesians Paul wrote, "By grace you have been saved through faith, and this is not your own doing; it is the gift of God" (Eph. 2:8).

Saved by grace, I love to tell,
What the love of Christ has done.
He redeemed my soul from hell,
From a rebel made a son.

Oh, 'tis grace, 'tis wonderful grace,
My ransomed spirit sings,
Oh, 'tis grace, 'tis wonderful grace
That full salvation brings.

Not for His Sake Alone

Now the words, "it was reckoned to him," were written not for his sake alone. Romans 4:23

Reading this verse one feels like blessing Paul for this insight of the Spirit. These words weren't written for Abraham's sake alone. God's work is extended to all who open themselves to him. He is not partial. Neither is God capricious, acting on a whim, but he is trustworthy, consistent with his own holiness and integrity.

This word is our assurance. Others who have walked with God are examples. They may be our mentors, but we do not simply copy them. We open our lives to experience the same spiritual realities that transformed the lives of saints who walked with God in the past. I have studied the Anabaptist movement of the sixteenth century with great appreciation. In many ways, men like Felix Manz and Michael Sattler are my mentors. They are long gone, both martyrs for their faith, but the reality of transformed living that characterized their lives is also my experience. Four hundred and eighty years later I walk with the same Jesus. I live in this continuum. This same Jesus is our Lord, our Savior, our Mentor.

Walking in the resurrection,
one's mortal body quickened by his Spirit;
being risen with Christ,
participating in the new life.
This is the dynamic of fellowship with him.
In baptism we symbolize this truth.
We are baptized into his death,
a break with the old life as definite as death,
but, like Christ, raised from the dead.
We, too, rise to walk in newness of life.
The power of the resurrection is at work in us;
We are a new creation.
The old, the reign of sin, is gone, the new is now.

April 12

If We Believe

. . . but for ours also. It will be reckoned to us who believe in him who raised Jesus our Lord from the dead. Romans 4:24

For each of us who believe in the God who raised Jesus from the dead, there is a quickening in our own lives. Our faith is credited by God as "rightness" with him where we lacked godliness without him. The words "but also for us" are inclusive words; they open the door to each of us.

In the Anabaptist movement one of the first synods among Protestants was held at Schleitheim, February 24, 1527. In the Schleitheim Confession—drawn up by Michael Sattler, who died a martyr later that same year—approved by the assembly, we find his statement that "baptism is for those who will walk in the resurrection of Christ." Our covenant is to live now in the transforming power of this new relationship with our Lord.

A friend from Switzerland entrusted his daughter to us to be surrogate parents for nearly two years while she attended Eastern Mennonite High School. This was an extension of our covenant of grace. We enjoyed the relation with this lovely teenager very much. In addition to this responsibility was our work in the church. Esther worked with a group of artists and conducted art classes for inner-city children and filled the duties of a pastor's spouse. I was very busy in pastoral work, elders' meetings, deacons' meetings, and work with a new associate pastor. While we enjoyed our time with our Swiss daughter and have a continuing friendship with her, the need for God's grace in the heavy load was important. We walked together with God, sharing our discipleship of Christ with others.

The God who raised Jesus from the dead
*   is the God who saves us and walks with us.*
He releases us from the death-dealing influence of sin
*   and enables us to walk in the freedom of Christ.*
Ours is a new life through believing and trusting,
*   through honoring him in leaning on his Word.*
He is our Savior, our Redeemer, our Companion;
*   in his grace we will trust him to give us strength.*
His unwavering love cloths us in the robe of righteousness.

Raised Again for Our Justification

[He] was handed over to death for our trespasses and was raised for our justification. Romans 4:25

This text is a wonderful statement of the gospel in a nutshell. Christ died for our sins and was raised again for our justification. We are represented before the Father by the Savior who has completed the work of redemption. It is not only the cross but the empty tomb which is the guarantee of the love-value of the cross.

Our text is a concise statement of the atonement: "He was delivered for our offenses and raised again for our justification." His death is the result of our offenses, but it is his self-giving love that is redemptive. Enacted once on Calvary, the meaning of his sacrifice extends throughout all history. Our hostility did not overcome him, for he rose from the dead in victory, overcoming the most serious thing we could do against him. His nonviolent response to our hostility exposed our offense while confronting it with love.

As the Suffering Servant he is also the essential model for us. As we cross cultural and denominational lines, we can be effective in a style that serves. For over twenty years as a Mennonite preacher, I spoke annually in the Lenten services at St. Andrews Episcopal Church, Wilmington, Delaware. My latest meditation was "The Mastery of Service," as a pattern for global sharing.

We were blessed by a letter from a woman who found help in a meeting in Montana where Esther and I spoke. We had observed the woman at the edge of the crowd. She was something of a hippie. Later she wrote of the meeting and her release in finding forgiveness and in forgiving another for wounds she had suffered. One line in her letter stands out in my memory: "He will carry the scars of his love forever!" When we have been wounded, we can forgive, but we recognize with realism that we carry the scars; yet we can take them as tokens of Christ's love. As Charles Wesley wrote in his hymn "Arise, My Soul, Arise":

> *Five bleeding wounds He bears;*
> *Received on Calvary;*
> *They pour effectual prayers;*
> *They strongly plead for me.*

Justified by Faith

Therefore, since we are justified by faith, we have peace with God through our Lord Jesus Christ. Romans 5:1

This text gives us the wonderful assurance of salvation. In the Lenten season we think especially of Christ's suffering for us. I am impressed with the momentous words of Jesus from the cross: "*Tetelestai!*" (Greek for "It is finished" [John 19:30]). It was a shout of victory, which means the atonement is accomplished. We are redeemed! We now belong to him.

The prophecy of Isaiah 53:6 is finished, "All we like sheep have gone astray; we have all turned to our own way, and the LORD has laid on him the iniquity of us all." Genesis 3:15 is finished, "He will strike your head, and you will strike his heel." The victory over the tempter is now complete. Above all, the way into the presence of God is open, the veil is torn in two, and we can meet God at his mercy seat.

Our text is a central affirmation of the Christian faith. "Justified by faith, we have peace with God through our Lord Jesus Christ." How can we have peace with God when we were the cause of the death of his Son? This is only possible if God was acting in Christ on our behalf. Note carefully the further phrase in the text: justification is a gift, and we accept it by coming in faith. Peace is a gift, and we experience it in a new relation with God with our rebellion ended. And all of this is through the Savior, Jesus of Nazareth, the Christ, and therefore our Lord. We come to God in him and live our lives in relation with him.

We are justified by faith and not by our works. It is his grace that provides us with salvation. Paul begins with the word *therefore,* and studying the passage we know what the word is there for. It ties this declaration to his whole argument: faith is the only way to come to God, the only honest expression from ourselves.

> *Thank you, O God,*
> *for this wonderful gift of your Son, Jesus,*
> *for redemption, and for his willingness*
> *to bring us victory over death! Amen*

April 15

Access into This Grace

Through whom we have obtained access to this grace in which we stand; and we boast in our hope of sharing the glory of God. Romans 5:2

We observe Black Saturday as the day of sadness, recognizing the day that Jesus was buried in the tomb. Peter tells us that in his death he went in his spirit and made a proclamation to the "spirits in prison," an announcement that the atonement had been completed, the sacrifice of mercy had been offered (1 Pet. 3:19). By his presence in Sheol, the Savior experienced and defeated death itself.

The Apostles' Creed states, "He descended into hell," or into the realm of death. Calvary was not a myth; he actually died. The cross was not the death of an idle dreamer, nor primarily the martyrdom of a great man. It was actually the self-giving of God in his Son, giving his life as a ransom for us. Being redeemed, we now belong to the Redeemer.

I once met a man sitting on a bench along the street in Washington, DC. As I started talking with him, he suddenly asked, "Are you a preacher?" I said, "Matter of fact, I am." He almost sneered as he asked, "What difference does it make in my life that Jesus died on a cross two thousand years ago?" I asked, "Do you have some friends?" He said, "Of course, I have friends." I said, "And one gets into trouble?" to which he responded, "You help him out." I continued, "But it gets really difficult, when can you cop out?" He bristled a bit and said, "If he's your friend, you never cop out."

My response was, "God came in Jesus to be our friend, and we were in trouble; it got really difficult, but he hung in with us. It got really severe. When could he cop out?" It was as though lights went on in his eyes as he responded, "Is that why Jesus had to die?" I said, "That is one reason. Jesus came and said, 'Your problem is now my problem,' and he hung in all of the way to death." The man got up, squared his shoulders, nodded his head, and walked off down the street. As I watched him go, I chuckled to myself, thinking, "Man, you don't know it, but you've been evangelized. Once you know a God who says your problem is now my problem, you can never be the same." Or as Charles Wesley wrote:

And can it be that I should gain
An int'rest in my Savior's blood?
Amazing love, how can it be
That Thou, my God shouldst die for me?

April 16

We Rejoice, Even in Suffering

And not only that, but we also boast in our sufferings, knowing that suffering produces endurance. Romans 5:3

His resurrection is our assurance that there is victory beyond suffering. Easter brings hope. It was always a joy to share worship on Easter with the believers of Washington Community Fellowship. Although we celebrated Christ in each worship service, the Easter service always began with "The Lord is risen." "He is risen indeed!"

I believe in the actuality of the resurrection because of the witness of Scripture, the accounts of the disciples, and the contemporary transformation of lives in fellowship with the risen Christ. I do not agree that it doesn't matter whether Christ arose as long as we believe in new life. The disciples did not create the resurrection. The resurrection was a reality which created the disciples.

Resurrection follows death and is experienced beyond the suffering of death. Jesus engaged the whole gamut of human experience, including death. Paul concludes that we can rejoice in our own suffering because already we know the victory. Suffering refines our spirits in our faithfully looking forward to his return as consummation.

Easter has special meaning for both Esther and me with both of our parents having died. We find assurance and hope in the reality of the resurrection. Jesus said, "[God] is not God of the dead, but of the living" (Matt. 22:32). In these words he invites us to think of those who have died in faith, living in the presence of God and awaiting resurrection.

During the Russian Revolution, a Dr. Bukarian traveled to various cities lecturing on atheism. In Kiev, speaking to a large crowd, he gave his declarations against belief in God. At his conclusion, an Orthodox priest asked whether he could say a few words. Granted permission, the priest came to the podium, raised his hands in the traditional Christian sign and shouted, "Christ is risen!" The crowd, with one voice, came back with the words, "He is risen indeed!" The priest bowed and stepped off the platform.

Lord, help us in this interim period awaiting your coming
to know your grace for faithfulness in discipleship,
to accept any suffering we have as a moral exercise
in and by which we are strengthened to trust you. Amen

Perseverance Produces Character

And endurance produces character, and character produces hope. Romans 5:4

For us as a couple, our life together is enriched when we take short breaks for rest and relaxation. I remember an occasion when Esther and I drove from Washington, DC, to Harrisonburg, Virginia, on Sunday afternoon and got a room at the Sheraton. After a relaxing evening with the refreshment of the pool and a good night's sleep, we called my brother Don and his wife, Martha, to join us for breakfast. Family and fellowship are very important aspects of life, providing meaningful community as we walk together in love. Life is a process in which God is at work in us to produce character and quicken hope.

Age itself, when we walk with the Lord, is a special witness of his grace. Following our night at the Sheraton, we paid visits to my mother, who was ninety-two years old at the time, and Esther's mother in her mid-eighties. Mother Kniss, with her husband, Lloy Kniss (deceased by the time of this visit), had a very meaningful history of mission work in India and also in Bible studies with James Madison University students. Until three days before her death, at age ninety-four, she continued to pray daily for a long list of persons by name.

Paul says that character comes through persevering. We are indebted to parents who carefully practiced Christian disciplines in prayer, which affected our lives for the graces of Christian character. They have been mentors, along with many others, who have inspired us. Yet the fruit is possible only by the inner resources of the Spirit of Christ in each of us. As I heard Bishop Zulu of Zululand say in a conference in Pretoria, South Africa, in 1979, "The only branch that bears fruit is the one attached to the vine."

Ephesians 3:18   John 3:16
We know how wide God's love is, ... *for God so loved the world.*
We know the length of his love; . . . . *he gave his only Son.*
We know how deep love reaches, ... *for whosoever comes to him.*
We know the height of his love, ... *should have eternal life.*

April 18

The Spirit Whom He Has Given Us

And hope does not disappoint us, because God's love has been poured into our hearts through the Holy Spirit that has been given to us. Romans 5:5

His Spirit is given to live within us. Yet, occasionally I have one of those days when, emotionally drained and physically tired, I have a feeling of being down. Once at lunch I asked Esther if she ever thought it would be helpful just to have a good cry. She asked what I wanted to cry about. I said, "Nothing in particular. I just feel wrung out."

As we prayed at the table, I thanked God for the truth of today's text and asked for his refreshing through the inner presence and renewal of the Spirit. He is faithful. He answered my prayer. How thankful we are for God's gracious presence. He has shed his love into our lives by the Holy Spirit, that is, by being present with us.

Paul says that the Spirit has been poured into our hearts. The image of pouring used here and elsewhere in Paul's writings is the biblical basis for our administering baptism by pouring. Baptism is, from this text, a symbol of the outpouring of the Holy Spirit, of baptism with the Spirit. However, this text is not suggesting a mode of baptism, but is simply saying that God isn't stingy; he pours out his Spirit upon believers. Similarly, being immersed in baptism is a good symbol. But impressive as it is, the text "buried with him by baptism into his death" (Rom. 6:4) is far more than a symbol for water baptism; it is being baptized into or identified with his death.

The Spirit-filled life is our privilege, but it is costly. We live in a spirit of yieldedness to him. That which our Anabaptist forefathers spoke of as *Gelassenheit* is an active yieldedness that obeys. They recognized two baptisms: the outer baptism by water as symbol only, and an inner baptism that saves and changes persons. This is a baptism *with* the Spirit. The Spirit is the baptism given by Jesus, who does the baptizing.

> *Thank you, Lord, for presence,*
> *for the gift of your Spirit.*
> *Although John and others baptize with water,*
> *you baptize with the Holy Spirit.*
> *I thank you. Amen*

April 19

Christic Died for the Ungodly

For while we were still weak, at the right time Christ died for the ungodly.
Romans 5:6

This reference to the ungodly includes all of us. Yet, while we were away from God, traitors to his cause, he came to express his love for us. Love means to open one's life intimately to another and to do so whatever the cost. And God did just that in opening himself to us, sharing our plight, absorbing our hostility to the death. His love was and is shared to the ultimate. He died for us. In love he hung in with us in our sin.

Jesus said that he came, not to call the righteous, but the unrighteous to repentance. His story of the one lost sheep, which caused the shepherd to leave the ninety and nine in the fold and go out to find the lost one, illustrates how deeply the Good Shepherd cares for the erring. God is a God of love and mercy, but this doesn't mean that he takes it lightly. The cross is evidence of how seriously God takes sin, how genuinely he loves sinners, and how much he is willing to suffer in substituting himself for us. This is the character of the cross. God, the innocent, taking on himself his own wrath for the guilty and releasing us.

A lawyer who was an agnostic came to hear one of my lectures on ethics. At the close he thanked me, then explained that he was not one of these "blood Christians." He didn't believe in the innocent suffering for the guilty. I held his hand a bit longer and said rather emphatically, "Man, I'm sorry for you. You can't have a happy marriage or a happy family. You are not an angel, and you will blow it. Only if your wife and your children suffer and forgive you, can you have any happiness in your home." He said, "I'll have to think about that." He came back in the evening, and I preached on the cross, where God in Christ carried his wrath on our sin in forgiveness. The man came to Christ. I will always remember his words in the prayer room: "For the first time in my life I can subject the Christian faith to my lawyer's mind." John Newton wrote:

> *Amazing grace! how sweet the sound*
> *That saved a wretch like me!*
> *I once was lost, but now am found,*
> *Was blind, but now I see.*

Daring to Die

Indeed, rarely will anyone die for a righteous person—though perhaps for a good person someone might actually dare to die. Romans 5:7

On occasion I have joined a group of preachers for an hour of prayer at The Cedars in Arlington, Virginia, on the western edge of Washington, DC. The prayer time was searching as we sought accountability before the Lord. At lunch, as each shared, the focus moved to how these suburban pastors could share with us of the inner city in our ministry among the poor. I emphasized the need to see the poor as persons, not as a class. We need to help our congregations to share an authentic identification with people and avoid any condescending compassion. Our love must be authentic, as was Christ's love.

Our text today reminds us that Jesus identified with humanity in our perversions, even when we were aliens from him and from his will. Paul says some might dare to die for a good person, but the intrinsic worth of a person is that they have been created in the image of God, whether attractive to us or not. Our privileges do not put us in a special class, but call us to mutual enrichment. The cost of serving persons, even those not so good, is a cost from which we instinctively back away.

One morning during my college days, in a prayer meeting, the librarian, Miss Sadie Hartzler, spoke. She said that there are two ways of learning compassion: one is to move among suffering persons; the other is to be close to someone who has a friend who is suffering. Compassion can be learned by being close to God, who has many friends who are suffering. Love for the poor gives evidence that we share the character of our Father.

For what would I be willing to die?
Or, for whom would I be willing to die?
What an amazing question of the ultimate.
It focuses the matter of highest values.
I'm not sure that I can know,
Except to say that God will give grace,
Should the test actually come to me.

God Demonstrates His Love

But God proves his love for us in that while we still were sinners Christ died for us. Romans 5:8

For some years we quite regularly traveled to Lancaster, Pennsylvania, to meet at the Willow Valley Restaurant with the board of InterChurch, Inc., on which I served. This board has for over forty years given direction to InterChurch missions, which we have held in evangelistic meetings in several hundred settings, and for Esther's conferences for Christians in Art in Asia and Eastern Europe. The text of God's love has special meaning in thinking of each person at these board meetings, persons we care about beyond our own interests.

Evangelism is not merely program. It is the extension of the love of Christ. Evangelism is sharing the good news of God's love. It is making faith in Christ a possibility for persons. It is announcing to all that in Christ they can become children of God. In our text, "While we still were sinners, Christ died for us." What a word of grace.

In Esther's art classes for neighborhood children near our church on Capitol Hill, one little girl in the class was from a very difficult life. She was the daughter of a prostitute who didn't care for her. She was found eating from a garbage can and brought to the class. One day she made a small clay sculpture of a little girl. Later, when Esther picked up the sculpture to place it in the kiln, she read the inscription, "The Lord luves me like I am." God's love, shown to this girl through Esther, made all the difference.

> *Love gives one a sense of worth;*
> *to be loved is to belong,*
> *to be affirmed.*
> *For love compliments the other,*
> *brings to the other our strength,*
> *shares with the other our resources.*
> *Love participates with the other as person,*
> *not for what we get out of this,*
> *but because the other is important.*
> *God is love!*

April 22

Justified by His Blood

**Much more surely then, now that we have been justified by his blood, will
we be saved through him from the wrath of God. Romans 5:9**

Our salvation is not cheap. We are justified by his blood. That is, he gave his very life to save us. And we who share this life must regard allegiance to Christ our highest priority. In turn, we who share this message must do so in a style and quality that befits such a wonderful and amazing self-giving Savior.

Serving for the Council of Christian Colleges and Universities, I spoke on many campuses, including a chaplains' conference in Philadelphia. Their mission is to involve thousands of students on some ninety campuses across the country in firsthand Christian faith. We concentrated on the mission of the Christian college in the global community. Using Colossians 2:2-3, I sought to show the relationship of Christology to the whole of life, spirit, thought, and action. In the freedom of Christ, we must discover how to think in a Christian spirit and to serve in a style true to him. Christ calls us to love God with our minds as well as our heart, soul, and strength. Our educational work should go beyond indoctrination to interpretation, and in this to relate a Christian worldview to the whole of life and thought.

Our salvation is not in our heritage, in our religious identity, or in moral deeds, but is in relationship with Christ. He is the one Mediator who reconciles us to the Father, the one who has certified our forgiveness through his blood. This is the reason we preach Jesus; not to negate other values in God's created order, but to show that he is the greater answer to our search for life.

We should relate ethics to Christ
just like we relate salvation to Christ.
We are saved in relation to Jesus,
and we behave our relation to Jesus.
It is theological rather than doctrinal—
not relating faith and works in the old style,
but recognizing the relational dynamics of faith.

April 23

Reconciled by His Death, Saved by His Life

For if while we were enemies we were reconciled to God through the death of his Son, much more surely, having been reconciled, will we be saved by his life. Romans 5:10

This text is the heart of the gospel: reconciliation in Christ. It means to be turned back to God. Turned from our rebellion, yes, but primarily we are turned *to* him. Our new life is an identification *with* God. It is positive. We are converted through the death of Christ, and confession of Christ is a positive identification. At the cross we know how deeply God cares, how much he loves us. On God's part, this is accepting us with integrity. On our part, it turns us to him in honesty. In dealing with the problem of our estrangement, he is not unjustly ignoring our rebellion, but is justly correcting it.

This salvation is not only from our trespasses, but is into his fellowship. The text moves to that glorious phrase, "will we be saved by his life." That is, beyond the cross, we find the full dimension of a new life with God. We relate now to the risen Lord. He certifies, sitting at God's right hand, that the price is paid in himself, that we are liberated from our estrangement from God, that Satan is silenced and his grip on us is broken.

This very day we need to affirm our covenant with Christ. We are in him *now,* which makes the difference in what we would be without him. In his life we have our salvation. Because he lives, we live in his quality of life, and we shall also live forever.

> *Justification by faith, yes,*
> *   this is Christian theology.*
> *But, reconciled to God in Christ,*
> *   this is the basis for justification.*
> *It is the work of Christ on our behalf,*
> *   the redemption that has changed all.*
> *For, in coming to Christ, our search is ended;*
> *   in him we are coming to God.*
> *He is our Redeemer;*
> *   having been redeemed, we belong to him!*

April 24

We Rejoice in God

**But more than that, we even boast in God through our Lord Jesus Christ,
through whom we have now received reconciliation. Romans 5:11**

Joy is an inner strength of spirit. To boast in God is to have the strength of joy, of inner harmony with God at the very core of one's being. In Jesus we have received "at-one-ment" with God. We do not *make* atonement; we *receive* it, *respond* to it, and *rejoice* in the new union. We now participate in the relationship for which we were created.

We have come home to God. We experience what Paul Tillich called a relation with "The Ground of Being," but not an impersonal ground, for God is Person, our Father. Ours is a wonderful fellowship with God, not simply a dependency.

One evening while teaching a seminary class in Romans, to aid in the discussion on how we think about God, I led the class in a review of God's attributes. With Tillich, I asked about a hierarchy of his attributes, and we reflected on an order of God's dealing with us. It makes a difference whether one's first premise is his sovereignty, his love, or his holiness. Beginning with his holiness, we move to his justice, next to his mercy toward us as offenders, then to sovereignty as his self-determining patience, then to fellowship in his love, and so on. While we are very limited in thinking about God, we do discover these attributes in the gospel, especially that God shares himself with us in love.

The best informed mind is so limited that we need to be very humble. My friend Elam Hertzler served as assistant to the Honorable T. H. Bell, former U.S. Secretary for Education. He shared Bell's insightful comment: "Education is the movement from cocksure ignorance to thoughtful uncertainty." Our best thinking about God would be limited to mere humanism except for the disclosure in Christ. The truth is in Jesus.

God is not an impersonal force,
A universal vitality without being;
God is known in Jesus the Christ,
"He is the image of the invisible God." (Col. 1:15)

Sin Entered the World Through One

Therefore, just as sin came into the world through one man, and death through sin, and so death spread to all because all have sinned. Romans 5:12

Through one person's disobedience the whole world has been subjected to sin. This is not to say that God punished the world because of that one trespass, but that in one person's estrangement from God, all who follow are born on the deficit side of the ledger. This means that our problem as humans, self-determination, which is being one's own god, entered humanness in Adam.

While we tend to moralize the nature of our depravity, thinking of what things we do that are immoral, we should see depravity first as a perverting of relationship. In breaking from fellowship with God, we then exalt ourselves as the higher authority for life. Consequently, we seek to use God for our own ends rather than approaching him in reverence. In very subtle ways this happens among the religious, as well as among the secular or nonreligious. The deepest levels of perversion are in our thinking and in our motives.

Sin entered the world by one person, so God's redemption came by one person. Is there a sense of God's justice in this? He chose not to invade the world with all of the resources of heaven, but in the second Adam (Jesus Christ) he met us on our own turf and condemned sin in the flesh. While fully identified with humanity, he demonstrated the God-intended pattern of decisions in the will of God. Jesus lived and taught the will of God among us. We see in him a quality of personhood we have not been able to match. Horatio G. Spafford wrote the hymn:

> *My sin! O the bliss of this glorious thought,*
> *My sin! not in part, but the whole,*
> *Is nailed to His cross and I bear it no more,*
> *Praise the Lord, praise the Lord, O my soul!*
> *It is well with my soul,*
> *It is well, it is well with my soul.*

April 26

Sin Was Here Before the Law

Sin was indeed in the world before the law, but sin is not reckoned when there is no law. Romans 5:13

Before and after, how often we think of such distinctions. God has given us three wonderful children, and we enjoy celebrating their birthdays. We love them deeply, but we can also think of our lives before children and our lives with children. In this relationship we have had both joy and pain. We rejoice in both, for even in the pain we would much rather have them than not have them. We would rather know this love than to never share the love of parent and child. And we believe it is much the same with God as he looks at his children.

My mother lived to be ninety-two. At her ninetieth birthday, I reflected with her on her influence in my life. I never knew a time that I had not known her. I frequently think of my mother, who read me Bible stories, who prayed with me when I made my early commitment to Christ, who taught me to help in the kitchen, and who often reminded me, "The man worthwhile is the man who can smile when everything goes dead wrong." That was before. Now, as I live out her influence, it is after.

In our text Paul speaks of before the law and after the law. Before, with no moral understanding, and after, with accountability for sin. Once we understand responsibility for the right, we are accountable. And this is awesome, for to be alive as a human being is to be one who can, in all eternity, recognize that I am the one who has done what I've done. This awareness magnifies God's wonderful grace.

> *Sin is the perversion of the good.*
> *It is the cheaper pattern of something better.*
> *Sin is turning my own way, a rejection of God's way.*
> *Sins derive from our basic sinfulness.*
> *Once I confess my sin against God, I respond to his call;*
> *Then I can deal with the sins, in therapy or through nurture.*
> *The first confession is theologically basic;*
> *Confessions that follow are psychologically healing.*

Yet Death Dominated

Yet death exercised dominion from Adam to Moses, even over those whose sins were not like the transgression of Adam, who is a type of the one who was to come. Romans 5:14

Whether we fully understand life or not, we are a part of it. Whether we understand death or not, we will experience it. Whether we understand God's law or not, we must live with it.

The text for today reminds us that death came with Adam's transgression, not with the law; it simply clarifies the grounds for this verdict of death. From Adam to Moses death was a reality, and before the law was a revelation of God's guidelines. In Paul's argument, death came from sin, and the victory over death, or the release from death, must come from the divine answer to the sin of humanity. The law explained the problem but it didn't correct it. The Redeemer has come to correct the problem. He doesn't remove the law, even though he interprets it and supersedes it. In exposing our problem the Redeemer moves beyond law and acts to destroy sin and death itself.

My in-laws tell of a fellow missionary family living in a jungle village of India who had Bible reading and prayer each morning with their workers. A Hindu woman from the village became their cook and refused to attend. Again and again she was told that it was a vital part of her working for them. Her excuse was that she needed to be about getting breakfast for them. The missionary told her that wasn't necessary. So, finally she came, leaving the bread toasting in the oven. Without a word, the family ate the burnt toast each morning. One morning she came to them in tears. "Sahib," she said, "I need your kind of religion! The one that makes you treat me in this kind of caring." Their love took upon themselves the weight of her wrong, and she came to the one whom she now began to understand. They moved beyond the law, as Charlotte Elliott wrote in the confession:

> *Just as I am, Thy love unknown,*
> *Has broken every barrier down;*
> *Now, to be Thine, yea, Thine alone,*
> *O Lamb of God, I come, I come!*

The Free Gift Abounds for the Many

But the free gift is not like the trespass. For if the many died through the one man's trespass, much more surely have the grace of God and the free gift in the grace of the one man, Jesus Christ, abounded for the many. Romans 5:15

In our congregation in Washington, a young man from Jordan was an active participant in a quiet way. He was a prayer leader and witness in discipleship. Later William Sahawneh, with his wife, Jeannie, invested many years of work in Jordan. On one occasion a group of persons from our congregation joined with persons from the Arab Baptist Church in a dinner at their building to identify with William and Jeannie in their plans to serve under Arab World Ministries to the Muslim peoples. On that occasion it was important to help our Arab brothers and sisters to see that we love and care for them equally with all others. Christians need to be pro-Palestinian as much as pro-Israeli.

Our text says that the free gift abounds to many. Paul has made clear that the giving of this gift includes Jew and Gentile without partiality. Sin has perverted many, so the free gift of love abounds for many. God is open to all who respond.

As we move to God, we are not presumptuous, but we come on his terms. We come to God in reverence, in awe, in submission, in obedience, in fellowship, and in joy. We are coming to God! He wills to be our God, our Lord, our Redeemer. A basic difference between us as believers and those who are nonbelievers is that believers worship; we open ourselves to God's love in praise and adoration.

Love unlimited,
Love impartial,
Love equally open to all,
Love including each of us,
Love accepting prodigals,
Love making no distinction,
Love respecting yet not coercing.

April 29

The Gift Follows Many Trespasses

And the free gift is not like the effect of the one man's sin. For the judgment following one trespass brought condemnation, but the free gift following many trespasses brings justification. Romans 5:16

"He will carry the scars of his love forever." What a thought! With our text this statement is a special word to me. God's gift of grace follows many transgressions, and I claim this as the gospel, the good news of his forgiveness, covering my many sins. We celebrate the gift of God's wonderful acceptance.

Paul is showing us in the text God's answer to Adam's sin, and the consequence of sin in all of us. He says man's sin, generic for men and women (he doesn't say "Eve's sin," although she usurped the leadership, in acting in a way that Adam mimicked with his eyes open! [1 Tim. 2:12-14]). The answer is God's forgiving grace, moving to forgive and overcome sin. Since forgiveness is a gift, it excludes partiality, for God offers the gift to all alike. It excludes limitation, for God forgives to reconcile us, not just to deal with a list of our transgression. Our Savior suffered willingly that we might come to God freely. It was unconditional love that God suffered for our transgressions.

Life in Christ is a life in fellowship, in covenant, and as such it is a life of transforming grace. This day one can claim his presence and power for the new life that Peter describes as our being partakers of the divine nature! (2 Pet. 1:4).

This day I can walk in Christ's love.
This day I can walk in his freedom.
This day I can walk with my wife in his covenant.
This day I can walk in his promise for our children.
This day I can walk with integrity in vocation.
This day I can walk with his Spirit in his work.
This day I can walk in joy in fellowship with him.

April 30

Reigning in Life

If, because of the one man's trespass, death exercised dominion through that one, much more surely will those who receive the abundance of grace and the free gift of righteousness exercise dominion in life through the one man, Jesus Christ. Romans 5:17

"How much more. . . ." God's abundant grace is expressed in Jesus, grace for those who will receive God's abundant provision of grace; therein is life. Rather than death reigning in our lives, we now reign in life through Jesus Christ. To reign means to rule, to be in charge, to transcend the death-dealing power of sin by his righteousness.

Paul's emphasis is on the quality of the new life in Christ. He is careful to use terms that focus on a present relationship. He does not use legalistic terms lest we institutionalize Christianity and make it a religion of law. He doesn't even use the word *church* in the epistle until the last chapter, where he speaks of the church as "the people of God" or as "believers." The triumph of which Paul speaks here is the victory of Christ replacing what Adam lost in the fall. True, we live in a fallen world, but in a redeemed world. We don't live by our fallen state but by a new dynamic relationship with Christ.

The story is told that one day when Queen Elizabeth was a young girl, and her father, George VI, was King of England, the princess held a lawn party at Buckingham Palace for her friends. On that afternoon it began to rain, and so everyone was invited inside the palace. The princess was showing her friends around the palace and in a room, used by King George VI, she pointed to a picture of Jesus on the wall and announced "That is the man that my daddy says is the real King!"

Lord, King of my life, help me today to claim your gift,
to know the resurrection power in Jesus,
to walk in the resurrection
and to live free even with my sinfulness.
While I acknowledge my fallen state,
I confess my new identity;
I am now in fellowship with the King of kings!
Thank you for this reality and power. Amen

Life for All Peoples

Therefore just as one man's trespass led to condemnation for all, so one man's act of righteousness leads to justification and life for all. Romans 5:18

In his one redemptive act Jesus Christ brought life for all. Everything changes because of Jesus. He changes everything for all who identify with him. He has redeemed us, restored us to fellowship with God, and re-creates in us the righteousness of God in a new quality of life. We are an expression before the world of life as it was meant to be.

The church has too often emphasized the human fallen state or sinfulness as though it determines our pattern of life, rather than emphasizing redemption in relationship as a new pattern. As disciples of Christ we share the life of Christ, the new quality of life.

Family and friends are primary relationships where we express this quality by doing. While living in Washington, Esther and I traveled frequently to Harrisonburg, Virginia, to teach a seminary class and to have lunch with our sons who lived there. Occasionally, Ann Strong, a hardworking mother of four from Germany, in an interracial marriage, went with us to visit her daughter, Carmen, at Eastern Mennonite High School. Esther had helped Ann cope with many serious family problems as a mentor and a friend, even at Esther's own physical safety and sometimes with police protection. Ann, not only found a friend in Esther; she also came to a commitment to Christ. We rejoiced to see the victory of Christ in this relationship and learned in this more of what it means to walk with Christ in a covenant of love for one another.

Lord, help us to live beyond ourselves,
above all in a close relation with you,
then with family and then for others.
Help us to bring your joy and hope to all peoples. Amen

Many Will Be Made Righteous

**For just as by the one man's disobedience the many were made sinners, so
by the one man's obedience the many will be made righteous. Romans 5:19**

These are great words, but greater yet is to participate in this righteousness, this rightness. We hardly need Paul's reminder of the fall and our subsequent sinfulness.

But he is pointing out that the disobedience of the one man, Adam, is defeated by the obedience of the One, Jesus. How wonderful! Through Christ's obedience we are made righteous. He sets things right between us and God, between each of us, and between us and others. Implicit in the text is choice between the disobedience of Adam and the obedience of Christ. Jesus is our answer and our mentor, and to be in Christ is to walk in his way, in his righteousness.

The revival we need is new obedience to the Word and will of Christ. He calls us to walk in his will, to walk with him. We won't do it perfectly, but we will clearly walk with him in the same direction, walking by his side. To walk in the Spirit is to walk in the will of Christ. When I am doing my daily exercise walk in the morning, I enjoy repeating the Apostles' Creed. It is a great statement of faith. The first part speaks of God the Father. The second part speaks to us of Jesus Christ, his Son. Here I take the liberty to make an addition in the fourth line, which I think has been missing:

I believe in Jesus Christ, his only Son, our Lord;
who was conceived by the Holy Spirit,
born of the virgin Mary,
lived and taught the will of God,
suffered under Pontius Pilate,
was crucified, dead and buried.
He descended into hell.
The third day he rose again from the dead.
He ascended into heaven, and sits on the right hand
of God the Father, Almighty; from thence
he shall come to judge the quick and the dead.

Grace Increased All the More

But the law came in, with the result that the trespass multiplied; but where sin increased, grace abounded all the more. Romans 5:20

Where sin increases, grace increases the more! This is a wonderful word. God's answer is in grace, which reaches beyond the problem to the person. God isn't uptight because of our sin; he is up to the challenge of reaching beyond the sin to the sinner.

To appreciate the depth of his love, the extent of his grace, we must understand the seriousness of our sin. Paul states that the law was given to expose our sin; in fact, the law actually increases our conscious awareness of our sins. Those rules which point out the will of God make us aware of how far away we have been in our own will. Laws which point out what we shouldn't do simply expose the fact that we have done those very things. But beyond law is the Person of love and grace. We are not a society of perfection, but a fellowship of persons honest in our need and relation in grace.

This grace is boundless. It is able to meet us in any situation. God loves the world, sinners all. Christ died for the world, for us, while we were yet sinners, and acted to redeem us from sin. The Holy Spirit calls us initially and keeps calling us, first to the Lord and consequently away from our sin. Our subconscious urges are inclined to selfishness, but we come to God with the conscious commitment to live for his honor and praise. Johann Heermann wrote the verse:

> *O God, Thou faithful God,*
> *Thou fountain ever flowing,*
> *Without whom nothing is,*
> *All perfect gifts bestowing,*
> *Grant me a healthy frame,*
> *And give me, Lord, within,*
> *A conscience free from blame,*
> *A soul unhurt by sin.*

May 4

Eternal Life Through Jesus Christ

So that, just as sin exercised dominion in death, so grace might also exercise dominion through justification leading to eternal life through Jesus Christ our Lord. Romans 5:21

Eternal life is a life of quality before it is quantity. In the text, quality is an intrinsic characteristic of exercising dominion, or in some translations, to reign. We can live and reign with Christ over and against the negatives. We can live positively with him. We live our lives as up, not as under, the circumstances.

Frequently we have been involved in premarital counseling and wedding plans, enjoying the pleasure of working with young couples, seeing their love, and sharing their dreams for the future. We recalled our own dreams as we celebrated our fifty-fourth wedding anniversary this year. We talk about what it means to share love, including our imperfections. We are to relate to each other in and through Christ, that is, in the awareness of his presence in our union. He brings a special quality into our relationship.

The eternal life of which Paul writes is quantity with an unequalled quality! As to quantity, we will live on with God, and countless billions of years from now we'll be young souls with him! But as to quality, we live *now* in the power and quality of the eternal.

One of the most amazing things about Christian faith is sharing in God's abundant resources. Again, Christian faith is simply the attitude that permits God to be himself in one's life. It is participating in his richness.

Life and death, what does it mean?
We have forever the eternal years of God.
These, God shares with us!
Life: Jesus is the way, the truth, and the life.
His Word gives us hope;
For God is not the God of the dead but of the living.

God Forbid!

What then are we to say? Should we continue in sin in order that grace may abound? By no means! Romans 6:1-2

Since we are saved by grace, does this not imply that our behavior may be presumptuous? Shall we go on practicing sin that grace may continue to be expressed in answering our sin? Paul's answer is emphatically stated: "*By no means!*" Some translations use the strong expression "God forbid!" Forbid what? That we should be presumptuous toward God's grace. In saying that salvation is not in the law but in grace, Paul does not minimize obedience to the spirit of the law.

There are two kinds of obedience: the servile obedience of the law and the filial obedience of the child to the Father. So wrote Michael Sattler, martyr for Christ in the sixteenth-century Anabaptist movement. Filial obedience is the more dynamic, for it is a relation of love. Grace is not a cover-up for sin. Rather, it is a powerful acceptance which delivers us from sin. Dietrich Bonhoeffer emphasized that "cheap grace presumes on God's love in disobedience or carelessness; while costly grace meets Christ at the cross to be delivered from sin and to live in his freedom."

Esther is an artist, a sculptor. Sometimes with my help she loads the car with sculptures and pedestals to set up an exhibit, and I watch her drive away. Or, sometimes I bid her adieu as she leaves for a speaking mission. Even more often, I have left for preaching missions with Esther staying at home. We both rest in God's grace and assurance that he will be present in our travel and our mission. Accidents do happen, and we are not careless, but God cares for us. God wants us to call on him in dependence and allow him to manifest his grace as seen in these ideas from A. W. Tozer:

In grace we are disciples not legalists.
The legalist works up to the cross,
seeking to gain God's acceptance.
The disciple has been to the cross
and works out from there in obedience.
The legalist is hard on others and easy on self.
The disciple is easy on others, hard on the self.

May 6

We Have Died to Sin

How can we who died to sin go on living in it? Romans 6:2

The change spoken of here is a change in us. Sin doesn't die to us; we die to sin. That is, we stop responding to sin. This is the character of life in Christ. With this change we no longer live in rebellion, in the perversion of self-seeking that pursues our own way.

This has both personal and social dimensions. Samuel Escobar of South America is a friend of ours. In one of his lectures he reviewed Latin American history and spoke of the liberation of the peoples through nonviolence. In his presentation he pointed out the sins of oppression, of power used to dominate rather than to serve, and the sins of inequity among peoples. He also reviewed the form of much religion where Jesus is seen as a mystical being rather than known as Lord—a mythical experience rather than a master in life. No one people should behave to coerce another; the gospel confronts us with Jesus as a new way.

Paul affirms that in our identification with Christ, we die to sin, die to the old life. Our break with the ways of our past sin is as definite as death. This is the true liberation, freedom from the past life in sin, and a new freedom to walk in the new life in grace.

The questions we face are What is the new way? What is the new character? We find the answer in Jesus. The new life comes by our recognition of his lordship. We have one mentor; he is our model. We are his disciples, walking with him in the way and learning from him. We draw on him for power. This walk with Christ we call discipleship, following Jesus in life, as confessed by the sixteenth-century Anabaptist Hans Denck:

> *No one can truly know Christ*
> *Except one who follows him daily in life,*
> *And no one can follow Christ daily in life*
> *Without first knowing him.*

Baptized into Christ

Do you not know that all of us who have been baptized into Christ Jesus were baptized into his death? Romans 6:3

Christian baptism is not simply to be baptized into a church, into a religious order, but to be baptized into Christ. We join covenant with him; we take on his identity. We are now in the family of Christ. We are commissioned to be his ambassadors in our particular setting. To be baptized into Christ means that we now find our identity in him.

This time of the year we celebrate Mother's Day, a day of respect for one who gave us the privilege of life. Three times I have stood beside Esther as she went through that deep valley of suffering to give birth to our three children. We've enjoyed them so much, even though some experiences have not been easy. But to not have had them would be to have missed the experience of sharing life and love with them, of knowing their love and respect, of walking together in the grace of God.

What does Paul mean by the phrase baptized into Christ? The word *baptism* in the New Testament is used in five expressions: baptism with fire, a refining experience; baptism with suffering, a purging experience; baptism with water, an initiation into the fellowship of believers; baptism with the Spirit, being given his presence and being brought under his control; and a baptism into the body of Christ by the Spirit, being identified with and under accountability to the community of Jesus.

Baptized into his body we come under his leadership, come under the experience of dying to our self-centeredness, and come under his control. This baptism is into his death and consequently resurrection into his life. *Baptism* is a word picture, but it is a good one. We give up our autonomy and take on his identity.

> To share with Christ is demanding;
> For, it includes sharing his death;
> A break from the old life, as definite as death.
> This death is the way to freedom!

So We Too Might Walk in Newness

Therefore we have been buried with him by baptism into death, so that, just as Christ was raised from the dead by the glory of the Father, so we too might walk in newness of life. Romans 6:4

In the sixteenth-century confession of faith by Anabaptists at Schleitheim, they spoke of baptism for those who will walk in the resurrection of Christ. Baptism is the public sign of having been delivered from the old life and having become a participant in the new life in Christ. Baptism is symbolic of what God is doing in us by his grace and Spirit.

In my own baptism as a young lad on a Sunday afternoon in a flowing stream, kneeling on a grate placed in the water, I shall always remember the words of the pastor as he completed the baptism. They still ring in my mind as he said, "Arise, and as Christ was raised from the dead through the glory of the Father, you also shall walk in newness of life." These were thrilling words of direction and of assurance, and through the years I have continued to seek this resurrection power.

Our text calls us to live this new life. We are not only forgiven for our sins; we are also called into fellowship with our Savior. The sanctification of life in this text and in the next chapters is the awareness that the totality of life is set apart for him. This is the meaning of holiness, that we belong completely to him.

Resurrection power, now!
An amazing reality.
God's power, the Spirit's power,
this is the resurrection power in Christ!
The new life is not something I achieve
but, a quality of life given to me.
This life we claim by faith.
This life we know in identity with him.

United with Jesus

For if we have been united with him in death like his, we will certainly be united with him in a resurrection like his. Romans 6:5

United with Jesus means a holistic relationship. This is more than a cerebral confession of doctrine; it is a confession of identification. In covenant with Jesus we are united with the whole Person, not just with particular aspects of his work. We do not select his forgiveness, or his promise of heaven, and then go our own way. We covenant with him to walk in the mutual integrity of relationship.

In this solidarity with Christ, we share his death and his resurrection. This relationship we must engage. In this relation our eternal life is as certain as the fact that he lives. Paul's argument in this passage is an emphasis on the freedom of the disciple of Christ to live a new life now. The same power that raised Christ from the dead is at work in us to raise us above the death-dealing power of sin (Eph. 1:19-20).

In the same way, as we are justified by faith rather than by works, so also, we live by union with him and not by our own efforts. God has forgiving grace and transforming grace. The church has made much of his forgiving grace but tends to excuse our failures as our humanness. We should recognize our failure to draw on his transforming power. Each victory becomes a testimony to the presence and power of the Spirit of Christ. We are united with him, not just professing a religion. We are transformed. What a privilege!

> *A new creature in Christ,*
> > *born anew into a new family,*
> > *claims a new order of life.*
> *Born from above, entrance into his kingdom,*
> > *ours is, in the words of Peter,*
> > *a living hope by the resurrection.*
> *It is to an inheritance incorruptible*
> > *reserved for us who are kept by God.*
> > *(cf. 1 Pet. 1:3-4)*

May 10

Crucified with Him

We know that our old self was crucified with him so that the body of sin might be destroyed, and we might no longer be enslaved to sin. Romans 6:6

This is one of the more dynamic texts in the Scripture on freedom in Christ. But this text is seldom understood because people equate the old self with the body of sin (or sin tendency). It is as though the two, the old self and the body of sin, are the same. Some people believe that when the old self is gone the body of sin is also gone. The text does not say this. The old self is the old life, in which sin reigned. That reign is now over. The new self is life in which the Spirit reigns. The tendency to sin is a continuing part of our humanness, but now is devitalized. It now has lost its power to control.

We now live the new life by our union with Christ. The only thing the Word of God ever says concerning the old self is that it needs to be crucified, put to death. We are now a new creation, participating with Christ as the new self to grow by life in the Spirit.

In Colossians 3, Paul talks about stripping off the old self. It is a definite action. We, as believers, are now to put off all of these things which he lists, sins which reflect the human nature without the victory of the Spirit. There are still problems in the Christian life that we need to deal with. Having gotten rid of the old self does not mean that we no longer have an earthly nature, but rather that we are free from its control. It is devitalized. We can choose to put off any sinfulness which would seek to control us. Self-defense, violence, hatred, and ill will are all a part of the old life. "For freedom Christ has set us free" (Gal. 5:1).

During the intense violence in Ireland, a mediation group met with persons from both parties for a discussion. Suddenly, a man in a wheelchair rolled forward into the aisle. Pointing to the men in the other group he said, "These are the men who set the bomb that blew off my legs. But I forgive them and want them to know this." A man in the other group stood up and said, "I'm the man who set that bomb, and he has forgiven me. I know this because when I suffered the loss of my wife, he is the man who came and gave me comfort and support." This story, related by Douglas Gresham, the stepson of C. S. Lewis, expresses the power of the new life as expressed in Galatians 5:1:

> *For freedom Christ has set us free.*
> *Stand firm, therefore,*
> *and do not submit again to the yoke of slavery.*

Freed from Sin

For whoever has died is freed from sin. Romans 6:7

Our freedom is an inner, personal release. We are the ones who have died to sin; it is not sin that has died to us. In dying to sin Paul means that we no longer yield to it.

This marvelous text on our liberation is a continuation of the preceding verse. Dying to the reign of sin, we no longer function in that realm. Our primary loyalty is not to the earthly or sensual realm. We are citizens of heaven while living here on earth (Phil. 3:20). We are seated with Christ in heavenly places (Eph. 2:6), that is, at the feet of him who reigns. He has made us kings and priests (Rev. 1:6, KJV) to reign over the things that once mastered us.

To be freed from sin means that we are no longer its slave. Our sins happen because we are very human, but in Christ when we sin our union with him leads to a confession and repudiation of the sin. John writes, "Those who have been born of God do not sin, because God's seed abides in them; they cannot sin, because they have been born of God" (1 John 3:9). We are free in Christ but not in ourselves, in union with him but not in our wisdom, in grace not our grit.

The wonderful truth is that in Jesus, our Master, we are free from all lesser masters. This freedom is first inner, and then it is an ethic that guides us in life. We are free from addictions by a greater affection, free from selfish pursuits by the pursuit of God. We do not stand fighting sins, but we turn our back on the sins by becoming actively engaged in the will of God. This is good psychology and good theology.

> *Help me, Lord, to accept the mastery of Christ,*
> *to know the freedom of the Spirit,*
> *the freedom to which I have been called,*
> *and the freedom in which I can grow.*
> *Teach me, Lord, how to appropriate your power,*
> *to participate in your Spirit's work,*
> *claiming the liberating power you provide*
> *to become the person you mean for me to be.*
> *Hold me, Lord, in the circle of your love. Amen*

May 12

We Live with Him

But if we have died with Christ, we believe that we will also live with him.
Romans 6:8

To speak of dying with Christ makes us uncomfortable; this is not easy nor welcomed, but the choice is made easier with the understanding that we can live with him. Dying with Christ and living with Christ are parts of one holistic experience. By active relationship we participate in the freedom of his fellowship.

When we counsel young couples for marriage, we encourage them in the meaning and joy of sharing their total lives in the covenant of love. To live their new life in the freedom of love will mean dying to the self-orientation so that each can share intimately with the other. So also in our relation with Christ, we share a covenant of love, a covenant of expected fidelity, but one of unbelievable intimacy with God.

There is a depth to this passage that many Christians miss. We are often hesitant to move into the experience of intimacy, to be totally set apart to God, to belong wholly to Christ. All things are ours in Christ if we will but appropriate his provisions by faith. We live in intimacy with him.

In the Old Testament God said of Canaan, "All of this land I have given you." Then he added, "Every place that the sole of your foot treads upon, that I have given you." So it is with God's promises: they are all given for us, but we must claim them and walk in them.

Lord, I claim your grace as I live for you.
You have promised to accept me, and I claim it.
You have promised to forgive me, and I claim it.
You have promised to be with me, and I claim it.
You have promised to guide me, and I claim it.
You have promised to enable me, and I claim it.
Lord, I honor your grace, depending on you. Amen

May 13

Beyond Death

We know that Christ, being raised from the dead, will never die again; death no longer has dominion over him. Romans 6:9

Once Christ was raised from the dead, there was no further threat of death. So too, once resurrected into the new life, we are released from the fear of being overrun by sin; we are liberated in Christ. Ours is an actual freedom, not just an idea. We walk in the fellowship of Christ. We are his disciples, and we walk with Jesus at the heart of life.

Covenant in marriage is similar to covenant in union with Christ. In a wedding meditation I have often spoken of the beauty of marriage when a couple is united in Christ. From Paul's statements in Ephesians 5, there are three points of emphasis: covenanting together in faith, changing together in sharing, and maturing together in loving. Marriage marks the beginning of a new order of life. A couple never goes back to life as before. Social change becomes the occasion for a deepening of our faith.

Paul says we die to our old life and share a transition of grace and freedom in our personal lives. United with Christ we live in and by the freedom of his gift of life. Let us share his freedom with one another today, especially respecting the freedom of the other, and avoid violating their space. The symbol of death is used in our text to make transition.

> *Death is a passage beyond the present.*
> *Death to the past enables a move into the new today.*
> *Death, as terminus of our earthly life, is*
> *a transition into the larger eternal life.*
> *Death as an unknown is an enemy,*
> *but Jesus has destroyed the enmity.*
> *He has given us assurance of life extended.*
> *He promises to share his glory with us.*
> *He is our Light in the shadow of darkness.*
> *O death, where is your sting? O grave, where is your victory?*
> *(cf. 1 Cor. 15:55)*

He Lives to God

The death he died, he died to sin, once for all; but the life he lives, he lives to God. Romans 6:10

Jesus's death released his life to appear in the presence of God for us. He not only died for us; he also lives for us. His life in glory is the authentication of his lordship. This is the certification that God accepted his sacrifice on the cross for us. This is the declaration that he is now the mediator of our relationship with the Father. This is an affirmation of his authority. His headship is in the kingdom he is creating today throughout the world.

In Paul's letters to the Colossians, and to the Romans, he lists persons whom were close to him. His emphasis is on community, a new people the Lord is creating. Here are friendships that last a lifetime, that express the quality of the Christ-life we share. We do not come to Christ and then walk on in isolation. We walk in community.

When Paul Tournier, the famous Swiss psychiatrist, began study at Vienna, on the first day of classes his psychology professor asked the class if anyone believed in God. Tournier raised his hand, looked around, and discovered that he was the only one with his hand up. The professor said, "You believe in God?" Tournier answered that he did. According to the story, the professor said, "I have an assignment for you. Go to your room and write an essay on why you believe in God." As he struggled to write, he attempted a philosophical answer. Unsatisfied, he tore it up, tried again, tore it up, and simply wrote his personal testimony of what it meant to walk with Christ. He took it to the professor, who sat reading it, then lifting his face with tears said, "I, too, believe in God." Tournier asked, "And when did that happen?" He answered, "Just now; reading your paper."

Jesus said, I am the way, the truth, and the life.
Lord, let me share your life this day,
in all its joy and power.
Let me walk in your path of love,
in reaching beyond myself to others.
Help me to be sensitive to your Spirit,
for victory in release to be my best for you. Amen

Reckon Yourself Alive unto God

So you also must consider yourselves dead to sin and alive to God in Christ Jesus. Romans 6:11

In Virginia, where we've lived a major part of our lives, the word *reckon* is quite commonly used. In a rather unique way, in the King James Version, we are told to reckon ourselves dead to sin but alive to God through Jesus Christ. This word *reckon* means "to count it so." It is a word of affirmation, of decision. To respond, "I reckon" is to agree, to put one's word to something. This word means to count this as actual in our experience. God has provided freedom, and now we claim it.

Esther was a board member of the Mennonite Board of Missions from 1980 to 1988, which meant frequent travel to Elkhart, Indiana. Her real interest was in discovering creative ways to communicate the gospel with integrity. Her concern has been that the quality of the way the gospel is presented is consistent with the quality of the gospel; that the witness participates in the meaning of the gospel itself.

With so much compromising of integrity among religious voices on TV, as well as voices in the secular and political arenas, the need for quality of life and integrity is especially acute. With the evangelical church tending to buy into conservative nationalism, and with some TV preachers given to huckstering the gospel, there is need for a corrective voice in the church. We must reckon ourselves dead to the ways of the world and alive to the way of his kingdom. E. Stanley Jones said, "We do not build the kingdom, which is God's gift to us; we build the church." We should do this in faithfulness to Christ. We recognize the kingdom as the work of the Spirit. We discover what God is doing, so we identify with his work as we build his church.

Some of the greater activities of the mind
are in the areas of selectivity.
The test is not only in what we use or do
but often in what we pass over.
If we are committed to quality
it will be evident in our choices.
The Christian life offers the greatest quality.

May 16

Do Not Let Sin Reign

Therefore, do not let sin exercise dominion in your mortal bodies, to make you obey their passions. Romans 6:12

To exercise dominion is to be in control, to rule or order life. The marvelous freedom of our life in Christ means that the dominion of sin is broken. We now live under the liberating reign of the Spirit. His power at work in us counteracts the power of our sinfulness.

Since our old self, the life in which sin reigned, has been crucified by our identification with Christ, we have been resurrected into a life with Christ. And this wonderful change has happened by conscious, voluntary identification and solidarity with Jesus as our Lord. Now as we walk with him, the suggestions of our human nature that would turn us back to the way of sin are exposed. We simply continue to affirm, and reckon on our continuing commitment in the Spirit that says, I still mean it!

Walking with Christ makes victory possible. Jesus himself said, "My yoke is easy, and my burden is light" (Matt. 11:30). We yoke ourselves with him, and he shares in the weight of the task.

Nelson Mandela, as he stepped from prison door where he had been kept over twenty-seven years, expressed a flush of anger on his face when he saw the crowd watching him emerge. However, quickly the anger disappeared, not to return again. Bill Clinton, then governor of Arkansas, had been watching the news and remembering this later asked Mandela about it. Mandela's reply was that he had found faith in Christ through a Bible class in prison. His anger that day was countered by the Spirit saying to him, "Nelson, while you were in prison, you were free. Now that you are free, don't become their prisoner!" He became a model of forgiving grace.

There is freedom in a cleansing of memories, from failures and even from the enjoyment we got from sin. As Jean Stapleton has reminded us, we must walk down the halls of our memories, stand before each picture, and acknowledge it. Then we can take the memory picture down, put it under the blood of the cross, and walk on in freedom.

Lord, help me today resist becoming a prisoner to my memories.
Give me strength to still mean it,
To continue my walk with you. Amen

Present Yourselves to God

No longer present your members to sin as instruments of wickedness, but present yourselves to God as those who have been brought from death to life, and present your members to God as instruments of righteousness.
Romans 6:13

During my pastorate in Washington, DC, I met for an hour of prayer with the elders of the congregation once a week. It was always a lift in my own spirit to join with them in praying, especially for members of the congregation and others. As shepherds we offer ourselves to God in prayer for others.

This text calls for the offering of our whole lives, our bodies, as well as our minds. We asked God to be a reality for each person in our congregation. The very use of our physical powers, the sanctification of our drives and passions, the proper use of our energies with right priorities, is a part of our Christian discipleship.

Christian faith is to be fleshed out in life. It is to be lived in deed as well as word. Our standard is more what we do than what we say. It is in the doing that others see the evidence of our faith. Our discipleship in life gives visibility to our faith.

We can pray with John Wesley's Covenant Prayer:

> *I am no longer my own, but yours.*
> *Put me to what you will,*
> *Rank me with whoever you will.*
> *Put me to doing, put me to suffering.*
> *Let me be employed for you,*
> *Or laid aside for you,*
> *Exalted for you, or brought low for you.*
> *Let me be full, let me be empty.*
> *Let me have all things, let me have nothing!*
> *And now, O Father, you are mine and I am yours.*
> *So be it. And the covenant I am making on earth,*
> *Let it be ratified in heaven. Amen   (abridged)*

Under Grace

For sin will have no dominion over you, since you are not under law but under grace. Romans 6:14

Grace is God's graciousness, it is found in his accepting us and in his identifying with us. We need to recognize both his forgiving grace and his enabling or transforming grace. It is the power of his presence that enables us to live a new life.

The meaning of grace is not simply assuring one another that God forgives, as though we may go on sinning, presuming on that forgiveness. The deeper meaning is in sharing the presence of God. This presence is as transforming as light penetrating darkness. Sharing our covenant with God in this new relationship is its own therapy.

Our text says that we have freedom from the reign of sin in our lives because we are under grace. Paul here contrasts law and grace: law making us aware of our sin and grace liberating us from sin. This is the joyous affirmation of faith, that we are free in Christ, free to live as children of God.

In any temptation, we can affirm this text. Sin shall not be my master! I am under grace! The longer I live and walk with God, the clearer it becomes that the Christian life is all of grace. The text is a very personal claim, for I must affirm freedom in Christ, and break the tyranny of sin by honest confession, for Christ makes me free.

Philip Yancey's book *What's So Amazing About Grace?* is a wonderful testimony to the truth of the gospel. He says that there is nothing we can do to make God love us more, and there is nothing we do that will make God love us less. How fantastic!

Yet as I read, I asked, "Yes, but, is there no therapy in grace, no transformation, no healing?" Of course, there is a remarkable change; one cannot enter covenant with God to walk with him and not be changed. Our fellowship in grace is a transforming dynamic.

Thank you, Lord,
for this wonderful dynamic for life today!

Should We Sin?

What then? Should we sin because we are not under law but under grace?
By no means! Romans 6:15

The legalist cannot trust grace to keep one in the will of God. The legalist is only comfortable with laws. An assumption in this text is that many persons would like an excuse to sin because God so freely forgives. Paul's answer is an emphatic "By no means." To sin is to pervert life, to live at less than our best. We are called to walk with God.

Vance Havner, a friend and great preacher, often said, "A thing is never settled until it is settled right, and a thing is never settled right until it is settled with God." We should not look at sin as a pleasure that we have to give up, but as a perversion of the good, the cheapening of something better. Righteousness is walking in the will of God, in the good that God intended for us to enjoy. Sin is a compromise of the good life, turning selfishly to shortcuts of pleasures that rob us of the good and wholesome life.

Jesus said, "I came that they may have life, and have it abundantly" (John 10:10). His redemption is the enrichment of life by what may be called "spiritual direction," or abundant living.

Discipleship is not following a new law. It is engaging a new relationship. We are called to walk with Jesus, the same Jesus who lived and taught the will of God in his incarnate life. It is this same Jesus who is risen and is at God's right hand. Therefore, as we walk with him, we are walking with the Jesus who walked and taught in Galilee. This is the same Jesus we can understand in the Word. We do not interpret him only as a subjective sense of spiritual presence, but more concretely as the Lord whom we serve.

Lord, help me walk with you today
in honesty and openness,
in faithfulness and love,
in victory and joy,
in fellowship and integrity,
in service and witness.
Lord, I would be true to you. Amen

Obedience to Righteousness

Do you not know that if you present yourselves to anyone as obedient slaves, you are slaves of the one whom you obey, either of sin, which leads to death, or of obedience, which leads to righteousness? Romans 6:16

We are what we obey. We become like that to which, or like the One to whom, we give our obedience. Slaves to sin move only in the path of death. Those who live in obedience to Christ move in the path of life. Obedience is the affirmation that, as disciples of Christ, we are committed to follow him, to obey him in love.

Esther served on the Board of Trustees of Eastern Baptist College and Seminary for more than a dozen years. I traveled with her to Philadelphia on the Metro-Liner train for an evening banquet honoring Dr. Robert Seiple, who was leaving the college presidency to lead World Vision. I sat by a young fellow, an illustrator for several book publishers, who spoke of the off-beat life that he had known in New York City. He spoke of drugs, alcohol, sexual promiscuity, speaking of the crucial youthful decisions. "One leads to another," he said, "until one is so trapped from one to the next that there is no way out."

"No way out," I replied, "except for Jesus—he comes into one's life and makes possible the road to freedom!" It was a privilege to share this good news with him, to help him to see that when Jesus comes to us, his call makes possible a decision for obedience in discipleship. How often I have been blessed by this truth. When I could not come to him on my own, he has come and made a response possible. This is a new freedom; to live with his power of selectivity.

Obedience is too often thought of as bondage rather than freedom. We all obey something, and if that is self-interest, it will close us off from God's abundant resources. Micah 6:8 reminds us that in obedience to God, life could not be better:

> *He has told you, O mortal, what is good;*
> *And what does the Lord require of you*
> *But to do justice,*
> *And to love kindness,*
> *And to walk humbly with your God.*

We Have Obeyed from the Heart

But thanks be to God that you, having once been slaves of sin, have become obedient from the heart to the form of teaching to which you were entrusted. Romans 6:17

The best life is in being an inner-directed person. Transformation of life begins within the person. Laws may be held over a person, yet behavior at its best is not by outward coercion, but by inner direction. We must own the principles we have been taught so they become our standards freely owned. We do not want to live on a borrowed religion, but our own. To be inner-directed rather than outer is true liberation.

Our behavior is never perfect in action, but it can be proper in attitude. We can, from the very heart or core of our person, seek to glorify God. Once we were slaves to our self-interests, but in his grace we have a new center, a new focus; we now seek to live in faithfulness to him. This is the dynamic of love, the deep sense of belonging to him. Commitment to Christ is similar in nature to commitment to another in love. Esther and I have walked together for fifty-four years. Many times I have been away, even overseas, and she at home with the children, but I have never been out of the awareness that I belong to Esther and she belongs to me. This is love guiding from the heart.

"After those days," says the Lord, "I will put my law within them, and I will write it on their hearts; and I will be their God, and they shall be my people" (Jer. 31:33). Our privilege in Christ is to be transformed at the heart or center of life and motivation. With transformed minds, we not only think *about* God, but we think *with* God.

This text is a before-and-after statement. In the past we were servants of sin, but we have obeyed from the heart and are now servants of righteousness. This is a new lifestyle. This is more than religious rites and performances; it is rather a right spirit and attitudes. No other passage is so clear on this as is the Sermon on the Mount, where Jesus blesses those whose heart is right toward God. We can have a righteousness that exceeds that of the scribes and Pharisees. This is a righteousness that moves beyond an obedience to law and that lives in the willing obedience of fellowship with Christ (Matt. 5:17-20).

Blessed Father, may your love so fill my life today
that in turn I may love you sincerely
as a response-love in freedom and joy. Amen

Slaves of Righteousness

And that you, having been set free from sin, have become slaves of righteousness.
Romans 6:18

This text might be termed life's greatest contrast. Once slaves to sin, now we are slaves to righteousness. This is life's most remarkable transformation. Philip Paul Bliss in one of our hymns says, "Once I was blind, but now I can see; the light of the world is Jesus."

This text needs to be read with the preceding one if we are to grasp its impact. It has well been said, "A text without a context is a pretext." The context says that we have been released, liberated. We are released from the servitude of sin, slavery to lust, greed, anger, injustice, violence, and addiction. We are free in Christ, in contrast to the old order, free to now live as servants of righteousness.

The Christian church has not given enough attention to this quality of the new life in Christ. We are not only forgiven sinners, we are made new creatures who share a new life in the Spirit. Our freedom is that of the Spirit working within us to counteract our tendency to sin. In fact, the power of the Spirit in our lives is stronger than the power of sin (Gal. 5:16-17). The choice is ours: we can walk in the Spirit, we can walk in righteousness.

God calls us to himself, to belong to him, and thus to walk with him. With the risen Christ we are enabled to walk in the resurrection, to say no to sin.

> *His amazing grace has laid hold on me,*
> *has claimed me for his own;*
> *has created my inner self anew,*
> *a place for the Spirit's abode.*
> *My freedom is to cry, "Abba, Father,"*
> *and know that I belong as his child.*
> *My purpose is now to live in his will,*
> *to live in worship, in service, in joy. Amen*

. . . *and to Holiness*

I am speaking in human terms because of your natural limitations. For just as you once presented you members as slaves to impurity and to greater and greater iniquity, so now present your members as slaves to righteousness for sanctification. Romans 6:19

Jesus's teaching on freedom in John 8:34 declares, "Very truly, I tell you, everyone who commits sin is a slave to sin." But in verse 36 he says, "If the Son makes you free, you will be free indeed." While we once lived in sin, using our bodies in slavery to impurity, we have been set free in Christ. The bondage of sin is broken—greed, lust, covetousness, disbelief, and idolatry are defeated. In the new life we offer our bodies in righteousness unto holiness.

Psychologically, we find release from one obsession to become involved in another, the Magnificent Obsession, doing the will of God. By belonging wholly to God, we pursue righteousness, and in turn the pursuit contributes to our wholeness. Our priorities are set by his holiness, and our goal is the holiness of life enjoyed in freedom.

"Yet whatever gains I had, these I have come to regard as loss because of Christ. More than that, I regard everything as loss because of the surpassing value of knowing Christ Jesus my Lord. For his sake I have suffered the loss of all things, and I regard them as rubbish, in order that I may gain Christ and be found in him, not having a righteousness of my own that comes from the law, but one that comes through faith in Christ, the righteousness from God based on faith" (Phil. 3:7-9).

A friend of ours, who was a missionary in India, tells of being visited by an American who had never been in another culture before. They were invited to dinner one evening to the home of a wonderful Christian woman. Typically for that culture, they sat on the floor and ate with their hands. Indian people never eat with the left hand, as that is used for toilet roles. The guest being left-handed and not knowing Indian custom, began to eat with her left hand. There was a pause of silence around the group. Then, in quiet dignity, the hostess began to eat with her left hand. All the rest immediately did the same. The hostess had the freedom from a cultural law to adjust for the sake of the guest, extending Christian love.

Lord, give me the freedom of heart to adjust to the needs
and feelings of others with whom I relate. Amen

Under What Control?

When you were slaves of sin, you were free in regard to righteousness.
Romans 6:20

The question is, Which controls our lives, the pursuit of righteousness or the pursuit of sinful gratification? We cannot pursue both for they are going in opposite directions.

Jesus said, "No one can serve two masters" (Matt. 6:24). Long ago, the prophet Amos asked, "Can two walk together, except they be agreed?" (Amos 3:3, KJV). We cannot serve sin and God too. Paul's message in this chapter is a call for a total break from sin, a break as definite and as decisive as death. We now can share the resurrection quality of life with Christ.

This is not a new legalism, a blunt requirement to do what is right. Rather, it is a new covenant of love, an actual, meaningful relationship with God. Through the righteousness of Christ we are enabled by the Spirit to live right in relation with others.

John writes that the one who dwells in love dwells in God, and again, "whoever does not love does not know God" (1 John 4:7-13). This is from his Master, for when Jesus was asked about the greatest commandment, he answered with an enlarged focus on love:

> *The great commandment is first to love God*
> *with all one's mind—attitude,*
> *with all one's heart—affection,*
> *with all one's soul—ambition,*
> *with all one's strength—activity.*
> *The second commandment is to love one's neighbor as one's self*
> *with esteem,*
> *with genuine concern,*
> *with mutual support,*
> *with encouraging participation.*

What Advantage?

So what advantage did you then get from the things of which you now are ashamed? The end of those things is death. Romans 6:21

To look back in one's life brings both celebration and regrets. In the honest review of our lives we have so much for which to be thankful, but we also have things that we regret and must face honestly. This is recognizing my failures along with my blessings and privileges.

Each of us needs to objectify our lives for analysis and decision, to learn from the past and avoid working only from subjective elements. We cannot deny the latter, for the subjective is the sum total of all of our composite experience and preferences. But decision making calls for an objective analysis: Who am I, what am I doing, where am I going, what should I be doing, and how do I get there? All of these questions and more become the unique expression of the higher level of humanness, of self-transcendence.

Decisions call for selectivity, which means giving up some things for other things that we decide are the better for us. Esther and I have enjoyed hearing the National Symphony Orchestra at the Kennedy Center on occasion. A symphony is a good illustration of community, for individuals are disciplined to do together what no one could do alone. The hours of discipline they have put into practice means they had to say no to other things.

Paul asks, What advantages were won by our past choices in sin? The answer is quite evident. Values that enrich and abide are quality factors, not the perversions that reduce self-interests to mere selfishness. We are called to be authentic selves in fellowship with God.

> *For me to be yours, my Father,*
> *   is life's greatest privilege.*
> *For to belong to you, Lord,*
> *   frees me from belonging to any other.*
> *To walk with Christ as Master*
> *   releases me from any other master.*
> *To live in the Spirit*
> *   is to be inner-directed.*

May 26

You Have Been Freed

But now that you have been freed from sin and enslaved to God, the advantage you get is sanctification. The end is eternal life. Romans 6:22

Free as a servant of God—this is a good description, for we have been redeemed, and we belong to him. The redeemed belong to the Redeemer. In this there is freedom.

Yes, this text is true, but if today I become impatient and my attitude is expressed in hasty words, I have not engaged the freedom of self-control granted me in Christ. True, we repent, but in the experience we see how limited is our progress in holiness (sanctification). We may become angry at ourselves for failing to live by this freedom which we know. I am thankful for God's grace. I can close the door on the failure and reach out anew to him.

By faith we can affirm that we have been set free. Again, by faith we allow God to be himself in our lives. In fact, apart from him there would be many more failures. Even in our limitations, we share the new life in contrast to the old, which was under sin.

This freedom is the quality of eternal life, a life which begins by coming to Jesus and which will never end. Paul wrote to the Ephesians that it will take the ages of the ages for God to unfold all of the marvels of his grace, our amazing inheritance in Christ.

"Fifty billion years, what a horrible thought," Betty Wicks said to me during a crusade in Salt Lake City. She said that she didn't want her life extended in such a scope, not life as she knew it. But, during that week she met Christ in a new way and her perspective changed; the thought now became one of joy. Fifty billion years *with God*!

Months later, traveling from the west in the Denver airport, I met a gentleman from Salt Lake City. As we chatted he suddenly asked, "Do you remember Betty Wicks, who helped in advertising the crusade? She has died of cancer." "Yes," I said, "I remember her." After a moment of silence I said softly, "Fifty billion years … what a wonderful thought."

Lord, help me to claim my freedom
in you each day. Amen

The Gift of God Is Eternal Life

For the wages of sin is death, but the free gift of God is eternal life in Christ Jesus our Lord. Romans 6:23

God's promise of eternal life is such a great gift. We have been created in his image; we have been redeemed; he promises us that we can share all eternity with him.

The rich young ruler, in Mark 10, asked, "Good Teacher, what must I do to inherit eternal life?" Interestingly, the word *inherit* means that one is receiving a gift, although the ruler may have used it as a benefit to follow a particular work. Life is a gift of God, received by letting God be God in one's life.

The contrast in the text speaks volumes. Sin has its wages—death, but the gift of God is life. In him we live, *now*. In him we are in fellowship with the Eternal One; we share our God-intended destiny, life with him.

Jonathan Edwards said in his diary on May 1, 1723, "Lord, grant that from thence I may fix my thoughts, affections, desires, and expectations upon the heavenly state; where there is fullness of joy; where reigns heavenly, sweet, calm, and delightful love without alloy; where there are continually the dearest expressions of their love; where there is the enjoyment of the persons loved, without ever parting; where those persons who appear so lovely in this world, will be inexpressibly more lovely and full of love to us. How sweetly will the mutual lovers join together to sing the praises of God and the Lamb." The Job 19:25-27 verses confess:

> *I know that my Redeemer lives,*
> *and that at the last he will stand upon the earth;*
> *and after my skin has been thus destroyed,*
> *then in my flesh I shall see God,*
> *whom I shall see on my side,*
> *and my eyes shall behold, and not another.*
> *My heart faints within me!*

The Authority of the Law

Do you not know, brothers and sisters—for I am speaking to those who know the law—that the law is binding on a person only during that person's lifetime? Romans 7:1

The law has authority, yes, but if one is dead or has died to the law, he is free. Is that not the implication of this verse? The chapter presents a searching analysis of the law in a person's life and of the characteristics of legalism.

This chapter is a careful argument for the freedom we have in Christ. In the chapter we will find the despair of persons who live under the law rather than in the freedom of grace. As to whether this happens before or after conversion, it seems that it happens at any stage when one sinks below the level of freedom in Christ, to live by the mandate of law. The bondage to legalism is broken by our commitment to Christ.

Paul begins his argument with an illustration from the life and context of the Hebrew community. The law is the authority for life and is binding so long as a person lives. Once one dies to that realm, the law cannot be the authority.

Here Paul helps the reader to understand that the law was the authority for the old order, the old life under the reign of self. But once we die to that order and live in a new order of freedom in Christ, we are free from the law by belonging to Jesus Christ. To make this argument clear he uses marriage as the illustration. The point he is illustrating is that the law is authority for those who live in the realm of law. Another illustration could be that the Constitution of the United States is authority for us who are citizens of the United States. We, citizens of the U.S., need to be committed to the constitution, but we are also citizens of another kingdom—the kingdom of God, and this is our first loyalty.

Heavenly Father, you are gracious.
Thank you that you love and care for us;
not in laying a guilt trip on us
but rather, you provide freedom for us;
the freedom to be citizens of your kingdom.
We rejoice in being your subjects.
God, our Chief of State, we thank you. Amen

Discharged from the Law

Thus a married woman is bound by the law to her husband as long as he lives; but if her husband dies, she is discharged from the law concerning the husband. Romans 7:2

A number of years ago, our surrogate daughter from Switzerland, Patricia Leuenberger, graduated from Eastern Mennonite High School. Esther and I drove to the Shenandoah Valley to attend her commencement exercises. We stayed overnight, visited each of our mothers, had dinner with our son Mike, and the next morning had a chat with our oldest son, John. He shared with us that his wife of twelve years was beginning divorce proceedings, to be free to follow other interests. What pain we shared with him over a marriage that died. What disappointment for John and for us. We each had to bear the tragic pain of their divorce. In fact, it was so heartrending that I have at times felt like I should quit preaching.

In the text Paul is illustrating the demands of the law, that one partner must die for a marriage to be ended. But beyond his point there is, for me, a cold hard fact—a marriage can die. The law holds a person to the covenant with the spouse. But if there is a break of the covenant, if the love is dead and the covenant is broken (sinfully of course, but broken), the law holds them responsible. The law can't rebuild it. Paul's point is that, in death the other is free, for we are held accountable by the law so long as we live.

The primary meaning here is that death to the old life makes one free to engage the new life. In the new relation there is no residual tie to the old life. God is the Creator of the new, and in our coming to him the old passes away; all of life is made new. We have a new Master, new relation, new heart, new motive, new purpose, and new goal.

> *God is the God of a second chance.*
> *In this statement I find grace,*
> *In this perspective there is hope.*
> *In God's grace we can begin again.*
> *We can build again.*
> *When we fall we can get up.*
> *God is there to help us up.*

Accordingly

Accordingly, she will be called an adulteress if she lives with another man while her husband is alive. But if her husband dies, she is free from that law, and if she marries another man, she is not an adulteress. Romans 7:3

This is a word of the law, clear and unambiguous. The previous meditation is carried to its completion in this text. Reflecting further on Paul's illustration, we are now shown the immorality of breaking covenant. The meaning of adultery is "covenant breaker." The German word for adultery means marriage-breaker. This is more than sexual immorality. It is the more serious act of breaking covenant.

Breaking covenant is the violation of one of the higher levels of our being made in God's image. For example, we have the ability to make covenant with integrity. Paul's point is that to break covenant and form a relationship with another person is to be untrue to one's primary commitment. It is breaking covenant that is committing adultery.

Yet I must add some thoughts on the serious aspects of his illustration of the sin of adultery. The focus is on covenant breaking, not so much on sex, for divorce and remarriage is a covenant breaking, and this is the serious aspect of the sin. Yes, Jesus forgave the adulteress, but he said, "Go, and sin no more." Do not break covenant (John 8:11). But what if a second covenant is formed that we need to deal with? Broken because of sin, yes, but the gospel calls them to now live by the kingdom standard.

Can their old life be dead and we meet them where they are in grace? Does God's forgiveness not liberate a person and help them build a new life? Can we not provide the forgiveness and acceptance for a new life without condoning the sins that preceded the present? Billy Graham has said, "You can't unscramble scrambled eggs."

The text is an illustration that cannot be modified, but it is used here as an illustration. Other passages in the Scripture help us work with the problems of sin and brokenness without hopelessness. Paul wrote, "This is what some of you used to be. But you were washed, you were sanctified, you were justified in the name of the Lord Jesus Christ" (1 Cor. 6:11).

God, help us to understand all that it means
to live under your grace and forgiving love. Amen

May 31

We Have Died to the Law

In the same way, my friends, you have died to the law through the body of Christ, so that you may belong to another, to him who has been raised from the dead in order that we might bear fruit for God. Romans 7:4

In Christ we have died to the law. Here Paul is making the application of his illustration and relating it to the life of faith. He does not say that the law has died to us. If you sink beneath the level of the law in behavior, the law is there to condemn. But in walking with Christ we live above the level of legalistic constraint; we live in his fellowship.

Paul's illustration is primarily to show the finality of a break from one order of life when we die to it. We are now free to live by a new order. He is building here on his statements in chapter 6 that we die to the old life by identification with Christ.

Back in the 1960s I wrote a historical novel called *Pilgrim Aflame*. It is the story of Michael Sattler who, as prior of St. Peter's in the Black Forest, was converted and became a leader in the Anabaptist movement which took place in the time of Martin Luther's reformation. He was burned at the stake in Rottenburg on the Neckar River in Bavaria on May 20, 1527. His wife, Margueritha, was drowned three days later for her faith in Christ. A film-producing group called Sisters and Brothers asked to use this book for the basis of a film, presenting the Anabaptists to the public.

I joined Michael Hostetler on a short trip to Switzerland and South Germany to scout out historical settings for sites to use later in filming. This led me to review the commitment of a man who left one denomination, the Catholic Church, to become a leader in a new order among the Anabaptists. He was the spokesperson for one of the earliest, if not the first, Protestant Synod in the Reformation, Schleitheim, February 1527, with its unique confession of faith. Sattler became a martyr for the freedom he knew in Christ.

The phrase which changed Sattler's life and which brought him physical death was John 8:36:

> *If the Son makes you free,*
> *you will be free indeed.*

June 1

Sin's Control Is Now in the Past

While we were living in the flesh, our sinful passions, aroused by the law, were at work in our members to bear fruit for death. Romans 7:5

The remarkable contrast between the old life and the new life in the preceding text is expressed again in this one. The contrast: we bear fruit for God or bear fruit for death. The path of sin leads to death; the identification with Christ leads to life.

One day in Washington, DC, Esther called me to tell me that one of her art students was shot at school! The girl was still living but was in critical condition. The student was only age thirteen. In a quarrel with her girlfriend, the friend shot her. Esther told me the news by phone with great concern, for this girl was from a broken home in the black community and had come to love God. The meaning of this text is not just a theory; it is actually the stuff of life.

Paul is saying that, controlled by our sinful nature, even the presence of the law can offer only directions for restraint. It may actually serve to arouse an inner stimulus to do the things the law condemns. We are not good people with a few mistakes; we are sinful people whose lives are perverted by selfishness. We need a Savior, not simply a code of conduct, but one that saves us from living only for ourselves.

On our trip to Switzerland to find potential sites for the film about the early Anabaptist movement, we visited several areas in the region of Interlaken, one of which was a castle taken over by a group of Protestant "monks" and a "Landes Museum." The glorious view of the snowcapped Alps was a lift to my spirit and left me with an exhilarating feeling—very different from the Washington, DC, streets. Just so, the new life in Christ opens new vistas of the spirit. The grandeur of creation is a stimulus as we think beyond creation to the God of which it is witness. So we must think beyond the law to the God expressed in the Helen H. Lemmel words of a simple chorus that I learned as a young man:

Turn your eyes upon Jesus,
Look full in His wonderful face,
And the things of earth will grow strangely dim
In the light of His glory and grace.

Serving in the New Way of the Spirit

But now we are discharged from the law, dead to that which held us captive, so that we are slaves not under the old written code but in the new life in the Spirit. Romans 7:6

One cannot be totally neutral; we always serve something. We either serve God or our selves. Paul contrasts service in the new way of the Spirit with the old way of the letter. Many Christians have failed to grasp this contrast and have placed the primary emphasis on the fallen state of our lives rather than on the redemption Christ has brought to us. We are released from the control of our fallen state; we are participants in a new order.

When Paul speaks of the law as so limiting, he is speaking of the nature of code without spirit, of letter without life. In Jeremiah, God promised a new covenant written in our hearts by the Spirit. As inner-directed people, our minds are set on Christ and his will.

On the investigation trip to Switzerland for the film *The Radicals*, we traveled from Basel to Colmar in France. We then crossed the Rhine to Freiburg and north into the Black Forest to St. Peter's Monastery, where Michael Sattler was prior in the early 1520s. After a visit there we traveled east to Horb, the center of Sattler's work, where he and Margueritha had lived and he had served as a pastor. I saw a road sign to Lahr and remembered from my studies a letter from the pastor, Ottelinus, newly Protestant, written to Martin Bucer, the prominent reformer at Strasbourg. He wrote of Michael Sattler's ministry in the region impacting his parish and said of Sattler, "He teaches that there is a spirit of Scripture which we are to follow; rejecting those of us who follow the letter of Scripture."

The prayer that we should pray
as we study the Word written
is that the Spirit will show us
in the words the inerrant meaning,
that we meet and understand the Living Word,
and in him grasp the knowledge of God.

Is the Law Sin?

What then should we say? That the law is sin? By no means! Yet, if it had not been for the law, I would not have known sin. I would not have known what it is to covet if the law had not said, "You shall not covet." Romans 7:7

The law reveals not only also our sin, but our sinfulness. By having the law we are fully aware of the contrast between the right to which it points and the inner urging to which our selfishness points us. It is not the law that is sin; the law is only a reminder; it is our self-centeredness that is sin. Our sinfulness is present, whether there be knowledge of the law or not. The law enables us to understand and recognize our sinfulness.

This is a humbling insight. If the law were our order of life, every success in keeping any part of it would be met with a response of pride. But once we are aware that it exposes our bent to sin, it is very humbling. Jesus said that not only is the breaking of the law to be regarded as sin, but actually anything that leads to the sinful act is already sin in the heart. This is expressed in Jesus's words: "Everyone who looks at a woman with lust has already committed adultery with her in his heart." He has broken covenant (Matt. 5:28).

Michael Sattler, an early Anabaptist leader, left the state church when he saw the immorality of fellow priests. While in the Benedictine Cloister at St. Peter's Church, Sattler was prior. He had been a "lord of men," but he resigned to be true to his faith relationship with Christ. What a price he paid for his moral integrity as a disciple of Christ, as expressed in the Fannie Estelle Davison verse:

> *Purer in heart, O God, help me to be;*
> *That I Thy holy face, one day may see.*
> *Keep me from secret sin,*
> *Reign Thou my soul within;*
> *Purer in heart, help me to be.*

June 4

Sin Seizes Opportunity to Control

But sin, seizing an opportunity in the commandment, produced in me all kinds of covetousness. Apart from the law sin lies dead. Romans 7:8

"Apart from the law sin lies dead"—what an amazing statement! Sin, seeking our own way, has no challenge until a higher standard is introduced. The law is not sin in itself, nor does it produce sin, for the sin is already there. The sin takes opportunity to express itself in response to the new insights the law offers.

Does this mean that we are better where there is no law? Where there is no standard? No, for we are sinful and depraved whether there is a law or not. When the law is expressed, when the higher standard for life is introduced, sin resists this higher standard. Sinfulness seeks comfort, in not wanting to change for the better. The knowledge of the higher standard becomes the occasion for selfishness to express itself.

When we completed our short film location survey north of Switzerland in France and Germany, we returned to Basel. Just before leaving there, my friends Peter and Erika Leuenberger gave me presents to bring to Esther for us both to enjoy. Among them was some of the best Swiss chocolate. Wonderful! However, as to calories, the chocolate provides the opportunity, as Paul says, for one to be a nutritional overachiever. Their presence is a test of our freedom, much as the standards of the law provide a test of our choice for the higher will of God.

True religion is relationship,
not just rites or rules.
Beyond the rites and laws
is fellowship and love.
Salvation is not just from something;
it is fellowship with someone.
Jesus is our Redeemer,
and he is our friend.

June 5

But the Commandment Came

I was once alive apart from the law, but when the commandment came, sin revived and I died. Romans 7:9-10

At this time of the year we celebrate Pentecost Sunday, the giving of Christ's gift, the Holy Spirit. On Pentecost Jesus baptized with the Spirit those who confessed him as Lord. He became present with them in the person of his Spirit. Our risen Lord continues to baptize with the Spirit those who accept him as Lord, confirming his promise to be with us and in us. The Spirit enables us to live a new life in freedom.

To live by law alone is to live beneath life in the Spirit. The Spirit gives life, enabling us to live by and in his righteousness. We can live in fellowship with the Spirit and in fellowship together with others who truly know life in the Spirit in any circumstance. An example of two persons who were not slaves to the law of their particular religious order, but who were of the same Spirit in a difficult circumstance, is found in this moving story:

Under Stalin's persecution of Christians, a Mennonite preacher, Hans Rempel, was arrested for continuing to preach in spite of the prohibitions. Sent to one of the large prisons, he was jammed into the crowded facilities. Once a day they were served a bowl of thin soup, and on the first day, jostled by prisoners near him, he spilled most of his soup. The next day, seeing a table in the corner of the room, he got his soup and stooping, he crawled under the table. He bowed his head in silent prayer, then looking over he saw a bearded man had joined him. The man asked, "What were you doing just now?" He replied, "I am believer and was thanking God for this food." The man cried, "I'm a believer, too." They chatted a bit, the Mennonite preacher and the new acquaintance, a Russian Orthodox believer. Suddenly the stranger said, "We can have communion together." Hans said, "Communion? Where do we get the wine and the bread?" The man responded, "We have bread and soup, and we are all three here." "Three?" Hans asked perplexed. "There are two of us." "Yes, we two and the Lord," the new friend replied. Later Hans said that of all communions he ever shared, this was one of the most meaningful.

Lord, thank you for your gift of the Spirit
that brings new life. Amen

<

June 6

Life Proved to Be Death

And the very commandment that promised life proved to be death to me.
Romans 7:10

When the commandment comes, I die; that is, the death-dealing aspects of self-fulfillment are now evident and dominating. The commandment that promises life cannot deliver. Paul discovered something more than mere direction; he found empowerment.

Unless Christian faith becomes personal, it cannot be transforming. If it stays only within the person, it cannot impact society. Paul expresses what we today refer to as the psychological aspects of the inner workings of sin and of grace. Of sin, in that it kills the self which wants to be free; of grace, as in the graciousness of God we are accepted.

The primary emphasis of the text is on the inner working of law and gospel. From his own background Paul knew the constraint of law, but he knew that the deeper aspects of the struggle are when one thinks that keeping the law is the way to achieve a right relationship with God. This tension between law and grace brought Martin Luther to see some of the greater understandings of faith that started the Protestant Reformation.

The law's constant reminder of God's demands and our failures kills our hope, our confidence, and our assurance. Something dies within us, and we are left with despair over knowing the God beyond the law. In grace, we meet God in Jesus. He is our mediator.

To live is quality life,
a life in fellowship with God.
It is life with meaning and hope,
assurance and fulfillment.
There is nothing about dying that we want,
unless it be in dying to selfishness.
For life is the essence of being.
Of Jesus it is said,
"In him was life, and the life was the light of all people!"
(John 1:4)

Sin Seizes Any Opportunity

For sin, seizing an opportunity in the commandment, deceived me and through it killed me. Romans 7:11

While sin is already there, it is when the commandment comes to go God's way that sin asserts itself in calling us to go our own way. In fact, the full expression of our stubbornness is only shown when we have something we prop our feet against. It is the very tug of God upon us that becomes the occasion for our rebellion against him.

Frequently we see persons rather ignorant of God and his will who are living quite blithely or freely, without a care in the world. Alongside we may see one who knows something of the will of God and who seems in contrast to be living under a heavy sense of constraint. What causes this burden? Is it the knowledge of the will of God? Or is it that this knowledge provides occasion for our selfishness to express itself? If the knowledge of God's law provides conflict, would it be better not to know the law?

Paul says that the problem is not in the law, but in us; not in the ethical standard, but in the selfish preference. Sin, our perversion of selfish pride, finds opportunity to actually kill the authentic self that God intends for us by obsessing us with rebellion against the divine will. This chapter of Paul's letter is one of the deeper treatments of the psychology of religious experience. In these verses he depicts the struggle in a depth of theological and psychological insight beyond the thought systems of his day.

It was not until Augustine that a great mind dealt explicitly with the psychology of religious experience. From him we learn a deep truth. Having been quite sensual, having a mistress and a son at the age of nineteen, he later converted to Christ, and wrote his *Confessions*. Analyzing the nature of sin, his illustration of the most expressive disclosure of his sinfulness was that he had crawled up in a neighbor's pear tree and picked pears and threw them to the hogs. This, he said, was not because of any need he had, but just out of plain mischief. It is not what we do, but rather why we do what we do.

Lord, help us to understand ourselves,
to be honest with ourselves,
to recognize our need for your forgiving grace,
and also for your transforming grace today. Amen

June 8

The Law Is Holy

**So the law is holy, and the commandment is holy and just and good.
Romans 7:12**

The problem is really not with the law; it is with us. Confronted by God's standard we become aware of our failure. It is in this sense that John Wesley said, "Before I preach grace, I must preach law." Too often we do not sense our need of the guidance and importance of the law.

Paul says that the law is holy, just, and good. The problem is not with the law. The fact that the law becomes the occasion for more overt expressions of sin does not mean that we ignore the law. We need to regard it in its proper role. It cannot be the mediator of a right relationship with God. Its impact is to expose and thereby condemn our alienation. We need the mediator, Jesus.

It is important for the thinking person that we recognize that there is a standard of right. It is not true that everything is relative. We are called to walk with God and not against him, called to seek his will, not our own. We are called to live by God's standards, not by the desires of self. Freedom is not license to do as we wish, but a release from being dominated by perversion. We can, by the law, maximize our potential in the will of God.

I recall the story of a teacher calling a boy to account for cheating. She told the chap that she was sure he had cheated on his exam because the answers were just like those of his fellow student. He responded, "That is simple; the other fellow copied mine." She replied, "I thought of that, but the answers were all alike until I got to the last one. The other student wrote, 'I don't know,' and you wrote, 'I don't know either.'"

The law holds us accountable. In "Rock of Ages! Cleft for Me," Augustus M. Topladt writes of our release:

> *Nothing in my hand I bring,*
> *   simply to the cross I cling.*
> *Naked, come to Thee for dress,*
> *   helpless, look to Thee for grace.*
> *Foul, I to the fountain fly,*
> *   wash me, Savior, or I die. Amen*

June 9

Working in Me What Is Good

Did what is good, then, bring death to me? By no means! It was sin, working death in me through what is good, in order that sin might be shown to be sin, and through the commandment might become sinful beyond measure. Romans 7:13

The subtlety of sin is its ability to pervert everything, even religion, causing it to become idolatrous in expression. For some, the law has become an end in itself. Anything that keeps us from coming to God becomes an idol to us, no matter how good it may be. In our exercise of religion, when we want to put it into systems of belief that we can master, we actually close ourselves off from reaching beyond it to God himself.

Faith is not synonymous with belief. In faith we reach beyond proof. Faith is response to evidence; this is not proof. When one has proof, the leap of faith is not needed. Paul writes, "Now we see through a glass darkly" (1 Cor. 13:12, KJV). Jesus told Thomas that he was blessed in seeing, but he added, "Blessed are those who have not seen and yet have come to believe" (John 20:29). That includes each of us.

Sin is not only in breaking the commandment, but the way in which we arrogantly relate to the law. We approach the law as though to say, "Show me the way and I will do it." But we cannot. For the *meaning* of the way is not fulfilled in law. The way is to reach out to God himself. Jesus said, "I am the way, and the truth, and the life. No one comes to the Father except through me" (John 14:6). The search for a way to God is ended in Jesus.

Today's verse is a profound argument that when we stand in the light of God's revelation, we are exposed. We understand more fully and authentically our sinfulness. Adam and Eve, in their finitude, anxiety, and independence, reached for the forbidden in order to become like God. We are called to be like God by identification with Christ.

To paraphrase the words of the early church father, Athanasius, of the fourth century: "In Jesus God became like us so that in turn we in Jesus can become like God."

Lord, I pray this day
that I may be conformed
to the image of your dear Son. Amen

The Law Is Spiritual

For we know that the law is spiritual; but I am of the flesh, sold into slavery under sin. Romans 7:14

Honesty with one's self is a basic principle of finding meaning in life. Paul says, "I am of the flesh." This is the crux of the issue. Some translations use the word *carnal*, by which Paul means an inner perversion through the dominance of self-interest. To be carnal is in contrast to being spiritual; it is to be self-oriented rather than God oriented. For the carnal person, the law, or the claims of God, actually create a civil war within one, for the mind acknowledges that the law is spiritual, while the self-interest is to have one's own way.

In that magnificent messianic chapter, Isaiah 53, the Old Testament prophet defines sin, saying, "We have all turned to our own way" (v. 6). And while sin dominated our lives before we came to faith, now as a people of faith we are called to freedom in the Spirit. This freedom from slavery to sin is not found in the law, but in subjecting ourselves to the Spirit of Christ.

This power of the Spirit is the only source of release from being slaves to things that are contrary to the law. Paul is making clear that we understand the depth of the conflict and why we so desperately need the Holy Spirit. We can, of our own selves, do nothing. Only the Spirit frees us to say, "I can do all things through him who strengthens me" (Phil. 4:13).

Once while riding to the airport in a van from the college where I was president, I opened conversation with a passenger. He learned that I was a minister and began to tell me of his conversion to Christ. He was a businessman and described his new life and the difference it made for him. In a strong voice, which the other passengers could hear, he emphatically said, "It isn't easy. There is so much greed and compromise in the work I'm in, and it isn't easy to do the will of Christ. But," he declared, "I've found something that works. I've found, with Paul, that I can do all things through Christ who strengthens me." I saw the others look at each other and smile. At the airport we each went our way, but he had given his witness.

> *Help us, Lord, this day,*
> *to live by the strength and grace of Christ.*

June 11

What I Hate, That I Do

I do not understand my own actions. For I do not do what I want, but I do the very thing I hate. Romans 7:15

How often have we said, "Why did I do that? I know better"? Yet, so often there is a gap between what we know and what we do. Relationship with God is far more than intellectual perception or simple academic awareness. Relationship has to do with respect, love, esteem, and openness to the other. Faith is openness to God.

Many arguments have been given over whether Paul was speaking of his current life or his preconversion life. After considerable reflection on the context, it seems to me that Paul is describing what happens at any time when one sinks to live under the law rather than in the freedom of Christ. In the context, he has been showing us how the law exposes sin and how it actually creates the occasion of sin. In this text he carries this into the psychological depth of the inner struggle between perception and personal decision—"I do the very thing I hate."

Some Christians who fail to understand Paul's further teaching on victory in Christ quote this text as an excuse for their sins. But Paul is giving this as a *problem* and not as an *answer*. At some point, we have all experienced what this text says. Until we become this honest about our sinfulness, we won't fully recognize our need for a Savior. I have often prayed that, even though subconsciously I may have selfish motivations, consciously I *will* to serve for the glory of God. If we pray in faith, he will grant inner freedom "both to will and to do his good pleasure" (Phil. 2:13).

This passage is an exposure and rejection of legalism. The idea that if we only know God's will, God's commandment, we can do it. This notion is undercut by the insight of this text. Knowing the law does not enable one to practice it. The only answer to our dilemma is in participation in the resurrection power of Christ. To join in solidarity with Christ means being engaged by faith as in John 15:5:

I am the vine, you are the branches.
Those who abide in me and I in them
bear much fruit, because apart from me
you can do nothing.

June 12

I Consent unto the Law

Now if I do what I do not want, I agree that the law is good. But in fact it is no longer I that do it, but sin that dwells within me. Romans 7:16-17

Are my actions a conscious choice or the expression of my unconscious self? Paul sees the inner struggle as confirming his earlier point that the law is spiritual, but human nature is sinful. The voice of the inner consciousness that we are in a struggle, doing the very thing that we don't want to do, is a recognition that there is a higher law, a law of God. Perception of the mind is one factor, the expressions of life may be another.

To consent with the law is to agree on the common foundation of ethical principles on which life is to be built. The precepts of righteousness become our guide, but we live only by the power of the Spirit of Christ. We live by his freedom rather than by constant struggle with the constraint of law.

Many Christians emphasize our fallen state, our sinfulness, to the exclusion of adequate emphasis on redemption. The fact is that we have a Savior. Our fallen state is our condition, yes, but not our confession! He has set us free, restored us to fellowship with God. Now we know, as Paul says, "It is no longer I who live, but it is Christ who lives in me" (Gal. 2:20).

Ours is a call to identify with Christ, not just to be religious. We are not simply practicing religion; we are enjoying fellowship with God. Such fellowship is not an achievement in living by law, but is in-depth sharing in God's grace. We confess that wrong behavior is not the true me, but sin dwelling in me. We also confess that right behavior is not truly of me, but of Christ living in me.

To confess sinfulness means that we renounce any trust in that sinfulness. We are to place our trust in him, for he promises to forgive if we but ask him. In so doing we honor him so that all may know that victory is not in our achievement, but is God's work in us. The invitation to come to Christ is the affirmation of the Spirit that one can say yes to God. Evangelism is everything that makes faith in Christ a possibility for a person. Preaching is one of those things, but our walk with Christ may itself be evangelism.

Dear Lord, let my life communicate
the meaning of my faith in Christ this day. Amen

June 13

Now to Perform That Which Is Good

For I know that nothing good dwells within me, that is, in my flesh. I can will what is right, but I cannot do it. Romans 7:18

Immanuel Kant gave us categorical imperatives as a basis for ethics, which means that we treat every person as an end and not as a means to an end. Behave so that your behavior could be a universal law. But noble as these are, where does one get the strength to live them? This is a philosophical legalism, an ethic of duty. We may acknowledge the right, but to live it is the real issue.

Of ourselves, we have no power to walk with God. Salvation is a work of God's grace; he comes to us and calls us, and as we respond, he changes us by his grace. This is a special word for the legalist. But having come to God in faith, as Paul writes, we are to "work out [our] own salvation with fear and trembling; for it is God who is at work in you, enabling you both to will and to work for his good pleasure" (Phil. 2:12-13). That is, we work out in life's expression what God is working into our experience.

Paul's very candid treatment of our sinfulness calls us to honesty before God. We are made aware that we are hopelessly sinful apart from God, and that only by his work within us can we be made new creatures.

The evangelistic appeal in meetings in which I often preach, is the good news that we can become children of God, that he will forgive us and accept us into his family. For the people gathered, I have regularly announced a new relationship, a new Master, new motivation, new purpose, new principles, and new power in the Holy Spirit to live differently, to walk with him in life. Harry Emerson Fosdick expressed this new birth as the power of grace for:

> *God of grace and God of glory,*
> *On Thy people pour Thy pow'r;*
> *Crown Thine ancient church's story;*
> *Bring her bud to glorious flow'r.*
> *Grant us wisdom, Grant us courage,*
> *For the facing of this hour.*

June 14

Of Ourselves We Do the Evil

For I do not do the good I want, but the evil I do not want is what I do.
Romans 7:19

One under the law can only live with this kind of struggle. Paul writes, "What I do is not what I want to do." This is what it is like to live by law rather than by the freedom of Christ. When one lives without the inner transformation of the Spirit, one is left with the struggle between the mind, which recognizes what ought to be, and the lack of power to live by this "oughtness." Left only to ourselves, perceptions of the higher level of right notwithstanding, we have only the abilities of the sinful person.

A father and his son went camping, and the father asked the son to clear a place for the tent while he gathered firewood. Upon his return the young lad said, "I've cleared it all but one large rock in the middle of the area. I can't move it." The father replied, "But son, you haven't used all of your resources." His son replied, "Of course I have; I've tried with all my might!" "No," his father said. "You have more: you have yet to use me." So, our efforts to live righteously by the law leave us defeated. We have yet to call on God!

While attending a conference on Christology, I met a good friend, Lawrence Burkholder, former president of Goshen College in Indiana. I asked him how he felt about the conference. An ethicist with his doctorate from Princeton, he replied, "Some of these participants want a Christology for ethics, but I still need a Savior!" Knowing the right is important, but his power to do the right is imperative.

Our behavior is the expression of our beliefs,
for belief is not what we say but what we do.
Salvation by faith through grace is not empty;
rather, faith is an identity in grace.
When one confesses Jesus as his Lord,
the same will live as a servant of Christ.
To believe is to commit, to enter covenant;
believing is confessing, identifying with that confessed.
Our confession is our stance.

June 15

The Problem Is Sin Dwelling in Us

Now if I do what I do not want, it is no longer I that do it, but sin that dwells within me. Romans 7:20

What other system of faith, what other religion of the world, deals with sin and transformation in such an honest and redemptive way? This is one of the strengths of Christianity. We are all prodigals who, in becoming honest, return to the Father and his gracious acceptance.

Honesty is a basic essential to a meaningful life. The level of trust between friends is high because of honest sharing. Our text says that we recognize that we are sinful, not just that we have sinned. That is, we are sinful persons who cannot but make mistakes. We are not sinners for what we have done so much as we are sinners for what we are—persons living with a God-vacuum in our lives.

Does this mean that we are no good? No, we are created in the image of God, with the reminders and potential to be made new by identification with God. But to think that we can become truly good apart from God is the very nature of sin. We have been created in the image of God. When that is violated, it is reborn only in his grace.

Confession is hard on our pride, but only when we recognize that we are sinful can we actually know the meaning of God's transforming work. Such confession calls us to come to the Lord in full honesty. The story is told that two students were late to school and when the teacher asked the reason for their being tardy, they answered that they had been delayed by a flat tire. The teacher asked each separately, "Which tire was flat?" We often have dishonest excuses for our wrongs.

Lord, help me to be honest about my own sin,
*   and my very sinfulness.*
I need the Savior, not only to wipe my slate clean,
*   but to fill my life.*
Free me from what limits me
*   by your indwelling presence.*
Make me new as your child,
*   transformed by and conformed to Jesus.*

I Find This Law at Work

So I find it to be a law that when I want to do what is good, evil lies close at hand. Romans 7:21

Once again, Paul shows us the way of honesty, to recognize and admit the law of evil at work in us. Only as we are honest about sin do we understand our need of the Savior. We need forgiveness, not just for mistakes, but to save us from living in sin.

This section of the letter uses the term *law* in multiple ways: the moral law, the law of sin, the law of sinfulness in one's members, the law of righteousness, and ultimately, the law of the Spirit of life. The wonderful news is that the law of the Spirit supersedes the law of sin.

The moral law, the law of God, does not in itself remove the law of sin, but makes us more aware of its presence and power. The law of sin determines our actions more than does our good intention, and that determination continues until we know the superior law of Christ. This helps us recognize daily that we need him to enable us to walk with God. Jesus is saving me today from being what I would be without him!

God's work in us, to empower a new life, fits our understanding of the psychology of personality. He doesn't just expose the evil, but he places something good in its place. He overcomes evil by good and asks us to become participants in the same, replacing our selfishness by the pursuit of the good.

In 1 Peter 2:21-25 we are told why Jesus had to die. His death at our hands exposes our sinfulness. Further, his death expresses his love for us: "He bore our sins in his body." Third, his death extends his forgiving acceptance to us: "Now you have returned to the shepherd and guardian of your souls." We are restored to fellowship.

> *Love is self-giving.*
> *It doesn't stumble at the cost.*
> *For love delights*
> *in the other in mutual sharing.*
> *"God so loved the world,*
> *that he gave his only begotten Son."*
> *(John 3:16, KJV)*

I See Another Law

For I delight in the law of God in my inmost self, but I see in my members another law at war with the law of my mind, making me captive to the law of sin that dwells in my members. Romans 7:22-23

We are created in the image of God. One aspect of the *imago Dei* is the function of the mind, the ability to think creatively, have moral discernment, and to exercise self-transcendence. The mind is capable of recognizing evidence and interpreting it, a function essential for faith, for faith is response to evidence.

The text speaks of a war in one's inner being. It is a war between one's sinful nature and the ideals of the mind. War is brought to an end by one side surrendering. The sinful nature must give up its control, and the mind must have its ideals set on God.

In evangelistic meetings I share that saving faith is normal faith placed in the Savior. It is not something within us that saves, but it is the Savior himself. This faith is not a mystical exercise, different from faith in friends, in the postal system, or a banking system, for faith responds to evidence. Our faith in the Savior is response to evidence, in one whom we meet in the Word. This evidence engages the mind in believing. Faith and reason are like two sides of a zipper: they interlock with one another.

The presence of sin perverts the process in the mind as well as by other parts of our person. Paul says that there is another law within us, and it wages war with the law of the mind to make us a prisoner to itself, to the law of sin. Such an imprisoned mind is not free to think God's thoughts. The following lines come to my memory from a moving poem by Theodore Monod:

> *Oh, the bitter pain and sorrow,*
> *That a time could ever be,*
> *When I proudly said to Jesus,*
> *"All of self and none of Thee."*

> *Higher than the highest heaven,*
> *Deeper than the deepest sea,*
> *Lord, Thy love at last has conquered:*
> *"**None** of self, and **all** of Thee."*

What a Wretched Man

Wretched man that I am! Who will rescue me from this body of death?
Romans 7:24

Caught up in the civil war of the soul, between the consciousness of God and his will on one hand, the sinful struggle for autonomy on the other, we are thoroughly wretched. There is no misery so great as the lack of peace within one's self. When one is at peace with God and self, one can face anything.

In the words, "Who will rescue me from this body of death," Paul speaks of the despair of one bound to the body of death. In his day, prisoners were punished by being chained to the body of the person killed. For such there is no freedom, no life. The law of sin, like a chain, binds us in the awareness of sinfulness.

"Who will rescue me?" This question focuses on why we need a Savior. It is not just to pardon a few mistakes, but to save us from being enslaved to our sinful nature. This awareness is very devastating to most of us. In our sophistication we would rather believe that we have been trained so well and brought up in such good order that we haven't been very bad sinners. As though, when God called some of us, he got a bargain.

John Wesley was a religious man with very high principles, but he lacked assurance of salvation. In distress of soul, he went to a Moravian meeting and heard a reading of Luther's "Preface to Romans". After this Wesley wrote, "At about a quarter of nine I came to understand that Christ died for my sins and that my sins, even mine, are taken away by the blood of Christ." This was Wesley's transformation, to become one of the greater eighteenth-century voices for God. One cannot save one's self from one's self by one's self.

Lord, I have struggled against you,
I've sought to live by my own preferences and power,
I've been at war with your higher calling,
I've said no to your Spirit.

I now surrender myself to you,
I give up my autonomy and become your servant,
I commit myself to walk in the steps of the Master,
I want daily to say yes to your Spirit. Amen

Through Jesus Christ Our Lord

Thanks be to God through Jesus Christ our Lord! So then, with my mind I am a slave to the law of God, but with my flesh I am a slave to the law of sin. Romans 7:25

Jesus said, "No one knows the Son except the Father, and no one knows the Father except the Son and anyone to whom the Son chooses to reveal him" (Matt. 11:27). This is an amazing statement of the one way in which we can come to know God and have fellowship with him.

Jesus is our Savior. This means he saves us from being slaves to sin. The whole argument of Romans 7 leads to this climax. Deliverance from sin is not by law, but by the Lord himself. This deliverance is in his turning us from going our own way and back to God. Reconciling us to God frees us from self-orientation.

Paul says, with the mind one can recognize and affirm the values of the law of God, but if left to one's self, we are only a servant of the self and consequently a slave to our sinfulness. The question is not simply what one knows, but whom one serves.

Intellectual perception is necessary, but that alone is not enough. I may have an intellectual understanding of aerodynamics, but I must have more than that to fly an airplane. I understand something of music, but I cannot play the violin or piano by that understanding alone. I may understand something of God through his laws and even try to live by them, but I must move beyond the law to the Lawgiver and become a participant with God.

The conclusion in this text on the psychology of religious experience shows that in one's self, the mind is slave to the law of God, but the flesh is slave to the law of sin. Only by the action of God can we be brought into the freedom of God.

Let us celebrate:
The love of God, so abounding,
The grace of God, so amazing,
The peace of Christ, so abiding.
How wonderful!

June 20

No Condemnation

There is therefore now no condemnation for those who are in Christ Jesus.
Romans 8:1

No condemnation! What wonderful words. What an amazing transition from the survey of our problem in the preceding chapter to this section of the epistle about the life of freedom in the Spirit. We are forgiven, accepted, and liberated to walk with God.

One of the searching texts I have used in evangelistic meetings is Hebrews 9:28, "An Appointment with God." Our primary appointment with God is at the cross, in his coming to us as an expression of grace. When we have entered into his peace of forgiveness, we need have no fear of meeting him in his second coming.

With joy, I have used the text for today, "There is therefore now no condemnation for those who are in Christ Jesus." By faith I can say, "I am in Christ." How do I know? Because I have come to him and he has said, "Anyone who comes to me I will never drive away" (John 6:37). We take Jesus at his word. This is our assurance. He will do what he says.

To be children of God, participants in his family, is life's greatest privilege. And this is our calling —to live as the family of God and so to invite others to accept his grace and be adopted into his family. And in this relationship we are free, joyfully free in belonging to him.

Assurance of salvation is the privilege of the believer. Jesus accepts us; he is as good as his promise. This assurance is no self-claimed boast; for it is not something we have achieved by keeping his laws, but is ours by accepting his love. One who lives only by seeking legalistically to achieve will never have assurance. One can never be sure of doing well enough. Our salvation is not dependent upon perfection; it is a response to God's accepting love. We are not perfect, but we belong.

In his insightful style, Bruce Larson has said:

> *Perfectionism will drive you up the wall.*
> *You can't be all right and be well.*

June 21

The Law of the Spirit of Life

For the law of the Spirit of life in Christ Jesus has set you free from the law of sin and of death. Romans 8:2

Life has many contrasts, but none so great in its internal meaning as that between the law of the Spirit of life and the law of sin and death. In chapter 7 there are many laws: the moral law, the law of sin, the law of self or the flesh, the law of conscience, the law of contradiction, and the law of the mind. But Paul here adds the law of the Spirit of life. This law of the Spirit is greater by far than the law of sin and death.

The law of the Spirit conforms the law of the mind to God's will as we obey. It programs the conscience by new directions (as a computer is programmed). It interprets the spirit of the moral law by conformity to the person of Jesus. It releases us from the law of the flesh by crucifixion of the self in our surrender to Christ. It frees us from the civil war of contradictory laws by enabling us to surrender to the will of Christ.

The formerly wretched man is now the liberated man. We are made new creatures in Christ, made free in Christ to live by the will of God, to enjoy life in the Spirit. This chapter is an answer to all of the problems surveyed so far in the book. Paul spoke first of our condemnation in sin (Rom. 1-2), then, of our salvation from sin (chaps. 3-4), then of justification by faith that reconciles us to God (chap. 5), then of the freedom from the old life (chap. 6), then of the honest recognition of our impotence before the law (chap. 7), and now he introduces the holy life by the fellowship and power of the Holy Spirit.

In a hymn written by my great-grandfather Bishop J. M. Shenk, there is a stanza of this power of the Spirit. Let's pray it with him:

> *O gracious Redeemer, be with us we pray,*
> *Breath on us thy Spirit to show us the way,*
> *And fill us with goodness, with peace and delight,*
> *That all to thy glory may shine as a light. Amen*

And So He Condemned Sin

For God has done what the law, weakened by the flesh, could not do: by sending his own Son in the likeness of sinful flesh, and to deal with sin, he condemned sin in the flesh. Romans 8:3

Laws expose and guide, but God's presence will identify and accept. The marvel of grace is that God both exposes and accepts us. To make this clear, he came to us in Christ, the full exposure of our sin. Christ showed in his suffering the consequences of our sin without his participation in sin. In doing this he condemned sin when in the flesh, condemned it in and for humanity, exposing sin as a rejection of God.

What amazing love, what fantastic engagement, doing what the law was powerless to do—free us from sin. God, in his Son, acted to liberate and reconcile us. As the British preacher P. T. Forsythe has said, "How can we keep striking back at one who takes the blow with such a spirit." At the cross we meet a suffering God who identifies with our plight, a loving God who acts for us in our problem, and a victorious God who overcomes our problem by sharing it without surrendering his integrity.

He condemned sin; there was no minimizing the problem. In fact, he showed the depth of sin as far more serious than a simple violation of law. Sin at its depth is an attack on God, the rejection of his order for us and of his very person. Yet God reaches beyond the problem to the person and draws us into his circle of love. This, the moral law could not do in itself. But in grace, the redeemed belong to the Redeemer.

Lord, we come to you in faith,
Believing and responding to the gospel.
We confess our sin, our rebellion,
Asking for your costly forgiveness.
We respond to your grace with welcome.
We worship to enjoy your fellowship.
We commit ourselves to serve you,
To walk as disciples of Christ.
We will seek as a community of faith
To witness of your love and grace.
This is our prayer, through Christ our Lord. Amen

The Just Requirement of the Law

So that the just requirement of the law might be fulfilled in us, who walk not according to the flesh but according to the Spirit. Romans 8:4

Jesus said that he did not come to destroy the law but to fulfill it (Matt. 5:17). That is, to fill it full in its meaning. Here Paul refers to the just requirement of the law, which is the right requirement of the law to live in the will of God. Having said that, we do not enter fellowship with God through the law. Paul now affirms fellowship through Christ. Then we can actually live in right relationship with God, a relationship to which the law could only point.

The key is in the last phrase of our text: "who walk . . . according to the Spirit." The power of the inner presence of the Holy Spirit confirms and guides us in the righteousness of Christ. In Philippians 3, Paul tells of once seeking his own righteousness, which is of the law, until meeting Christ and finding that in him he could know the righteousness of God by faith, an actual right relatedness.

Righteousness is more than a moralistic achievement; it is a rightness of relation with a corresponding rightness of behavior. The new life in Christ is not a cheaper life than life under the law; it is a more costly life as seen in the cross. Like Dietrich Bonhoeffer, we need to avoid an approach of cheap grace, which is to live with license, and we need to know the costly grace of yieldedness and of obedient faith.

We walk now according to the Spirit and not according to the flesh. Paul focuses more on this terminology; defining sin as the way of the flesh or the self and contrasts this with the way of the Spirit. Our sin problem is much closer than relation to some external law. It is anything in which we seek our own way rather than God's way. His purpose for us is to live in worshipful devotion and obedience to our Lord. Archbishop William Temple says, "Worship has the power to transform." Worship thus will

Quicken the conscience by the holiness of God.
Free the mind with the truth of God.
Purge the imagination by the beauty of God.
Open the heart to the love of God.
Devote the will to the purpose of God.

Minds Set on What the Spirit Desires

For those who live according to the flesh set their minds on the things of the flesh, but those who live according to the Spirit set their minds on the things of the Spirit. Romans 8:5

Christianity needs to be understood to be fully enjoyed. While it is holistic, it is not unfocused. The mind is to be transformed to think in a God-centered rather than a self-centered perspective. In the work of higher education, I have become convinced that conversion makes a difference in the way we think and learn. A teacher is responsible to integrate the understanding of faith within the arts and sciences, to show its relevance and bring a wholeness to those fields. But Christian experience also involves the emotions and the will of the individual. We respond to God in a loving relationship as Jesus said, "You shall love the Lord your God. . . . This is the first and greatest commandment" (Matt. 22:37-38). That means to open one's total life intimately to him. This isn't automatic: it is a choice, it is volitional, we make a conscious decision to yield to God.

Paul wrote to the Corinthians that the gospel is God's "Yes" to us (2 Cor. 1:17-19), and faith is our "Yes" to God. In grace, God has moved to us, and he does so today. Now it is as though we hear his voice saying, "It is your move next."

In Christian growth we walk in the Spirit by a "Yes, Lord. Yes, Lord" attitude. As we discern God's will in the Word, as we pray and open our lives to him, we respond by decisions of yes to his will. Much like a skill course in which we learn by doing, so we learn meanings of faith and love by practice. Obedience itself is a way of knowing.

Life is a journey in which we are constantly confronted with new challenges and opportunities. As we mature through the experiences of our journey, we are able to see new dimensions of meaning and fulfillment. Knowing God is more than knowing some ideas *about* God. It is participation and awareness of covenant love that permeates our lives with the sense of belonging and becoming.

There is a rest for the people of God. (cf. Heb. 4:9-11)
A rest of trusting his completed work in redemption.

The Mind Controlled by the Spirit

To set the mind on the flesh is death, but to set the mind on the Spirit is life and peace. Romans 8:6

As an educator, this verse has become a remarkable assurance and a tremendous challenge. It is our privilege to not only bring every thought into the captivity of Christ, as Paul writes elsewhere (2 Cor. 10:5), but to have the mind controlled and guided by the creative power of the Spirit. The educational experience is thereby broadened, while the secular closes out the spiritual. The spiritual mind includes the secular with the spiritual focus.

John writes that we have an anointing of the Holy One, and we all know spiritual things (1 John 2:20). This anointing releases us from the narrower confines of the secular mind, which excludes the spiritual. God broadens our scope as he opens for us the additional realm of the sacred, an interpretive and selective influence.

As we think of the work of the Spirit, we recognize that some persons assume that it is primarily emotional, ecstatic, and uncontrolled. But Paul's emphasis here is other than that. He emphasizes guidance, security, vitality, and peace. The dynamic of the Spirit-controlled mind is contrasted with the mind of the sinful person as limited in a selfish death process.

We are a people of faith, of love, and of peace. The life in the Spirit is in contrast to the bondage to human sinfulness described in chapter 7. In the Spirit, we have the liberty and power to live in the freedom and fellowship of Christ.

One aspect of being made in the image of God is the ability to think, to reason and solve problems, to be logical and consistent, to be creative and constructive. What a wonderful gift and what a reminder of the calling for thinking persons to take God with utmost seriousness. Only the proud mind would assume that there is no larger sphere to be known by including God. Only the small mind would think of self-interests as an end. God still says, "Come now, and let us reason together" (Isa. 1:18, KJV). He asks us to open our minds and our hearts, as in the Cleland B. McAfee verse:

There is a place of quiet rest,
Near to the heart of God.

The Sinful Mind Is Hostile

For this reason the mind that is set on the flesh is hostile to God; it does not submit to God's law—indeed it cannot. Romans 8:7

The mind of secularism closes God out. I do not mean the truly secular, which is neutral, but secularism which is an end in itself. The secular is essential to the nature of education but is not limited to that. It is not to say in the words which David attributes to the atheist, "There is no God" (Ps. 14:1). The sophisticated front appears indifferent to God, tolerant toward those "weaker" ones who need God, but boasting in their attitude of not needing God. Yet, with this implied tolerance, they are rejecting God; and before the claims of Christ, their mind is not neutral but hostile.

As it is said, "One cannot turn his back to the light without increasing the darkness in his own soul." In closing God out, the consequence is limiting oneself to the realm of one's own knowledge and experience. In interpersonal relations, you never come to know another so long as you close them out. In the verse for today Paul writes, "The mind that is set on the flesh is hostile to God," for one who lives only for the self finds God to be an adversary.

To know God is more than philosophical reflection about God; it is opening one's self to God. Our text says that one who lives by the sinful mind, hostile to God, refuses to submit to the law of God. One who walks with God respects God's law, living in relation to God and his laws.

What is God's law to which Paul here refers? It does not necessarily mean the Ten Commandments or the moral law; it is variously presented by Paul and by John as the law of love. This designation is more personal, more relational, and therefore more dynamic. God's law is not static, for his primary concern is the well-being of persons.

"If any want to become my followers, let them deny themselves and take up their cross and follow me" (Matt. 16:24).

We are to make up our minds,
give up our autonomy,
take up our identity,
and engage our obedience.

Controlled by Self, One Cannot Please God

And those who are in the flesh cannot please God. Romans 8:8

The contrast Paul presents is between a life controlled by the Spirit and a life controlled by self. The only release from sin controlling the self is in the greater control by the Spirit. This is the answer of grace to the sinfulness described in chapter 7. But this chapter presents the normal Christian life, not the life of Romans 7.

To be a disciple of Christ is to walk with him in life, on "the way" with Jesus, to walk in the Spirit. We are not imitators, but participants with Jesus. The new life is enabled by the inner quickening of the Spirit. We truly become inner-directed persons.

To be controlled by the Spirit is to walk in the Spirit, to be filled with the Spirit, to live in obedience to the Spirit. This transcends living according to our own self-interests.

As children our behavior was shaped by the controlling influence of our parents because there was always a mutual love between us. Yes, at times we wanted to do some things contrary to their wishes, but our parents' love was always there to keep us from going the wrong way.

We can share from Ephesians 1:17-20 with Paul:

I pray that the God of our Lord Jesus Christ,
the Father of glory,
may give you a spirit of wisdom
and revelation as you come to know him,
so that, with the eyes of your heart enlightened,
you may know what is the hope to which he has called you,
what are the riches of his glorious inheritance among the saints,
and what is the immeasurable greatness of his power
for us who believe,
according to the working of his great power.
God put this power to work in Christ
when he raised him from the dead.

June 28

The Spirit Lives in You

But you are not in the flesh; you are in the Spirit, since the Spirit of God dwells in you. Anyone who does not have the Spirit of Christ does not belong to him. Romans 8:9

What a contrast in this text to the earlier language of the law! What marvelous affirmation of our life with God! This is fellowship, not legalism, freedom, nor bondage. This reality engages us in magnanimity, not mediocrity.

The power to become Christlike comes from the Spirit of Christ. Our freedom from the control of sin is through the control of the Spirit. Victory comes through the dynamic of the Spirit's work. Of all the gifts of God's grace, the greatest is the gift of the Holy Spirit.

John the Baptist said of Jesus, "He will baptize you *with* the Holy Spirit." The Spirit *himself* is the baptism, and the one doing the baptizing is Jesus. When we accept Christ as Lord, he first of all forgives and accepts. He has extended his acceptance to make our coming to him possible. But the accompanying gift is his baptism with the Spirit. Sharing his reconciliation, he now gives us his Spirit to indwell our lives.

Paul says here, "Anyone who does not have the Spirit of Christ does not belong to him." If we fully accept Jesus and not just his gifts of forgiveness and peace, we also accept his Spirit. Jesus has promised to give us his Spirit, and he is as good as his word. We have now become the temple of the Holy Spirit. Our responsibility is that of obedience to his word and will. We are to be continually filled with the Spirit (Eph. 5:18). He doesn't violate our persons, but responds to our attitude. We are just as filled as we want to be.

> God is not a God far removed;
> He is here within us.
> He has moved in by his Spirit.
> He is creating a community of the Spirit.
> He is sovereign in his rule of his Body.
> He is resident, and in this
> He is President.

But If Christ Is in You

**But if Christ is in you, though the body is dead because of sin, the Spirit is
life because of righteousness. Romans 8:10**

The risen Christ is at God's right hand, and yet he dwells in us by his Spirit. The Apostles' Creed says, "The third day he rose again from the dead. He ascended into heaven and sits on the right hand of God the Father Almighty." Yet this Christ abides in our hearts by his Spirit, given to us (1 John 3:24).

It is important for us to distinguish clearly between our own spirit and God's Spirit. In salvation, the Spirit takes our inner spirit and quickens it from deadness toward God to a new life united with God. This is a radically new relationship, "For in the one Spirit we were all baptized into one body," united with Christ (1 Cor. 12:13). The new birth begins the new relation of our spirit with the Lord, while the baptism with the Spirit is Jesus's gift of the Spirit to be present within us as our Lord.

Paul suggests a dualism within us even though we are unitary beings and parts cannot be separated. This spiritual dualism of our text is created by the presence of Christ. He makes us aware that our body carries the death-dealing aspects of sinfulness and in itself is dead to God, that is, alienated and irresponsive. But one's spirit, when quickened by God's Spirit is made alive to God. The flesh (self), incapable of living in the will of God, is transformed by a quickened spirit to live by the power of his Spirit. Under his authority this self is made alive in him, alive in thought and deed, in word and act, in belief and behavior. He makes all things new.

A new relationship,
A new quality of life,
A new focus,
A new heart,
A new Master,
A new community,
A new future!

Life for Our Mortal Bodies

If the Spirit of him who raised Jesus from the dead dwells in you, he who raised Christ from the dead will give life to your mortal bodies also through his Spirit that dwells in you. Romans 8:11

In contrast to the human nature carrying a death influence (Rom. 8:10), Paul now affirms that the Spirit quickens life in our mortal bodies. This life, this fellowship of spirit with Spirit, is expressed in our mortal bodies *now*. In the context, it appears to be related to the present experience of salvation. In the fellowship of the quickening Spirit, our spirit is changed by our being made alive to him. This is a holistic salvation.

In this text we are made aware that the resurrection power that raised Christ from the dead is at work in us. Paul says, "If the Spirit of him who raised Jesus from the dead dwells in you." The *if* being not so much a question as an affirmation: *Since* he is dwelling in us, the result is life here and now.

In this verse there is reference to the entire Godhead, the One who raised Christ as Father, the Christ of God, and to the Spirit of God. In God there is oneness without this meaning a numerical one, a "perichoric community." And similarly there is three-ness without this being a numerical three. In this chapter, each manifestation of God is identified with us for our redemption. God is for us, Christ is for us, the Spirit is for us.

> *God is so totally other in his majesty*
> *that none of us can fully know him.*
> *The Scripture says, "No one has ever seen God.*
> *The only begotten Son, who is in the bosom of the Father,*
> *He has made him known." (cf. John 1:18, KJV)*
> *"Now we see through a glass darkly;*
> *but then, face to face.*
> *Now we know in part,*
> *but then we shall know" his awesome Majesty!*
> *(cf. 1 Cor. 13:12, KJV)*

We Are Accountable

So then, brothers and sisters, we are debtors, not to the flesh, to live according to the flesh. Romans 8:12

"So then" are transition words. Since it is true that we have life through the Spirit, we have an obligation to fulfill this new life. The words "so then" are a bridge from the argument to the application.

We are accountable, we have an obligation. New insight adds new responsibility. New responsibilities add a new sense of accountability. Granted a new life, we are free from the old life under the control of sin, and we enjoy a new life controlled by the Spirit.

In many expressions of theology, more attention is given to the Fall and our sinfulness, than to redemption as our freedom to live in the will of God by the Spirit. As believers, disciples of Christ, we do the world the most good by our walk with the Lord, for we thereby heighten their consciousness of a higher order of life.

We, as believers, are called to live by his will, ethic of freedom, and love. Empowered by the Spirit, we are enabled to do so. Even our mortal bodies experience his quickening in life's testing and suffering experiences. The joy of the martyrs on the burning pier is testimony of this victory in suffering. A remarkable account of actual deliverance was told to us by our friend Oleg Artimiev, a pastor from Syktyvkar, Siberia, about six hundred miles northeast of Moscow in Russia.

In one of the Siberian prisons with many believers, a father and son discovered each other. When the guards learned of this, they called both to the gate, opened it, and commanded them to run. After the father and son ran some distance, the guards called the killer dogs and ordered, "Get them!" The men knew what was to happen. Looking back and seeing the dogs, they dropped on their knees and began to pray. The dogs ran up, dropped to the ground about ten feet from them, inched forward on their bellies, and began to lick their feet and hands. Then they ran back and attacked the guards. Many prisoners witnessing this came to faith!

Lord, thank you for your faithfulness,
and the strength to live by your will. Amen

On the Way to Die

For if you live according to the flesh, you will die; but if by the Spirit you put to death the deeds of the body, you will live. Romans 8:13

To be carnally minded is to participate in the process of dying. The Greek form in this phrase means that if we, as disciples of Christ, should turn to live by the sinful nature, we are on the way to death. Although Christ provides security, sin does not.

True, once one is born, he cannot be unborn, but he can die. While it is inconceivable to me that a saved person who has known Christ would then turn from him, a relationship can deteriorate from self-interests. Relationships can be taken for granted and broken. We are secure only in Christ, and as we keep ourselves in the love of God (Jude 21), he keeps us. Our election is in Christ, and our security is in him.

The positive note of this text is that we, through the Spirit, can put to death the misdeeds of the body—we can live! As we walk in the Spirit, we are released from the misuse of the body. Paul writes in 1 Corinthians, "Your body is a temple of the Holy Spirit; . . . you are not your own. For you were bought with a price" (6:19-20). Paul says that consequently we are to avoid immorality, idolatry, and covetousness —particularly the sin of immorality. He says it is against one's own body and has physical consequences. Sin is a perversion of the good, the cheap route, but God intends the better in his will.

> *Dear Lord,*
> *At every fork of the path, in every decision,*
> *help me to seek your will,*
> *to hear the Spirit's prompting,*
> *to choose the way that honors you.*
> *Help me to say no to self-interests*
> *by saying yes to your Word and will.*
> *Lead me in the way of holiness,*
> *engaging fully the fellowship of grace. Amen*

July 3

Led by the Spirit of God

For all who are led by the Spirit of God are children of God. Romans 8:14

Children of God—what a fantastic reality and what a revolutionary statement! Our assurance of salvation is not measured by a legal code, but by living communion. The prophet said, "Not by might, nor by power, but by my spirit, says the LORD of hosts" (Zech. 4:6). Grace is not an It; grace is God's participation with us. Salvation is not a package that we receive and run away with; it is a participation in which we share.

The greatest privilege in life is to be a child of God, to belong, to be in the family of the redeemed. John writes, "To all who received him, . . . he gave power to become children of God" (John 1:12). Again, in his first epistle he writes, "See what love the Father has given us, that we should be called children of God; and that is what we are" (1 John 3:1). We are brought into this reality by the Spirit of God. He calls us, transforms us, and directs us in our walk with him.

Our text is both a statement of privilege and a statement of delineation. We are God's children by virtue of being in Christ, in relationship. We are God's children if we are led by the Spirit of God. This is the dynamic of costly grace, a gift that forgives and accepts us and redirects us in the way of the cross, the way of the Suffering Servant.

Heavenly Father,
Thank you for accepting me in Christ,
for making me your child,
for giving me your Spirit.
Help me to be sensitive to the Spirit's voice,
to hear it in your Word written,
and to test it by your Word, Jesus.
Empower me to do your will,
to live by your grace,
and to worship you with my love.
Let this be my greatest joy. Amen

Abba, Father

For you did not receive a spirit of slavery to fall back into fear, but you have received a spirit of adoption. When we cry, "Abba! Father!" Romans 8:15

Jesus brought into human experience a new understanding of God and a new relationship with him. This is expressed in his use of the word *Abba*. It is the word of closest, familial relationship: Abba, my Father, my very own Father in personal relationship. Jesus used this word in his prayers. It is the heart cry of those born into the family of God. We are actually God's children.

A. W. Tozer has said of our discipleship that we've *been to* the cross and now we work out *from* the cross in the expression of our new life. In the sixteenth century, Michael Sattler, a prominent leader of the free church, or Anabaptist movement, wrote a tract entitled *Two Kinds of Obedience*. He contrasts the obedience of the slave, an obedience of fear, and the obedience of the son, an obedience of filial love. We are disciples of Christ, not living in fear. We share his love. We are in the family of God. Our obedience is that of a child to its Father, not of a slave to his master. As Michael Sattler wrote:

> *Obedience is of two kinds, servile and filial.*
> *The filial has its source in the love of the Father,*
> *even though no other reward should follow,*
> *yea even if the Father should wish to damn his child;*
> *the servile has its source in a love of reward or of one's self.*
> *The filial ever does as much as possible,...*
> *and is never able to do enough for Him.*
> *The servile looks to the external and to the prescribed command of his Lord;*
> *the filial is concerned about the inner witness of the Spirit.*
> *The filial is not contrary to the servile, as it might appear,*
> *but is better and higher.*
> *And therefore let him who is servile seek for the better, the filial;*
> *He dare not be servile at all.*

The Inner Witness

It is that very Spirit bearing witness with our spirit that we are children of God. Romans 8:16

John Calvin, the great theologian of the sixteenth century, wrote of the inner witness of the Spirit as assurance that one is truly among the elect. The elect, or called, are those who are in Christ as participants in grace. My understanding of election is a designation that we are not saved by our efforts, but by the calling of God, who elected that, in Christ, we are saved. My assurance is in Jesus's words, promising that whoever comes to him, he will not cast them off, and Jesus is as good as his word. I have come to Jesus, and on the authority of his word I am assured that I am accepted (John 6:37).

When we deal with the subjective aspects of Christian experience, they need to be aligned with the objective reality of his Word. The Spirit is the presence of God as an objective reality known in subjective experience. This witness of the Spirit calls for a calm attitude of our spirit to recognize the witness of the divine Spirit.

The writer of Hebrews states, "The word of God is living and active, sharper than any two-edged sword, piercing until it divides soul from spirit, joints from marrow; it is able to judge the thoughts and intentions of the heart" (4:12). When asked what is meant by "divides soul from spirit," I prayerfully responsed. The Scripture helps us to know whether an experience is merely soulish or whether it truly engages the spirit. An experience of beauty in a sunset, in art, music, or liturgy may be enjoyed by the soul, mind, and emotions. But whether we worship or not is dependent upon our spirit.

> Love is knowing beyond the mind,
>   for love is a holistic embrace.
> Love engages the heart of the person,
>   as well as the consciousness of the mind.
> Love is felt in the core of one's soul,
>   permeates one's being as a radiance of warmth,
>   and so assures one of belonging.

If Children, Then We Are Heirs

And if children, then heirs, heirs of God and joint heirs with Christ—if, in fact, we suffer with him so that we may also be glorified with him. Romans 8:17

An heir is a recipient of benefits from predecessors. Adopted into God's family, we are given equivalent relation with Christ; we are joint heirs with him. This is so amazing that it is hard to believe. The remarkable thing about being children of God is that we now share the inheritance of the resources God has expressed in Christ.

In Ephesians 1:18, Paul writes of the inheritance we share in the beloved, that is, in Christ. The unique statement in our text is that we are coheirs with Christ. That is, all of the familial benefits that Christ has from the Father are being shared with us. To be a coheir is to be a recipient of God's purpose and mission as it converges in each succeeding generation.

This text emphasizes our full identification with Christ. Being baptized into Christ (Rom. 6), we share his death and his resurrection. But walking with Jesus in life means to accept as well the opposition to Jesus that is often expressed in our society. Walking with Jesus means to be baptized with the baptism he is baptized with, to bear the cross he gives, the cross that cuts across the way of self-pursuits, cuts across the way of the world. We are coheirs with Christ by our participation in the very mission of God.

> *To suffer is to be robbed of freedom;*
> *   it is to be prevented from social fulfillment.*
> *But one can lose external freedoms in life,*
> *   yet know the inner freedom of mind and spirit.*
> *"Stone walls do not a prison make,*
> *   nor iron bars a cell."*
> *   (Richard Lovelace)*

Glory That Shall Be Revealed

**I consider that the sufferings of this present time are not worth comparing
with the glory about to be revealed to us. Romans 8:18**

Paul matches his reference to suffering with a statement of hope. Often in his writings he refers to faith, hope, and love—a trilogy of expressions that convey divine reality. In our text, faith moves to articulate the hope that extends this faith into the future. Hope is not wishful thinking; it is a dynamic anticipation of what faith perceives.

Faith in God is faith that God will fulfill all that is promised. Above all, his promise is for us to be participants in his fellowship and presence. This is both a present and a future reality, for there is the "already" and the "not yet" of his kingdom. His rule is expressed among us by the walk in faith, but the full meaning is yet to come.

The kingdom is a spiritual reality; we are born into it by the Spirit, for "he has rescued us from the power of darkness and transferred us into the kingdom of his beloved Son" (Col. 1:13). Jesus is ruling, and when he completes the kingdom, "he hands over the kingdom to God the Father. . . . For he must reign until he has put all his enemies under his feet" (1 Cor. 15:24-25).

The text contrasts present suffering and future glory to be revealed. Jesus spoke of this as the glory he had with the Father before the world was (John 17). When our goal is clear of sharing this glory, the difficulties along the way seem small. We enjoy life more when we minimize problems and rejoice in God's victory and purpose. Even in the "valley of shadow" we celebrate his presence.

I know very little about suffering,
compared to brothers and sisters beyond,
whose lot in life has been so different,
threatened by the tyranny of others;
in India, in China, in Siberia, and Africa,
many have paid a price for their faith.
Yet I share a small bit, suffering what it means
to give up my self, my preferences,
and do so again and again for God's work.

July 8

The Creation Waits

For the creation waits with eager longing for the revealing of the children of God. Romans 8:19

Philosophers look at the created order and ask numerous questions. Is God good but weak and not able to prevent the problems in creation? Or, is God strong but not good and simply doesn't choose to safeguard his creation? Or, is God both good and strong and in his goodness he created us in his image with freedom? This contains the risk that we would mess things up; yet in his goodness he will not violate the freedom of humanity, but will cope with our mistakes another way. I believe the latter. In grace he involves himself with us, works with our choices, doing the best with the conditions he has permitted.

The consequences of the human fallen state have impacted the created order itself. The world was designed for human life, in God's good creation, and when humanity rebelled against God, to have its own way, the whole world suffered the consequences. The misuse of creation by humanity brings about consequences we do not fully recognize. Does underground nuclear testing strain fault lines of the earth to increase the earthquakes? Does our use of chemical sprays cause an increase of cancer and illness?

The creation is waiting for the full extension of redemption. Creation awaits the full purpose of God to be revealed, the full experience of the glory we anticipate as his children. Although futuristic, we should recognize that since our goal is to be conformed to the image of God's Son (Rom. 8:29), we already share in aspects of the transformation and anticipate full restoration. Christians should be oriented to ecology, stewardship, and longevity in the use of material things. We should be concerned for the generations to come (Ps. 78). Together we can sing with the psalmist (19:1-4):

> *The heavens are telling the glory of God;*
> *and the firmament proclaims his handiwork.*
> *Day to day pours forth speech,*
> *and night to night declares knowledge.*
> *There is no speech, nor are there words;*
> *their voice is not heard;*
> *yet their voice goes out through all the earth,*
> *and their words to the end of the world.*

Subjected in Hope

For the creation was subjected to futility, not of its own will but by the will of the one who subjected it, in hope. Romans 8:20

One man's failure, Paul wrote in chapter 5, has affected all others. Paul states that one man's sin affected creation. In fact, God, in making evident the seriousness of the Fall, pronounced the curse passed upon all creation as an altering of its compatibility with humanity. Creation is to be subdued by humans, his fallen creation. We are to have dominion and responsibility for creation and are accountable to God for that dominion.

We enjoy so much the beauty of the created order in life, the harmony and precision that allows space travel, the intricate designs of the smallest things like computers, the wonderful experiences of travel and cross-cultural and interracial exchanges, the richness and variety of foods, the minerals and riches of the earth. Yet in these there is temptation to be selfish, to horde, and to misuse when, as a part of a world of over six billion persons, we are called to share and to participate in the value levels of the human family. But we fail to distribute, to share with any semblance of equity. Some 7 percent of the world's population use at least 70 percent of its available resources. To speak of mutuality is a foreign concept.

The second part of the text says that God subjected the creation in hope; that is, it will not always be this way. This passage anticipates a future restoration, a culmination, a telos, in which the created order will be restored. "But, in accordance with his promise, we wait for new heavens and a new earth" (2 Pet. 3:13). God's work of redemption will touch every area of the universe that has been impacted by sin.

Ron Sider spoke to the conscience of the Christian in *Rich Christians in an Age of Hunger*. Far too commonly, the Christian community is simply a reflection of the worldly mind that uses the world in a way that abuses it.

Lord, help me to recognize that you are Lord of all creation,
and that I am a steward of your trust. Amen

The Creation Itself Will Be Liberated

**In hope that the creation itself will be set free from its bondage to decay
and will obtain the freedom of the glory of the children of God. Romans 8:21**

One cannot understand all that this means: sharing the freedom and glory of the children of God. One cannot look at perversion and poverty without crying out "Hasten the day!" To be liberated from disease and decay, perversion and suffering, handicap and limitations, poverty and want is the cry of our helplessness. God frequently administers a healing liberation as a reminder to his children to maintain hope.

The freedom of being children of God means we no longer groan in uncertainty. Instead we expect to see the created order released from its groaning of limitation into the fullness of God's family life pattern. We are participants with God in liberating creation from bondage and decay. This is an aspect of our mission as Christians, which is often overlooked as though mission is just telling others rather than serving others. Mission involves engagement in stewardship, concern about ecology, creative involvements in overcoming poverty, famine, inequity, and a rejection of social or racial dominance.

We cannot live with this text and not be concerned about the nuclear buildup and danger, monies that go to armaments for war, a lack in creative work to meet needs in food and health in many areas of the world. In the conclusion of the General Assembly of the Mennonite Church at Purdue University in Indiana, about 3,000 youth and as many adults, after days in worship and reflection, affirmed that our mission includes care of the environmental. The Quaker artist, Edward Hicks, has depicted in his painting *The Peaceable Kingdom*, this hope as expressed by the prophet Isaiah (11:5-6, 9):

> *Righteousness shall be the belt around his waist,*
> *   and faithfulness the belt around his loins.*
> *The wolf shall live with the lamb,*
> *   the leopard shall lie down with the kid,*
> *the calf and the lion and the fatling together,*
> *   and a little child shall lead them. . . .*
> *They will not hurt or destroy on all my holy mountain;*
> *   for the earth will be full of the knowledge of the LORD*
> *   as the waters cover the sea.*

July 11

The Whole Creation Has Been Groaning

We know that the whole creation has been groaning in labor pains until now. Romans 8:22

We do not see the same level of conscious intelligence in creation as God has given to humanity. But Paul does use a basic life-figure, childbirth, to give us a feel for the life-struggle in creation. The anticipation of liberation is illustrated with the groaning of pain preceding the birth of a child. Creation is seen to be in labor, anticipating the birth of a new order, in which we already share.

Liberation theology arose from this kind of groaning. Although we have politicized this consciousness and thereby found ways to avoid its prophetic voice, the cry for liberation on the part of the poor and dispossessed is consistent with this text.

As Christians, we need an understanding of the life-element in creation, yet refraining from worshipping creatures rather than the Creator. Focusing on the Creator frees us from pantheism and from thoughts of reincarnation, which worship life itself. The promise of this text is that God, distinct from creation, is *acting in* creation. The future is not repeated cycles of life to achieve higher levels, but creation liberated to enjoy fully the privileges of its purpose. These verses from 1 Corinthians express our privilege as already sharing this level as children of God:

> *Indeed, even though there may be*
> *so-called gods in heaven or on earth—*
> *as in fact there are many gods and many lords—*
> *yet for us there is one God, the Father,*
> *from whom are all things and for whom we exist,*
> *and one Lord, Jesus Christ,*
> *through whom are all things and through whom we exist. (8:5-7)*
> *Not everyone, however, has this knowledge.*

We Ourselves Have the First Fruits of the Spirit

And not only the creation, but we ourselves, who have the first fruits of the Spirit, groan inwardly while we wait for adoption, the redemption of our bodies. Romans 8:23

We were created for God's glory and fellowship and this has already begun through Christ. God has given to us the first fruits of all that we anticipate by giving us the earnest of the Spirit; the first installment of the fullness that is to come (Eph. 1:14). The presence of the Spirit is our freedom and our assurance that God will fulfill everything which he has promised.

This verse recognizes the full promise in our adoption to include the redemption of our bodies. That is, we currently suffer physical limitations, we get weary in our work, and we groan in our illnesses. We do so knowing that the full redemption of our bodies is promised. Our hope is to have glorified bodies like that of our risen Lord!

This is in marked contrast to Greek philosophy of immortality of the soul or the rational aspect of the self in a future escape from the body. It is in similar contrast to Hinduism and Buddhism in the cycles of reincarnation, which they deem necessary until the life is released from a body and rests in nirvana. We, however, believe in resurrection and in a transformed body. We will have our identity in all eternity. Jesus said, "Many will come from east and the west and will eat with Abraham and Isaac and Jacob in the kingdom of heaven" (Matt. 8:11). Again, of the resurrection, "He is God not of the dead, but of the living" (Mark 12:27).

Immanuel Kant, the philosopher, believed that we are immortal, for there is too much potential in one's mind and life to fulfill it in a mere seventy years and it be all over. It is inconceivable that we should live and think and love and die and then suddenly there be nothing more. On the other hand, Jesus in John 14:2-4 promises life:

> *I go to prepare a place for you, . . .*
> *So that where I am, there you may be also.*

July 13

In Hope We Are Saved

For in hope we are saved. Now hope that is seen is not hope. For who hopes for what is seen? Romans 8:24

The word *hope* in Scripture means the conviction of a reality that is to come. It is not wishful thinking with the consequent insecurities that are actually hopelessness. Paul talks of faith, hope, and love as presenting three dimensions of our walk with God—faith as the relationship with him in Christ, hope as the anticipation of the culmination of God's plan, and love as the participation with God in his caring and presence.

In this hope we have our salvation, our full redemption. This is not a hope-so salvation without assurance. We are actually in a saving relation with Christ. This is the assurance that we are saved in hope of God's fulfillment of his redemptive purpose for all creation. We do not have, as yet, the full redemption of the body, of the physical or material world, but we live in the hope that this too will come. Our present problems of suffering, illness, heartbreak, or insecurity are all reminders of our hope, of assurance in God's promise to restore creation to its full harmony and wholeness.

The Lord who came, who lived among us, who suffered and died at human hands, who rose from the dead and ascended to the right hand of God, will not now forsake his mission and his followers. He—this LORD saw his mission in light of God's purpose, the future being a present influence, and so we live today in this *eschaton*, in hope of ultimate glory.

Peter says, "Since all these things are to be dissolved [with fire], what sort of persons ought you to be in leading lives of holiness and godliness" (2 Pet. 3:11). John confesses this hope with very clear words of assurance in 1 John 3:2-3:

> *Beloved, we are God's children now;*
> *what we will be has not yet been revealed.*
> *What we do know is this:*
> *when he is revealed, we will be like him,*
> *for we see him as he is.*
> *And all who have this hope in him purify themselves,*
> *just as he is pure.*

July 14

We Wait for This Patiently

But if we hope for what we do not see, we wait for it with patience.
Romans 8:25

To wait patiently for something promised is the expression of trust. Impatience is an expression of our desire to control. It is an expression of our ego-centeredness; we want everything to happen by our desires. We find it hard to make room for others, to wait on others, to provide them space. Impatience is not just an emotional problem; it is an attitude that relates to others by my preference to be the controlling person in the situation. But God is in control and we wait patiently on his promise.

Patience is an expression of love, as well as trust. We can adjust our attitude even in the press of time. As Sam Shoemaker has said, "There is enough time in every day to treat every person as a person." Patience is respect for the importance of another and of their space. Patience in relation to the promises of God is actually worship.

Our text expresses the character of our hope in God's plan as patience in waiting for the fulfillment of his promise. Hope reaches beyond what we already see, what we already have, and patiently waits on God for what is yet to be seen. One test of our faith in experiences of prayer is whether we can patiently wait for God to move. Or, as parents, we live with the prayer and hope for God's fullness in the lives of our children. We pray with hope and we await the answers with patience. As missioners or workers in his kingdom, we continue to work, to sow the seed, awaiting in hope the harvest which he promises. He is faithful to his promises as expressed in Hebrews (11:8-10):

> *By faith Abraham obeyed when he was called*
> > *to set out for a place that he was to receive for an inheritance;*
> > *and he set out, not knowing where he was going.*
> *By faith he stayed for a time in the land he had been promised,*
> > *as in a foreign land, living in tents, as did Isaac and Jacob,*
> > *who were heirs with him of the same promise.*
> *For he looked forward to the city that has foundations,*
> > *whose architect and builder is God.*

July 15

The Spirit Intercedes for Us

Likewise the Spirit helps us in our weakness; for we do not know how to pray as we ought, but that very Spirit intercedes with sighs too deep for words. Romans 8:26

As a part of the created order, we are limited in our exercises in God's grace. This is true in our prayer life, our understanding of how to best engage God in our experiences. We do not know how to pray as we ought.

Having spoken so clearly of the Spirit's work in the early part of this chapter, Paul then extends this to elaborate on the bondage of creation. But he returns here to his emphasis on the work of the Spirit. He has made clear that we are indwelt by the Spirit, we are liberated by the Spirit, we are led by the Spirit, we are secured by the Spirit, and now, in this verse, we are supported by the Spirit. The Spirit makes intercession for us; that is, the Spirit engages the divine power for our freedom far beyond what we are able to comprehend.

Paul does not say with utterances of other tongues, but with groaning—deep feelings of concern that cannot be uttered. We often become aware that we are confronted with issues and powers with which we are helpless, and we agonize in hopeful prayer, in assurance that the Spirit's work is far beyond our efforts. Only as we believe in a divine activity in the world's trauma, can we live in hope and enjoy our salvation. It is a comfort to know that, beyond our perception, the Holy Spirit intercedes for us and represents us to the Father.

Prayer is worship, my expression of love;
it is my identification with God as Lord.
But prayer is my expression of dependence,
my sense of incompleteness without God.
But I don't often know how to ask,
except for his presence and guidance.
I can offer praise, humbly worship,
and bow before him as my Lord and Master.
I can acknowledge the presence and sovereignty
of the gracious Holy Spirit, who lives in me.

July 16

According to the Will of God

And God, who searches the heart, knows what is the mind of the Spirit, because the Spirit intercedes for the saints according to the will of God. Romans 8:27

Jesus prayed in his darkest hour, "Yet not what I want but what you want" (Matt. 26:39). This statement is not a lack of faith; it is rather the full affirmation of faith. Our trust is not in our discernment, but in God and his wisdom. The three Hebrew youths said in essence, "We don't know what God will do in this situation, but we know God and we will trust him and not compromise" (Dan. 3:16-18). We must be true to God and believe that as we open our lives to him, he will do what is best for us.

The Spirit intercedes for us according to the will of God. What a marvelous comfort. We are not alone. He prays for us, intercedes for us. This is the most amazing relationship conceivable: the Savior is at God's right hand, representing us. The Spirit is with us, representing God for the achievement of his will.

God searches our hearts and knows the mind of the Spirit. We may have mixed signals from our hearts, but our conscious affirmation of the Spirit and of wanting his will is heard and accepted by God. That is, we are accepted on the basis of our conscious decisions for Christ. We don't just look back and bemoan our failures, but we look forward in faith and hope. Gordon Allport of Harvard University said our intentions for the future have more power to shape our lives than the experiences of the past.

Heavenly Father,
My unconscious bias I don't fully understand,
but consciously I will do the will of God.
This alone is my confession as I come to him,
forgive me for those unconscious urges
and accept my conscious choice to will your will.
Hear me pray, "Not my will but yours be done."
But hear even more the intercession of the Spirit,
who knows your will and affirms this as mine.
Far beyond my awareness or understanding,
yet by faith I own this to be mine in your grace.

God Works for Good in Those Who Love Him

We know that all things work together for good for those who love God, who are called according to his purpose. Romans 8:28

Probably no one Scripture on divine providence is quoted more frequently than this text. Our assurance of hope is that God is at work in our lives and in our circumstances. God works even in difficulties for the good; he moves in and through circumstances to bring the best possible for us out of them. The key phrase is "for good for those who love God"; that is, God has committed himself to us, to his children, to work out his best for us.

When we take this text seriously, it becomes our bulwark in times of difficulty, our relaxing comfort in times of stress, our hope in times of despair. In difficulties we do not ask the Lord, "Get me out of this," but rather, "Lord, what can I get out of this?" From the book of Job, we can also refer to "God my Maker, who gives strength in the night" (35:10). With Psalm 23 we are assured with the people of God for centuries, "The Lord is my shepherd."

We have been called to move beyond a mere conceptual belief in God to a personal relationship with God. The last phrase provides assurance in the purpose of God. In this word we are sure that he will continue that purpose-work in us, for above all, his purpose is that we be conformed to the image of Christ.

Freedom in Christ is more than release from sin, for freedom is the opportunity to become, to exercise one's potential in the will of God, to walk with Christ rather than against God. This is God's purpose for each of us, as we come to him in faith, to open ourselves to the presence of his Spirit, to seek his will and his glory. We rejoice in assurance of his grace and worship him in praise and devotion.

> *Ours is a new life in the Spirit,*
> *Living above the dominance of fleshly interests,*
> *Knowing the true nature of essential being,*
> *And living as inner-directed by his Spirit.*

Conformed to the Image of His Son

For those whom he foreknew he also predestined to be conformed to the image of his Son, in order that he might be the firstborn within a large family. Romans 8:29

We are predestined for one basic thing: to be conformed to the full humanness expressed in Christ. In him we have a vision of what God intended us to be: conformed to the image of his Son. This is God's goal for each of us. He is creating a family in which Jesus is central, but a family to be conformed to Christ. Our heart's cry should be as expressed in the verse of Thomas O. Chisholm:

> *Oh! to be like Thee, blessed Redeemer,*
> *This is my constant longing and prayer;*
> *Gladly I'll forfeit all of earth's treasures,*
> *Jesus, Thy perfect likeness to wear.*

In the text the two difficult words "foreknew" and "predestined" are not to be separated from the phrase that follows, "conformed to the image of his Son." God has a definite plan. He intends that the incarnation should be followed by many adopted children, who are to be like Christ. As we become believers, we discover that we are predestined in Christ to be conformed to his image. It is preplanned that identifying with Christ in faith, the basic result is already determined; we will be conformed to his image.

Predestination can be considered almost mechanical and deterministic, like the joke of the man who fell down the stairs, got up, dusted himself off, and said, "Well, I'm glad that's over." More dynamic ways to think of this term are relational ways of understanding it. The nature of a child born into a family will be determined by the genes of the family line, to be short or tall, heavy or slim. But he still has responsibility for the person he becomes. Those born into the family of God are foreknown to have Christlike gifts. The believer is predestined to be conformed to Christ, but this is realized by an appropriating faith. We should rejoice in this, the work of God's grace, not react as though it undercuts our responsibility.

Again and again, Lord, we thank you for this wonderful grace of God!

July 19

He Calls and He Glorifies

And those whom he predestined he also called; and those whom he called he also justified; and those whom he justified he also glorified. Romans 8:30

Being justified does not come first in the above list. Before justification, God predestines and calls. Paul's understanding of God's grace is so profound that we stand in awe before this truth. God has his own purpose, then he takes the initiative and calls us; God acts on our behalf in Christ and justifies us. God fills our lives with his Spirit and thereby shares his glory with us. We hear again Jesus's high priestly prayer of John 17 the marvelous words, "The glory that you have given me I have given them, so that they may be one, as we are one" (v. 22). The unity of the body of Christ with its diversity is a glory to God.

To glorify means to be honored with the full essence or potential of one's being. To glorify God is to recognize him for who he actually is. For God to glorify us is to affirm us for what we actually are in Christ: children of God. There is nothing so great as being God's child, to know it and to enjoy it. There is nothing so powerful in relating to another as to see her as God's child and to treat such as a child of God.

Dietrich Bonhoeffer writes in *Life Together* that Christian community is a gift of grace. We relate to one another in and through Christ, not directly. A genuine community of faith is our greater strength for holy living above greed, covetousness, sensuality, violence, status, and inequity, for in this community we relate in Christ.

Our salvation is full and abundant. God calls, justifies, and glorifies. He doesn't just squeak us through. We are united with him and will share the ages with him. We sing in the old doxology:

Glory be to the Father,
and to the Son, and to the Holy Ghost.
As it was in the beginning,
is now, and ever shall be,
world without end. Amen

If God Be for Us

What then are we to say about these things? If God is for us, who is against us? Romans 8:31

The questions Paul raises have their answer implicit in the verses which speaks to them. Since all of the preceding is true, that God is so gracious toward us, who can be against us? That is, since God has moved to us, has bridged the estrangement, who can interfere and spoil our hope?

I once heard C. F. Derstine, a Mennonite evangelist, say that he would like to preach a sermon on "Why it is easy to be a Christian and hard to be a sinner." I never heard the sermon, but I could preach it from this text. As believers, we are not trying to come to God, rather we come to God in response to his grace, walking in the loving care of God. It is for us, as Jude writes, simply to keep ourselves in the love of God.

The positive spirit of faith should be the shield for us as Christians. This is the power for aggressive action in the world. The early disciples "with great power gave witness of the resurrection" (cf. Acts 4:33, KJV), so this assurance gives us power to declare God's work. He is at work in calling people, and we only serve as heralds of this message. We pray for an anointing of the Spirit, but with assurance that the Spirit is at work. This dynamic of grace is expressed by the beautiful hymn text:

> *I sought the Lord, and afterward I knew*
> *He moved my soul to seek Him, seeking me;*
> *It was not I that found, O Savior true,*
> *No, I was found of Thee.*
>
> *Thou didst reach forth Thy hand and mine enfold,*
> *I walked and sank not on the storm-vexed sea;*
> *'Twas not so much that I on Thee took hold*
> *As Thou, dear Lord, on me.*

He Gives Us All Things

He who did not withhold his own Son, but gave him up for all of us, will he not with him also give us everything else? Romans 8:32

Wow! What an argument, what a conclusion! God has given his best, his Son, for our redemption. Could we think that he will not follow through? With salvation provided in his Son, everything else is serendipitous. This provision is *with* Christ, not apart from him. Paul asks, "Will he not with him give us everything?" God's grace is in Christ, by him and in him and through him. We do not "get saved" and then go off on our own. We come to walk with the Savior.

We must be careful that we do not make of belief a mere intellectual assent when it is a holistic identification. If I believe something, I bind my whole life to that conviction. When I believe in Jesus, that he is the Christ of God, I bind my life to him. This is covenant, the relating of two persons in a oneness with accountability for both.

That God has given himself to us makes of the Christian faith the most unique faith among religious understandings. This is so wonderful that it can't be a human creation; it is so profound that it can't be other than true. Walking out of the Kennedy Center in Washington, DC, after listening to a rendition of Handel's *Messiah*, I commented to Esther, "That is so wonderful that if it hadn't happened it would need to." But it has happened: Christ has come and redeemed us to God by his blood. Our response is well expressed in the words of a hymn by Lauchlan M. Watt:

> *I bind my heart this tide*
> *To the Galilean's side,*
> *To the wounds of Calvary,*
> *To the Christ who died for me.*

> *I bind myself to peace,*
> *To make strife and envy cease,*
> *God, knit Thou sure the cord*
> *Of my thralldom to my Lord!*

July 22

It Is God Who Justifies

Who will bring any charge against God's elect? It is God who justifies.
Romans 8:33

I recall a unique experience in New Orleans when I led workshops on "The Spirit and Peace." As a Mennonite pacifist, I was asked to serve in this charismatic conference on world evangelization. That was quite a privilege and challenge. The crowd of Catholics and Protestants was almost unbelievable, for some 70,000 people had gathered. With all of the variety of views, this verse had special significance for my presentations—it is God who justifies. It is God who calls us to live in his will, in love and justice and peace. As Martin Luther King Jr. said, we should not only avoid violence of deed, but also violence of spirit. It is the inner harmony of grace which makes peace possible.

Paul asks: Since salvation is by God's gracious action, who can raise an accusation against us that will stand before what God has done in his Son? He engaged the full meaning of forgiveness in love to the death that he might be just in justifying the one who believes in Jesus. When he justifies us, no other power in the universe can come between us. This is our security.

Our relationship with God, our heavenly Father, has an in-depth assurance. A man was walking down a lonely street in the dusk hour of the evening. He came upon a little boy who stood on the street corner. He asked the child, "It's getting dark and no one else is around. Don't you think you should go home?" "No sir," replied the boy. "Aren't you afraid out here alone in the dark?" asked the man. To this the boy, pointing up to a man high on a telephone pole, said, "No sir; my father's up there!" His relationship with his father was in complete confidence that he was okay.

In my teens I was a songleader for J. Otis Yoder, an evangelist. My life was touched by the words of a theme song by Julia H. Johnson that we used in the services each night:

> *Marvelous grace of our loving Lord,*
> *Grace that exceeds our sin and our guilt,*
> *Yonder on Calvary's mount outpoured,*
> *There where the blood of the Lamb was spilt.*

July 23

Christard Jesus Intercedes for Us

Who is to condemn? It is Christ Jesus, who died, yes, who is raised, who is at the right hand of God, who indeed intercedes for us. Romans 8:34

Christ represents us before the Father and intercedes for us. This phrase "for us" is used in triune reference to the Godhead: Father, Son, and Spirit, who are committed to our support. In verse 26, Paul refers to the Spirit's intercession for us. In verse 31 he refers to God the Father, who is for us. Now in verse 34 he says that Christ intercedes for us. Are we covered, or what?

Christ died for us, is resurrected, is exalted to God's right hand, and intercedes for us. Before the present form of the Apostles' Creed its content was expressed. Christ is the mediator of right relationship with God, who has "made us to be a kingdom, priests serving his God and Father, to him be glory and dominion forever and ever. Amen" (Rev. 1:6).

Leading a seminar at the Congress on Evangelism in New Orleans, I had much interchange with both Catholics and Protestants in the charismatic movement. While I had not moved in these circles, not myself emphasizing tongues, I do share the emphasis on a personal experience with the Spirit and a Spirit-filled life. I stressed that only in Christ do we really know the Spirit and only by glorifying Christ are we in the stream of the Spirit. The Spirit has come to glorify Christ.

There are two baptisms, if not three. The outer baptism with water is a sign, the inner baptism with the Spirit is given by Jesus, and the baptism with suffering comes to many. The focus of each is on Jesus, who is our Redeemer: the outer baptism is witness of our covenant with Christ, the inner baptism is the presence of the Spirit of Christ, and the baptism of suffering is for the cause of Christ. To be baptized is to come under the power of Christ, in grace, to walk with him, indwelled with the Spirit, and to live by undivided loyalty to the King of kings.

Lord, thank you for sending us a Redeemer to whom we can belong.
We are his disciples, and he looks out for us.
In his family he represents us to you.

Separated from the Love of Christ?

Who will separate us from the love of Christ? Will hardship, or distress, or persecution, or famine, or nakedness, or peril, or sword? Romans 8:35

The first-century church existed under intense persecution. The strength of their faith was the immediacy of their relationship with the Lord, an immediacy that is also ours in a firsthand relationship with Christ and his Spirit. As Paul reviews the causes of suffering, tribulation, distress, persecution, famine, nakedness, peril, and sword, my mind goes to the suffering church today in China, Ethiopia, Sudan. An amazing miracle of this century is the emergence of a strong church in China, probably 100 million believers, as oppressed people have sought the Lord. What a prophetic word to us who are so involved in the materialism and secularism of the Western world.

As I shared officiating in an interracial wedding at our congregation in Washington, DC, I prayed for the two extended families to accept and support the couple. I recognize, in this setting, how relevant the emphasis on peace I have been teaching. We know that each of us alike is created in the image of God; it is now ours to be secured in the love of Christ. We do not ask that there be no problems in life, but that God be with us in the problems. And we ask that we can pray with St. Francis of Assisi:

> *Lord, make me an instrument of Thy peace.*
> *where there is hatred, let me sow love;*
> *where there is injury, pardon;*
> *where there is doubt, faith;*
> *where there is despair, hope;*
> *where there is sadness, joy.*
> *O Divine Master, grant that I may not so much seek*
> *to be consoled, as to console;*
> *to be understood, as to understand;*
> *to be loved, as to love.*
> *For it is in giving that we receive;*
> *it is in pardoning that we are pardoned;*
> *it is in dying that we are born to eternal life.*

July 25

As It Is Written

As it is written, "For your sake we are being killed all day long; we are accounted as sheep to be slaughtered." Romans 8:36

Holy Scripture is the foundational truth for our security in faith. God has acted in history, unfolding a revelation of himself. When Christ came in Jesus of Nazareth, he didn't just drop in out of nowhere; he came as a fulfillment of God's prophetic word. Paul reaches into history and quotes the psalmist in understanding the suffering that accompanies our walk of faith. Our security is in Christ interceding for us.

In a congregational worship service in Washington, DC, I recall preaching from the well-known passage on the encounter between Jesus and an expert in Jewish law. The man sought to put Jesus to the test, but Jesus turned the man's questions back to him in the moving story of the Good Samaritan (Luke 10). In his conclusion, Jesus turned the lawyer's question completely around. The question is not the lawyer's "*Who* is my neighbor?" but rather Jesus's question, "Which man *was* the neighbor?" In other words, are we willing to be neighborly? Martin Luther referred to Jesus as our Good Samaritan, helping us in our suffering, in our helplessness, and we are to follow the example of Jesus.

We should note the words, "for your sake" in this verse. We are suffering, not just because of our own simplicity, foolishness, or selfishness. Living by the will of God, we are an affront to those outside his will, and we suffer persecution. We serve Christ for who he is and not primarily for what we seek to get from him. This is not a "success gospel," a support for our materialism and selfish pursuits, but a life in the integrity of faith.

It helps in suffering to keep our perspective,
for what happens to us is not so serious
as is what happens in us in our reaction.
It also helps to have a plan of action,
to overcome evil with good,
to do to others what we'd like done to us.
It takes grace to live in the spirit of Jesus;
grace beyond ourselves, for it is from him
that the grace of God is given by our faith.

July 26

More Than Conquerors

No, in all of these things we are more than conquerors through him who loved us. Romans 8:37

The victory of Christ becomes our victory. He has conquered the depth of evil, its attack to the death. He carried our sins in his own body on the cross; he has conquered death in his resurrection from the dead. His victory is total, Satan is defeated, evil is overcome, and we can walk with him in his victory!

Paul exclaims, "We are more than conquerors through him who loved us." We not only conquer, but we also walk on in the freedom of the new life with new dimensions of love and joy in the fellowship of Christ. This is a freedom as we pray and worship. We live in a fallen world, but also in a world where there is redemption. We live in a world in which the victory of Christ is a reality, enabling us to live in victory. This perspective is realistic, for it recognizes the problems, but stands with Christ in his superior power.

Victorious living,
we are overcomers.
He enables us to walk faithfully,
even though we do not walk perfectly.
Victorious living means
we are honest about the problems,
we confess our failures,
but we affirm our faithfulness to him.
Victorious living means
he has overcome the evil one,
and we can resist, saying no, having said yes.
Victorious living means recognizing the problems;
it means drawing on our resources to cope.
Those resources are the riches of his grace.

July 27

I Am Convinced

For I am convinced that neither death, nor life, nor angels, nor rulers, nor things present, nor things to come, nor powers.... Romans 8:38

Christian faith is not only a feeling of the heart, but a conviction of the mind. True, it is a matter of the heart, of the core of one's life, of wanting God in our lives, of loving or opening our lives intimately to him. But faith is also a matter of the mind, of thinking with God, understanding the evidence for faith-conclusions. "I am convinced" is a move from doubt to certainty, of question to conviction, which builds strong disciples.

Augustine said, "For it is better for them to find you and leave the questions unanswered than to find the answer without finding you." In faith we can say with Anselm, "Faith seeks understanding." In this we can say like Paul, "I am convinced."

There is nothing wrong with doubt and question so long as we do not park there. Doubt should stimulate the pursuit of reality; questions should stimulate our search for answers. Doubt and question are also important in aiding us in humility, for questions will keep us from premature and inadequate answers.

Our text lists adversaries which faith overcomes—death, life, angels, demons, the present, the future, and powers—all of which are realms or realities beyond ourselves. Yet we are secure in the love known supremely in the self-giving of Jesus our Lord.

My father-in-law, Lloy A. Kniss, was a missionary in India. On one occasion he was visiting a village in the jungle where the people had never heard the gospel. As he spoke to the group around a campfire, he noticed an older woman near the back with a glowing smile on her face. He thought to himself that there must be one believer here. After the meeting, she came up to him and said, "Sahib, I have never heard that before, but I believe it. Long ago I discovered that there was no peace in my religion, and I started to pray to the God beyond all religion to hear me and to give me peace." God answered, and she found this peace in the grace of God. Now she learned how to call God by his right name, for that day she learned of him in Jesus.

Lord, help me to work through my doubts and questions
and say with Paul, "I am convinced."

Nothing Will Be Able to Separate Us

. . . nor height, nor depth, nor anything else in all creation, will be able to separate us from the love of God in Christ Jesus our Lord. Romans 8:39

When we are in Christ, nothing can come between us and God, for God identifies with Christ fully. The love of God is extended in Jesus, and in this love we are included. To be in Jesus is to be in God's love. In him we are secure.

As Paul completes his list, including height and depth, in an attempt to be universal, he sums it up by saying that nothing in all creation will be able to separate us from the love of God. We do not fear the material order, for it cannot separate us from God's love. He is the Creator, present and active in his created world, redeeming, transforming, and securing.

The striking affirmation is that this love is known in Christ Jesus our Lord. Should one ask why we preach Jesus, the answer is that in him we are meeting God. The message of the gospel is that in Christ, God reached down to lay hold on us. Having gone to the length expressed in the love of Christ, it is inconceivable that God would allow anything to come between his children and himself.

In Ephesians 3:18-19, Paul writes of the extent of God's love. He says that we can know by *experience* what is impossible to know simply by *perception* (from two Greek words Paul uses for knowing: *ginōskō* and *oida*). This reference, to the breadth and length and depth and height of the love of God, I interface with John 3:16. I repeat it here for emphasis and to note that this arrangement can be sung it to the tune of "O Sacred Head, Now Wounded."

> *We know how wide God's love is,*
> *For God so loved the world;*
> *We know the length of his love,*
> *He gave his only Son;*
> *We know how deep love reaches,*
> *For who so comes to him;*
> *We know the height of his love,*
> *Should have eternal life!*

Conscience Confirmed in the Spirit

I speak the truth in Christ—I am not lying; my conscience confirms it in the Holy Spirit. Romans 9:1

Conscience is the tribunal of the mind. It passes judgment upon our actions according to the values by which it has been conditioned. But conscience is not the ultimate authority; God is. The conscience expresses itself in accordance with the way it has been programmed. We need to educate (program) our conscience by the Word of God. The Scripture is the standard; the conscience is to be "standardized" by the Word of God.

In one sense, conscience is an expression of the spirit aspect of our being. It is a part of the *imago Dei* and keeps calling us to God. Even though different consciences speak in different ways because of their different programming, there is one thing that is universally consistent: conscience in any and all cultures casts its vote on the side of what a people believe to be right. This fact, that there is a sense of the right, calls us to think about the ultimate right.

In our verse today, Paul speaks of his conscience being confirmed in the Holy Spirit. This is a marvelous reality that one's conscience has the illumination of the "truth in Christ" and the witness of the Spirit. This is our highest authority, the ground on which we operate in his mission. This is also our joy and our peace, the answer of a good conscience.

We are not bound by one another's conscience; each one is to live at peace with his own. However, if others have conviction that I do not have, I should humbly and honestly examine the issue. But the fact that I do not have their conviction calls for them to examine the issue again as well. We should each bow before the higher will of God.

I do not count Romans 9–11 as a parenthesis, as though a focus on the Jews and excluding the Gentiles. God's reconciliation in grace is for both Jew and Gentile. Chapter 9 shows the place of historic Israel in reconciliation, chapter 10 shows the place of Christ, and chapter 11 shows the place of election and faith in reconciliation.

Lord, help us to see your plan in history,
in Christ, and for each of us. Amen

July 30

The Anguish of Compassion

I have great sorrow and unceasing anguish in my heart. Romans 9:2

Family is our most important social identity and association. We have frequently joined Esther's maternal family, the Luther clan, at reunions. The extended family of her grandparents now numbers in the nineties. Of their ten children who lived, two of them in 2004 are still with us, with grandchildren and great-grandchildren, even great-great grandchildren. Many of them are walking in the faith of Christ. However, when persons close to us are not enjoying life in Christ, we yearn for their faith.

This is the focus of our text and Paul's anguish in relation to his people. No doubt among his own immediate family were those who rejected Christ. Paul lived with them weighing heavily on his heart, caring and praying for them. We do know of his nephew, his faith, and his empathetic concern for Paul. When Paul was a prisoner, his nephew came to tell him of the plot to take his life; therefore, he was not adversarial to Paul (Acts 23).

Paul's depth of caring is beyond levels that I have known. Similarly, Mother Teresa gave herself beyond the pattern of any of us. I have found as an evangelist the importance of looking beyond people to focus on persons in sharing God's love.

> *Help me, Lord,*
> > *to know your love for persons,*
> > *to care for each one holistically,*
> > *not just for souls as impersonal,*
> > *but for persons as living souls.*
> *Help me, Lord,*
> > *to be more clear in sharing Christ,*
> > *more free in conversation about him,*
> > *above all to live by his Spirit,*
> > *and to invite others to share this joy.*

I Could Wish

For I could wish that I myself were accursed and cut off from Christ for the sake of my own people, my kindred according to the flesh. Romans 9:3

In reading this text there is no reason to doubt Paul's sincerity, and yet we stagger when he "could" wish himself to be cut off from Christ for the sake of his own race. To think that he could give himself to be lost if it would turn Israel to faith in Christ! Referring to them as his brothers, we are given a glimpse into Paul's heart of compassion. Paul's compassion took him across the Roman world with the gospel. He lived with compassion, giving himself totally to the ministry to reach his own people. What a striking expression of what it means to love one's neighbor as oneself.

To the Corinthians Paul says, "Therefore, knowing the fear of the Lord, we try to persuade others" (2 Cor. 5:11). This is the passion that comes from the awareness that all alike are accountable to God. To place one's person in the breach as willing to be excluded so that others should be in Christ is compassion that comes only from Christ (cf. Exod. 32:32).

In the 1960s at a church in an Oregon city, a hippie entered and started down the aisle, looking for a seat. No one moved over to make space. He continued until he got to the front, and then he sat down cross-legged in the aisle. A rustle in the congregation expressed the resentment toward this strange newcomer. Suddenly an elderly man from back in the audience got up and started down the aisle with his cane. The audience watched almost breathless. When he came to the hippie, he sat down beside him, cross-legged, in the aisle. The pastor went to the pulpit and said, "What I say this morning you will not long remember, but what you have just seen you will never forget." Compassion means identification.

We are responsible to others
rather than being responsible for them.
Each person is responsible for oneself,
responsible to God for one's decisions.
And we are responsible to God in his mission,
to share his love, the good news of grace.
We can approach others as we'd like to be approached,
in a winsome sharing, not a judgmental put-down.

To Them Belongs the Adoption

They are Israelites, and to them belong the adoption, the glory, the covenants, the giving of the law, the worship, and the promises. Romans 9:4

A heritage is a wonderful resource. We are what we are because of God's grace at work through others, as well as in our personal lives. In fact, we experience nothing apart from history. And yet we are not children of yesterday, but of the future.

Paul articulates the values of Israel's heritage: their being purposed for adoption, their privilege of being the people who witnessed the Shekinah glory of God, their being a people of covenant to whom God moved in grace again and again, their being the recipients of the law at Sinai, their high experience of temple worship of Yahweh, and their promises of God. What a heritage! What an opportunity, yes, and what a special responsibility.

Paul's appeal in this text is for a contemporary people to recognize and respond to the acts of God on their behalf. As we look at evidences of God's grace in our own history, we cannot turn our back and rob ourselves of the privileges and meanings of our heritage. We are actually free to choose a heritage of faith, own it, and be enriched by it.

I never met a sixteenth-century Anabaptist; yet as far as I understand them and their interpretation of the Scripture, I identify with them and believe as they did. And in this heritage I stand: emphasizing solidarity with the risen Christ, participation in the kingdom of Christ now, enjoying the inner baptism with the Spirit, and seeking to walk as a disciple in daily life. I choose this heritage, this faith. Each of us comes to faith with presuppositions, recognized or unrecognized, they condition us. And while we reinterpret in our context, we own this heritage and work from this premise.

Lord, thank you for my heritage and history.
Help me to own my heritage and use it for your glory. Amen

From Them Comes the Messiah

To them belong the patriarchs, and from them, according to the flesh, comes the Messiah, who is over all, God blessed forever. Amen. Romans 9:5

Paul continues his emphasis on heritage, its climax being that from them comes the Messiah. Uniquely, he refers to the patriarchs as of Israel, but in this reference to Christ he speaks of the Messiah "according to the flesh," a reference to the incarnation, which he expresses so magnificently in Philippians 2:5-11. Christ as the Son of God is over all and, as in Romans 1:3, he is of the seed of David "according to the flesh." God has fulfilled his promise. The Messiah is come. Jesus didn't just appear on the human stage out of nowhere; he came as the climax of a long prophetic history.

The ultimate affirmation in the text is of Christ with the declaration that he is God over all, forever praised! This is a most daring affirmation of faith, based on the witness of the resurrection and exaltation of Christ. Our text is a gem of the gospel, placed here to make the Jewish community aware of their privilege. They could be jealous that many of them were missing out while Gentiles were entering into a faith that was the Jews' right. In Philippians 2:5-11, Paul praises the Messiah as Savior and focuses his eternal glory!

> *Let the same mind be in you that was in Christ Jesus,*
> > *who, though he was in the form of God,*
> > *did not regard equality with God as something to be exploited,*
> *but emptied himself, taking the form of a slave. . . .*
> *And being found in human form, he humbled himself*
> > *and became obedient to the point of death. . . .*
> *Therefore God also highly exalted him*
> > *and gave him the name that is above every name,*
> *so that at the name of Jesus every knee should bend,*
> > *in heaven and on earth and under the earth,*
> *and every tongue should confess*
> > *that Jesus Christ is Lord,*
> > *to the glory of God the Father.*

God's Word Has Not Failed

It is not as though the word of God had failed. For not all Israelites truly belong to Israel. Romans 9:6

This is a key statement for the understanding of the larger passage. The essential declaration of God's Word is his covenant of grace. Because of his own nature, not because of any merit in the human family, God moves to us in reconciliation. He chose a channel of disclosure through Israel. He bound himself to his covenant, even to death on the cross, certifying his love by total self-giving. Yet among those to whom his revelation was so clearly given, "not all who are descended from Israel are Israel."

As we recognize the theology of reconciliation in these chapters, we will see how Israel and believing Gentiles are invited to the reality of God's reconciling grace. To understand the in-depth nature of God's calling, of his electing us to reconciliation, we must see this in several ways, in the history of Israel (chap. 9), in the person and work of Christ (chap. 10), and in the free election of God's sovereign mercy (chap. 11).

God is as good as his word. He said to Abraham that in his seed all the families of the earth would be blessed (Gen. 12:3). So here, his promise is good of our election in Christ.

God so loved the world,
    and that includes me;
that he gave his only begotten Son,
    and there is no greater expression of love;
that whosoever believes in him,
    and that whosoever is open to me!
should not perish but have everlasting life,
    and this is my assurance of salvation.
This is God's action,
    not for one people but for all peoples,
the intent and action of God,
    witnessing to this in history
and calling all peoples, not just one group,
    to share his wonderful reconciling grace.

August 4

Through Isaac, the Promise

And not all of Abraham's children are his true descendants; but "It is through Isaac that descendants shall be named for you." Romans 9:7

Abraham, the "friend of God," is the father of all who come to God by faith. Standing in the tradition of Abraham, in the heritage of faith, is not a matter of flesh-and-blood relationship, but is a relationship of faith. This is for each of us. Paul sets forward his argument from the Old Testament story (Gen. 16:21).

Abraham and Sarah had been promised a son, but as Sarah was unable to bear a child, she presented her maid to Abraham, and they had a son by this surrogate wife and mother. Abraham's prayer became, "Oh, that Ishmael might live before thee." But God said no to this human fulfillment and gave them the son of promise, Isaac. Now Paul is stating that God does not accept all who have human relationship to Abraham, but accepts those who are members of his family because of his gracious promise. We must beware of placing any "confidence in the flesh" (Phil. 3:3), of wanting God's acceptance because of our religious identity or our achievements. We are called to faith.

A priest, Alexander Men, was an instrument of God for renewal in the Russian Orthodox Church. One morning while walking to a speaking appointment, two men attacked him with an ax and he died. One of his disciples, a friend, Vladimir Illiouchenko from Moscow, continues Men's ministry, calling for personal reconciliation with God in Christ. In spite of the KGB and Orthodox hierarchy, the message lives on.

To live by faith	*is to trust Christ,* *is to respond to him,* *is to celebrate his acceptance.*
To live by faith	*is to join covenant with him,* *is to be in solidarity with him,* *is to take up identity with him.*
To live by faith	*is to follow him in life,* *is to practice his love,* *is to witness of his grace.*

Children of the Promise

**This means that it is not the children of the flesh who are the children of God,
but the children of the promise are counted as descendants. Romans 9:8**

Corrie ten Boom often said, "God has no grandchildren." Each of us is to come to God for ourselves, by God's action to be born into his family. This is a work of the Spirit, in which we are born from above, born of the Spirit (John 3:3-5). When we open our lives to Christ, we have a new Lord, a new relationship, a new purpose, and a new direction.

Here in our text, Paul makes it clear that we become children of God by entering into the promise God has expressed and now fulfilled in Christ. We are not God's children by human lineage, but by a relationship of faith. We do not trust in our religious heritage or ethnic identification, but we trust alone in the grace of God. "To all who received him, who believed in his name, he gave power to become children of God" (John 1:12).

In our text we are truly Abraham's offspring when we stand in the same faith as Abraham. In this faith we "make [our] calling and election sure" (2 Pet. 1:10, KJV). That is, with the integrity of our faith we identify with God, who justifies the believing person. This faith, uniting us with God in the obedience of faith, enables us to walk with him daily in life as did Abraham. Faith also unites us with all others who, in the same way, believe in him and identify with him. This faith extends the people of God across racial, cultural, and national lines, a community encompassing the world. To believe God, to accept and honor his word, is the highest praise we can offer him.

> *"Lord, I believe, help thou my unbelief." (Mark 9:24, KJV)*
> *With the honesty of these words*
> *many of us have needed to identify.*
> *Faith is not manufactured; faith is response.*
> *We are responding to him,*
> *to his word of promise.*

August 6

In His Appointed Time

For this is what the promise said, "About this time I will return and Sarah shall have a son." Romans 9:9

God makes the promise, but Abraham and Sarah needed to wait by faith. Within a few months she had the evidence that God's promise was being fulfilled. The New Testament account of this confirms the Old Testament story that Abraham and Sarah laughed when God made the promise. When God confronted Abraham and Sarah about the laughter, she denied laughing. God responded by asking them to name the child of promise Isaac, meaning "he laughs" (Gen. 17:15-21; 18:9-15). Day after day, Sarah must have been amazed at the incredulous happening that she had a child at her advanced age and of her laughter at the promise. Isaac's name was a constant reminder of God's grace.

From this account we recognize that God performs the work of reconciliation, both because we are incapable of achieving a saving relationship with him unless he moves to us, and also because by his providing salvation, he puts all humanity on one level and makes salvation equally possible for all. This is marvelous news, the gospel, the announcement that "whosoever will" may come to God in Christ. How fair and equal is God's offer of acceptance; his grace is open to all peoples.

We are each alike invited into a new freedom in God's grace. In the days of slavery in America, Mark Twain wrote a story of an event when, due to heavy rains during the night, the Mississippi River cut a new channel through a neck of land. In the morning, a black man found that he had gone to sleep in one state a slave and awoke in another state a free man! God has acted to cut us off from the old life of estrangement and to grant us freedom to live a new life in fellowship with him. As Paul wrote the Galatians, "For freedom Christ has set us free" (5:1). Ray Palmer expressed a desire for Christ's freedom in his wonderful hymn text:

> *My faith looks up to Thee,*
> *Thou Lamb of Calvary, Savior divine:*
> *Now hear me while I pray, take all my guilt away,*
> *O let me from this day be wholly Thine.*

The Promise Is Not One Time Only

Nor is that all; something similar happened to Rebecca when she had conceived children by one husband, our ancestor Isaac. Even before they were born or had done anything good or bad (so that God's purpose by election might continue).... Romans 9:10-11

The legalist always has an answer to perspectives that call for a change of thought or stance. Paul could well imagine a legalist saying, "Of course, the child of covenant is Isaac and not Ishmael, for Ishmael was born from Hagar, who was not truly Abraham's wife." Paul moves next to Isaac's family and to Rebecca who gave birth to twins, showing that God chose Jacob and not Esau to be the line of promise or of faith. Esau was of the same fleshly line, but God was choosing one, and evidently not the more impressive one, to demonstrate his electing promise. Deceitful though Jacob was, God saw in him a bit of faith that he could use to transform Jacob's life.

This passage is a clarification of the nature of salvation. Among the Jews, salvation is for those who have faith in God, and the Gentiles come by the same faith in God. "For by grace you have been saved through faith, and this is not your own doing; it is the gift of God" (Eph. 2:8). We are in Christ, who is the Elect One in whom we are elect to salvation.

God is not an "it" but is, "Thou." He is the Thou of the universe. As such we ask of his person: is he unfeeling, judgmental, demanding? Or is he compassionate, merciful, and forgiving? Is he withdrawn, unresponsive, and uncaring? Or is God present, suffering, and redeeming? Is he capricious and unpredictable? Or is he consistent and faithful to his Word?

In his revelation we get to know him:
a God of glory and of grace,
of steadfast mercy and of love,
of self-giving to the death,
of reconciliation and fellowship!

Not by Works but by His Call

(Not by works but by his call) she was told, "The elder shall serve the younger." Romans 9:12

We need to regain a sense of awe before the sovereign Lord. The modern church, the average evangelical Christian, has become somewhat presumptuous, even cocky with God's sovereignty. It is as though they can order God to exercise his power and do certain things for them. Some of the "success gospel" spokespersons sound as though they can give God orders and have him serve them. We need a new sense of humility, of being ones who only receive from God by his will. He is sovereign, he is in charge. Paul's phrase, "but by his call" places the priority on God in his choice to act.

Our text carries the illustration further in God's word to Rebecca, that the "elder shall serve the younger." This did not follow the rights of the eldest son. This statement expresses God's right to designate our place in life. Someone has said that God's cure for envy is for us to accept his right to appoint our brother his role in life.

As parents, we need to recognize God's sovereign role and not predetermine the roles of our children. I have a sense that God will do something greater through our children when it is clear that it is of God and not just because they are our children.

Faith that accepts God's sovereign role is not easy. Our human nature is inclined to seek to be in control. We like to be in charge. We want a God who will serve us and fulfill our interests, when we should surrender to the sovereign work of his Spirit. The Spirit-filled life is costly for it surrenders the claim to self-determination, as Judson W. Van de Venter wrote in his popular hymn text:

> *All to Jesus I surrender,*
> *All to Him I freely give;*
> *I will ever love and trust him,*
> *In his presence daily live.*
> *I surrender all, I surrender all,*
> *All to Thee, my blessed Savior,*
> *I surrender all.*

August 9

As It Is Written

As it is written, "I have loved Jacob, but I have hated Esau." Romans 9:13

This phrase "As it is written" throws us back on the history of God's actions. Paul's argument is not some isolated idea that he has come up with. This insight is a part of the whole process of God's unfolding revelation, a covenant in both Testaments. It has been well said, "The New is in the Old contained, and the Old is in the New explained."

Paul's account of God's choice of Jacob, rather than Esau, is used here to show that God was acting in his right to chose as he purposed. However, the forms in the Greek language suggest that there was a reason for the choice, the conditional clause suggesting such. God, seeing into the future, had a reason to choose Jacob. He expressed mercy on Jacob, and he became a transformed man, Israel, a prince with God. To bypass Esau is to say that God's purpose in history of calling a people is God's choice and not by human initiative.

This is not an easy passage for us. We want to know why God does what he does. In accidents, suffering, unexpected deaths, we can only be at peace when we rest this with God. In faith we believe God will work for good in his purpose. We do not think of God as the cause or accountable in our problems, but we worship amid them as did the patriarch Job.

I read Job to see his faith in suffering,
and to hear God's words to him
when finally, in his patience, he listens
and affirms God as God, and bows before him.
I read the words of his miserable comforters,
some of the best humanists of his day,
not that God is speaking in all of their words,
but in them, with Job, I too find I need God.
I need to hear him, the sovereign Lord,
and listening to him, honor his Person and Word.

August 10

Is God Unjust?

What then are we to say? Is there injustice on God's part? By no means!
Romans 9:14

Is God unjust to bypass one in choosing another? No, God's choice is for the sake of expressing his role, fulfilling his promise, and to do that through a particular people he has chosen. God's choice is made by foreknowledge. But his mercy shapes his justice.

In a story of a woman convicted of an offense, she appealed to the judge: "It isn't justice I want, but mercy." But with God, mercy guides justice for God's justice works to set things right. God in mercy exposes our sin and acts to forgive us and accept us in grace. God works to set things right as creative justice. He forgives to achieve reconciliation. The Old Testament prophet asks, "Who is a God like you, pardoning iniquity?" (Mic. 7:18).

On one occasion when I was in the Far East, I was chatting with a high-class Hindu, a Brahman. Upon his claim that Hinduism incorporates values from all religions, I asked him what he found in relating to the Christian faith. He responded that Jesus taught forgiveness, and this concept was not part of Hinduism. They needed to borrow forgiveness from Jesus,

But, we ask, how can God be just in forgiving? It is by his love acting to set things right, a love that moves beyond the issue to the person in restoration. God is just in releasing us in that he has dealt with the issue. He has taken into himself the cost of solving our problem. God expresses his mercy to whomsoever he wills, without a special privileged group: he opens his love to all humankind. His justice is conditioned by mercy.

Salvation by grace is the good news that God is interested in all humanity. A special work through some people is not to be exclusive, but is an evidence of grace which will in turn speak to others. Salvation by grace, the basic principle of the Reformation, affirms grace for all peoples as expressed in F. M. Lehman's verse of God's love:

> The love of God is greater far
> Than tongue or pen can ever tell;
> It goes beyond the highest star,
> And reaches to the lowest hell.

I Will Have Mercy on Whom I Have Mercy

For he says to Moses, "I will have mercy on whom I have mercy, and I will have compassion on whom I have compassion." Romans 9:15

A striking thing in this verse is that God begins with mercy, not with judgment. Humanity has alienated itself from God, has written its own judgment, but God comes to us with mercy by his own decision. We often begin our prayers, "Merciful God . . ."

Paul here quotes God's word to Moses, his response to Moses's daring request (Exod. 33:18-23). Emboldened by his fantastic privilege of talking with God face-to-face, Moses dares to request, "Show me your glory, I pray." In response, the divine act was to have Moses stand in the cleft of the rock as God walked by. Moses could see God's glory, but he could not look on God's face. God said to Moses that it was God's divine decision to be merciful. Great in faith as Moses was, God revealed himself to Moses by God's own mercy.

We see here how Moses was made aware of God's grace. God had called him at the burning bush, used him before Pharaoh, and manifested his power through him for Israel's deliverance in the exodus —all because of God's mercy. In reviewing Moses's prayers for Israel, his acts as intercessor, we see his understanding of the mercy of God.

But we have a more complete revelation in Christ, as John writes, "The law indeed was given through Moses; grace and truth came through Jesus Christ" (John 1:17). As forgiven sinners, we stand only in his mercy. We have not deserved his grace, but we respond to his claim by giving ourselves to him as disciples, persons who will walk with him in life.

We worship you, Father, Son, and Spirit,
Redeemer, who gave yourself for us all;
Heavenly Father, who welcomes us into your family,
King of kings, who calls us into your kingdom,
Lord of lords, to whom we give our allegiance,
Thank you for grace, mercy that forgives and accepts,
and for the grace that makes us your own.

August 12

But on God's Mercy

So it depends not on human will or exertion, but on God who shows mercy.
Romans 9:16

This remarkable statement opens the door for each of us, for anyone to come to God. Our salvation is not dependent upon our heritage, on being a part of historic Israel. It is upon our total and utter dependence upon the mercy of God. He will have mercy upon whomever he wills.

This chapter, the first of this section of three, deals with God's acts and his manner of reconciliation. God has moved into history to win humanity to himself. God has come to us, and as Paul is showing here, although we were not a part of the Jewish community, God in mercy calls us as Gentiles. His plan was to use Israel to introduce the larger world to himself, not to select Israel as the end in his plan. While Gentiles did not desire or seek God, the divine plan did not await such desire. God moved to us when we were yet enemies, moved to us because of who he is, because of his mercy.

And now that he has moved, it is our move next. Confronted by such mercy, we can do nothing more intelligent than to respond to him. We were enemies, but grace has overcome our rebellion and transformed us into children of God. This is our unique joy.

> *There is a therapy in grace:*
> *no one can enter covenant with God*
> *and not be changed in this covenant.*
> *Grace is acceptance into fellowship,*
> *and fellowship with God is transforming.*
> *Grace is free, but it is not cheap;*
> *for grace cost God in the cross.*
> *Paul has written that we share his cross*
> *by our identification with Christ.*
> *There is therapy in grace, our healing.*

August 13

That My Name May Be Proclaimed

For the scripture says to Pharaoh, "I have raised you up for the very purpose of showing my power in you, so that my name may be proclaimed in all the earth." Romans 9:17

God is sovereign over all the earth. He is not limited to work only among those who seek him. He acts among and even through unbelievers to confront all with the realities of his kingdom. God's purpose is for all the earth to know and respond to him. His purpose is not prevented by those who oppose him; it is only cause for a detour as he takes another path to achieve his goal.

The children of Israel were delivered from Egypt by God's mighty acts, but not so abruptly that they would miss the lessons of the confrontation between Yahweh and a Pharaoh who claimed to be divine. God confronted Pharaoh on his own terms, meeting his claims and making clear who is divine, who is actually God. The miracles through the hand of Moses exposed one false deity after another. That the interaction led to further hardening of Pharaoh's heart is a process that happens to any person who rejects the truth. Paul's quotation is that God placed Pharaoh in power, and that could be any Pharaoh, but in exposing him as a mere sinful man, the majesty of God is seen.

The confrontation with Pharaoh is spoken of as a message to all the earth. This comes not through the Jewish group in defense of their religion, but by interaction with Pharaoh as a word to the world. Understanding God's confrontation with tribal gods, by victories by his people, is to be regarded in this manner also. God now makes known who he is as sovereign Lord, not through military victories elevating one nation over another, but by calling all alike to come to God through his gospel. God has no favorites.

Our vision is to be for the world,
God's mission encompasses all peoples.
And God has no racial preferences;
no ethnic group is to be bypassed.
God is no respecter of persons;
he welcomes all on the same ground,
his unfailing love and grace.

August 14

God Has Mercy on Whomever He Chooses

So then he has mercy on whomever he chooses, and he hardens the heart of whomever he chooses. Romans 9:18

We tend, consciously or unconsciously, to think in terms of class or heritage. The Jews, to whom Paul was speaking, were overconfident in their heritage as granting them special status with God. Paul shows from their own history evidence of God's choices and actions, that his expressions of mercy are based on his own will to be merciful and in no way on human merit. Open hearts, whoever they may be, are invited to come to God, for he expresses his mercy because of who he is and in his own freedom.

The story of the Syrophoenician woman who came to Jesus for mercy is a good illustration. Jesus had been speaking with the Jewish leaders, who thought they were guardians of God's favors. The woman's request for mercy for her daughter, being a Gentile, provided a setting for illustrating his marvelous grace. In turning down her request at first, he was making application of the Jews' patterns of behavior toward Gentiles. This was so inconsistent with the character of Jesus that it makes the story a clear illustration. Jesus replied: "It is not fair to take the children's food and throw it to dogs." The woman comes back with an amazing response: "Sir, even the dogs under the table eat the children's crumbs" (Mark 7:27-28). Jesus responded in kind, with mercy, and commended her faith as being far beyond that of many in Israel. Here the heart of God is shown, the God who has mercy where he wills to have mercy.

But there is a caution in today's text, for God also hardens the heart of whomever he chooses. That is, in being presumptuous toward God, assuming special favors, God has no choice but to say no to such, for they thus pervert the message of mercy by implying that it is not for all peoples. He will harden whomever he chooses, even though they may have the heritage of a great people, a great faith, or a great denominational history.

God is not capricious.
His work is not to be construed
as having favorites but as Favor.
His free offer of covenant is covenant,
asking response from us.
We are only saved as we want to be saved.

August 15

Why Does God Still Hold Us Accountable?

You will say to me then, "Why then does he still find fault? For who can resist his will?" Romans 9:19

The question in our text is that of the more shallow mind: "If God is sovereign, then what will be will be." This means that the questioner has moved immediately to a determinism that escapes personal responsibility. That is to say, if God so chooses, why am I to be blamed for things that are decided for me?

Such an approach is presumptuous. It is God of whom we are speaking, and sovereignty is one of his attributes consistently related to the attributes of his holiness and of his mercy. Understood in this way, sovereignty is God's self-determination, his security, his function from himself, from his holiness and love, not from his reaction to us, or what we may have done. In this sense, the greater expression of his sovereignty is his patience with us. This very sovereignty actually provides us with freedom to be ourselves, for he will not violate our personalities.

We are responsible for the decisions we make by his gift of freedom. We are accountable to God for what we decide and do in our life experiences. We cannot claim our lot to be the way God has shaped us. We are responsible for our decisions.

Again, all alike are sinners, though we are not all sinners alike. Yet it is futile to grade levels of sin when the issue is our direction, not levels. The prophet says that we know that direction, we know whether our face or back is toward God. The question is not so much what we have done; it is rather, Do we want God in our lives? Our choice is one of relationship; it is letting God be our God, taking our place as his servants.

Walking with God, we are forever different,
persons who share his love and mercy
and who walk in the light of his Word.

August 16

Who Are You to Talk Back to God?

**But who indeed are you, a human being, to argue with God? Will what is molded say to the one who molds it, "Why have you made me like this?"
Romans 9:20**

Recognition of the sovereignty of God means to recognize at the same time our role as his servants. If God is sovereign, there can only be one Sovereign. It is for us to acknowledge this, not only intellectually but as a working relationship. We confess him as Lord and conduct ourselves as his servants. Service is a spirit of life that lets us go anywhere in the world and serve. In surrendering to God we also surrender any attempt to be in control in human relationships. We will treat others as we would like to be treated.

Paul is asking how we can dare to talk back to God or question his action. He is the Creator, not only in the sense of first cause, but in the sense of purpose.

I recall flying to Chicago to meet with some church leaders. We would design an Anabaptist Roundtable to interpret and project our faith into the future. As the chairperson, I opened the meeting by emphasizing that the kingdom is the Lord's and whatever we do must be in his will, must be by his Word, and must be in his purpose. We do not envy or compete with others in their roles, but we ask God how we can best serve him in the role to which he has called us. We do not question why God placed us in a particular family, race, nation, or stream of life, but rather we seek to do his will in our context. We enjoy the privilege of walking in this day with him.

*Our human tendency is to ask "Why?"
But there are many such questions
for which we will receive no answer.
The question may better be "What?"
That is, "What can I get out of this?
Or, "What can honor God in this?"
Circumstances are not to control us;
we are rather to rise above them,
or rise through them, by reaching up,
by seeking above all the glory of God.*

August 17

The Potter Controls the Clay

Has the potter no right over the clay, to make out of the same lump one object for special use and another for ordinary use? Romans 9:21

My wife is an artist, sculptor, potter, and painter. When Esther works on the wheel to throw a pot, she decides what she will make of the clay. From the same clay she may choose to make a vase, a bowl, a cup, or a plate. The potter determines what she will produce. God is the potter at work in creating us.

A parable is used to communicate one point. We do not seek to express some truth from each supportive characteristic of an illustration, story, or parable. We do not draw a secondary point from the clay as having no mind or response to the potter, for we as humans do have minds and wills. The clay must be pliable, suggesting yieldedness. The point is that the potter decides what she will produce.

As we look at our different gifts and aptitudes, we recognize that God has made us each with particular endowments. One may be gifted to sing, another not, but the gift should be received with gratitude to the giver. Jeremiah records a story of God as potter:

> *"Come, go down to the potter's house,*
> *and there I will let you hear my words."*
> *So I went down to the potter's house, and there he was working at his wheel.*
> *The vessel he was making of clay was spoiled in the potter's hand,*
> *and he reworked it into another vessel, as seemed good to him.*
>
> > *Then the word of the LORD came to me:*
> *Can I not do with you, O house of Israel,*
> *just as this potter has done? says the LORD.*
> *Just like the clay in the potter's hand,*
> *so are you in my hand, O house of Israel.*
> *At one moment I may declare concerning a nation or a kingdom,*
> *that I will pluck up and break down and destroy it,*
> *but if that nation, concerning which I have spoken,*
> *turns from its evil, I will change my mind about the*
> *disaster that I intended to bring on it. (18:2-8)*

August 18

God Endures with Patience

What if God, desiring to show his wrath and to make known his power, has endured with much patience the objects of wrath that are made for destruction? Romans 9:22

In this verse we are struck with the paradox between wrath and patience. Yet we must recognize that wrath is not the opposite of love, for the opposite of love is indifference. God's wrath and love are two sides of the same coin. Wrath exposes and rejects evil, but is balanced by a love that will not coerce or violate another's freedom.

One of the great expressions of God's sovereign self-determination is his patience. God does not manipulate us; he does not violate our personalities. Being sovereign, that is being fully self-determined, he is patient toward us. Patience is the extension of love that respects another; it is counting the person as more important than the misdemeanor.

In God's creation, as with the potter, many objects may be created for various purposes, and in his patience he respects each. Some will be the occasion of making obvious God's wrath of rejecting misdemeanors, and others will be the focus of his love expression. This is to say that God is to be known as a whole being, with love and wrath. These two are not so far apart, for both evidence the depth of God's caring. Wrath is God's love respecting humanity's freedom to say no to him without his approving it. Love is authentic in exposing the full nature of the offense and the depth of God's rejection of that which violates love, but is expressed in the face of evil as grace.

We share his love—his strong love, his just love—that exposes and condemns the unholy even while he reconciles. This is the amazing wonder of the cross, for here God in Christ exposed the depth of human sin in his being crucified by us, while at the same time speaking back the word of forgiveness as an expression of his reconciling love.

I have felt his wrath, the condemnation of my sin,
and I have been embarrassed, and led to repentance.
Through this experience of his wrath, he has led me
to share his love, to experience his forgiveness,
and to know and enjoy his fellowship.

August 19

Prepared in Advance for Glory

And what if he has done so in order to make known the riches of his glory for the objects of mercy, which he has prepared beforehand for glory? Romans 9:23

Only in his gracious love can I come and stand before him, forgiven, accepted, changed, renewed, transformed, and empowered by him. All of this is to make known the riches of his glory, the magnificent, unfathomable glory of acting by his own holiness and marvelous grace that transforms our lives.

Paul's reference "which he has prepared beforehand for glory" makes clear that we are not an afterthought. God foreknew his church, his people, and he is including us as he calls us into the body of Christ. God is not one who is difficult to approach, but one who has moved to us in Christ and has opened the way for us to engage him in our lives.

I have enjoyed a rich life. I have had mistakes and sins, yes, but God has forgiven me and has granted me wonderful privileges in his service, and I celebrate his grace. Esther and I have been blessed so richly by God; our prayer has been to find his victory in adjustments. Our confidence is that he will fulfill his purpose in our lives, in our family of three wonderful children, our grandchildren, and those with whom we have been privileged to minister.

Heavenly Father,
forgive us for being self-centered,
for failing to glorify you,
and reducing you in our thought to be
an extension of ourselves.

Heavenly Father,
we depend on you;
we only live through you;
we reach out to you by faith,
and ask you to be yourself in us. Amen

August 20

Including Us!

Including us whom he has called, not from the Jews only but also from the Gentiles? Romans 9:24

The gospel is the one universal message for faith. It is for all peoples, not just for the people of Israel. This is Paul's argument in this chapter. He is showing God's intention through Israel to bring his word to the world, to Gentiles as well as Jews.

The little phrase "including us," is an answer to any tendency to spiritual pride. None of us is deserving of God's salvation, but in his mercy he has called even me. The experience of his grace is personal, but it is never private.

Paul was a Jew, and yet his identification with the people of God was his primary relationship rather than his ethnic Jewishness. This led him to identify with the Gentiles, and he does so in the words "including us" as identifying with those not of Jewish background. We also need to identify with people across racial and cultural differences.

God's purpose is that all the world may know and have the option of faith. In Christ there is neither Jew nor Greek (Gal. 3:28). There is no Christian culture as such. We are part of a global fellowship called the body of Christ. This network of disciples is international, transracial and transcultural. We must reject a civil religion and avoid the nationalization of the Christian church while we live as good citizens.

Wherever we go in the world, it is especially rewarding to find a fellowship of faith in which people express the same joy in Christ. This is empirical evidence that the risen Christ meets people wherever they are and at different levels of perception. He has met me in his love, and I celebrate this, especially today, which is my birthday.

Lord, thank you for including me in your plan.
Thank you for life and your amazing grace. Amen

I Will Call Them My People

As indeed he says in Hosea, "Those who were not my people I will call 'my people,' and her who was not beloved I will call 'beloved.'" Romans 9:25

Paul's quotation is to show that the exclusiveness of Israel was not consistent with their own prophetic witness. God expressed himself as a God of grace in the amazing story of Hosea. After his wife left him to live in sin, God asked Hosea to take back his erring wife in forgiving grace (Hos. 3). This should have been understood by the people of Israel.

While there is little clear teaching in the Old Testament on world mission, there are references that God has always wanted the world to know of him. He purposes that the nations will come to the light of his glory and that people of other tongues shall hear and speak the gospel of faith.

I read in *Progressive Vision* several years ago that the leading rabbi of Washington, DC, stated, "We Jewish people are thankful that you Christians have taken our values and evangelized them around the world, something we could not do as we are communities of law. . . . The main difference between us is that you believe that Jesus is the Messiah and we don't. . . . We'll see when Messiah comes." The issue Paul is raising of faith in God through Jesus Christ is still with us.

Many Christians need to read this passage as an answer to idolizing denominationalism. Although a denominational heritage is valid as an example of how the Spirit has met a given people at a given time, we do not idolize a denomination. We must always move beyond symbols to meaning.

Jesus said, "Other sheep I have, which are not of this fold: them also I must bring" (John 10:16, KJV). In further confirmation of his mission, Jesus gave the great commission: "Go therefore and make disciples of all nations" (Matt. 28:19). Today's verse tells us of God's marvelous grace to accept people who come in faith, any people, of any culture or race. John 3:16 affirms that "whosoever believeth" may "have everlasting life" (KJV). Christ died for all. Julia H. Johnson expressed God's "infinite grace" in verse:

> *Marvelous grace of our loving Lord,*
> *Grace that exceeds our sin and our guilt.*

Called Children of the Living God

**And in the very place where it was said to them, "You are not my people,"
there they shall be called children of the living God. Romans 9:26**

The greatest privilege thinkable is that of being a child of God. "See what love the Father has given us, that we should be called children of God; and that is what we are" (1 John 3:1). Being born into God's family, we enjoy full privileges as family members and express our belonging with "Abba, Father."

Paul's primary point is that we Gentiles, those not in the heritage of God's special mission with Israel, are now by grace "children of the living God." The purpose of divine revelation was that the world may learn of Jahweh through his people, Israel. As shown in the book of Jonah, this truth was lost to Israel, yet God sent Jonah to Nineveh even though Israel had come to think of themselves as exclusively the people of God.

I have been impressed with the story of Apollos (Acts 18:24–19:7), a man whose education and eloquence needed to be perfected by the full word of God. This is important for all of us who as professionals have considerable knowledge in a particular field. One function of God's law is to kill our self-sufficiency so that the Spirit may give us life (2 Cor. 3).

As children of God our greatest joy
is to reflect the image of our Father.
Our highest wish is to be like him,
to have our character conformed to him.
Our greater purpose is to bring him glory
and in all of life to honor him.
Our sincerest thanks is that he has called us,
when not his children, to become his.
Our deepest worship is to respond to him,
to be shaped into his likeness.
Our prayer is that we may know him better
and follow him faithfully in life.
Lord, minister within us by your Spirit
and empower us to do your will.

August 23

Only the Remnant Will Be Saved

And Isaiah cries out concerning Israel, "Though the number of the children of Israel were like the sand of the sea, only a remnant of them will be saved."
Romans 9:27

This quotation from Isaiah may be the more searching in Paul's argument. If there is only a remnant to be saved, where does that put me? How is it that I am one of the elect? Paul is clear that being God's people is by faith in Christ, not by ethnic claims.

The concept of "remnant" is not so much to emphasize a small number as it is to emphasize the uniqueness of God's true community within the larger ethnic or social community. Isaiah saw hosts of descendants of Israel, but cried out against presumption, declaring that only the remnant who are chosen in faith are truly a people of God.

Paul's argument opens the door for Gentile and Jew alike to make up the people of God. To be a part of God's called ones, God's remnant, is the wonder of his grace. When Jesus said, "For many are called, but few are chosen" (Matt. 22:14), he was saying that many hear the word of invitation, but only those who come are seated with the bridegroom. Petrus Herbert wrote:

> *Faith is a living power from heaven,*
> *Which grasps the promise God has giv'n.*
> *Securely fixed on Christ alone,*
> *A trust that cannot be o'er thrown.*
>
> *Faith to the conscience whispers peace;*
> *And bids the mourner's sighing cease;*
> *By faith the children's right we claim,*
> *And call upon our Father's name.*

August 24

The Lord Is in Charge

For the Lord will execute his sentence on the earth quickly and decisively.
Romans 9:28

The Lord's sentence, his judgment, is the fulfillment of his Word, the expression of his holiness and integrity in dealing justly. This justice includes mercy, for justice works to correct the problem. But when humanity refuses to respond to the mercy that changes us, the only response justice has is to pass sentence according to our decision.

Paul's statement is a declaration that God will act in accord with his word. God is not capricious; this means that he is consistent with himself; we can extend our understanding of his past actions as projections for the future. Our prophetic utterance is the pronouncement that God acts consistently with what we read in Scripture. When we respond in faith, his action reconciles; but where persons respond in nonfaith, God judges to condemn the unbelief. This is God's judgment even now on the earth.

I would rather be judged by God than by any other. God is fair. He is consistent with himself, that is, with his Word, and we can know what is expected. God is just and knows the intent of the heart. We will in no way achieve perfection, but God expects us to respond in a spirit that honors him. As Abraham rhetorically asked, "Shall not the Judge of all the earth do what is just?" (Gen. 18:25). This is our security.

None of us should presume on God. With David we should pray, "Keep back thy servant also from presumptuous sins" (Ps. 19:13, KJV). We honor God by recognizing him for who he is, a God of grace, and then by responding to him. This we can each do today.

> *"In wrath remember mercy." This is our prayer.*
> *None of us can avoid the exposure,*
> *but in being exposed we appeal to grace.*
> *God's wrath is unavoidable as judgment,*
> *but we can repent of that which he judges.*
> *One need not live in dread of God's wrath*
> *when we know the power of his love;*
> *for there is no fear of judgment, as*
> *"perfect love casts out fear" (1 John 4:18).*

August 25

Unless the Lord

And as Isaiah predicted, "If the Lord of hosts had not left survivors to us, we would have fared like Sodom and been made like Gomorrah." Romans 9:29

Unless the Lord of Sabbaoth (hosts) had left a remnant, we, Israel, would have been destroyed like Sodom. This is not pessimism as much as realism, the recognition that with all of Israel's sin, it is only of God's mercy that a remnant remains. In our sins it is God's mercy that continues his work with us and in us. Ezekiel also describes unbelieving Judah, as like her "sister Sodom," showing the sinfulness of Israel (Ezek. 16).

We recall God's word to Moses in the face of Israel's rebellion: "Let me alone that I may destroy them. . . . I will make of you a nation mightier and more numerous than they" (Deut. 9:14). Moses's response was to appeal to God's mercy and the glory of his name before the nations. In his mercy, God spared Israel. Now, in the argument here in Romans 9, Paul is showing that in reconciliation to God, the key is not who Israel is but who God is! The key is God's pardoning grace, extended to whomsoever he will. It is not only a wonder that Gentiles are included; it also is a wonder that people of Israel can be included in their rejection of the purpose of God.

In the fall of 1987, Esther and I flew to Maui, Hawaii, on the first leg of a four-month trip, including New Zealand, Australia, Japan, China, Hong Kong, Thailand, and India. En route we shared many seminars and then taught a semester at Union Biblical Seminary in Pune, India. It has been our privilege through the years to share the gospel in many countries, contextualizing in various contexts. God cares equally for all peoples.

History is God's story, telling us what happens
when we hear God and respond to him,
or when we hear God and disregard him.
Our salvation is not in what we do,
but it is in what God does in us;
for it is God who calls us to himself,
who forgives and accepts us in his love,
owning us as his children and sharing his life.

Righteousness Through Faith

What then are we to say? Gentiles, who did not strive for righteousness, have attained it, that is, righteousness through faith. Romans 9:30

I recall with pleasure spending four days in balmy Maui, one of the beautiful Hawaiian islands. Friends of ours from Indiana granted us the use of their condo. We drove into Lahaina and saw some of the historical sites, the old whaling port, the churches, and the large banyan tree planted by the missionaries to celebrate fifty years of their work. We were told of the conflict in the 1800s between the whalers and missionaries. The whalers turned the town into a place of drinking and revelry, and didn't want the gospel preached because it changed the lives of the people they were misusing.

Paul speaks of a "righteousness through faith." Gentiles actually came to share a right relation with God simply by faith and not out of a long history of knowing God's law. In contrast, the Jews knew of this righteousness and yet failed to come to God in their obsession with the law. Righteousness is not a legalism, it is a relationship. This consciousness can bring us to God in faith. In this we are reaching beyond the commandment to meet the one to whom the commandment points. With Paul we marvel that often those without a heritage of knowing God may reach honestly for God.

How do we come by faith into righteousness?
By hearing his Word,
by answering the call of his Spirit,
and joining in covenant with Christ.
This means joining in solidarity with Christ,
in a response righteousness,
walking daily with him,
affirming our discipleship with integrity,
opening ourselves to his Spirit, and
living by the guidance of his Word.

August 27

But Israel Did Not Succeed

But Israel, who did strive for the righteousness that is based on the law, did not succeed in fulfilling that law. Romans 9:31

We have emphasized that righteousness means right relatedness with God. The question has inevitably followed, "How does one come to this relationship authentically?" Our text says that Israel tried to do so by fulfilling the law, but failed in the attempt. Paul's argument here, is that there is actually something greater, and that is faith. This faith, Paul wrote the Philippians, is not of oneself, but is a response to God as he expressed himself in Christ. God has opened himself to us, reconciling us in love.

Our verse today refers to the Jews who live by works and not by faith. It is not the law that is incorrect, but the assumption of our ability to fulfill the law. Paul says that Israel pursued a righteousness based on the law and failed to follow God. God did not give the law for us to worship it, but that we would worship him. He is the sovereign Lord, choosing to dwell among his people.

To a young Jew, Jesus said, "Keep the commandments," and as a further word he quoted the last six to him. When the youth said honestly, "What lack I yet?" (Matt. 19:20, KJV), Jesus in essence reinterpreted the first commandment to say, "All of life is to begin with God."

"Purity of heart," said Søren Kierkegaard,
"is to will one thing"—the will of God.
God first identified with Israel,
then he gave Israel his law.
"I am the LORD your God, who
brought you out of the land of Egypt" (Exod. 20:2).
God then gave to Israel his commandments.
God first identifies with us, and
in turn he expects us to first identify with him.
To commit oneself to Christ is this identity;
it is to say, "Jesus is my Lord,"
and in this covenant of faith we live,
walking with him as disciples.

Stumbling over the Stumbling Stone

Why not? Because they did not strive for it on the basis of faith, but as if it were based on works. They have stumbled over the stumbling stone. Romans 9:32

At the core of a healthy personality is a marvelous self-esteem. In Abraham Maslow's hierarchy of personal attributes, he places self-actualization at the top. Beginning first with physiological needs, he speaks of safety and security, then he moves to love and affection, then to esteem, and then self-actualization. But this esteem is readily perverted into pride. Rather than actualizing the *imago Dei*, it expresses arrogance and independence.

The answer to this perversion is found in being reconciled to God. The stumbling stone in today's verse is to make us aware of our own limitation. Stumbling over it means that we fail to see our limitation and our need of faith. In a restoration with God, we can actualize a new relationship, a new character of godliness. This godliness is modeled in Jesus, the true expression of genuine humanness. The more godly we are, the more we are like Jesus.

When we attempt righteousness by our own performance rather than by our partnership with God, we fail. When in pride we avoid the partnership of faith, we sever the very relationship which is itself righteousness. Christ, the righteousness of God to us, confronts us with the open hand of grace; but for those set on their own achievement, he is a stumbling stone. He causes us to stumble that in our plight we might trust in him. We pray with the words of this old hymn by Richard Redhead, based on Psalm 51:

God, be merciful to me,
On Thy grace I rest my plea;
Plenteous in compassion Thou,
Blot out my transgressions now;
Wash me, make me pure within,
Cleanse, O cleanse me from my sin.

Gracious God, my heart renew,
Make my spirit right and true;
Cast me not away from Thee,
Let Thy Spirit dwell in me;
Thy salvation's joy impart,
Steadfast make my willing heart.

The One Who Trusts in Him

As it is written, "See, I am laying in Zion a stone that will make people stumble, a rock that will make them fall, and whoever believes in him will not be put to shame." Romans 9:33

The stumbling stone is a person; "whoever believes in him," in the man Christ Jesus. Paul, in his identification, moves from the descriptive language of a stone, to the designation of *him* as the object of stumbling. Significantly, as we check the source of his statement in Isaiah 8:13-15, it is the Lord who is the rock of stumbling. This is to say that Israel stumbled over the very privilege that was theirs, over the one to whom the law pointed, over the knowledge of the Holy One.

Idolatry is the tendency of putting our god into a form that we desire, into a box. Then we seek to manipulate him for purposes that we make to be ultimate in our lives. A mere "success gospel" does this; selfish prayers do this. With this perception of God, we can no longer submit ourselves to the authentic God of the Scriptures. We have, instead, a simple god that we can use. We have a prosperity god, a humanistic god, or a nationalistic god of civil religion, and we stumble when the God of the Scriptures known in Jesus Christ confronts us: a God of peace, justice, equity, and self-giving love.

Esther and I visited Kona, the Big Island in the Hawaiian chain, where we shared in lectures with Youth With A Mission (YWAM) in their training school at Pacific Asian Christian University. Friends at the school, Paul and Bertha Swarr, having returned from thirty years of mission service in Israel, took us on a tour of the island. We enjoyed viewing the volcanic crater, the rain forest vegetation, waterfalls, and the impressive ranches. We marveled at the greatness of our creator God and his goodness. This was worship in the context of nature. But beyond nature, his special word in Scripture and above all in Jesus Christ is his word of grace. The blind hymn writer, Fanny Crosby, expressed this well:

> *Blessed assurance, Jesus is mine!*
> *O what a foretaste of glory divine!*
> *Heir of salvation, purchased of God,*
> *Born of His Spirit, washed in His blood.*

August 30

That They Might Be Saved

Brothers and sisters, my heart's desire and prayer to God for them is that they may be saved. Romans 10:1

This text convicts us all. As we meet peoples in the world, the uppermost concern should be of our interest in the spiritual wholeness of all people. As Paul looked at his fellow Israelites, his highest concern was that they might be saved and enjoy fellowship in the kingdom of Christ. His magnanimous expression at the beginning of the previous chapter lets us know that the earlier word was not a passing burst of emotion. Paul lived to see people brought from estrangement into fellowship through Jesus.

The word *saved* is something of an affront to people quite sure that they are not lost. For those who make of religion a moral, or ethnic, or doctrinal identification, to speak of being lost is so out of sync that it seems irrelevant. But the biblical perspective is the lost state of human estrangement from God; being saved is to be reconciled to God.

Salvation is not simply to avoid hell, but to know God. It is not having a religion that we hold, but in being open to God who holds us. Anything other than this openness is an affront to God, an expression of human pride maximizing one's own achievement. This is a serious affront; not everyone can achieve the same level, and yet God loves us all alike. God meets humanity on other terms than our achievement, so that he is fair to each. God has planned salvation by faith. In this way all persons are on the same ground regardless of privilege and knowledge. *The Mennonite Hymnal* prayer (742) expresses God meeting persons at their level of understanding, hence building the kingdom:

> *Lord Jesus, when You have drawn all men to Yourself,*
> *there will be peace on earth.*
> *When we try to get things for ourselves, . . .*
> *we fight and push, and are angry and cruel,*
> *and everything is made less happy than it was meant to be,*
> *and Your kingdom does not come.*
> *So give us Your Spirit,*
> *to make us people who build Your kingdom,*
> *not people who pull it down. Amen*

August 31

A Zeal That Is Not Enlightened

I can testify that they have a zeal for God, but it is not enlightened.
Romans 10:2

God has given me the privilege of participating in preaching missions on each continent except Antarctica. I have witnessed many forms of religion and the zeal with which the adherents carry out their religious rites. With Paul, I feel that they have a zeal for God, but it is not based on knowledge. In many religions in the world, people reach their groping hands, seeking to find God; but the gospel announces that God has reached down to lay hold on us. This is the gospel which says, "[The] truth is in Jesus" (Eph. 4:21). Searching in other sources is now over. God is fair to us; he has not left us in darkness. Jesus came and said, "I am the way, and the truth, and the life. No one comes to the Father except through me" (John 14:6).

When we dialogue with the adherents of another religion, our approach should not be to negate the values they have, not to do a put-down, but, rather, to show them what Jesus has to offer that is far greater. He came to share the more complete understanding of God, as well as to reconcile us to God in his love.

This revelation is essential for our perception and for the consequent experience of faith. As in any field of knowledge, we couldn't even ask the right questions if we didn't first have some understanding, some answers. Similarly, we couldn't ask intelligent questions about God if God had not already given us some answers, his Word.

Sharing with Youth With A Mission in pastoral training, we discussed the call to contextualize the gospel without falling prey to a synergism that alters the true message. The gospel is the good news that God is reaching to us. All persons can open themselves to him when they understand that salvation is not in religion but in openness to God himself. God has made himself known in history and fully in Christ. Jesus can be presented in any culture when we avoid identifying him with our own culture. Jesus was not a Westerner; he was Semitic and has become a transforming influence in any culture. Contextualization is a philosophy of missions in which we Westerners need to share.

Lord, give me a zeal for you
and a willingness to share your gospel in all contexts
and with true knowledge. Amen

September 1

Seeking to Establish Their Own

For, being ignorant of the righteousness that comes from God, and seeking to establish their own, they have not submitted to God's righteousness. Romans 10:3

Human nature in its pride wants to achieve its own destiny. Our focus is beyond ourselves, a right relationship with God. Righteousness of God means that he deals justly with all peoples, expressing an equity for both the privileged and unprivileged to come to him. This reconciliation is "the righteousness that comes from God," his gracious acceptance that reconciles any and all who will respond in faith.

When persons refuse this offer of grace and seek to establish their own righteousness with God, they sin against God's grace. This perverts the message of God's righteousness and closes the door to reconciliation with God, both for themselves and for others who would learn from them of God's reconciliation. Human pride leads to a legalism that would boast of our achievements. This legalism fails to be evangelistic; it fails to magnify God's grace and thereby gives the sinful person occasion for despair and hopelessness. But into this despair comes the good news of God's grace, that we can become children of God through Jesus Christ, which is the basic theme of this epistle.

In these three chapters (9–11), Paul shows us how historically, redemptively, and doctrinally we share reconciliation with God. In chapter 9 he stresses God's call in salvation history, in chapter 10 he is stressing God's action in Christ for our reconciliation, and in chapter 11 he will show God's sovereign purpose in election. Both Jew and Gentile share God's electing call that through faith we now form one new body.

This same truth is expressed in Paul's letter to the Ephesians: "For he is our peace; in his flesh he has made both groups into one and has broken down the dividing wall, that is, the hostility between us. He has abolished the law . . . that he might create in himself one new humanity in place of the two, thus making peace" (2:14-16). Lesslie Newbigin, having served over forty years in India, said that he often saw a picture in Indian homes of three figures—Buddha, Gandhi, and Jesus—as though all three were to be revered equally. He said that this is wrong, that Jesus stands in a revelatory class as the Christ of God, to which these persons could only point. Jesus is our Savior, our Redeemer, and our Peace.

Lord, thank you for your revelation
and peace through your Son, Jesus Christ. Amen

September 2

Christy Is the End

For Christ is the end of the law so that there may be righteousness for everyone who believes. Romans 10:4

"Christ is the end of the law for righteousness" is the better translation, not just the end of the law. The law still functions as always to show us that we need righteousness. Where humanity once trusted the law to mediate righteousness with God, we now trust Christ to be our mediator. Where once Israel trusted their religious system to mediate between them and God, now Paul says they and we are to trust Christ as the one mediator. As such, he is the end of the role of the law to mediate righteousness.

If Christ is the end of the law's pursuit of righteousness, then he is the end of everything else that claims a mediating role. The law stands as the highest level of God-consciousness, of the claims of God upon our lives, and of our accountability to God. If Christ brings to an end the role of the law as mediator, he has also brought to an end the role of any lesser religious rite as a mediator. If we interpret *end* as the completion of the meaning of the law, then he is the completion of everything to which religions point.

If Christ is the end of the law for righteousness, he is then the answer for everything else for righteousness. In fulfilling all that the law pointed to, Christ has actualized the divine-human relationship. There is no expression of the righteousness of God that comes anywhere near the sublime expression in Christ. He is the answer to all other honest quests for God. With Paul, we say, "[The God] therefore ye ignorantly worship, him declare I unto you" in Christ (Acts 17:23, KJV). He is the one mediator for everyone who believes.

Esther and I were in meetings with the Cuna Indians on one of the tiny San Blas Islands off the coast of Panama. We enjoyed the time with them, a radically different culture. In the morning at about 4:30 a.m. the men left to fish and were back about 9:00 a.m., finished for the day. Young women took canoes, went to the mainland and up the river to fill their jugs with fresh water; that was their day's work. We met with the people for worship. Observing an American couple walking around the village, I invited them to the meeting. He declined. As we talked, I learned that he was an anthropologist from an American university studying these people. To my questions concerning what he was finding, he responded, "These people are in real trouble." I asked him, "What is that?" He answered, "Unemployment." What a perspective! He was seeing only material things and missed the simple joy in their lives.

Lord, we thank you for the end of the law for righteousness through Christ. Amen

Moses Wrote to Live by Them

**Moses writes concerning the righteousness that comes from the law, that
"the person who does these things will live by them." Romans 10:5**

If we claim that our achievement is by our keeping God's standards, we are accountable to a kind of righteousness, that, in its highest form, is impossible. When our righteousness is limited to what we can do, it is woefully inadequate. Isaiah says that "our righteous deeds are like a filthy cloth" (Isa. 64:6). When we offer to God our attempts at righting the broken relation with him on our own terms, our attempts are an insult to the grace that has reached out to accept us. The prodigal son returned to find, what Helmut Thielike, the great evangelical preacher of Germany, has called "The Waiting Father."

Paul's quote from Moses is to say that the divinely given law is to be followed. It is the divine imperative because it is God's law, but not if it is seen only as law. It must be seen as the divine will which focuses our response. Beyond the law is God himself, and we as sinners are in need of forgiveness and reconciliation with him. This is God's acceptance, rather than our seeking to be adequate by an obedience of his law.

The quote from Moses used in today's verse shows the impossibility of righteousness by the law. Such right relatedness would mean that we live by the law, that we keep that law in practice to be righteous. This claim is even more limiting, for if one practices a degree of righteousness by the law, such righteousness goes only as high as the law. This is not creating a right relatedness with God himself.

Righteousness that is from God by faith does not have the form of law, but has the form of covenant with Christ. In his covenant of grace we have genuine freedom, as Jesus says:

> *Come unto me,*
> *all you that are weary*
> *and are carrying heavy burdens,*
> *and I will give you rest.*
> *Take my yoke upon you,*
> *and learn from me;*
> *for I am gentle and humble in heart,*
> *and you will find rest for your souls. (Matt. 11:28-29)*

The Righteousness That Comes from Faith

But the righteousness that comes from faith says, "Do not say in your heart, 'Who will ascend into heaven?'" (that is, to bring Christ down) "or 'Who will descend into the abyss?'" (that is, to bring Christ up from the dead). But what does it say? "The word is near you, on your lips and in your heart" (that is, the word of faith that we proclaim). Romans 10:6-8

Righteousness of faith is in our response to God. It is in no way by our initiative. God initiates. Faith is opening oneself to the word and presence of God, who has come to us in gracious acceptance. We do not place ourselves at the center as though we can achieve. God is not to be found and used by our initiative. God is central and primary. We do not discover God; we do not create his Christ, the Messiah who came to us.

Faith is a covenant response to God's self-disclosure in his word. Eugene Nida has said that in some languages of the world, when you think *faith*, you must think *obedience* and when you think *obedience* you must think *faith*. Faith is an attitude of openness to God, letting God be himself in our lives.

When visiting Auckland, New Zealand, we spent some delightful hours with John O. Rymer, dean of the cathedral, and his wife. They showed us through the building, interpreting the progress and careful work that has brought the cathedral to this stage. One high point was when they showed us all of the vestments that had been carefully handmade by an elderly sister who had spent many hours in this painstaking and beautiful work. Rymer said of her, "She is a simple woman whose faith is expressed in this remarkable service. Every day for seventeen years she has performed a daily service." This work, not of law, was a work of devotion.

Today's verses tell us that we are not in a quest to find the Messiah. God has sent the Messiah. This has been verified by the death of Christ on the cross as an in-your-face dynamic confrontation with evil, and by the resurrection of Christ in overcoming evil. Now, ascended into heaven and at God's right hand, Jesus is our mediator.

This faith is biblical, reasonable, and historical. With the Anglican Church, we, too, should affirm a threefold cord: Scripture, reason, and tradition.

Lord, you have come to me.
Help me to reach to you. Amen

September 5

If One Confesses

Because if you confess with your lips that Jesus is Lord and believe in your heart that God raised him from the dead, you will be saved. For one believes with the heart and so is justified, and one confesses with the mouth and so is saved. Romans 10:9-10

This text probably stands next to John 3:16 in familiarity and popularity. These verses constitute a most concise statement of the way of salvation. It is one of the most prominent in personal evangelism. What believer has not used this text in helping another come to faith? It stands with the Alpine peaks of Scripture in majesty and beauty. In no way do we see this verse left for some future period for Israel; it is now! This promise opens the way to salvation now, for whoever will believe and confess Jesus as Lord.

When Norman Vincent Peale retired from the board of the Presbyterian Ministers' Fund, he shared with us his remarkable conversion story. As a young pastor, one day his wife said, "Norman, let's go for a walk." They walked along the sidewalk to Central Park in New York City and sat together on a park bench when she said, "Norman, you are my husband, my pastor, and my theological adviser, but you don't really know Jesus. I'm going home, and I want you to sit here until you meet Jesus for yourself and are converted." Norman Peale sat there thinking. With all that he knew about Jesus, if his wife didn't see in him evidence of personal faith, he needed to make a commitment to Christ. Right there and then he did just that. Each of us must move beyond knowing *about* him only and open ourselves to him as our Savior and Lord.

In verse 9 we are called to make a confession of faith. To confess is to identify with. Paul calls us to confess Jesus Christ as Lord. In doing so we identify with him as sovereign and give up all other lords, beginning with the self. We find that, in being our Lord, Jesus is our Savior. As Lord he has priority over any other earthly lord. This is not a surface confession but a living covenant—our commitment to serve him.

It is with the heart, the center of inner direction, that we believe unto righteousness. Here we enter right relation with God in Christ.

> *We confess Christ as Lord*
> *and in this confession we have salvation;*
> *we are brought into freedom.*
> *What a glorious truth!*

Whoever Believes Will Never Be Put to Shame

**The scripture says, "No one who believes in him will be put to shame."
Romans 10:11**

In southern New Zealand on a boat cruise through the Milford Fiord, we saw the majestic, rugged mountains slope thousands of feet into the sea. They have been so for millions of years. Yet, when this world is gone, the Word of God will live on.

We are called to faith in God's Word, and the text says that whoever believes in him will never be embarrassed, never be let down. When we come before God, we will not find that we accepted his promise in vain. God has bound himself to his word; it has been said, "We have a 'know-so' salvation, not a 'hope-so' salvation."

When Martin Luther came to die, he was asked, "Is your faith good enough to die by?" He answered, "Yes, a thousand times, yes."

Jesus the Christ is my Savior,
not just in pointing the way,
but in mediating the relationship.
His amazing act of redemption
means that I belong to the Redeemer.
I am not just saved from something,
that is, my sins, my selfish spirit,
but I am saved to and for something;
saved for fellowship with him.
My salvation is through confessing
that Jesus is now my Lord,
that I am his servant,
and in this solidarity with him
I shall walk, worship, and serve.

September 7

Everyone Who Calls

For there is no distinction between Jew and Greek; the same Lord is Lord of all and is generous to all who call on him. For, "Everyone who calls on the name of the Lord shall be saved." Romans 10:12-13

God is no respecter of persons. His love is open to all alike. God used the Jewish people as the channel to communicate a revelation of himself. His intent was that the knowledge of him should come to all peoples. The prophet looked for a day in which "the earth will be full of the knowledge of the LORD as the waters cover the sea" (Isa. 11:9). Paul affirms, "Everyone who calls on the name of the Lord shall be saved."

The special note in the text, that there is no difference between Jew and Gentile, places all of us on one level. This should bring to an end any ethnic superiority complex. Paul's intent, however, is to offer special encouragement to the Gentiles. Note the phrase, "The same Lord is Lord of all." It is basic for faith among the Gentiles and basic to the Jews' correct understanding of God. This brings to an end the prayer of the Jewish Pharisee who would thank God every day that he was not born a Gentile, a slave, or a woman (Luke 18:9-14). To the Ephesians Paul writes, "There is one Lord, one faith, one baptism, one God and Father of all, who is above all and through all and in all" (4:5-6). Further, he tells us in this text that God richly blesses all who call upon him (Eph. 1:3-4; Ps. 145). This expresses the character of God but assures us our prayer for salvation will not go unanswered.

When Esther and I flew to Sydney, Australia, in 1987, we were welcomed warmly by pastor Foppi Brower. We were driven north to Fennell Bay, where we served in five days of evangelistic meetings. He oriented us for our visit, recounting God's blessing in the work his wife and he shared. Being from the Netherlands, he was praising God for grace that is the same for all peoples in all of the world, even in that diverse and very secular-minded country. This is the emphasis of our text for today.

> *Thank you Father,*
> *that your love is universal,*
> *that you would exclude no one,*
> *that grace is for all people,*
> *and we have the good news to share.*
> *Help us, Father, to do so. Amen*

How Can They Call If They Have Not Heard?

But how are they to call on one in whom they have not believed? And how are they to believe in one of whom they have never heard? And how are they to hear without someone to proclaim him? Romans 10:14

Good news is to be shared. That God has taken the initiative and moved to us in grace is a marvelous declaration of the gospel. The legalist offers good views; the herald of God offers good news. This is what drove Paul to travel across the Roman world to preach the gospel of Christ. As it says in Romans 1, so it is reflected in today's verse. Paul is a debtor to others until all have heard the gospel.

Oswald Smith expressed it, "No one has the right to hear the gospel twice until all the world has heard it once." In Australia we shared the gospel in a very secular society. Only 8 percent of the people have any association with the Christian church. But many people have hunger for the Word.

Paul's questions are rhetorical: the answer is implied and expected. The sequence concludes that someone must declare the gospel; as persons hear the word, many will come to faith in God. In my years of evangelistic preaching, I have found that if we can get people to listen to the gospel, many of them will come to Christ. Our problem in evangelism is in moving beyond the in-group to share with unbelievers on their own turf, to identify with them as much as possible so they can authentically hear the gospel.

When we moved into the inner city of Washington, DC, in 1981 to plant a church, we identified with ghetto people by simply saying, "We are here because we care." We identified with professional people by saying, "We're here to hold an evangelical faith and social responsibility together." With this approach God enabled us to reach both ways in our public witness, developing a community with considerable diversity, yet a very basic unity.

One dear woman who lived on the streets would come shuffling in each Sunday morning and sit beside Esther. Esther would help her button her sleeve cuffs or straighten her several hats and make her feel warm and loved. She always joined in our carry-in dinners, and the young people would have birthday parties for her. She came to love her Lord, because she heard the good news and felt our love.

O Lord, you have created a diverse world.
Help me to enjoy, appreciate, and learn from all of your creation. Amen

September 9

How Beautiful upon the Mountains

**And how are they to proclaim him unless they are sent? As it is written,
"How beautiful are the feet of those who bring good news!" Romans 10:15**

The above quote is from Isaiah 52:7, the picture of the herald upon the mountaintops with the message of peace. How beautiful, the prophet declares, are the feet of one who brings good news, "who announces peace, . . . who announces salvation, who says to Zion, 'Your God reigns.'" This marvelous text is brought into a direct relationship with the gospel of Christ, the good news of salvation, his peace. For the one bearing the good news, its beauty and meaning makes it a joy to share. Paul is answering his question in the opening text, saying, "Yes, persons have been sent. How beautiful it is!"

During five days of preaching the gospel at New Castle, Australia, I had a remarkable and challenging privilege. Each day I spoke at different high school assemblies, addressing over two thousand young people. The unusual challenge was that in contrast to such an audience in America, where 60 percent of the general population would have some church involvement, I was told that perhaps only 3 percent had any church involvement. To hear a man unashamedly and forthrightly declare that he is a disciple of Jesus Christ was itself a new idea for them. For me, there was a new awareness that I am a sermon, just as much as the fact that what I say is a sermon. To say "I believe in God" is a message of faith to youth who have heard most persons they know deny belief in God.

It is good news that "God so loved the world, that he gave his only begotten Son, that whosoever believeth in him should not perish, but have everlasting life" (John 3:16, KJV). How profound this statement, yet how simple. Jesus transcends mere religion and calls us into a relationship of faith, as expressed in 2 Timothy 1:12:

> *For I know the one in whom I have put my trust,*
> *And I am sure that he is able to guard*
> *Until that day what I have entrusted to him.*

Who Has Believed Our Message?

But not all have obeyed the good news; for Isaiah says, "Lord, who has believed our message?" Romans 10:16

In further identification of the good news with Jesus as the Messiah, Paul quotes from Isaiah 53, the great messianic chapter of the suffering Christ. Not all of Israel are a people of faith, not all have heard this word as the word of God. Hence, not all have accepted the good news, even if they have religious conditioning in their history.

Ministering the gospel in New South Wales, Australia, I had never been in a setting where there was so much skepticism and cynicism. The history of this country, with the atrocities committed by the state church, had lead many to reject the church and its message. It is more difficult to get a hearing among people who have turned off the gospel than among people who have never heard the message of Christ.

Paul says that not all of Israel responded to God's good news. He refers to the remnant of faith, to those few who were actually hearing God in the message. His quote from Isaiah emphasizes the Christ-event, but years after Isaiah's time. In Matthew 22, Jesus engaged the religious leaders in an interchange, answering their testing with questions and stories exposing their unbelief. Theirs was the tragedy of people who had the form of religion but missed the meaning of opening their lives to God. The just shall live by faith, as Petrus Herbert wrote:

> *Faith finds in Christ whate'er we need.*
> *To save and strengthen, guide and feed;*
> *Strong in His grace it joys to share*
> *His cross, in hope His crown to wear.*
>
> *Faith to the conscience whispers peace,*
> *And bids the mourner's sighing cease;*
> *By faith the children's right we claim,*
> *And call upon our Father's name.*

September 11

Faith Comes by Hearing

So faith comes from what is heard, and what is heard comes through the word of Christ. Romans 10:17

Faith is not a blind wish, hoping something to be true that you are quite sure is not. Faith is the intelligent, thoughtful response to evidence when it is understood. The psychology of faith is seen between people, in marriage covenant, in doing business, or in trusting the banking system. So it is in trusting Christ. What makes faith to be saving is not that it is a different kind of faith, but that it is normal faith in the Savior. It is not the faith that saves; it is the Savior who saves us.

Faith happens in hearing the word of Christ. In the Word we are given God's self-disclosure. A faith response is impossible apart from this Word. If God had not moved to us, we could not move to him. This reference is an answer to the third point in Paul's series of questions: "Have they not heard?"

My mission in Australia confronted me with the limitations of secularism. Among the hundreds to whom I ministered, the knowledge of God's Word was absent or so minimal that they had little evidence for a faith experience. The secular is a narrow stance that rules the spiritual out. To quote Bishop Pike again, "Secularism means 'there-ain't-any-more-ism.'" The Christian worldview is broader, including both secular knowledge and the spiritual, all the works of God, as confessed by the psalmist:

> *It is good to give thanks to the* LORD,
> > *to sing praises to your name, O Most High;*
> *to declare your steadfast love in the morning,*
> > *and your faithfulness by night,*
> *To the music of the lute and the harp,*
> > *to the melody of the lyre.*
> *For you, O* LORD, *have made me glad by your work;*
> > *at the works of your hands I sing for joy.*
> *How great are your works, O* LORD!
> > *Your thoughts are very deep!*
> *The dullard cannot know,*
> > *the stupid cannot understand this. (Ps. 92:1-6)*

September 12

Did They Not Hear?

But I ask, have they not heard? Indeed they have; for "Their voice has gone out to all the earth, and their words to the ends of the world." Romans 10:18

The quote here is from Psalm 19. It expresses what we call general revelation or natural theology. This psalm affirms that creation itself is a silent witness to the Creator. This word has gone out into all the world. Gentiles who had not heard the special revelation were confronted by this general revelation. Thinking persons ask about creation and a Creator, design and a Designer, purpose and meaning. Numerous scientists in the space programs have come to faith by seeing and experiencing the fantastic evidence of a Designer.

While in Australia, on several early evenings we enjoyed the sight of the Southern Cross in the stars of heaven. Speaking to hundreds of high school youth, I drew on this, reminding them that science tells us that the stars we see have been there up to fourteen billion years, and at the rate they are disintegrating, they will be there billion years more before they are gone. Yet those stars can't think, can't laugh, can't love, can't fellowship, sing, or worship. It is inconceivable that I should live eighty or ninety years and that be the end. It doesn't make sense to think that one of these days the universe will be gone and there won't be a single intelligent being that remembers that we ever happened. If we truly want to know God, we can reach out to him and find him.

The universe is so vast, and I am so small.
Yet, God notices me and has acted to redeem me.
The psalmist speaks of considering the heavens,
the work of God's hands,
and then he considers humanity, the work of God,
made a little lower than the angels,
and crowned with glory and honor.
"What is man?" he cries. He must be something!
He is made in God's image.
We can think and laugh and love.
We can worship and fellowship with God. (cf. Ps. 8)

Did Israel Not Understand?

Again I ask, did Israel not understand? First Moses says, "I will make you jealous of those who are not a nation; with a foolish nation I will make you angry." Romans 10:19

Paul's quote from Moses is a direct point for his Jewish readers. Many in Israel who had this special revelation failed to enter into what the Gentiles were pursuing with only natural revelation. In Plato we see a highly reasoned concept of God as the ultimate beautiful, the rationality of the universe, the source of all meaning. Yet Plato did not know a personal God, a God with a face. The ultimate disclosure or revelation of God is the Word present in Christ. Karl Barth is reported to have said that either Jesus Christ was really God or we don't have a full revelation yet.

Our text is almost human to the extreme in its description of God. Paul quotes a statement about Israel forsaking God in unbelief and generating jealousy and anger in seeing God magnifying himself among the Gentiles. This faith will generate envy among the Jewish people over the Gentiles' seeking God without the insights of God's acts, which the Jews knew in the special revelation of the Scriptures.

At Perth, Australia, it was my privilege to be interviewed on a night-line talk show, speaking about the nature of faith to an audience which was mostly secular. I tried to present the whole Jesus, not just a narrow pietism, nor what they call "wow-ism," but a realistic spirituality expressed as discipleship of Christ. We met with Christian artists, and Esther gave a discussion on art and faith. They wanted to know how to be Christian and an artist. Some secular persons are more excited about reconciliation, justice, peace, and compassionate service than some pietistic, yet very materialistic, Christians.

Paul next quotes Isaiah saying that even people who are not consciously seeking God could not avoid running into the evidence for God. In turn, God revealed himself to them, almost as a surprise, for they were not consciously desiring God. C. S. Lewis, the agnostic who encountered Christ, described his conversion experience as being "surprised by joy." I heard another famous Brit, Malcolm Muggeridge, give his testimony as a move from agnosticism to faith. He said that confined in the dungeon of his own ego as in a prison cell, there was a ray of light that kept shining into this cell, and he kept looking into that light. As he looked into that light of love and truth, he met the Christ.

Holy God, I want the light of faith to illuminate my life and my walk with you. Amen

September 14

Found by Those Who Did Not Seek

Then Isaiah is so bold as to say, "I have been found by those who did not seek me; I have shown myself to those who did not ask for me." Romans 10:20

"Amazing grace! how sweet the sound, that saved a wretch like me!" (John Newton). Our verse today is a text of grace, for God is saying, "I revealed myself to those who did not ask for me!" Israel should have understood, for God revealed himself to Moses at the burning bush when Moses wasn't asking (Exod. 3), and revealed himself in Egypt when Israel wasn't asking.

This section of the epistle presents the truth of reconciliation; we are made aware that God's purpose is to reconcile all, both Jew and Gentile, to himself. He is creating one new community, for in Christ "there is no longer Greek and Jew, circumcised and uncircumcised, barbarian, Scythian, slave and free" (Col. 3:11).

The missionary message was introduced to Abraham in God's words, "In you all families of the earth shall be blessed" (Gen. 12:3). This was eclipsed by Israel's ethnicity. The ethnic Jew was not open to Gentiles sharing God's grace of forgiveness and acceptance. Many references in the Old Testament show God's concern for the nations. Even Israel's victories in war, in a day of tribal gods, was to show that Jehovah alone is the sovereign God! God did not continue to prove his sovereignty by defeating his enemies in war. In this Word there is progression in doctrine. The Bible is not a flat book. The Old Testament relates to the New Testament as promise to fulfillment.

In Croatia in the year 2002, we visited the city of Vukovar by the Danube River, which borders Serbia. We were amazed at the devastation of the war. Of a population of 30,000, over 22,000 people had been killed. Shells had been dropped; some were killed by snipers across the Danube River. After touring the city we met with the small congregation for worship. After the service, a young man in his thirties thanked me for the message and bid me a goodnight. As he walked down the sidewalk, the pastor told me, "That young man was a soldier conscripted by the Serb army and killed persons whose spouses are in this congregation. After the war, in grief he became alcoholic and a derelict. But people from this congregation extended loving help and forgiveness, and now he is a believer and a member of this fellowship."

Lord, you reveal yourself to all people.
Help me to do my part in responding
and entering into a relationship with you. Amen

All Day Long I Have Held Out My Hands

But of Israel he says, "All day long I have held out my hands to a disobedient and contrary people." Romans 10:21

Unbelief is more a matter of the heart than of the head. The primary problem of unbelievers is that they don't want God in their lives. Actually, the few who are intellectual agnostics are not so far from God, since they are constantly thinking about God as the problem. If we can get people to think seriously about God, it is often not long until they think with God.

The text is an expression of God's sovereign grace and amazing patience, continually holding out his hands of love to people who reject him. What a picture! When we recognize God's sovereignty as his own personal quality of wholeness, being totally controlled by his own character or principles, then we can see his patience toward us as the expression of his love and grace in sovereignty. He is sovereign, controlled by his own integrity, expressed especially by his patience more than by authoritarianism.

In Perth, Australia, I was privileged to lecture at the Baptist Theological School on Christology and ethics, and Christology and evangelism; I spoke on Christology and futurism at the Uniting Church. My thrust was to call us to a rigorous discipleship of Christ in a contemporary society, to show how such a discipleship will be one of reconciliation in grace. As we recognize our place in the global village and move into the twenty-first century, we must become consciously and creatively a part of the global network of faith. We are God's new people, witnessing in society to the wholeness which Jesus brings to life.

Our greater challenge is how to reach people for Christ in an age of pluralism. In fact, with the increased pluralism, the human tendency is to move to secularism in a promotion of tolerance toward persons of all religions. Rather, we should recognize that religion itself is a reminder of our need of God. But since secularism is the orienting of life around humanness, as if there is no personal God, we recognize that there is both humanistic secularism and religious secularism. The latter is the orienting of life around religion itself, but without a relationship with a personal God.

Being religious is not a substitute
for a relational faith to which we are called.
Lord, help me to practice my religion
through a personal walk with you. Amen

September 16

Did God Reject His People?

I ask, then, has God rejected his people? By no means! I myself am an Israelite, a descendant of Abraham, a member of the tribe of Benjamin. Romans 11:1

No! God is extending his people! In any case, it is not God who rejects a people, but rather, they reject God. Paul uses his own experience of faith as a Jew and his walk with God in the fellowship of Christ as argument that God has not rejected Jews as such. But no people have priority. God's arms are open to all who come to him.

Salvation by grace means that God opens the door, that God takes the initiative. God has moved to us, and it is our move next. There must always be response on our part, not achievement by works or merit.

This text reminds me of what Jesus called the sin beyond pardon, referred to as blasphemy against the Holy Spirit. This sin is not simply an activity which makes God so disgusted that he closes the door. Rather, the sin is our deliberately closing out the voice of the Holy Spirit, the one divine Agent who calls us to repentance and faith. If we close out the Holy Spirit and blaspheme him, there is no other voice that can bring us to God.

Paul's point is to give a word of assurance that God's love continues to include Israel. God has not rejected his people through whom he has unfolded his revelation, but he calls each person to respond in faith. The fact that he calls and accepts Gentiles does not mean that he has turned away from the Jews, for in his purpose each is called to come to him. "For whosoever shall call upon the name of the Lord shall be saved" (Rom. 10:13, KJV).

In John's vision in Revelation, Jesus said,
"Listen! I am standing at the door, knocking;
If you hear my voice and open the door,
I will come in to you and eat with you,
and you with me." (Rev. 3:20)

September 17

His People Whom He Foreknew

**God has not rejected his people whom he foreknew. Do you not know what the scripture says of Elijah, how he pleads with God against Israel? "Lord, they have killed your prophets, they have demolished your altars; I alone am left, and they are seeking my life." But what is the divine reply to him? "I have kept for myself seven thousand who have not bowed the knee to Baal."
Romans 11:2-4**

Sometimes we feel alone, as did Elijah, focusing on the problems in the world and the church. God is at work, and this is our assurance. It is important to see God at work and trust him to fulfill his promises.

God's plan to bring the revelation of his love, his reconciling grace, to all the world was that he would use Israel as this channel of communication. He knew that some would respond in faith and, as a remnant, they would be the ones through whom the world would be blessed. Paul could have turned to Abraham again as an illustration of God's promise to bless the world through his seed; instead, he turned to Elijah. In a period of extensive unbelief in Israel, in the day of the prophet Elijah, the remnant is still affirmed.

Paul's argument, inspired by the Spirit, is that God always works through a people of faith. They may be a remnant, a minority, a small community in the larger social community, but God still works through them. We need to be reminded that God doesn't bring in his kingdom through a majority vote. When Elijah felt alone as a servant of God, the Lord told him that God had seven thousand who had not bowed the knee to Baal. God had a remnant who said no to the idolatry of Baal, the idolatry of power, material gain, pleasure, and sensuality.

In 1987, we arrived in Tokyo from Perth, Australia, and rode the bus into the city. We gazed in awe at the size of this city. Having come from our inner-city church in Washington, DC, we were aware of urban dynamics and how a church body must work in a city like this. We discovered that in Tokyo, God has a remnant of faith. The presence of the church in any society enriches the larger society by its presence.

Lord, thank you that we can each be a part of your church.
Help me as a person of faith to reject the present-day god of Baal.
Fill me and inspire me by your Holy Spirit.
Grant me a renewed vision of your eternal kingdom. Amen

At Present There Is a Remnant

So too at the present time there is a remnant, chosen by grace. Romans 11:5

Our text is an existential expression, as Paul was speaking from the fellowship of believers who walked with God. He was able to look at history from the perspective of God's activity. God is at work in our time: "there is a remnant, chosen by grace." God has not panicked. He is not desperate or defensive in a world of such increased population, modern technological development, secularization, and indifference. God foreknew this, planning that in a people of faith he would express his transforming grace.

We had the privilege of leading a mission conference with Japanese and American missionary church leaders in Tokyo. In Japan only 1 percent of the population are Christians. Here Shintoism (emperor worship) and Buddhism are experiencing renewed vitality. Yet, we found a remnant of grace, a joyous word that others can come to Christ. When a secular Japanese person in this different culture and language meets Christ, the same changes happen in their lives that happen in ours.

In our world of over six billion people, the global village has mostly moved into an urban context. We have a whole new challenge in mission. In Tokyo, with its size, one is staggered by the question of how to reach these people for Christ. However, Christ is with his people, and he confronts others through those who are his disciples. In each community this remnant, chosen by grace, is God's channel of sharing the good news. Others, too, are invited to become children of God.

Having attended most of the World Congresses on Evangelism, convened by Billy Graham, I have seen their major influence for evangelism in the global community. In those meetings it was a thrill to see thousands of persons gather for fellowship, encouragement, and clarification of vision for the mission of Christ. From the inspiring first one in Berlin in 1966 to the most recent in 2000 in Amsterdam, persons have returned to their own country as more effective witnesses and ambassadors for Christ. We had the joy of meeting some of these persons in Japan, where they returned to share the good news of grace.

Saving God, thank you for choosing to keep a remnant.
Give me your grace to share and witness to others in my community. Amen

September 19

If by Grace, It Is Not by Works

But if it is by grace, it is no longer on the basis of works, otherwise grace would no longer be grace. Romans 11:6

God's plan, salvation by grace, is the great equalizer. If any of us could work for salvation, or merit it by our deeds, it would not be God's work but ours. True, in discipleship, with varying abilities, some achieve less or more maturity than others.

Attempt at salvation by works is an affront to God; it is an insult to his character. Salvation by works is to imply that God is some difficult personage to whom we can come only by intense and costly ways of entreaty. The gospel is the good news that God is love, and he stands with open arms to receive us. What we need to do is respond to his offer to accept and forgive us, and to join covenant with him.

Grace, as Dietrich Bonhoeffer emphasized, is costly and is not a cheap grace. Once we have worked through our sins at the cross of Calvary and have seen what our forgiveness has cost God, we cannot go back to sin lightly again. To live as though grace can be received without a commitment of fidelity is an affront to God. Bonhoeffer wrote, "Only he who obeys truly believes, and only he who believes truly obeys."

Obedience is first an attitude,
then it becomes an achievement.
The attitude is honest and uncompromising,
while the achievement is only partial.
We cannot do anything to make God love us more,
nor in whatever we do, will he love us less.
His grace is an extension of his person;
gracious, compassionate, merciful, accepting.
The therapy is that he cares for us as persons,
more for us than about what we have done.
His love moves beyond issues to the person,
enfolding us in his love,
then transforming us into his likeness!

September 20

The Elect Obtained It

What then? Israel failed to obtain what it was seeking. The elect obtained it, but the rest were hardened, as it is written, "God gave them a sluggish spirit, eyes that would not see and ears that would not hear, down to this very day." Romans 11:7-8

Israel could not, by simply being Israel, obtain fellowship with God. In their intense religious practice, they failed to reach beyond the form to meet God himself. Only those who respond to God himself know the joy of his salvation and share the fellowship of his elect. By recalling the birth narratives of Jesus, we see the witness of grace in persons such as the parents of John the Baptist, in Mary's wonderful Magnificat, Joseph's faith as surrogate father, and the faith of Anna and Simeon in the temple.

During our seminar on evangelism in Tokyo we went to visit the buildings and program of a rapidly growing Buddhist lay movement known as Rissho Kosei-kai. We wanted to understand its appeal to its followers and learn how to better present Christ to them. They do not have a message of a personal God as our Father in heaven, nor do they have a message of forgiveness and of reconciliation, nor of the kingdom as the rule of the Spirit, nor of resurrection and of eternal life. They do talk much of peace, of the circle of harmony, and have group counseling. We sat in a circle of twenty or more and heard them share their struggle to overcome suffering and to live in harmony. We listened to people share their problems and others shared as counselors, with much feeling and tears. It was a unique therapy, indeed.

This experience caused us to be deeply grateful to God for the Christian faith, for the community of spirit in which we have shared in the congregation in Washington, DC, and for our covenant groups, which have ministered similarly in the fellowship of Christ. As we shared with the Japanese pastors and the American missionaries in the seminar, we all joined in the quest to be truly God's remnant of grace in witness to those about us. Our mission is to make faith in Jesus possible for all people.

Lord, we want to be true servants,
Making possible the option of faith
in Christ to all peoples. Amen

September 21

Eyes Darkened, They Cannot See

And David says, "Let their table become a snare and a trap, a stumbling block and a retribution for them; let their eyes be darkened so that they cannot see, and keep their backs forever bent." Romans 11:9-10

The old statement comes to mind again: "There is none so blind as he who will not see." Again, "No one turns his back on the light but what he increases the darkness in his own soul." This is suggested by our text. Quoting David in Psalm 69, Paul says that when people don't want to walk with God, their eyes are blinded to the evidence of God all around them. While some look at creation and marvel at the handiwork of the Creator, others look at nature, stand in awe at the mystery, and see it simply as evolutionary.

On one occasion at a university in the midwest, following my lecture in the discussion period, a professor asked me a question on the nature of faith: "As my students here know, I am an agnostic. What would you tell me to do about this matter of faith?" I responded, "Why don't you experiment honestly for thirty days. Pray this prayer, 'God, if you are around, help me to recognize the evidence for you today.' Try that for thirty days, and if nothing happens, forget the whole thing." He thought a moment and then replied, "I'm afraid to pray that prayer. Something just might happen."

The evangelism seminar in Tokyo was with a fine group of Japanese Christian pastors of very small churches in difficult settings. One of their major challenges was to get persons to hear and to think with them on the Christian gospel. So many of the people accept the Shinto or Buddhist religion as a support system. They accept their symbols and rituals, but don't ask why. Evangelism in Japan is not a mass movement so much as a challenge to earn people's trust as we share the joy of the life we know in Christ.

> *John Mackay, a missionary of distinction*
> *and later president of Princeton Seminary, said,*
> *"The two greatest symbols of the church*
> *are the cross and the towel,*
> *symbols of salvation and service."*
> *These two must be held together if we are*
> *to succeed at making the gospel clear and attractive.*

Salvation Has Come to the Gentiles

So I ask, have they stumbled so as to fall? By no means! But through their stumbling salvation has come to the Gentiles, so as to make Israel jealous.
Romans 11:11

To the Ephesians Paul wrote of a hidden mystery: God's purpose to redeem Gentiles as well as Jews. Israel had failed to understand God's grace as his love for all people. As guardians of the Torah, they shaped their religion around the law rather than hearing the law as God calling them to put him first. The first commandment could well be translated, "I am Jehovah your God; all of life is to begin with me."

Paul's description of Israel, as stumbling and thereby opening the awareness of grace for the Gentiles, is a picturesque description. It is not a fall in which they have no hope of entering into this grace. The door is still open to them. But, seeing the Gentiles enter into the fullness of faith in Christ, their very joy in salvation will in turn make the Jews jealous. Israel may be made envious of the Gentiles who now are the evangelistic exponents of the faith of Abraham, a faith that is rightfully Israel's.

We traveled to Beijing, in China, a land of over one billion people. It is a land in which the church has grown with amazing strength and speed, now evident since the openness that followed the Cultural Revolution. There may well be over 100 million Christians in China today, perhaps one believer for every ten persons. One reason for the growth is that the Chinese people themselves are sharing faith with one another. In this way, Christianity is kept from appearing as a foreign religion.

A social interpretation of the dynamic growth of the church in China is that under the Cultural Revolution the young people of China were taught that the West was a long way behind them. When the new openness came they discovered that in many ways they were behind the West. They were both envious of the West and distrusted their leaders for not having told them the truth. Similarly, Paul sees Israel coming to faith through envy of the Gentiles' fellowship with God.

> [We have] the knowledge of the glory of God
> in the face of Jesus Christ. (2 Cor. 4:6)

September 23

Full Inclusion Is Far Greater

Now if their stumbling means riches for the world, and if their defeat means riches for Gentiles, how much more will their full inclusion mean! Romans 11:12

God has not given up on Israel. Paul's vision keeps him a debtor to his people, for as they become open to full inclusion, Jew and Gentile, how much greater will the circle of God's people be. Paul went to synagogue after synagogue, to the Jews and then to the Greeks. In Israel's stumbling the message has come to the larger world, but when Israel walks in the fullness of the Light, how much greater the blessing to the world.

Paul knew what theologians call "salvation history" and the reality of his own conversion to Christ. Consequently, he expected the same conversion for other Jews. We should hear this text and Paul's faith in a spiritual awakening within Israel and seek more effective ways of sharing Christ with them.

Visiting Beijing, we took a taxi north and climbed the Great Wall of China. What an experience! It was all that we had read about and expected to see: a wall 6,000 kilometers from the sea to the east, across mountains, valleys, and plains to the western side of China. Built to keep out the raiding hordes from the north and the northwest, it was breached several times by bribing the guards. The wall did keep the larger world from China, and in turn it kept China from the world until the first part of this century. Mission activity had earlier resulted in 100,000 Christians. The Marxist regime brought this mission to an end, and the cultural revolutionaries martyred and imprisoned many believers.

After dropping out of college in the fall of 1948, I wrote to the mission board of the Mennonite Church, volunteering to go to China. Unknown to me at that time, the door was closed. J. D. Graber, general secretary of the mission board, sent me an article by Dick Hillis entitled, "I Was Never Called to China." After eighteen years of mission work in China, he wrote, "I was called to teach the gospel; the door opened in China and I served there. Now it is closed, and I'll do the same elsewhere." Since then, China's Christian numbers have grown to the millions in both the Three Self-Patriotic Movement (self-supporting, self-governing, self-propagating) and in the hidden church. Each of us faces the challenge of calling, that is, to live in the service of Christ. The position is unimportant in itself.

Lord, help me to live in service to you
and your church. Amen

September 24

And Save Some of Them

Now I am speaking to you Gentiles. Inasmuch then as I am an apostle to the Gentiles, I glorify my ministry in order to make my own people jealous, and thus save some of them. Romans 11:13-14

This statement must be held in relation to the vision of full inclusion. Paul's concern is that he might save as many people as possible. He is addressing these comments to the Gentiles for their understanding of his strategy, stating that his work among the Gentiles could result in Jews coming to faith out of envy. While the statement sounds somewhat strange, he reminds the Gentiles that they should not become possessive of their privilege and make the same mistake the Jews made.

The suggestion that envy is a motivation for some to come to salvation must be read as recognition that the message had come through their own history. We do recognize that people are variously motivated to consider the gospel. Some people come out of a sense of guilt, some from a sense of being lost, some from being loved, some in a search for meaning or purpose. Some people come in very simplistic faith, and some with more philosophical reflection. Paul sees even cross-cultural envy as used by God.

In Beijing we visited pastor Kan Xueging, then went to the Beijing Seminary and visited with the president. He had been the pastor of the church where Kan Xueging was serving. Asking the president whether he knew of evangelist John Sung, he smiled. He had been converted under Sung's preaching, and Sung's daughters had participated in a village church where he himself had served earlier.

I heard the story of John Sung's conversion from a Methodist missionary of forty years in China, William Schubert. Sung's father was a minister; John was an agnostic. He went to America to study, and having completed his degree in veterinary science to please his father, he enrolled for a year at Union Seminary in New York City. At Calvary Baptist church he had a conversion; his new spiritual vitality and prayer life was neither shared nor accepted in this liberal seminary. One day Harry Emerson Fosdick personally walked him down the sidewalk to a psychiatric hospital and committed him. After three months, a Chinese friend negotiated his release. They returned to China, where Sung became a leading evangelist for the next several decades, preaching and developing churches in China and surrounding Asian countries.

Give me righteous envy of others' faith,
So that my own faith will be renewed and strengthened.

September 25

The Reconciliation of the World

For if their rejection is the reconciliation of the world, what will their acceptance be but life from the dead! Romans 11:15

Faith makes us eternal optimists. In the Jews' rejection of Christ, Paul saw God acting to extend grace to all the world. In Jesus's parable, when those invited made excuses, the Lord commanded his servants to go out into the byways and compel all they met to come to his dinner. Karl Barth says that Israel is serving God's purpose similarly to what Judas did in his unbelief—they make the world conscious of Jehovah.

Paul presents his unqualified conclusion of what was happening in the spread of the gospel as hope that the Jewish community will yet accept God's salvation in Christ and the result will be "life from the dead." He wrote the Ephesians that God has made alive those who "were dead through the trespasses and sins" (2:1-5). So here he uses similar language in a futuristic hope. We as Christians should be praying and sharing our faith with the Jewish community in this same confidence.

We attended a church service in Beijing; the woman preaching was a seminary student. She seemed very fluent and earnest, although we were listening to her through a translator. We caught her good spirit and could also sense the receptivity of the congregation. God has his people in every culture.

In many ways the service was an extension of the Western church, by whom they had been conditioned. We sang "This Is My Father's World," "O to Be Like Thee," and after the message, "Have Thine Own Way, Lord." As they now contextualize the gospel, they must be more post-Western in style and more and more Chinese as they express their faith as Christians. This is happening, for this church baptized 200 persons on Easter Sunday. God wants us to be authentic in our individual cultures.

Esther, in her artists' conferences, encourages the participants to be authentic in their particular culture. They should not reach to our Western patterns, which cannot be who they are. Once, while visiting an elderly artist in Japan, the famous painter Watanabi, she asked him why he painted a big red fish on the table in front of Christ at the Last Supper. His reply, in a voice of confidence was, "If Christ had been Japanese, he would have had a red fish on the table, for a red fish is for a special occasion!"

Lord, you call us to make the good news
attractive in every culture, language, and context.
Help us to move beyond religion to faith and a relation with you. Amen

September 26

Holy Roots, Holy Branches

If the part of the dough offered as first fruits is holy, then the whole batch is holy; and if the root is holy, then the branches also are holy. Romans 11:16

The figure in the text of the root carrying the branches is very similar to the word picture Jesus used of being the vine and our being the branches. The only branch that bears fruit is the one attached to the vine. The dead wood and encumbering shoots need to be trimmed off. We should recognize that fruit always appears on the new growth (John 15:1-11).

The figure, as Paul uses it, is to show how the Gentile Christians are branches from the root of God's work in historic Israel. We speak today of the Judeo-Christian heritage. If this root is holy, actually God's work, then the branches are holy. This means that Gentile believers are accepted as the seed of Abraham just as are Jewish believers.

Having visited in the Orient, I was impressed with how important it is that the church interpret our faith christologically and that this be grounded in the full sweep of salvation history. Christianity is not a Western religion. In Japan and in China, we clearly must reach back much further than Western history and our denominational histories. In China, the Three-Self Church speaks of the days before the Cultural Revolution, with many denominations. But with the ending of the Cultural Revolution, the church must be seen as one body, even with various denominational influences.

Eighty-year-old pastor Liu Chonghe shared with us extensively on the matter of a spirit of unity. He, formerly Anglican, with four other pastors who were formerly Presbyterian, serve at the Beijung Chong Wen Men Christian Church, which was formerly Methodist. He told of their administering the sacraments in a variety of ways. He believes that variety leads to contemplation on the meaning of the sacrament. They let people choose how they wish to be baptized: by immersion, sprinkling, or pouring. The openness, he said, has its appeal to the young.

We must always distinguish between symbol and meaning,
and not make the symbol absolute.
Our salvation is the covenant of faith we are engaging.

September 27

It Is the Root That Supports You

But if some of the branches were broken off, and you, a wild olive shoot, were grafted in their place to share the rich root of the olive tree, do not boast over the branches. If you do boast, remember that it is not you that support the root, but the root that supports you. Romans 11:17-18

Isaiah speaks of Israel as the vineyard that God planted (Isa. 5). Paul continues his use of this figure. The olive tree is his symbol, with the patriarchs and the prophets as part of this root of salvation history. The new olive shoots have been grafted into this root. We recognize how we came to faith in God; we enjoy our faith in appreciation for its source, its historic roots in the Israel of God's calling.

Paul says we are not to boast over our position in Christ, exercising a put-down to the Jews. This is an important word for our current sense of mission. As Gentiles, we should be seeking more effective ways of sharing faith with the Jewish community. In turn, we must be more effective in sharing with the other great historic religion, Islam.

Flying from Beijing across China to Hong Kong, one could see countless villages, many only eight or ten kilometers apart, and often with different language dialects. In many villages clusters of Christians are not in the Three-Self Patriotic Movement or registered with the government. How many? By 2004, Christianity's number has grown, with experts estimating from 30 to 100 million believers.

This universe is not a closed system;
it is open at both ends and quite drafty!
God has not forgotten nor forsaken us.
In our brokenness we are not experiencing
the absence of God, but often his silence.
God expects us to take his work seriously,
to hear his gospel and respond to his Word.
Listening, we can hear his voice,
the witness of the Spirit:
"Come unto me, all you who labor,
and I will give you rest." (cf. Matt. 11:28)

September 28

You Stand by Faith

You will say, "Branches were broken off so that I might be grafted in." That is true. They were broken off because of their unbelief, but you stand only through faith. So do not become proud, but stand in awe. Romans 11:19-20

God works for good, even out of human failures. With Israel's unbelief, God made clear that they didn't own the message of grace. The figure used in today's verses takes a difficult twist. Jewish branches were broken off so that Gentile branches could be grafted in, but both were dependent on the same root. Paul says that they were broken off because of unbelief. In Jesus's words, "Every tree that does not bear good fruit is cut down and thrown into the fire" (Matt. 7:19).

Herein is a note of caution. We are not to be arrogant or presumptuous, but fearful and reverent. Peter wrote, "If it is hard for the righteous to be saved, what will become of the ungodly and the sinners?" (1 Pet. 4:18). This is not to undermine our assurance of salvation, but it calls us to recognize that we are saved by God's grace. He has grafted us in because of his mercy.

In Hong Kong we witnessed evidence of God's mercy to a variety of people. In the morning I spoke at the Evangelical Free Seminary to a group of students. We shared with a member from our church in Washington, DC, teaching in China, who had come to Hong Kong to see us. At lunch we met with Mennonite church leaders to hear of God's work among them. I preached at the Mennonite church on "Evangelism as Reconciliation." Esther spoke about our respective work. Back at the YMCA, a Chinese friend met us to tell about his pilgrimage of faith. We shared in our diversity, yet a wonderful unity of faith.

What a privilege to meet people who have been a witness to God's marvelous grace and the challenge to contextualize our interpretation of the gospel. The people had some fear over the unknown in the release of Hong Kong to China in 1997. We encouraged them to stand together in faith in a political transition.

David Livingstone, a missionary in Africa,
lost his wife and officiated at her funeral.
At the conclusion he quoted from the farewell of Jesus:
"Lo, I am with you alway."
"Jesus," Livingstone said, "is too much of a
gentleman not to keep his word!" (cf. Matt. 28:20)

271

September 29

God Did Not Spare the Natural Branches

For if God did not spare the natural branches, perhaps he will not spare you. Romans 11:21

God is no respecter of persons. We can each come to him today and know that he will hear us and meet us, just as he does others. This is the faith in which we stand. His grace is extended to each of us. He only expects us to respond to him in the integrity of faithfulness. The text is a warning: if God did not spare those who stood in the tradition of his great acts in history, but cut those off who refused to walk in faith, he has less reason to continue work with Gentiles with no such history if we are not faithful.

What then is our security? It is alone in God's compassion, God's mercy. "God so loved the world, that he gave his only begotten Son, that *whosoever* believeth in him should not perish, but have everlasting life" (John 3:16, KJV). This is our security. Peter writes, "The Lord is . . . not wanting any to perish, but all to come to repentance" (2 Pet. 3:9).

We share in a global village with over six billion people, making the work of evangelism overwhelming. We need innovative ways to make faith in Christ possible for all peoples. In the Far East, with nearly two-thirds of the world's population, this need is evident. From Hong Kong and China's over one billion people, we flew into India with its population of one billion people, recognizing that the church must be transcultural.

For those of us in the Western world, with our freedoms and our affluence, we need to reexamine ourselves as to whether we are truly disciples of Jesus. Our materialism, secularism, political conservatism (possessing rather than sharing), psychologized gospel (feeling good rather than the cross), and success messages (health and wealth rather than sacrifice)—all stand judged by this text. Our highest calling is to be "ambassadors for Christ" in today's world (2 Cor. 5:20).

May we be a presence for Christ,
touching the society around us in faith,
a presence for your kingdom, God,
evidencing your transforming grace.
Let this be our witness for the Master.

September 30

Consider the Kindness and Sternness of God

Note then the kindness and the severity of God: severity toward those who have fallen, but God's kindness toward you, provided you continue in his kindness; otherwise you also will be cut off. Romans 11:22

Jesus said, "From everyone to whom much has been given, much will be required" (Luke 12:48). God has no favorites; he treats all alike in equity. His kindness is primary, but his severity is supportive. God's kindness to the Gentiles is an extension of his mercy toward people to whom little has been given. God's severity to Israel, correspondingly, is because they have been entrusted with so much. They had the heritage of patriarchs and prophets sharing God's special revelation. Israel was made its custodian. But it is to be shared with the world. When a people become ingrown, possessive, and judgmental, they pervert the message. They make it impossible for their word to be heard.

On visiting Calcutta, one is immediately immersed in its wonderful people, but also its heat, filth, poverty, and a hundred smells! Esther grew up in India and we have been there numerous times. I have served as a speaker for the Evangelical Fellowship of India in their conventions several times, and we knew what to expect this time. Driving to the guest house of the Mennonite Central Committee, the streets were filled with people celebrating the Hindu Puja, their highest celebration of the goddess of many arms, who is to have overcome evil. In each section of the city the people had built a special cloth covered temple to house the beautifully designed statues of the goddess, the animal symbols, and the prince and attendants who make up the story. We stopped at one temple to observe the ritual, so elaborate that though they were in poverty, they still spent 450,000 rupees in its construction (about $35,000 U.S. dollars).

The major question is, How can God's mercy and grace be shared in a loving witness in this setting? We need to be caring and clear so that people may respond in simple faith. Our approach dare not be one of rejection of persons, but of showing what Jesus has to offer beyond mere religion for any of us. As in Psalm 138, we are to exalt him above the gods, and that means all gods, including ours in the Western world. The mission of the Christian church is to share the joy of the Lord with the world.

The joy of the Lord is my strength!
(cf. Neh. 8:10)

God Is Able to Graft Them In

And even those of Israel, if they do not persist in unbelief, will be grafted in, for God has the power to graft them in again. Romans 11:23

Christianity is not simply a religious system over against other religions. It is rather, confidence in God's grace, in his act to reconcile humanity to himself. This is in contrast to religions seeking in their own way to find God, and or even our offering vain sacrifices to appease God or to win his acceptance. Such is an insult to the self-giving God of love and grace.

Paul's confidence that Israel has a continuing place in God's work was based on his understanding of God's sovereign grace. But there is a condition: "If they do not persist in unbelief." This phrase is key, for while God has taken the initiative in coming to us, we are responsible for our response. When one understands the biblical revelation, God's self-disclosure in his acts in history, it is more difficult to live by disbelief than by belief. It takes a lot of arrogance and presumption to live as if there is no God. The unbeliever is one who doesn't want God in his life.

While in India, observing people in this land of a billion people, we were moved with compassion, praying that they may know the freedom of Christ and his release from their strong fatalism. We visited a Hindu temple to observe their worship, especially the Durga Puja, the most important festival for Bengalis. We were turned away at the entrance because we were not Hindu. Even though their philosophers boast that Hinduism is open and incorporates the values of all religions, we were not welcome.

> *"It is for freedom that*
> *Christ has set us free."*
> *It is for the present life,*
> *free to walk with him.*
> *Our deterministic society*
> *would shape our lives;*
> *whether that be philosophical fatalism,*
> *psychological, or social fatalism.*
> *But, confronted by Christ, we can choose.*
> *We are free to say yes.*

October 2

Much More the Natural Branches

For if you have been cut from what is by nature a wild olive tree and grafted, contrary to nature, into a cultivated olive tree, how much more will these natural branches be grafted back into their own olive tree. Romans 11:24

The word picture of the olive tree continues to express Paul's message. The image of the stump is the Israel of God in history. The tree in the midst of history brought the fruit of God-knowledge into the world. We can't push an illustration too far, for grafting means the supply from the root may make for better production, but the branch itself determines the character of the fruit, and it is still Gentile. Having made his point that Gentiles have been grafted in, he now turns to Israel to show that their life is dependent upon being grafted back into the trunk of God's special work. This is "their own olive tree." They belong here, on this root. Their heritage of faith carries the history of God's redemptive acts from the call of Abraham, to the exodus, to the prophets, and to Christ.

The reference to faithful Israel as the "cultivated olive tree" is in contrast to the wild olive, from which the Gentiles have come. This expression describes Israel's historical privilege. The expected development is that the Jews would come to faith in Christ. How easy it is for people to make religion an end and not come to God oneself.

In the context of India, one could not but reflect on Buddha's search for God and his philosophy of life, tied very closely to the Hindu philosophy in which he was seeking a spiritual reality. How empty to observe people worshipping Buddha, rubbing the toes on his statue, and then placing their hand on their head, when at best they might be motivated by Buddha to seek the light of God. It is a very inadequate Christology when persons affirm that Buddha was the Christ for these people. At best, they might compare him to a prophet in Israel, like Amos and his higher emphasis on God's call to justice. We don't worship the prophets; they only point us to God, to the One who became Incarnate in Jesus.

I laid a foundation, and someone else is building on it. . . .
For no one can lay any foundation other than the
one that has been laid; that foundation is Jesus Christ.
(1 Corinthians 3:10-11)

275

The Full Number of Gentiles

So that you may not claim to be wiser than you are, brothers and sisters, I want you to understand this mystery: a hardening has come upon part of Israel, until the full number of the Gentiles has come in. Romans 11:25

The insight of this text Paul calls a mystery. The writer of Ephesians speaks of the mystery of Christ, that through the gospel the Gentiles are heirs together with Israel (3:2-6). In this text, the mystery is the hardening among Israel, which led to turning to the Gentiles with the good news of grace. Now, since the Gentiles are a special focus of mission, we are not to become conceited or possessive of the privileges we have in Christ, but be conscious of a calling of grace to the Jewish community. The hardening is only in part, not the fate of all Jews until "the full number of the Gentiles has come in." The full number is achieved to fulfill God's justice in equity of mission to the world.

This passage cannot find its fulfillment other than through God's sovereign grace. We must recognize this as a mystery, just as we bow before the mystery. God hasn't turned his back on us nor on Israel. It is only human unbelief that turns God off, and Paul sees this unbelief as supporting the expression of God's grace in turning to the Gentiles until their belief fulfills his goal of stimulating belief in Israel.

Our calling is to so maximize our joy in Christ that others will want to know the same freedom. This means a mission of presence and of integrity so that others will see the spirit of Christ in us. Paul wrote the Thessalonians, saying, "You know what kind of persons we proved to be among you for your sake" (1 Thess. 1:5). The freedom of Christ is communicated by example—not of ourselves, but by the work of the Spirit.

God moves where people are open to him.
Great revivals happen where people cry to God.
Parts of the world may be steeped in unbelief,
as their indifference prevents God from moving,
which does not mean that God will stop his work.

And So All Israel Will Be Saved

And so all Israel will be saved; as it is written, "Out of Zion will come the Deliverer; he will banish ungodliness from Jacob. And this is my covenant with them, when I take away their sins." Romans 11:26-27

Let us read this text carefully; there is a mystery here. It must be interpreted consistently with the larger passage. What is the interpretation of "and so"? Does it mean "therefore" or "ultimately"? Or does it mean, "in this way," "in this manner," or "by a return to faith"?

If the meaning is the former, we are saying that all Israelites will have the gift of salvation. This would mean a contradiction of his word of rejection for unbelief. Is this all Israel through the centuries? Or is it all Israel as the people living at some future time of salvation? Should we better interpret "and so" to mean "in this way" or "in this manner"?

We may well read this text meaning "in this manner." We believe that the incarnation is final. We do not find salvation other than that provided in Christ. Paul's hope was that belief would emerge again among his people in spite of part of Israel being hardened in unbelief. The gospel moves people from nonfaith to faith, and in this perception of God's grace, all Israel shall come to salvation with the believing Gentiles.

Paul's several quotations from Isaiah and Jeremiah are from messianic passages, which add to this interpretation. These passages point to the Deliverer, the Christ, whose work and word from Zion opens the new covenant in which God saves his people from their sins. This focus on Christ emphasizes the way of salvation as God's own openness in grace. With Paul, we believe that God's salvation is for the Jews, but for all people as well. Our goal as we ministered in India was to make faith in Christ intelligible, visible, and desirable.

As people reach out to God,
honestly dependent upon his grace
and not on religious rites,
the salvation they come to know
is what we know in God's grace
expressed in Jesus Christ.

October 5

God's Gift and Call Are Irrevocable

As regards the gospel they are enemies of God for your sake; but as regards election they are beloved, for the sake of their ancestors; for the gifts and the calling of God are irrevocable. Romans 11:28-29

God is as good as his word! He will fulfill his promise. He has accepted us in Christ, for Jesus said, "Anyone who comes to me I will never drive away" (John 6:37). In Ephesians we read that we are chosen, adopted, and accepted in the Beloved (1:3-11). We rest in this assurance, for God's gifts and call are irrevocable. Sharing in Christ, we are elect to eternal life.

Today's verses introduce again the concept of election, tying what Paul is saying to the special calling of our sovereign God in history. Peter wrote, "The prophets who prophesied of the grace that was to be yours made careful search and inquiry, inquiring about the person or time that the Spirit of Christ within them indicated" (1 Pet. 1:10-11). God's sovereign purpose was to bring the Redeemer into the world for all peoples. Paul sees the estrangement of Israel as opening the door for Gentiles, but he also sees a continuing offer of grace to the Jews, just as God declared and promised their fathers.

I taught a course in systematic theology at the Union Biblical Seminary in Pune, India, with ninety students. It was a challenge to help prepare national church leaders. My approach called for consistency, coherence, and completeness, and I set the work of theology in the context of missions, as in the book of Acts and in the early church and as we see here in our Scripture.

We are not only to have knowledge about God, as did the Jews in their history, but also, such knowledge calls us walk with God by faith. This is not only thinking about God, but also by the insights of his Spirit, it means thinking with God.

The prophet Isaiah says to all who are of faith;
God has inscribed us on the palms of his hands. (cf. Isa. 49:16)
What an amazing word-picture of grace,
He has claimed us and can't forget us.
We rest in this confidence of love.
Jude writes that we are to keep ourselves in the love of God,
knowing that he will keep us. (cf. Jude 21)

October 6

That He May Have Mercy upon All

Just as you were once disobedient to God but have now received mercy because of their disobedience, so they have now been disobedient in order that, by the mercy shown to you, they too may now receive mercy. For God has imprisoned all in disobedience so that he may be merciful to all. Romans 11:30-32

The Old Testament prophet cries out, "Who is a God like you, pardoning iniquity?" (Mic. 7:18). This is one of the unique things in the Judeo-Christian faith. A holy God expresses himself in mercy beyond his judgment.

Our text says that humanity's disobedience becomes the occasion for God to show mercy. In fact, the argument of this chapter is that both Jew and Gentile have been guilty of disobedience. Paul here calls his Jewish compatriots to recognize that they too have been disobedient so that the mercy of God may be recognized by all. God has bound all peoples to their disobedience so that he may have mercy upon all, treating all peoples in grace. God, as no respecter of persons, holds all alike accountable, but assures us that no one has an edge over the other in receiving mercy from him.

We tend to note culture, education, class, or status differences between people, but God sees those factors only as the framework in which a life is being expressed; it is the person that he loves. Teaching theology at Union Biblical Seminary in India was a new challenge, with the amazing variety in my classes of different levels of reading ability and theological awareness. But those differences are only conditioning elements in the development of their faith. This is, of course, a process, and I sought to help each one to grow in their understanding of God, of humanity, and of relationship with God, whose grace is equally expressed to each.

The wisdom of God's plan is to first expose all as disobedient; this is the great leveler of humanity. Then it is clear that we alike need his grace.

There are none lacking need of a Savior.
How amazing is the wisdom of God's
unfolding plan in the universalizing
of his message and his openness to every person.

O the Depth of the Riches of God!

O the depth of the riches and wisdom and knowledge of God! How unsearchable are his judgments and how inscrutable his ways! "For who has known the mind of the Lord? Or who has been his counselor? Or who has given a gift to him, to receive a gift in return?" For from him and through him and to him are all things. To him be the glory forever. Amen. Romans 11:33-36

There are times, when overwhelmed with the wonder of God's grace, we must burst out in praise that defies adequate words. Paul gives us such an expression at the end of this chapter, a lyric of praise similar to the end of chapter 8.

These verses are a form of poetry, rejoicing and marveling at the majesty of God. It is unfair to this section to break it down into smaller units, so we will include all four verses in these moments of reflection. They should become our own outburst of praise.

Paul is reflecting on the mystery of God's purpose in expressing mercy to all peoples, blessing Israel as the avenue of special revelation, having brought the Messiah through them. Now in Israel's rejection of the Messiah, God has made it clear that salvation is not in their religion, but in his grace as Redeemer. In their disobedience, God expresses mercy for disobedient people, and therefore his mercy includes the disobedient Gentiles as well. "O the depth of the riches and wisdom and knowledge of God!"

As we stand amazed before his marvelous grace, we ask with Paul, "Who has ever given to God, that God should repay him?" Our salvation is in no way a response to our giving to God, but it is the gift of God. This means it is for everyone!

The conclusion of this poetic praise hymn is a declaration of the sovereignty of God. Everything is *from* him, for he is before all things, and by him all things now exist. Everything is *through* him; he is the Creator, and distinct from the creation. Everything is *to* him, for all creation, and all humanity created in the image of God, is intended as an extension of his goodness, a participation in his loving purpose, a sharing of his glory.

> *It is in the recognition of your glory that we cry,*
> *"All hail the power of Jesus' name!" (Edward Perronet)*
> *In this we declare praise to you, God of love and glory.*

October 8

Living Sacrifices

I appeal to you therefore, brothers and sisters, by the mercies of God, to present your bodies as a living sacrifice, holy and acceptable to God, which is your spiritual worship. Romans 12:1

Our salvation is the gift of God's free grace. In response to this gift, it is logical that our reasonable worship is to give ourselves to him. This very practical section of the epistle, chapters 12–16, begins with a call to consecration. Salvation is a relationship. We come to his cross that we might share in the cross. Our response is to give our loyalty and service to him. This is worship.

This text calls for decisive, positive action. It has long been a favorite text in my tradition in the Mennonite Church. I heard this text used in many sermons from a child into my mature years. We are to present our bodies, our persons, to God. This is not a mystical spirituality in which one can retreat from real life, from the physical order, but a spirituality of wholeness, of presenting one's whole self to be a disciple of Christ. It is a spirituality of active yieldedness. It is what my Anabaptists forebears called *Gelassenheit*, a yieldedness to walk in obedience. The presenting of ourselves to God is our spiritual worship, not a periodic rite of religious exercises, but a lifestyle of devotion to God.

Paul's reference to our dedication being a living sacrifice takes us back to Old Testament images of sacrifices, the selection of the best offering to be presented to God. Here we are told that, in response to God's mercy, we should present, not some lesser gift, but our very selves to God. Dedication is a response not an entreaty.

Paul has here laid the groundwork for a Christian ethic. Redeemed in Christ, we are to live out this relationship to Christ. This relation keeps ethics from being legalistic.

> *Herein is a christocentric ethic.*
> *We relate ethics to Christ the same way*
> *in which we relate salvation to Christ.*
> *We are saved in relation to Christ,*
> *and we now behave in relation to Christ.*

Don't Let the World Squeeze You into Its Mold

Do not be conformed to this world, but be transformed by the renewing of your minds, so that you may discern what is the will of God—what is good and acceptable and perfect. Romans 12:2

As disciples of Christ, we are called out of the world to be sent back into the world as a presence for Christ. We use the world, but do not abuse it. This spirituality is other than a withdrawal from the world, other than a retreat from the material. It is what the South African theologian, David Bosch, called "a spirituality for the road." The transforming power of grace enables this, for the change is within us, not simply in our physical or social withdrawal. When we understand the world and its orientation toward sin as the perversion of the good, we can also understand redemption as a re-creating of the good and our presence in the world as salt of the earth, and as the light of the world.

Our text says, "Do not be conformed to this world," that is, don't let your life be shaped by or fashioned by the world. J. B. Phillips translates, "Don't let the world squeeze you into its mold." The Greek word means that we are not to be "schematized" by the world. We must not be shaped by the same individualism, selfishness, materialism, civil religion, violence, racism, or sensual perversity that characterizes the world.

The next phrase of the text is the key to our victory: "But be transformed by the renewing of your minds." The Greek word for *transformed* is the word from which we have metamorphosis—a total change resulting from the character of the life principle within. Once we are born of the Spirit, there is within us a new divine life, which is now to be worked out in the totality of our lives, through transforming power by the Spirit of Christ. Significantly, Paul says that the renewal is in the spirit of our minds. Now we can discern the perfect will of God and walk in his path.

> How we think includes the spirit or attitude,
>   the intention of our thought.
> As we think God's thoughts after him,
>   our lives will be shaped by him.
> By transformation we can exercise ourselves
>   in the good and perfect will of God.
> We can participate in Spirit-wrought metamorphosis.

October 10

Think with Sober Judgment

**For by the grace given to me I say to everyone among you not to think of yourself more highly than you ought to think, but to think with sober judgment, each according to the measure of faith that God has assigned.
Romans 12:3**

As children of God we are members of his family. We are not lone individualists. We are part of the new community of the Spirit. Having a common salvation in the grace of God, we have a common relationship in the people of God. When we are truly the church, we think in terms of how we enhance another's walk in Christ, of how we enable others and bear one another's burdens—personal, economic, social, and political.

The church is much like a symphony; each persons masters his or her own instrument so that they can do together what no one could do alone. This calls for respect for each others' role, whether one instrument is more well known than the other or not; they function together in a harmony engaging all. Each of us should think soberly, clearly, and honestly about our role in the community of faith. We should not think too highly of ourselves. Our gifts are for the good of all and not for personal status.

Some years ago, a small rural hospital in India was closed by decision of the Mennonite church workers. One of the leaders then helped carry out the beds and load the medicines onto the truck, told of his reflection on what actually remained of the service the dedicated physician, Dr. Shellenberg, had given in that place. He suddenly realized that her life could not be measured by the crumbling buildings, the few iron cots, and the small pile of medicines in the corner of the truck, but was to be measured by the lives of the many people in the villages who had been blessed by her ministry. Similarly, as we attended a Sunday morning worship service at a city church, we were impressed again with how the gospel changes, inspires, and directs lives across cultural differences.

It is not simply in the words we speak,
but also in the deeds of love
which God has assigned to us.

October 11

Each Member Belongs to All the Others

For as in one body we have many members, and not all the members have the same function, so we, who are many, are one body in Christ, and individually we are members one of another. Romans 12:4-5

The church in its diversity is compared to the body with its many parts. As the body of Christ, it gives visibility to Christ in the world. Paul says that each member belongs to all of the others. As in a body, there are many members, but all function as one body; so it is with the church. None of us can say to another, "We can get along without you." As one body, the church makes the spirit of unity a genuine work of grace.

The story is told of a musician conducting a great orchestra. During their practice he suddenly stopped conducting and cried, "Where is my piccolo?" He missed hearing the smallest instrument of all.

The human body is made up of many cells, in a thousand shapes, round, flat, square, short, and long. Some are hair cells, some skin cells, some blood cells, some bone cells, some tissue cells. But each has its own special task. So it is in the body of Christ. We come in many shapes and sizes, colors and cultures. There is always the danger that the parts of the body refuse to work together, that cancerous cells appear and attack other cells. The church has been crippled by members who are not willing to take an active role in the body.

Lifting an overly full suitcase once in our travel, I experienced a muscle cramp in my lower back. For a week I suffered pain, and during the first days I could neither stand straight nor walk freely. It took extra time to do simple things that are normally done instinctively. I was daily reminded of this text, for the freedom of the body of Christ is often limited by some strain of relationship in the body.

Health is the normal condition of life, not something sought only to correct an illness. Just so, the reconciling spirit is to be the norm for our relationships of service, as different personalities in the body of Christ, and not just sought when we have problems.

Will you let me be your servant,
Let me be as Christ to you?
Pray that I may have the grace
To let you be my servant too.
(Richard Gillard)

We Each Have Different Gifts

We have gifts that differ according to the grace given to us: prophecy, in proportion to faith; ministry, in ministering; the teacher, in teaching; the exhorter, in exhortation; the giver, in generosity; the leader, in diligence; the compassionate, in cheerfulness. Romans 12:6-8

God enriches each person for the good of the community. Our gifts from God are gifts to use as individuals, for our fulfillment and joy in service. But they are not to be used selfishly. As gifts of God, they find their highest expression when they are used for the glory of God, in full identification with his work and his kingdom.

There are a number of specific passages on gifts that are given us by divine grace. Here Paul speaks of how we are gifted by God for service in the body of Christ. In Ephesians 4 he speaks of gifts "to equip the saints for the work of ministry" (4:12). In 1 Corinthians he speaks of gifts of the Spirit for the enriching of the church (chapters 12 and 14). These passages enumerate at least eighteen gifts. Paul reminds us in the conclusion of 1 Corinthians 12:31 that we may be seeking the more impressive gifts (considering this a present tense verb), but he emphasizes the more excellent way, the way of love. Gifts of the Spirit are to be graced by the fruit of the Spirit (Gal. 5:22-23).

The gifts stated in our text are clearly relational gifts. The focus is on the covenant community and the interfacing of our gift with mutual enrichment.

In these gifts there is an evident relational quality. The work of the Spirit in the community of faith is to unite us in Christ. This unity is not static, but a unity in diversity, engaging these differences as an enriching composition for the whole body.

If the gift is prophecy, speak from proven faith.
If the gift is serving, serve in Christian grace.
If the gift is teaching, teach to inspire to learn.
If the gift is encouraging, encourage.
If the gift is contributing to others, be generous.
If the gift is leadership, be diligent in leading.
If the gift is showing mercy, do so cheerfully.

Love Must Be Sincere

Let love be genuine; hate what is evil, hold fast to what is good. Romans 12:9

Love means that one's life is intimately open to another. God opened himself fully to us, sharing himself to the death on the cross, of which Paul says, "in Christ God was reconciling the world to himself" (2 Cor. 5:19). His love invites our love and calls us to open our lives fully and totally to him.

Jesus said the first commandment is to love God with the whole of one's person, opening one's heart (affection), one's soul (ambition), one's mind (attitudes), and one's strength (activity) to God. The second commandment, he said, is like the first, to love one's neighbor as one's self. For in opening one's life to God, we also open our lives to all that God is doing in and for the neighbor, friend or enemy.

There is a cost in love, for when you love someone, their experience is shared with you, their problems become your problems. Love is far deeper than tolerance; it calls for repentance while tolerance doesn't require change. Love does not select. Love shares totally with the person. When we love we identify honestly, openly, fully. Paul states his admonition simply but profoundly: "Let love be genuine." No sham, no shirking, no selfishness in our relationship. This is important in marriage, but also in social relationships.

The text shows us that love is not only emotional, but is also intellectual and volitional. It is intellectual in that it is discerning, and volitional in that it involves choices. Expressed sincerely, though imperfectly, love grows. Love is discerning; it hates the evil that harms the loved one.

> *True love calls for transparency and is not selfish;*
> *nor will it misuse another for dominance.*
> *Love equalizes relationships, encouraging the other.*
> *Love seeks the other's fulfillment*
> *and supports the other in their role.*
> *But we are not perfect persons,*
> *even though love is the nearest perfection we achieve.*
> *Love does mean accepting our responsibility.*
> *It does include saying "I'm sorry."*
> *It calls for and thrives on forgiveness.*

October 14

Be Devoted to One Another

Love one another with mutual affection; outdo one another in showing honor. Romans 12:10

Community is a gift and a creation of grace. It doesn't happen automatically. There are essentials for the development of true Christian community. Bonhoeffer wrote of community as a relationship beyond relating to others directly, but, rather, we relate in and through Christ. If we relate directly without Christ as the mediator of oneness, we will be tempted to use, to manipulate, to intimidate, and to dominate. As we relate through Christ, each one is free to be her best; we respect the integrity of each.

Tertullian, one of the great early church fathers, wrote that the world in observing the Christians said, "Behold, how they love one another!" Jesus said, "By this everyone will know that you are my disciples, if you have love for one another" (John 13:35). This is our greater witness.

The second clause of the text calls us to honor one another above ourselves. This is the positive answer to selfishness—to become engaged in seeking the dignity and well-being of others. The courtesies of life grow from being considerate of others, of honoring them. Our tendency is to focus upon ourselves, our interests, our accomplishments, our ambitions. We therein fail to adequately consider others, to listen and truly hear them, to seek ways to enable them in their fulfillment. Listening itself brings a healing gift to another, for it is affirming and participating with the other.

It is the Holy Spirit who pours the love of God in our hearts (Rom. 5:5). He is the one who enables us to be an authentic community, who creates a spirit of oneness, of community by his presence. As we relate to one another in the Spirit of Christ, his common-unity becomes our privilege and our life together.

Someone has said, "When the spiritual tide gets low, every little shrimp has its own puddle." A spiritual revival always brings the church into a new freedom of relationship, a more vital sense of fellowship. Individualism prevents our sharing in community.

Lord, help us to love one another with honor.

Keep Your Spiritual Fervor

Do not lag in zeal, be ardent in spirit, serve the Lord. Romans 12:11

We are to work with zeal, but not arrogance or independence. Zeal is a spirit that we recognize when expressed, but we do not often think of promoting it. Yet, in this text, Paul is urging us to be zealous in the service of the Lord. The word denotes not only continued faithfulness, but an aggressive action in following Christ. Embodied in this word is the call to take the initiative, to be creative in finding ways of effective service. This means more than intense activity; it calls for careful thought and planning.

Zeal is a matter of maintaining integrity in a cause. In our text, zeal is directly related to maintaining our spiritual fervor. This admonition is of importance to those of us who have been Christians for many years, for there is a tendency to become matter-of-fact, routine, or even professional about our religious exercises. We may be honest when singing the lines, "Where is the blessedness I knew when first I saw the Lord?" (William Cowper). We need the revitalization of the Spirit, the reflection and prayer that will renew our love and joy.

There are many keys to keeping up our spiritual fervor, of maintaining our zeal. We should note that this is spiritual fervor, not fever! This is more than simple emotionalism. It is a deeper passion of commitment and fidelity. We must keep our priorities in proper order: relationship with the Lord, with our family, with our work, and with our leisure. By work, I do include "church work," for I had to learn that exercising such duties is not synonymous with putting Christ first. Our priorities are to be set in the context of worship, of serving the Lord, in the awareness that all of life is to be an act of worship. This is a discipline of selectivity in our daily activities as one's eye is focused on the glory of Christ.

> *One's service expresses commitment, true,*
> *But it also confesses who is Lord.*
> *We serve Christ because we belong to Christ.*
> *Knowing that one is serving God*
> *is enough to quicken our zeal.*
> *An ardent spirit becomes contagious,*
> *communicating by the spirit in which we serve.*

October 16

Be Joyful in Hope

Rejoice in hope, be patient in suffering, persevere in prayer. Romans 12:12

Attitude is of major importance in our lives. Often technical or professional expertise may qualify one for a good position, only to have advancement thwarted by a poor attitude. In the exercise of faith, the same dynamic is to be recognized, for even in holding to the faith of Christ, one may project a defensive, a legalistic, or a negative spirit that denies the victory of Christ, of whom we witness.

In the preceding verse Paul called us to keep a fervent spirit. Now he follows with three ingredients to make this a reality. (1) We are to be joyful in hope—rejoicing in the assurance that God will fulfill his promises. (2) We are to be patient in suffering—to look at life whole rather than to seek instant gratification for the immediate. (3) We are to be faithful in prayer—seeking to know and to identify with God's will and purpose. These three elements will keep our zeal for God's glory from atrophy.

The Christian life is not an unrealistic life. We are not on Fantasy Island spiritually. We do not convince ourselves of a bliss that makes an artificial euphoria. We live in hope, we live with affliction, and we live with dependency. But we are inspired by the nature of our hope, a hope grounded in the resurrection of Christ. We rejoice as though our resurrected future were already our experience. Our affliction, suffering, pain, and difficulties are genuine; and similar to those of anyone else. But we can exercise patience, knowing that God is working through the affliction to achieve greater partnership in his grace.

We need to come to God in and prayer, draw close to him for inner strength, rather using God for an escape. We walk with him in both bliss and pain. We are faithful in prayer, even if we don't feel like praying. The awareness of God will energize our faith.

We rejoice in him. The prophet Nehemiah said,
"The joy of the Lord is your strength." (8:10)
The stronger one is within,
the more stable in storms without.
There is a rest for the people of God,
a rest in his completed work. (cf. Heb. 10:9)

October 17

Practice Hospitality

Contribute to the needs of the saints; extend hospitality to strangers.
Romans 12:13

The new community of disciples has been described in Scripture as the family of God. The Scripture speaks of God as our Father, Christ as our Elder Brother, and each of us as sisters and brothers in the family. In this family relationship we avoid sibling rivalry; we encourage and help one another. This includes our finances, for our text says to share with God's people who are in need, to practice hospitality.

When the church was born on the day of Pentecost, one characteristic of this new community was that they "were together and had everything in common" (Acts 2:44). One of the first institutional concerns of the church was to organize and appoint deacons for the express purpose of seeing that the needs of members were met equitably. Paul wrote of gathering funds from the new churches in Asia Minor to assist those in Judea who were suffering. Paul reports his dialogue with Peter, John, and James at Jerusalem. They examined Paul as a recent convert to Christ. Endorsing his gospel, they added simply, "[Continue to] remember the poor" (Gal. 2:8-10).

In the sixteenth century, Felix Manz, one of the earliest leaders in the Anabaptist movement in Zurich, was accused of teaching the "community of goods." This he denied, but he said that he had taught, "What is mine is the church's when my brother or sister has need." He was drowned for his faith at the hands of the Protestants. They tied his hands together, brought his knees up between his wrists, and a stick through so that he could not wriggle, or swim, and then threw him into the Limmat River.

India, like China, also has a billion people, and many are poor. We must recognize that in the global village of well over six billion people, over one billion of them have basic needs for survival. In developing countries, 80 percent will never see a doctor personally; 50 percent will never see a clinic. In India it is estimated that 23 million children die every year from inadequate food and health needs. At the same time, the gap increases between those who have and those who have not. There is no easy solution, but we can begin by refusing to be selfish, by practicing a hospitality of sharing, and by helping our leaders recognize the importance of an economy of development rather than militarism.

Lord, give us a faith that is generous and giving.
Show us ways we can be more hospitable and less selfish. Amen

October 18

Bless and Do Not Curse

Bless those who persecute you; bless and do not curse them. Romans 12:14

How positive is God's word and how clear, how simple, and yet how profound! God meets us in story and guides us in counsel, as expressed again in this verse—a positive approach to life even in difficulties.

Not everyone likes us! Sometimes this is because we are Christians and are truly a reminder that they, too, could walk with Christ. Sometimes it is just because of the way we are, the traits of our personalities or of our lifestyle don't always make it easy for people to like us. Once in a meeting with Walter Wilson, he said to me, "I love all people, but I don't like everybody. There are a lot of people I'm glad I'm not married to."

When negativism is expressed and we are hurt or are made to suffer by others, we are to respond in love, not retaliation. We should not let the attitude and actions of others determine our action in reaction. Paul's words are reminiscent of Jesus's words, "Bless those who curse you, pray for those who mistreat you" (Luke 6:28, NIV).

Martin Luther King Jr. once said, "Nonviolence means avoiding not only external physical violence but also internal violence of spirit." The key is in the positive action through which we extend the goodness of God to others. We are agents of shalom, of his peace. As we seek the well-being of others, we will bring them good and not ill. Our attitude will be a blessing, not retaliatory cursing. We need the love of Christ to enable us to meet others in love. This is the way of freedom, of not having one's behavior determined by the opposition.

In India, the Christians make up only 3 to 4 percent of the population; persecution has become more intense, especially in Gujarat and Orissa, where Christians have died for the faith. Young Hindus have become aggressive in opposing Western religion. A few years ago, missionary Graham Staines and his two sons were burned, along with their van, by young Hindu fundamentalists. The wife and mother, Gladys Staines, declined to leave India. On TV she shared her faith in Christ, offering forgiveness to those who had killed her husband and sons. In her expression of grace, many persons in India heard the gospel.

That which lives to triumph is forgiving love.
Lord, help me to bless and forgive,
As you have blessed and forgiven me.

Rejoice and Weep with Others

Rejoice with those who rejoice, weep with those who weep. Romans 12:15

Empathy is a strange word. It means more than offering sympathy, for it means entering into the experience of others. Being members of the body of Christ, we are members of one another. In this partnership we share common joy in the blessings another receives, and we share common pain when another suffers. Our text calls us to empathize with others.

We are more inclined to speak of compassion, of caring when another has difficulty, than we are to speak of rejoicing in another's good fortune. It is easier to share from our privilege to assist another than to rejoice with another in their promotion. The latter is often an occasion for envy. But this text calls us to rejoice with those who rejoice and to mourn with those who mourn. Someone has said, "God's cure for envy is to respect his right to appoint another person her role in life."

The text is a call to positive action. We are on the same team, and their success or good play is ours. Their fumble or hurt is ours as well. Being partners, the important thing is that they feel we are with them. Rejoicing with another is a liberating experience, for psychologically it frees them to rejoice. Our sharing helps them set their joy in the larger context and purifies it from being simple pride.

Paul writes to the Philippians of the inner dynamic of rejoicing in the Lord (Phil. 4:4), for this sanctifies our joy, making us aware that it is God's goodness that we celebrate and not our selfish gain. In turn, we weep with those who weep. This is liberating. True caring is to say, "Your problem is also my problem. I own it with you."

Joy is an exercise of spirit;
it is a therapy for our moods.
We find joy in our relationships;
we get pleasure in things.
We rejoice in relationship with God,
and in fellowship with God's people.
Joy-happiness is a tonic for living!

October 20

Don't Be Proud

Live in harmony with one another; do not be haughty, but associate with the lowly; do not claim to be wiser than you are. Romans 12:16

Pride is our basic sin, even while it is a basic power. There is a proper self-esteem, but it is not to be idolized or misused. This basic sin, described by Reinhold Niebuhr, is expressed in two ways: dominance and sensuality. Both are a quest for power over another by self-indulgence.

Community means that we are one people in Christ and relate in common respect. Just as we are all alike sinners but not sinners alike, so we are alike disciples but not disciples alike. Our unity is in oneness with diversity. This also becomes an occasion for problems. Recognition given to gifted persons may lead to feelings of class or status roles. Respect for the abilities of others means that we rejoice in their privilege without being jealous or being competitive. The one with five talents is to be faithful, and that in proportion to the one with two talents. This keeps integrity in the community.

Gifted persons, with the privileges of winsome personalities, good minds, good voices, educational achievements, or management abilities, are not to be proud. They are to take their place with others, working for the good of the whole. Paul says we are to associate with people of low position, a statement that may be translated, "Be willing to participate in manual labor." He concludes by saying pointedly, "Don't be conceited." We might say, "Don't be stuck-up; don't look down on others in their role."

Over fifty years ago, as a young minister at the age of twenty-one, I was conducting evangelistic meetings in Arkansas. The pastor, Clarence Horst, took me to visit a family that had a number of teenage sons. We invited them to the meetings. The father, pointing to a field of hay, mowed and dry, now ready to take in to the barn, said that they had no time for church. In my effort to identify, I said, "Suppose I come tomorrow and help put the hay in the barn. Will you come to church?" He may have had doubts as to whether this young preacher would work in the hayfield, but with surprise he said, "If you help us, we'll come and hear you preach." The next day I had a demanding but enjoyable workday with them. In the evening they came, and several of those young men responded to the invitation to come to Christ.

Thank you, Lord, for every walk of life
and for the many different people you have created.

Good for Evil

Do not repay anyone evil for evil, but take thought for what is noble in the sight of all. Romans 12:17

Love is not simply an abstract principle. It is a spirit of life expressed in concrete situations. We, however, do not let the situation determine our attitude, for we come into every situation with the prior commitment of discipleship of Christ. We seek the way of love for whoever is involved and in ways appropriate to the occasion. This love frees us to act in the will of God rather than to have our behavior determined by the opponent's situation alone. To repay evil for evil is evil; to repay good for good is human. But to meet evil with love is the way of Christ. This quality love is shown at Calvary, in Jesus accepting the cross. Jesus was nonresistant to his enemies, absorbing their hostility as the cost of love.

The verse also calls us to be careful to do what is right in the sight of everybody. We are to be sure that evil done to us is not because we have done evil; rather, we are to express righteousness. This is a work of the Spirit. When Jesus promised to give us the Spirit, he said that by our lives the Spirit will convince the world of their sin of unbelief, of righteousness by our right relationship with God, and of judgment by showing that Satan and evil have been judged and defeated in our lives (John 16:8-11).

This text sounds like Jesus's words in the Sermon on the Mount (Matt. 5:38-44). Jesus stated that God had limited revenge in the Old Testament to a measure of equity, only "an eye for an eye and a tooth for a tooth" rather than tribal havoc (Exod. 21:23-25). Then Jesus said, "*But I say to you*, Do not resist an evildoer. . . . Turn the other cheek. . . . Go also the second mile. . . . Love your enemies." The answer to how we confront evil is to not meet it on its own grounds, but with a strategy of love. In turning the other cheek, we show that we are free to behave differently than the offender.

Turning the other cheek
is not the way of the wimp;
it is the strategy of love,
the way of the disciple.
Love does not necessarily win now,
but its victory is its focus.
Love triumphs by transcending hate.

Live at Peace with All

**If it is possible, so far as it depends on you, live peaceably with all.
Romans 12:18**

Seek every possibility of living at peace. The injunction has only one qualification: "If it is possible, so far as it depends on you." We cannot determine that the other person will respond and come to peace, but we can determine our own action. The King James Version reads, "As much as lieth in you, live peaceably with all men." Someone has said, "When the Holy Spirit is in you, filling you with his fruit as expressions of love, so much is possible." The question then is, What are the principles that make for peace?

Jesus said, "Blessed are the peacemakers, for they will be called [recognized as] children of God" (Matt. 5:9). Paul says, "For the kingdom of God is not food and drink but righteousness and peace and joy in the Holy Spirit" (Rom. 14:17). As we think of peace with the Old Testament word *shalom* meaning the total well-being of a person, these three words, "righteousness, peace, and joy," are the interrelated characteristics of shalom.

The text is not an idealism which is never experienced; it is a practice for daily living. We are to do as much as is possible to be at peace with everyone. The gospel is not perfectionistic; it is realistic and relational. Jesus lived in the will of God, yet he did not experience peace with everyone. Even in cleansing the temple court to make room for the common people and the Gentiles to come to worship, he used discretion. He drove the sheep and the oxen out of the temple, overturned the tables of the money changers, and spoke in his anger to the men who were defiling the temple. We do not know that he laid the whip on any person. It was a drastic action, but it was a moral choice; he could not fail the Gentiles, who should have access, nor would he avoid confronting the Jewish hucksters about their irreverence and injustice.

"So far as it depends on you!"
That is, do all that is possible
to promote the shalom of God for everyone.
This, too, is our witness for Christ.
We are his disciples, and therein
we are called to the life of peace.
"Blessed are the peacemakers." (Matt. 5:9)

Do Not Take Revenge

Beloved, never avenge yourselves, but leave room for the wrath of God; for it is written, "Vengeance is mine, I will repay, says the Lord." Romans 12:19

What we call justice is too often paying back in kind and is actually revenge. Justice has in it more than punishment. It constitutes a correction of the problem. This must take into account all of the related factors that created the injustice, hold the person accountable, but work for correcting the problem itself.

Revenge focuses on the offender and is set on punishing such a person for misdeeds. In more primitive days, if a person of one tribe was violated by someone from another tribe, the person offended would be avenged by his own tribe going and working havoc on the offending tribe with a revenge going far beyond the original deed of ill. Through Moses, God placed a limit on revenge, only "an eye for an eye, and a tooth for a tooth" (Lev. 24:20; Deut. 19:21). Jesus taught that we are to wish blessing on the persecutor, even while working for justice. Leviticus gives an admonition, not to seek revenge, but to "love your neighbor as yourself" (Lev. 19:18).

There are a number of reasons why we should leave revenge to God rather than seeking to execute it ourselves. First, only God can understand all of the aspects of an offense, including not only circumstances but motive, whether premeditated or spontaneous, with malice or committed in a moment of passion. Our courts do seek to discern these factors. Second, only God can be fully just in the proportionate execution of punishment. Third, revenge is not only in actions we perform, but is internalized and becomes an attitude that perverts the lives of those who engage it. Fourth, patterns of revenge create social associations governed by fear rather than by love and freedom. Revenge is left to God, who holds all people accountable for their actions (Deut. 32:35).

An early Anabaptist preacher was being persecuted by a few young men to pressure him to move away. In the wee hours of the morning, he heard the noise of men on the roof, tearing off the shingles. He asked his wife to prepare a good breakfast for guests, then went out and called to the men, "You've been working hard. Please come in and have breakfast with us." They came down and filed in around the table. He offered a prayer of thanks and of blessing for each of them, and then they began eating. But in a few minutes the men were unable to eat. They stood up, went out, put the shingles back on the roof, and slipped away.

If Your Enemy Hungers

No, "if your enemies are hungry, feed them; if they are thirsty, give them something to drink; for by doing this you will heap burning coals on their heads." Romans 12:20

Abraham Lincoln is thought to have said, "We should destroy our enemies by making friends out of them." The higher level of life is community and fellowship, and this is achieved by following Jesus words, "As you would that others should do unto you, you should become busily engaged in doing to them" (paraphrase of Matt. 7:12). This is not negative; it is a positive principle to inject a healing spirit into life's situations.

Our text is actually almost an exact quotation of Proverbs 25:21-22. Here the wise man has stated this principle of behavior among his ethical axioms. Paul quotes this passage as a part of what I call a "Jesus ethic." That is, we behave according to the ethic of Christ, seeing his example as expressing the full word and will of God.

As a boy I remember a story from my father's experience while foreman on a construction project in Newport News, Virginia. Another carpenter was jealous of Dad and had wanted his promotion, and so consequently caused him trouble. Due to hard times, the head office reduced the number of men on the job, and dad's enemy was one of those who lost his job. Work was not easy to find and each morning when Dad went to work, a group of men would be waiting at the gate, among whom was Bob, each hoping that he might be hired again. One day Dad negotiated a work arrangement that permitted him to rehire two men. He went to the gate, and told the men that he needed two workmen. He looked them over, pointed toward one good carpenter, and told him to get his tools. Then he turned to his enemy and said, "Bob, get your tools." In this he won the man's friendship and respect.

The text closes with the word picture of "heaping coals of fire on his head." In the cultures of the East, when your fire has gone out, you go to a neighbor with a pot on your head to get some live coals to start your own fire. It is a great favor to be given coals of fire when in need. So we are to extend special favors even to our enemies with acts of love.

October 25

Overcome Evil with Good

Do not be overcome by evil, but overcome evil with good. Romans 12:21

This is one of the shorter and more effective formulas for social transformation. It is a central characteristic of reconciliation. This pattern of love is the method to which God has bound himself in our redemption. The gospel says God has no other approach to us than to overcome evil with good, to overcome our rebellion and hostility by his self-giving love: "While we still were sinners Christ died for us" (Rom. 5:8).

To say that we are to overcome evil with good is not a guarantee that we will always win or come out on top. We may suffer by taking God's way, as seen in Jesus, in the way of the cross. First, it is victorious in that it is a refusal to have behavior determined by the evil. Second, it brings goodness into the situation as influence surpassing the evil. Third, it triumphs in leaving an example that will spread in the community.

As Christians, we are to take the initiative in love, reaching out to others. We should regard no one as beyond the transforming power of God's grace. Love is a strategy of building bridges. Goodness is the action through which love is communicated. To share in this way calls us to release hurts that we have suffered and to be able to extend love to the hurting. It has been well said, "Hurt people hurt people."

There is a remarkable story of a young man who stopped at a farmhouse asking for work. The farmer asked of his occupation, which was carpentry. At first the farmer said he had no work. Then, pointing across the road to the neighboring farm, he said, "That is where my brother lives, and we have become bitter enemies. He even took a bulldozer and cut a stream from the reservoir through the pasture between us. I'll hire you to take that lumber by the barn and build an eight-foot high solid fence between us, so that I don't need to be looking at him."

The farmer went to town for the day, and the young man went to work. When the farmer returned, instead of a fence, he saw a beautiful bridge across the stream, with handrails and all. At first irritated, he saw his brother walking down the hill to the bridge with his arms outstretched. As he walked to meet him, his younger brother called out, "You are a special brother, to think that you would build a bridge so that we can get together!" As the carpenter was walking away, the farmer called, "Hey, where are you going?" The man answered, "I'm going to build other bridges!"

Authority as Ordained by God

Let every person be subject to the governing authorities; for there is no authority except from God, and those authorities that exist have been instituted by God. Romans 13:1

Authority is ordained by God to maintain order in life. It is God who has and does set up authority. What is often overlooked is the fact that God, in doing the ordaining, is still above the authorities. Paul has just taught us that we are not to avenge evil, not to meet violence with violence. Now the question is, How do we live with such a lifestyle in a sinful world? Paul's answer is that God ordains government as the authority, to keep order in society, to police society, to punish evil and protect the good. I was once privileged to address the National Police Association in the Baltimore Convention Center, where I reminded them that we, at one time, spoke of the police as being "peace officers."

God, having established authorities, does not mean that we now give to them absolute loyalty. God establishes the authority therefore God is above it and is the highest authority. We obey authorities, but our loyalty is above all to God. At times we must say as did the apostles, "We must obey God rather than any human authority" (Acts 5:29). The early church rejected the request to offer the pinch of incense annually and declare "Caesar is lord." They did so by refusing and boldly declaring "Christ is Lord!" Our first loyalty is to Christ. Christians should live a more noble life than that which civil laws require. Yet civil laws can be consistent with Christian principles.

The relation of church and state has been a problem ever since Constantine merged the two and created a state church. This was a major issue in the Reformation. The Anabaptists insisted on a total separation and freedom to obey the mandate of Christ. The state church saw them as a threat and by violent persecution took the lives of thousands. Roger Williams first instituted this religious freedom in Rhode Island. With a free church perspective and an Anabaptist theology, we are in society as a support, not a threat. We serve the state by encouraging it to live up to the highest in its own claims.

During the Revolutionary War, Isaac Potts, a mill owner and minister near Valley Forge, sided with the British. But one day while walking through the trees, he heard a voice. Looking through the trees, he saw George Washington praying, tears on his cheeks, asking God to help him do the right things for this new nation. Potts was so impressed that he changed from being a Tory and became a supporter of the American cause.

Not Resisting What God Has Appointed

Therefore whoever resists authority resists what God has appointed, and those who resist will incur judgment. Romans 13:2

The disciple who walks in the Spirit is free and lives above constraints of law. But the disciple is not against law. Law serves a very special purpose in establishing order in society. Whenever one lives below the level of righteousness in Christ, the law is there to hold him accountable and to order or direct his life. We, however, are to be inner-directed, persons with the higher ethics of Christ rather than being outer-directed, or persons controlled primarily by the mores of society.

To rebel against authority is to rebel against something God has instituted. In answering to authority, whether it be government, police, societal, or parental authority, we are recognizing the larger relationships of life. We seek the good of all people, not just our own interests. As strangers and pilgrims, we do not find our total fulfillment in this world. We are not parasites upon society, but participants in the human order; we are in the world while not of the world. We serve for the moral, educational, social, artistic, economic, health, and welfare values that enrich any society. We seek justice, equity, and human rights for all peoples, thereby enabling any society to be the better.

John R. W. Stott wrote a book entitled *Christian Counter-Culture*, in which he argued for enriching society by infusing the values of Christian faith. Stott said that we recognize in Jesus's teachings that "the desire to rule is wrong." We are called to serve, to enrich others. Christians refusing to meet force with force, or violence with violence, are a salt to the earth and a light to the world (cf. Matt. 5:13-16).

We are citizens of the kingdom of Christ.
We have a global relation to balance our nationalism.
We care for the whole human family and its well-being,
not just for our own commonwealth alone.
True, we want order and freedom within our land,
desiring it for service in the kingdom, not selfishly.
America is great because of its freedom in sharing.

October 28

No Terror for Good Conduct

For rulers are not a terror to good conduct, but to bad. Do you wish to have no fear of the authority? Then do what is good, and you will receive its approval. Romans 13:3

I recall Bishop Festo Kivengere of Uganda telling a story of driving in England. He passed a car and went beyond the white line to where there was a yellow line. Just then, he met a policeman. Festo said, "In that moment I was overtaken with fear." Such is the meaning of this passage. Freedom from fear of the authorities is by doing what is right, and they will be your friend; they will commend you.

While the church is to operate by the higher level of the will of God, the state operates by the will of the people, of the governed. As Christians, we are a part of the governed, and we live in obedience to the state and join the people in calling the state to uphold the highest possible level of its claims. By sharing Christian insights, we actually enrich the level of morality and raise the expectation of the state. In the contribution of the Christian community, enriching and strengthening the state, we earn commendation from the authorities. But the church is never to be a political party in a competitive role.

When Christians need to say no to the idolatries of nationalism, to civil religion, to social perversions in the state with its variety of peoples, we do so with concern to help the state achieve justice for all. In the refusal by Christians to participate in war, because of our being conscientiously opposed to doing violence to any people, we still serve the state by helping focus its place in the global community. We serve by finding humanitarian ways in which to contribute. The church can transcend national lines and build a network of friends between nations by building bridges. The role of the state is to confront and negotiate with other nations by political diplomacy and power.

During the Vietnam War I had an appointment at the Pentagon with Secretary of Defense Melvin Laird. We talked for an hour of a higher honor than what he and President Nixon were seeking by war. He was very respectful, saying that my views made more sense to him than the position of preachers who led marches in Washington, crying "Victory at any price!" He added, "I could not be Secretary of Defense with your position." I well understood, and as he asked me to pray with him, I asked for humility for us both so that we could rethink our positions.

God's Servant to Do You Good

For it is God's servant for your good. But if you do what is wrong, you should be afraid, for the authority does not bear the sword in vain! It is the servant of God to execute wrath on the wrongdoer. Romans 13:4

While this text affirms that the role of government is in God's service, it also makes clear that there is one sovereign God, and that the government is under God as servant. With this understanding, the Christian looks at government in a positive manner. We seek to be good citizens, working supportively for the good of all. If we do wrong, we expect to be prosecuted by the government, for "it does not bear the sword in vain."

Many of us have deep convictions against abortion; yet our witness is not by violence at abortion clinics, but by teaching and helping those who have an unwanted pregnancy. Further, as my friend Vernon Grounds, president of the Conservative Baptist Seminary in Denver for many years, has said, "We are not only concerned for 'right to life' for the unborn. We are also concerned for 'right to life' for the born and are therefore against nuclear arms and warfare." In our text, Paul is respecting government as God's servant, saying that it is an agent of justice to bring judgment on the wrongdoer.

While this text explains the role of government as policing, in a democracy we also see government as enabling the welfare and order of society with very positive contributions. In the time of Paul, the rulers that he asked Christians to respect was the Roman government, the regime of Caesar. When Paul needed protection from the Jews, he appealed to Caesar; in so doing he utilized the government for his protection as a Roman citizen. As we travel in many countries, I am very thankful for a United States passport and its provisions. Our government is a minister of God to us for good!

We have been in areas where a government has a rule which says it is illegal to encourage another person to change his religion. In spite of this, the church in its own freedom continues to grow. Speaking in the Evangelical Fellowship of India Conventions in 1964, I went to Nepal. There I visited Pram Prahdan, in prison for converting and baptizing persons into the faith of Christ. The Nepalese believers answered their government by saying that they were not engaged in wrongdoing but were being loyal to God. The church in Nepal continues to grow. Voluntarism is not accepted by controlling governments because they are threatened by such an expression of freedom.

Subject Because of Conscience

Therefore one must be subject, not only because of wrath but also because of conscience. Romans 13:5

Fortunately, our government respects people's religious convictions. But since one's conscience speaks according to the way it has been informed, being programmed like a computer and informed that government is instituted by God and serves his purpose, many Christians are absolutistic about obedience to government. But conscience is to stand under the Word of God. Having been called to live at peace with all people as far as it is possible, the Christian conscience calls for a peaceful order of life in society. By this conduct the government will see Christians as law-abiding, supportive, not subversive, confrontational but not critical, and those who will sometimes abstain.

"But also because of conscience" means that as Christians we have an inner direction to live in the will of God as we know it. Rather than to be directed by guilt and fear, we are to be directed by freedom and love. This freedom is the liberty of the child of God, the freedom to live as members of his kingdom while we are sojourners, strangers, pilgrims, and resident aliens in this social order. But we are sent into the world, we are ambassadors for Christ, and our relation with the world is one of representing the highest good in love, compassion, justice, equity, service, and creative enrichment of society.

The phrase "but also because of conscience" is first a call for integrity, a call to our higher ethic of what is right in solidarity with Christ. In some cases, to be true to our Lord, we must say to governmental authorities: "We must obey God rather than any human authority" (Acts 5:29). As Christians, we are subject in all areas where we have agreement from the Word. But we can remind governments that they are servants of God, responsible to the highest authority. Our allegiance to God is a prophetic word. We are to seek God's will.

In the sixteenth century, the Anabaptists suffered and were martyred by the thousands across Europe. Yet they spoke to government officials and spoke of government itself as "Servants of God." In this recognition they called on government to live by the will of God in freedom for all. This is the respect to which we are called, even when in our commitment to freedom and to peace, we may disobey them to obey God.

October 31

This Is Why You Pay Taxes

For the same reason you also pay taxes, for the authorities are God's servants, busy with this very thing. Romans 13:6

We should pay our taxes with a smile, with gratitude for our privilege of economic freedom. The payment of taxes is based on the divine order. Taxes are the way in which a government is supported, but also the way in which the government may have resources to aid the needy. Our text says that we pay taxes because government is God's servant and we support God's order. Those serving in government give their time to govern and should receive support from those whom they serve. It is similar to the mandate for church leaders: "Those who proclaim the gospel should get their living by the gospel" (1 Cor. 9:14).

We Christians are not parasites, we are functioning members of society. We pay our taxes. However, at times governments raise taxes for causes, including warfare, which we as Christians do not support. The nuclear arms race has been a case in point or the general militarizing of our nation and of international relations. As Christian citizens we are responsible to exercise our freedom for confrontation, to speak to alternate patterns of international relations that build good neighbor relations rather than pursuing the path of power. We know from Jesus's teachings that violence begets violence. Even the agnostic Henry David Thoreau said, "If in a country its government acts wrongly, then a prison is the only place where a self-respecting person can live." For us in faith, John Howard Yoder speaks of "principalities and powers," which he describes by three words: Mars (the Roman god of war), mammon, and me; that is: militarism, materialism, and individualism. Such principalities should look at the church to see what God actually purposes in the world (Eph. 3:10).

As to Christian conscience on the matter of a government's uses of tax monies, some see this as "our money." But is it our money once it is paid as tax? Is it not the government's money? I do not believe that God intends for me to live with a guilt complex over the use of this money by government when it is *their* money. Once a tax is paid, it is no longer mine. But a tax refund is now mine since I paid income tax on my earnings. My witness is to free my conscience as a citizen in standing against violence.

November 1

Give Everyone What You Owe Him

Pay to all what is due them—taxes to whom taxes are due, revenue to whom revenue is due, respect to whom respect is due, honor to whom honor is due. Romans 13:7

Our goal is to live above reproach. This text speaks of four areas in which Christians respect political and social orders. We pay taxes to meet political services, revenue to meet services of economic benefits to us, respect for those in position with whom we deal, and honor to those whose position calls for special respect. We are to live as free people who first serve God, and in reverence for God we honor the authorities. Paul and Peter include leaders in the church as persons to be honored for their service. Paul says, "Let the elders who rule well be considered worthy of double [honorarium]" (1 Tim. 5:17).

In yesterday's meditation, attention was given to paying taxes. What do we do when a government is taxing us for a cause like war, which violates our conscience and in which we cannot conscientiously participate? While I affirm that the taxes paid are no longer my money but the government's, there is an alternative action that I can take. First, we have the government's approval that I can give as much as possible to charity and reduce the tax. Second, I can then pay my tax, knowing that I need to support much that is worthy. Third, I can calculate the percent of the tax I pay that the government will use for causes I cannot support and give an equivalent as a matching gift to a cause benefiting the needy. This is not just protesting taxes, but is a genuine human interest action.

Help me, Lord, to respect and pray
for those in authority,
who serve, often at risk to themselves,
diligent in seeking an ordered life.
Help me to look beyond this order,
beyond my material and social well-being
to the larger cause of the kingdom of Christ,
and set my order of life in this context.
Enable me to live in service to others,
that in this service they may meet you. Amen

November 2

Owe Nothing Except Love

Owe no one anything, except to love one another; for the one who loves another has fulfilled the law. Romans 13:8

We are to be free of debt except for one thing, the debt of love. This debt, Paul says, is always to be with us. As God loves us and continues to do so, we are to love one another—always. Paul uses this term similarly in Romans 1:14: "I am debtor both to Greeks and to barbarians" in sharing the gospel of Christ. Here he says that we who have received so freely from God are now debtors to share his love with those about us.

To share love sounds simple at first as we think of an attitude of caring, of compassion. But how do we share with people who are in need and at the same time respect their dignity and avoid insulting them? How do we share faith with sophisticated people who may be rich in means, but poor spiritually? While in India I wrote an essay emphasizing that we need an "oxcart theology," an understanding of a people tied closely to life, to basic human survival needs. Every day we saw men with oxcarts transporting their produce or tools, women with machetes cutting grass or wood and placing great bundles on their heads to walk miles to sell for several rupees, or workmen mixing cement with a broad hoe and women with basins on their heads carrying cement to other workmen for pouring. We observed contrasts in housing from the apartments being built to the tiny tent-like shacks in which the workmen and their families lived. As we walked the streets entreated by beggars, we would ask, how do we express love in this setting?

Just before we left India in 1987, Esther and I bought a poor man his freedom. He was a slave to loan sharks. He was paying 120 percent interest on two loans of 2,000 rupees, which he had borrowed for the weddings of his two daughters. It took his monthly income just to meet the interest payments. He was a slave in that he could never pay the principal. We arranged a gift to the Union Biblical Seminary (UBS) to establish an interest-free loan fund from which they were to pay the entire principal for him and set him free! This enabled him to pay on the interest-free loan. The fund could then be used to help others. Returning to UBS several years later, we found it rewarding to see the wonderful freedom in the man's countenance as he served others in his community.

Love Fulfills the Law

The commandments, "You shall not commit adultery; You shall not murder; You shall not steal; You shall not covet"; and any other commandment, are summed up in this word, "Love your neighbor as yourself." Romans 13:9

It is significant that this passage on love follows the treatise on respect for the authority of government. In fact, the passage on relation to government is sandwiched between two passages on love; one at the end of chapter 12 and this passage at the end of chapter 13. Paul says that living by love will be the fulfillment of the law. Someone has said, "If you have love in your life, it can make up for a great many things you lack. If you don't have love, no matter what else there is, it is not enough."

In our verse today, the laws of human relations are summed up in one law: "Love your neighbor as yourself." Jesus said that this is the second commandment, of the same nature as the first. When we open our life to God, we will then open to others the priority of love.

The power of love is shown in that if we live by love, we will not violate the commandments of relationship with our fellows. In the Sermon on the Mount, Jesus said that anything that leads to killing or to adultery is wrong. Now we are further made aware that it is love that prevents or "covers over" our tendency to do such sin (cf. 1 Pet. 4:8). That is, if we truly love, we won't commit adultery and violate covenant. If we truly love, we will not kill and destroy another. If we truly love, we will not steal and deprive another. If we truly love, we will not covet, but rejoice in the other's good fortune.

At Union Biblical Seminary we met Naba, a former Hindu from Nagaland. One of nine children of the leading orthodox Hindu, he was a member of the king's royal court, with his name in the select register of achievement. He lived in a court of dwellings totaling over two hundred family members, all Hindu. As a youth he became addicted to alcohol and was known for the perversions in his life. Hearing the gospel of a God of love was so different from the thousands of gods, who are all gods of fear, that he came to Christ. Upon his new birth he was set free, including his dependency on alcohol, a testimony his family could not deny. Now, although rejected by his family, he is a witness to the love of God.

November 4

Love Does Not Harm Others

Love does no wrong to a neighbor; therefore, love is the fulfilling of the law.
Romans 13:10

Because love does not harm the neighbor, it is the fulfillment of the law. The implication is that the righteousness of the law involves equity, justice, freedom, mutuality, and peace. Love does not violate another, does not coerce, does not manipulate.

"Love is friendship that has caught fire. It is quiet understanding, mutual confidence, sharing, and forgiving. It is loyalty through good and bad times. It settles for less than perfection and makes allowances for human weaknesses." In these lines someone has helped us relate the spirit of love to the relationships of life. Love always helps rather than hinders, encourages rather than intimidates. It corrects, but it does not demoralize or destroy initiative. It enriches by delighting in the good that lifts the level of life for one and all.

It seems that Paul cannot overemphasize the importance of this love-ethic. For a second time he says, "Love is the fulfillment of the law." As disciples of Christ, we are called to live in his love. Jesus told the disciples, "As I have loved you, so you should love one another" (John 13:34). John wrote, "Love is from God; everyone who loves is born of God and knows God" (1 John 4:7). Again, "God is love, and those who abide in love abide in God, and God abides in them" (1 John 4:16).

Jesus tells of coming judgment when all nations are gathered before the throne. This judgment is based on expressions of love in the Spirit of Christ. We should note Jesus's words to those whom he accepts: "Just as you did it to one of the least of these who are members of my family, you did it to me" (Matt. 25:40).

On my calling card I have had printed the following lines:

If love were possible without the gospel,
we would need no gospel.
If love is not possible by the gospel,
we have no gospel.
That love is possible by the gospel is
what Christian discipleship is all about.

November 5

Our Salvation Is Nearer Now

Besides this, you know what time it is, how it is now the moment for you to wake from sleep. For salvation is nearer to us now than when we became believers. Romans 13:11

Time for the Christian is linear; it is history moving to its climax. We do not see history as a cycle, ever repeating itself. We do not seek nonattachment as a means of peace, but rather we see history moving in God's purpose to a grand and glorious climax. "When he is revealed," John writes, "we will be like him, for we will see him as he is" (1 John 3:2). This eschatological hope adds a future dimension to the salvation we are already enjoying in our being reconciled to God. The future dimension is referenced in Paul's words in our text: "Salvation is nearer to us than when we became believers."

His appeal is for us to understand the present time in light of this eschatological hope. The time we have is given *now*. The impact of the kingdom of God in which we share is *now*. We know the end of history from the middle of history in Jesus Christ. We live each day in the light of the coming fulfillment of history. We live in what is called the *eschaton*: we live now in light of the coming of our Lord. The call of the text is for us to be diligent, to avoid the indifference of slumber. Jesus said we are to occupy until he comes.

In the parable of the talents, we are instructed to faithfulness, whether we have five or two or one special gift from God, we are called to be faithful. In the story, those who use their gifts are blessed by the master, but the one who wastes his gift is condemned.

When Paul says, "Salvation is nearer to us than when we became believers" (Matt. 25:14-30), he is expressing faith that Jesus can come at any time. But with our interest in eschatology, we are not date setters. Vernard Eller quips, "Some preachers act as if they are selling tickets to the battle of Armageddon!" We should live as though we'll be here a thousand years, but relate to Christ in a faithfulness that would welcome him today. We are to keep before us the ultimate fulfillment of our salvation, the actual presence of Christ coming to receive us into the glory of his eternal presence. True faith enables us to live as "resident aliens," to live responsibly in our daily walk as disciples.

November 6

Put on the Armor of Light

The night is far gone, the day is near. Let us then lay aside the works of darkness and put on the armor of light. Let us live honorably as in the day, not in reveling and drunkenness, not in debauchery and licentiousness, not in quarreling and jealousy. Romans 13:12-13

Ours is a lifestyle of righteousness. This theme, the righteousness of God, runs through the epistle and emphasizes a right relatedness with God and thereby with others in life. This is to walk in the light, that is, the light of his presence. Our conduct should be an expression of our relationship with God, characteristic of his family.

We have stressed that Christian ethics is not a means to achieve grace. It is the work of grace in our lives. We are set free in Christ, we are delivered from the old life and granted a new life, we are now led by the Spirit, and we yield ourselves to the Lord as our spiritual worship. Thus we "may discern what is the will of God—what is good and acceptable and perfect" (Rom. 12:2). As his disciples, we relate our ethics or behavior to Christ in the same way that our salvation comes by relating to Christ.

The two verses of our text call us to the careful application of this Christ-centered ethic to our personal lifestyle. Paul refers to "the day" as in contrast to deeds done in the dark that they might be hidden. Jesus called us to be watchful lest we become careless and not be prepared at his coming. We are to put on the armor of light, to know the defense of being transparent in God's presence. "God is light," and "if we walk in the light as he himself is in the light, we have fellowship with one another, and the blood of Jesus his Son cleanses [separates] us from all sin" (1 John 1:5, 7).

Paul describes the unrighteousness of darkness as both sins of the flesh and of the spirit, of personal life and social life. As unitary beings, we cannot compartmentalize our lives. In wholesome relationships we follow "whatever is true, whatever is honorable, whatever is just, whatever is pure, whatever is pleasing, whatever is commendable, if there is any excellence and if there is anything worthy of praise, think about these things" (Phil. 4:8).

The eminent Swiss theologian Emil Brunner said, "To live in love means concretely to let one's life be determined by the existence of others."

Put on the Lord Jesus Christ

Instead, put on the Lord Jesus Christ, and make no provision for the flesh, to gratify its desires. Romans 13:14

St. Augustine was in his youth an agnostic, a profligate, and a sensual person, but he had a praying mother, Monica. Studying in Milan, he was in a garden, wrestling with his own thought and unrest about his inability, as an intelligent person, to live a wholesome life when others with much less intelligence led better lives. Suddenly he heard a voice that sounded like a child, chanting, "Take and read, take and read." Hearing this as a word from God and looking at a scroll lying on the table before him in the garden, he opened it and read this very text: "Put on the Lord Jesus Christ, and make no provision for the flesh, to gratify its desires." This word led Augustine to a wonderful conversion in the exercise of faith.

The Christian church looks to the conversion of this North African man as one of the high-water marks of church history. He is seen as a theological source for both Catholic and Protestant thought. He is called the father of the Western philosophy of history, interpreting history as linear rather than in the cyclical manner of the Greeks. He is seen also as the earliest psychologist of Christian experience. His book *Confessions* is a psychological interpretation and is still read as a timeless message.

This text in Romans is for us a timeless word of God. We are to join solidarity with Christ, find our full identity in relation to him, appropriate the meaning of his presence, and be free to live as God's people. This is the key to transformed thinking, to what Kosuke Koyama, in his book *No Handles on the Cross*, calls the "crucified mind" and "the risen mind." A mind that is renewed with Christ does not give itself to thinking about gratifying the desires of the sinful nature. In Christ we are released from self-centeredness, from the perversions of a life driven by selfish or fleshly desires. Augustine said in his inimitable style:

> *For Thy glory we were and are created,*
> *and our hearts are restless*
> *until they find their rest in Thee.*

November 8

Accepting Those Who Differ

Welcome those who are weak in faith, but not for the purpose of quarreling over opinions. Some believe in eating anything, while the weak eat only vegetables. Romans 14:1-2

People come in many varieties, tall, short, heavy, thin, outgoing, timid, creative, musically gifted, or mathematically inclined. This is much more than physical differences. People come with different cultural conditioning and ways of thinking. The community of faith is made up of an amazing variety of peoples. Its dynamic is in accepting this diversity, in seeking the unity of the body with diversity of its parts.

To accept another without being judgmental becomes, in itself, a challenge to our own maturity. Often a judgmental attitude arises from our own insecurity. Our position is threatened if we accept another person who holds a different position. Each of us needs to work consistently to apply truth in our cultural and intellectual orientation. We are not all at the same place. This is not to say that truth is relative; it is to say that our understanding of truth is still through the grid of our cultural conditioning, and we should regard that understanding as relative. We do not remake others by our own mold. Having taught in various cross-cultural experiences makes me especially conscious of this.

In the second verse of our text, Paul speaks about one eating meat and another eating only vegetables. This we saw as a reality at the Union Biblical Seminary in Pune, India; in its dining hall, is a special table for those who are vegetarian. Many were conditioned as Hindus to avoid meat; conversion to Christ does not automatically change their culturally conditioned aversion to meat.

When Paul speaks of the weak in faith, we should better hear this as "tender" or even "immature" rather than as a personality classification. In mission outreach many new converts are weak in this sense. They have not yet matured in knowing how to prioritize issues. A small issue may be seen as challenging their whole faith. In conversation we are to be understanding, not judgmental, accepting, but avoiding condescension. In leadership roles we need to recognize the tension between excellence and inclusion. In leading our worship services, it is important that we seek participation from the community of believers, and this should include persons who represent other than the elite or highly educated. We together are the body of Christ.

God Has Welcomed Them

Those who eat must not despise those who abstain, and those who abstain must not pass judgment on those who eat; for God has welcomed them.
Romans 14:3

The church in a modern society and an international community must deal realistically with pluralism. Our emphasis must be unity with diversity. Only when we respect the diversity rather than seeking to remove it can we have unity of spirit. As Christians, we are not clones. Unity is a matter of spirit, not of sameness. The presence of differences helps stimulate our unity to grow in understanding and patience.

Someone has said that if two of us see things exactly alike, then one of us is unnecessary. This statement at least focuses for us the fact that we need differences for the enrichment of the body. We can look at issues where we differ, not so much as problems, but as opportunities, not only for our growth, but for the mission of the church. Different ones of us will be able to reach different types of persons in society.

The key in our verse for today is in the last phrase, that in our difference "God has welcomed" the other. If God has accepted him, for me not to do so is to defy God's judgment in the matter. Division in the church is a sin against God, a sin against the Holy Spirit, who is creating the body of Christ. Division is a power struggle between competing egos, but it is also a sin against the sovereignty of the Holy Spirit. Cross-culturally, persons converted to Christ do not immediately change all of their conditionings. We are not to force another person's conscience. Paul says that one with a more broad conscience should not intimidate others or make them feel inferior.

In Western society there is a tension between conservative and liberal thinkers. It helps when we recognize the possibilities of a third way, neither rightist conservative nor leftist liberal. Instead, we make selections from either and reject from either as we seek the way of the kingdom. Having a conservative theology does not necessarily mean a conservative political or social view, for a conservative theology takes the lordship of Christ, the priority of the kingdom of God, and the sovereign leading of the Spirit as ultimate. The disciple must be quite free and socially and politically selective.

Lord, help me to be true to you,
free in society because I am free in Christ.

Judging Another's Servant

Who are you to pass judgment on servants of another? It is before their own lord that they stand or fall. And they will be upheld, for the Lord is able to make them stand. Romans 14:4

God's cure for disunity is for each person to recognize that he and his brothers and sisters, are each alike accountable to God. It is not for us to align another person with our tastes or preferences, but to respect their orientation and accept them with their difference. Paul has said we are not to judge (Rom. 14:1), not to look down on another (14:2), and not to condemn (14:3); here he gives the theological base for his counsel.

This text calls for security, reverence, and faith. We need security in that we should not be threatened by differences that are not moral issues but arise from our own preferences. We are to think of how to enrich one another rather than to be judgmental. It is a call to reverence in that one's brother or sister answers like we do to the Lord. For us to judge the Lord's servant is disrespectful of the Lord and irreverent; we are assuming the role that the Master reserves for himself. The text calls for faith: we need to believe that the God we worship is at work in each of our lives. For long-range success, persons need inner strength from the Lord, who "is able to make them stand" (14:4).

Classes in India were made up of a variety of persons. There was wide variation in languages, knowledge, and theology. Some students were strong, but others were weaker, yet everyone needed to be stimulated to learn. If the more competent students would interfere with my role as teacher and intimidate or judge the weaker, they would spoil the spirit of the class and destroy the learning process. So it is in the community of faith. We encourage one another in Christ; we do not intimidate the weaker ones.

I have seen quite mediocre students helped to become persons of excellence just by being encouraged. Benjamin West, skilled painter of the Hudson River School, tells of the day his mother left him to care for his little sister, Billy. He got into some bottles of colored ink and made a painting, but also a big mess. When his mother came and saw his sketch, she said, "Why, it's Billy!" and kissed him. "Mother's love," West said, "made me an artist."

Help me, Lord, to see the face of Jesus
in each person with whom I relate.

Each Is Responsible for His Own Mind

Some judge one day to be better than another, while others judge all days to be alike. Let all be fully convinced in their own minds. Those who observe the day, observe it in honor of the Lord. Also those who eat, eat in honor of the Lord, since they give thanks to God; while those who abstain, abstain in honor of the Lord and give thanks to God. Romans 14:5-6

Having been made in the image of God, we have the ability to think, to analyze, to make decisions. We are not beings of chance or circumstance alone, but of choice. Even in the most dire circumstances, we can decide what attitude we will have toward others. In the concentration camp of Auschwitz, one of the noble choices that evidenced humanness was when suffering and dying men would still decide in dignity to break their crust of bread in pieces and share with those who were weaker.

Our text reminds us that our choices are to be made from our relationship in the Lord. Diversity is a fact, and we come to different issues from differing perspectives or conditioning. In this diversity, the one thing that unites us is our common praise to God. We each set our lives in an affirmation of conscious obedience to God and his will. What we do about things, neither right nor wrong in themselves, should be done with the desire to please God. Though our actions are different, we can participate in unity of spirit.

Paul's illustrations, respecting particular days as holy or not, eating meat or not eating meat, are examples of things that, in themselves are nonmoral. What makes such things moral issues is the spirit and purpose that we bring to their observance. Even circumcision, a sign of covenant with God, was made into a legalism that actually kept people from the God of covenant. Each person is to think through his interpretation of the will of God and be fully convinced in his own mind as we walk before the Lord.

A friend of mine, the late David Thomas of New Danville, Pennsylvania, once stated in a conference discussion, "It is more important that we see together than that we see alike." This is a prophetic statement, a call to a spirit of unity in the place of attempts at coercion.

Lord, give me an attitude that makes possible unity with diversity,
that helps to build others up in the knowledge and spirit of Jesus.

We Belong to the Lord

We do not live to ourselves, and we do not die to ourselves. If we live, we live to the Lord, and if we die, we die to the Lord; so then, whether we live or whether we die, we are the Lord's. Romans 14:7-8

The first of the Ten Commandments says that all of life is to begin with God. Our text affirms this truth that in life and in death we belong to the Lord. The unique thing in context is that Paul makes this affirmation with respect to our relationship with one another. He appeals to each of us to respect the differences we have and to accept one another in awareness that each is answering to God while being different. He undergirds this point by removing us from any claim to autonomy or to an absolute stance. All of us alike answer to God, for we belong ultimately to him and not just to one another.

I believe in the importance of community, of the dynamic of spiritual fellowship to create meaningful congregational life. Ultimately, fellowship is not experienced by our focusing on the group itself, but by focusing on the presence of God. Community is a gift, a gift of God's grace. As Jesus prayed, we become one when each is united with him as he is united with the Father (John 17). When all that we do, living or dying, is done in relation to God, we then share the meaning of belonging to him.

David Livingstone said, "All that I am and have I hold in relation to Christ and his kingdom." This should be our vision and our pattern, our stewardship, our mission. Everything we have, every potential of our lives, every plan for our future belongs to the Lord. We learn in geometry that two things equal to the same thing are equal to each other. Even so, as disciples of Christ, by each following Jesus, we are one in spirit and in purpose. Unity is not uniformity, but unity of faith and of purpose.

Unity, at times, is social before it is spiritual. The great Jewish philosopher Baruch Spinoza of Amsterdam found his philosophical stance and his emphasis against material securities rejected by his people. He turned to his friends in the Mennonite and the Quaker communities for fellowship. Their emphasis on ethics, on material sharing, and on pacifism is reflected in his writings. He said that the light of truth focused his mind on God.

> *Lord, help me to behave my beliefs,*
> *in a winsome style of love and acceptance,*
> *with the integrity that emphasizes accountability.*

In Life and Death We Answer to Christ

For to this end Christ died and lived again, so that he might be Lord of both the dead and the living. Why do you pass judgment on your brother or sister? Or you, why do you despise your brother or sister? For we will all stand before the judgment seat of God. Romans 14:9-10

There is no realm of existence where Jesus is not Lord. His death and resurrection make him Lord of the living and of the dead. This is our marvelous hope, our assurance that beyond this life Jesus is also Lord. Paul, in our text, calls us to leave all judgment to Christ. Jesus is the ultimate judge, and we each answer to him. We are not judges of one another.

Jesus taught us not to judge others, not to censor them in our attitudes, not to be judgmental. This does not exclude judgments of selectivity, of good and evil, or of truth and error, lest we incorporate the wrong thing in our fellowship. Jesus said, "By their fruits you shall know them" (Matt. 7:20, KJV). Jesus calls us to be peacemakers rather than prosecutors.

One who judges or evaluates thinks himself the stronger and the other as the weaker. This adds to the problem by creating class distinctions in our social relationships. But what appears to us to be weak in another may have its own strengths.

One day while we were in Pune, we took the train to Mukti Mission, an hour away. The tickets were a mere four rupees each; this was truly another culture. Here we visited a mission nearly one hundred years old, begun by Pambita Ramabai, a Christian widow from Hindu background. Her family died in the famine. After the death of her husband, she came to know Christ. In her new life, this small woman with great spirit began this mission to orphans, the blind, and the handicapped. As we talked with a blind woman radiating the love of Jesus and saw her caring for other blind young people and others who couldn't respond, I thought, "Who really is the weaker brother or sister?" Such service must be very specially blessed by God.

Once, because of theological differences between George Whitefield and John Wesley, Whitefield was asked whether he expected to see Wesley in heaven. He answered, "No!" as was expected. Then he added, "You must understand: Wesley will be so far up near the throne that I won't get to see him." Wonderful! Many simple servants will be recognized for their self-giving love in the name of Christ and rewarded beyond others (cf. Matt. 25:31-40; Mark 9:37, 41).

Each One Gives Account of Himself

For it is written, "As I live, says the Lord, every knee shall bow to me, and every tongue shall give praise to God." So then, each of us will be accountable to God. Romans 14:11-12

The quote in our text comes from the prophet Isaiah. The Word holds us accountable to God. In Philippians 2, in the great christological hymn, Paul affirms that every knee will bow in accountability to Christ, the exalted Lord. In our text, the emphasis is on bowing to God as the ultimate judge.

Here Paul is not discussing the future judgment, as much as holding us each accountable in life. Each of us answers for ourselves; we do not answer for others, and we should avoid acting as their judges. Implicit in this understanding is a second aspect. Since we each answer to God, we should help one another to walk with him and not discourage one another by judgmental attitudes. We are to be supportive rather than creating problems, recognizing that there are some differences in the community of faith.

In the book of Ecclesiastes, an expression of Hebrew philosophical wisdom, we are called to accountability before God (12:13-14). We do need to submit some of Solomon's statements to God's full disclosure in Christ. Some positions that Solomon takes leave us with problems. However, his conclusion is right on. Having examined the futility of life from a human perspective, he concludes that each of us is personally accountable to a personal God. Wow! Compare this conclusion with the views of the Greek philosophers of his day, and its uniqueness is apparent.

Once a farmer in England saw a group of men riding after the hounds approaching his fields. He called his son and told him to close the gate and not open it for anyone. The young lad hurried and did so, then he stationed himself by the gate. When the men rode up, one of them asked him to open the gate. He replied that he was under orders not to do so. The rider said, "The Duke of Wellington is in this group, and I'm asking you for him. Open the gate!" The young man took off his hat, bowed, and said, "If the Duke of Wellington is in this group, he will understand when I say that I am under my master's orders, and even though the Duke of Wellington asks it, I cannot open the gate." The Duke rode forward, took off his hat, and bowed to the lad, saying, "I want to honor a lad who is faithful to his master's orders. We respect you for not opening the gate."

Place No Stumbling Block

Let us therefore no longer pass judgment on one another, but resolve instead never to put a stumbling block or hindrance in the way of another.
Romans 14:13

After saying that "love is the fulfilling of the law" (Rom. 13:10), Paul shows that persons are more important than practices. We may do what we believe to be right, but if another sees our deed as a stumbling block, we should not exercise our liberty. Our higher standard is not only to avoid judging another for his convictions and becoming defensive in our position, but also to avoid causing another to stumble.

John Calvin wrote of this passage that there are two aspects: one is that we should not offend the other person; the second is that the other person should not be so easily offended! The truth of the text cuts both ways. By "stumble," Paul has in mind more than being offended, as in having one's sensitive spirit hurt. He is talking about becoming a barrier to the person's development of faith.

Jesus said: "Occasions for stumbling are bound to come, but woe to anyone by whom they come! It would be better for you if a millstone were hung around your neck and you were thrown into the sea than for you to cause one of these little ones to stumble" (Luke 17:1-2). How often lives have been altered, personalities intimidated, self-confidence destroyed, or improper decisions made in a child because of an aggressive, insensitive person.

With a lot of years in education, especially at college and university levels, I have seen the powerful influence of good teachers. I have seen the impact Esther has made in teaching art, helping students to discover themselves and to achieve. Success is not simply by the teacher's great knowledge, but by great encouragement and caring. Education is designed to excite others about learning. It expands one's life, and in doing so, touches so much more that we have not mastered. This makes the truly educated to be very humble. All education is done from some perspective, and for us this perspective is a Christian worldview. Jesus said that we are to love the Lord our God with our minds.

Lord, show me those things in my life
that are causing others to stumble.
For it is more important that my practice is pure,
than what I profess with my mouth.

Being Persuaded in the Lord

I know and am persuaded in the Lord Jesus that nothing is unclean in itself; but it is unclean to anyone who thinks it unclean. If your brother or sister is being injured by what you eat, you are no longer walking in love. Do not let what you eat cause the ruin of one for whom Christ died. Romans 14:14-15

Our identity is our being in Christ. We join solidarity with him, and we extend this solidarity in relationship with others. Paul says that food in itself is not unclean, that is, ceremonially unclean. It is ethically neutral. Christ said it is not what a person eats, not what goes into a person, that defiles, but rather the evil thoughts and lusts from within the person. Paul's understanding of Christ, that we are reconciled to God in Jesus rather than by religious rites, enables Paul to answer as he does.

Today's verses speak primarily of problems experienced by Gentiles in coming to Christ from a background of idol worship and living around idolatry. When sacrificed meat was sold in the market, their previous identification with obeisance to the idol would come to mind. This became a real problem for them. Also, Jewish persons, having a tradition from the laws of Moses that limited them from eating certain meats, now had a problem with the dietary practices of some of the Gentiles. Respect for each person with the differences was necessary to avoid distress in their fellowship.

The statement, "But it is unclean to anyone who thinks it unclean," is a key to understanding this whole passage. This is an insight in the psychology of personality. What one thinks to be true, is true for them until they have further revelation. Personal and social harmony depends on integrity, even if it makes one vulnerable. Finally, Paul brings to focus his primary concern: "Do not let what you eat cause the ruin of one for whom Christ died." Christ has a special claim on the sister or brother, and since we belong to Christ, we are supportive of even the weakest in faith. "A bruised reed he will not break, and a dimly burning wick he will not quench" (Isa. 42:3).

Give me, Lord, the grace to serve,
to help another in the journey of faith,
avoiding any tendency to be controlling
while meeting others at their point of need.

Be Consistent in the Good

So do not let your good be spoken of as evil. Romans 14:16.

"O consistency, thou art a jewel." It is not following our own preference that is the right course of action, but it is in seeking the good. We want our behavior to be identified with the will of God and not with selfish ambition. But our consideration of others and respect for them does not mean that we abdicate our own position. We are responsible to live consistently with our own convictions, but to be considerate of others. We give acceptance, not by compromising our convictions, but in respect of theirs.

Paul has said that the way in which we regard a matter becomes the basis of our behavior (14:14). We are responsible to live in harmony with our understanding and our cultural conditioning, so that our application of the faith to real life situations is authentic. In following Christ, each issue needs to be reviewed in its own right. In this same openness we can help others make applications in their life situation. We are to be models or interpreters of God's will rather than promoters of our own culture.

Just as we are not to destroy another (14:15), so we are not to have our own convictions destroyed. The truly good is in our commitment to Christ, and we cannot have this spoken of as less than the best because we run roughshod over others.

Although I consider it good to not drink alcohol and do not include such drinking in my lifestyle, I have Christian friends for whom this has long been a part of their pattern of dining. When Esther and I are with friends who use wine in a social context, we choose our nonalcoholic beverage, and they choose their wine. It is not always so simple to affirm friendship and full acceptance when you are a guest in a culture where the drink is an important social practice. Here our expression of friendship in other ways is very important. But now add to the problem by picturing yourself in this setting in the presence of another guest who is very rigid: you are going to offend one or the other. Or suppose the other guest has an alcoholic problem. In our love for that person we would not wish to cause him to stumble. We must express the spirit of Jesus and his love with sensitivity.

Dear Father, I belong to you and your kingdom.
Help me to live in that awareness.
Keep me from making an idol of my culture,
but let me serve in it by maintaining my integrity.

November 18

Kingdom Priorities

For the kingdom of God is not food and drink but righteousness and peace and joy in the Holy Spirit. The one who thus serves Christ is acceptable to God and has human approval. Romans 14:17-18

Jesus came announcing the kingdom, the rule of God. He presented the gospel of the kingdom because he was present as the King. At one point he said of the kingdom, "It is among you" (Luke 17:21). He could say this because he was there among the disciples. Where there is a kingdom, there is a king, and in Christ the King has come. In his death and resurrection he was exalted to God's right hand, the place of sovereign authority, and from this position as Lord he directs his church. He is our King, our sovereign. The early church expressed this by using the word "Lord" to designate his rule.

This reference to the kingdom of God is not strange for Paul. In Acts 20, he refers to preaching the gospel of the kingdom of God. In chapter 28 there are two references saying that in Rome he presented "the gospel of the kingdom of God" (20:25; 28:23, 31). To the Colossians, Paul wrote that God has "rescued us from the power of darkness and transferred us into the kingdom of his beloved Son" (Col. 1:13). To the Thessalonians, he says that God "calls you into his own kingdom" (1 Thess. 2:12).

Our text is emphasizing that the ultimate issue is not rules about meat and drink, but rather, the reality of the kingdom of God. This kingdom is an identification with God, not an organizational program or structure. It is a rule of God through his presence in the Holy Spirit. The character of the kingdom is righteousness (right relatedness), peace (the shalom of total well-being), and joy (the inner harmony of spirit in belonging to God). All of this, Paul says, is in the freedom and empowerment of the Holy Spirit.

One who serves Christ by the priorities of his kingdom is building a great life on a *sure* foundation. A man brought his son to college and, in conversation with the dean, asked whether they didn't have a short course. He said that he needed his son to help him at work. The dean replied, "Short course? When God grows an oak, it takes years, but he can grow a squash in six weeks."

Lord, you are the King of my life.
Help me to make you a priority in my actions
as well as my speech.

November 19

Every Effort to Promote Peace

Let us then pursue what makes for peace and for mutual upbuilding.
Romans 14:19

Peacemaking is never easy. It calls for a way to transcend differences. But God has done this in the bridge of love to us. We can learn from him and bridge differences between us and others. Jesus said, "Blessed are the peacemakers, for they will be called children of God" (Matt. 5:9). It is contrary to the defensiveness of human nature, but in Christ we learn the way of peace and also the cost of peace. *Agape* love is never easy because it respects another's freedom, including those who hate us. It never responds in ways other than nonresistant love, lest the expression of agape be altered.

In Romans 12 Paul says we are to live at peace as much as it depends on us, that is, we are to do our part even if the other person does not respond. We are responsible for only what lies in our power to perform. Love is always a success because of what it expresses, even though it doesn't always win in the day. At the cross, where Jesus made peace with and for us, his love was a success in absorbing the ultimate sin of murder. In human terms, he didn't win; he died, but he won the victory. To live by love is to be free in one's spirit, to not have one's behavior dominated or determined by the opposition.

Our work for peace is for the well-being of the other, to share in mutual edification. We rise or fall together. We grow by our fellowship with one another. Our worship, our nurture, and our service, as a congregation of believers, is a participation in mutual growth in the knowledge and love of Christ.

While in India, Esther built a large sculpture in the center of the Union Biblical Seminary campus to express their motto, "Speaking the Truth in Love." She first made a model of Jesus washing Peter's feet. She used the model and enlarged the work to nine feet, with the kneeling figure of Jesus about six feet. It was fashioned with reenforcement rods, then shaped with chicken wire, then filled and covered with cement. The final coat is of white cement. It is a beautiful piece, an expression of the servant love of Christ, a symbol of the spirit of the seminary, and a reminder to all the importance of serving one another in love.

> *Lord, give me agape love*
> *for my family, neighbors, church, and you.*
> *Show me how I can serve others*
> *and allow them to serve me, as well.*

Do Not Destroy God's Work

Do not, for the sake of food, destroy the work of God. Everything is indeed clean, but it is wrong for you to make others fall by what you eat; it is good not to eat meat or drink wine or do anything that makes your brother or sister stumble. Romans 14:20-21

Persons are more important than performance. This text is calling us to have our priorities straight. In the Gentile church, the issue of differences over foods, ceremonial days, and the drinking of wine and eating meat offered to idols had become divisive. Having said, "God will wreck the church wrecker" (1 Cor. 3:17, literal meaning), Paul here speaks about not spoiling the work of God by disunity.

The counsel that the apostle gives, calls for us to take a positive rather than a defensive course of action. We avoid practices that cause another to stumble, and we refrain from things that could cause another to fall. This avoids concentrating on who is the weaker, and at the same time keeps us from being slaves to the conscience of another.

Some make an application from this to abstaining from social drinking. My esteemed Presbyterian professor once said to our class, "Since in every group of eight or more people there is at least one potential alcoholic, to drink in a social setting has the possibility of helping put another person on the skids. If I truly love my neighbor as myself, I will avoid doing something that creates a problem."

However, this text calls for flexibility rather than rigidity. Our behavior is influenced by those to whom we are relating, not solely by our cultural preferences. Cultural difference increases with the pluralism in society and consequently in the church. As the Scripture says, "Love covers a multitude of sins" (1 Pet. 4:8). This does not mean that we like sins, but we help prevent them.

The church is God's special people;
its work is God's program, not ours.
It is a creation of the Holy Spirit.
We are called to serve, not to control,
to share in love without uniformity,
to pursue unity with our diversity.
We are united in being the body of Christ!

Behaving Our Beliefs

The faith that you have, have as your own conviction before God. Blessed are those who have no reason to condemn themselves because of what they approve. Romans 14:22

Carl F. H. Henry, an evangelical theologian of distinction, has said, "Christianity is personal, but it is never private." Being personal, it holds us each responsible to live what we profess. Paul has reminded us that our actions have social consequences, for we are a part of a Christian community and influence other members of the body of Christ. He is here addressing our personal stance of integrity.

While we each make adjustments or accommodations to others to promote unity and encouragement, we must maintain our personal integrity before God. I like the King James translation, "Hast thou faith? Have it to thyself before God." That is, put it into practice in your relation with God. Since the issues Paul has addressed here are not matters like killing, adultery, stealing, covetousness, or false witness, but are amoral issues, we can hold different preferences on such matters without compromise. With our preferences in lifestyle, we are to keep a clear conscience before God. On many things this is purely a private matter, but we are above all primarily responsible to God.

The last sentence of this text is a beatitude: "Blessed are those who have no reason to condemn themselves because of what they approve." Paul has asked us to limit our freedom wherever the exercise would cause another to stumble. Now he says, Don't compromise your true self. Don't approve practices that bring condemnation in your own life. We refrain from some preferences to respect another, and likewise we refrain from adopting another's preferences when it compromises our own life.

To believe is a response to something larger.
Truth is not controlled. Truth controls us.
Truth is larger than any human systems of thought.
It holds us humbly in its awesome claims.
Believing points to that which is believed.
We need to know that this is large enough
for a total commitment, that is, belief in Christ!

November 22

Violating Faith Is Sin

But those who have doubts are condemned if they eat, because they do not act from faith; for whatever does not proceed from faith is sin. Romans 14:23

The faith by which we are to live is a full identification with Jesus. Since we are disciples of Christ, we are, as Paul says, in Christ. We have our identity from him, and we live in solidarity with him. Jesus taught us that as branches we abide in the vine, for the branch absorbs its nutrition from the vine. But the branch is not merely a pipe through which nurture passes. The fruit is an extension of the vine's life. We are dependent upon Jesus; to be inconsistent with our faith relationship with Christ is sin.

Insisting on eating something to conform to social expectation, when done with deep inner personal doubt, makes eating a sin. Actions not prompted by a clear sense of being in the will of Christ are those of self-interest. The standard here is a very high one, applicable where there are no specific laws of "Thus says the Lord." This standard calls us to be true to ourselves as persons of faith. When we compromise our faith, we sin against the integrity of our own person. In doing so, we become weaker and thereby rob the community of faith of the very integrity and strength we should be bringing to it.

Recall now the statement in the previous verse: "The faith that you have, have as your own conviction before God." We answer to God, and we enjoy fellowship with God. And we pray with the hymn writer, J. Edwin Orr:

> *Search me, O God, and know my heart today,*
> *Try me, O Savior, know my thoughts I pray;*
> *See if there be some wicked way in me;*
> *Cleanse me from every sin, and set me free.*
>
> *I praise Thee, Lord, for cleansing me from sin;*
> *Fulfill Thy word and make me pure within;*
> *Fill me with fire where once I burned with shame;*
> *Grant my desire to magnify Thy name.*

November 23

Bearing One Another's Burdens

We who are strong ought to put up with the failings of the weak, and not to please ourselves. Each of us must please our neighbor for the good purpose of building up the neighbor. Romans 15:1-2

Martin Luther said, "The Christian man is the most free man, lord of all, subject to none." "But," he continued, "the Christian man is the most careful servant of all, subject to Christ in the service of others." In my thinking, this is a remarkable and true statement.

This text stands in contrast to human competition, whether in deeds or in spirit. Our goal is to encourage each other, to be positive toward one another, to avoid any intimidation of another. Strength in a given area of life is a blessing, and we should use our strength to help others. The church is a cooperative and not a competitive fellowship.

In 1963 it was my privilege to conduct a citywide evangelistic mission with the Protestant churches of Salt Lake City, Utah. Through the governor's kindness we held the meeting on the Capitol grounds, using the steps for the choir and platform, with three thousand chairs set down front. Many people of the Mormon Church attended, although they did not participate in sponsoring the event. In a TV program a spokesman for their faith did urge people to attend, saying, "We need a renewal of religion in America. Go to the meeting, but remember, we have all of this and more." My task was to show that no group has all that Christ offers, much less having more.

At the same time as I was ministering, I also learned some very important things from the Mormons, one of which relates directly to our text for today. I learned that if a farmer was not gifted with management and was failing, the local ward (congregation) would appoint two gifted farmers to be his counselors. They would guide him in what and when to plant, how to rotate crops, when to sell, and so on. They made these recommendations on the same basis as their own well-managed programs. The ungifted farmer achieved through their strength. This is bearing one another's burdens.

Lord, help me to see my neighbor's weakness.
Show me how I can help,
Then help me to do it.

November 24

Christis Did Not Please Himself

For Christ did not please himself; but, as it is written, "The insults of those who insult you have fallen on me." Romans 15:3

The work of Christ is centered on the obedience and glory of God. "He has not left me alone, for I always do what is pleasing to him" (John 8:29). Christ is the Son of God, but he is also the Son of man, and in his Incarnation he was exactly what God meant us to be, persons in free communion and harmony with God. Jesus lived a perfect life by obeying God and loving mankind, including his enemies. He loved in full respect for our freedom, not asking anything from us, that we might merit his love.

His love leaves us free, for forcing his love on us would contradict the very essence of his love. Jesus expressed this love the whole way to the cross, giving himself for others rather than defending himself. If his actions had been other than nonviolent, his expression would have been less than perfect love. He learned in experience the full extent of love. In Hebrews 5:8-9 we read, "Although he was a Son, he learned obedience through what he suffered . . . and became the source of eternal salvation for all who obey him."

It is upon this theology that Paul based his appeal for us as Christians: we are to look out for the good of others and "please our neighbor for the good purpose of building up the neighbor" (Rom. 15:2). Our text is similar to Philippians 2, where Paul presents Christ as the one who, being equal with God, made himself equal with us and then, as such, became a servant to us, being obedient in this love, even to death! The humility of Christ was so deep that he absorbed humanity's insults to God and carried them within himself.

> *To serve is an act of freedom.*
> *It is using one's gifts for others*
> *in unselfishness social participation*
> *for the enrichment of the whole body.*
> *To serve is an expression of selflessness,*
> *an indication that our vision is larger,*
> *doing more than seeking our own interests,*
> *for service is love complementing the other.*

Through Scripture We Have Hope

For whatever was written in former days was written for our instruction, so that by steadfastness and by the encouragement of the scriptures we might have hope. Romans 15:4

If our predecessors haven't learned anything important, there isn't much hope for us to do so. History is a testing ground in which we can check out the systems of thought that we encounter, find similar positions in history, examine their results, and then make our choice as to what we pursue. We have "time-binding power": we can reach back into history, select things that have proved good, and channel them into present history through our lives. In this same way, but with the special activity of the Spirit, Paul says that the Scriptures written in the past are to teach us. Ours is to be an informed faith, rich in the heritage of the history of God's acts.

I once asked the seminary class on Christology in India to contrast the Hindu doctrine of karma with the biblical doctrine of reconciliation. Karma means that all actions, good or bad, have their consequence in the law of retribution, which determines the life of the individual in the present. In the cycle of rebirths, one enters the future life conditioned to become better (even a god) or worse, (a snake, animal, or bedbug) depending on past good or evil acts. One's present life is fated, determined by behavior in a previous life. This is your karma; you cannot change it. Hindus lack the grace of a new creation in Christ.

The great mathematician Blaise Pascal said, "Jesus Christ will be in agony until the end of the age, and we dare not be silent all of that time." He wrote of his conversion, an existential experience with God, describing it as like waves of fire rolling through his soul until he needed to ask God to withhold the emotion. At his death, they found sown in the borders of his garment the words, "Not the god of the philosophers for me, but the God of Abraham, Isaac, and Jacob, the God and Father of our Lord Jesus Christ."

O God, you are our God,
awesome in holiness and grace,
so Other, yet so self-revealing
and so self-emptying for our salvation.

November 26

A Spirit of Unity

May the God of steadfastness and encouragement grant you to live in harmony with one another, in accordance with Christ Jesus, so that together you may with one voice glorify the God and Father of our Lord Jesus Christ. Romans 15:5-6

Prayer for the child of God is like breathing, and here in the middle of his admonitions Paul bursts out in prayer. Prayer is our recognition of total dependence upon God and his grace. Prayer unites us, for with one voice we glorify God together.

We live in harmony by our respect for and identification with one another in Christ. Whenever we stand over against one another, engaging in comparisons, we make unity impossible. Jesus prayed for us, "That they may be one, as we are one" (John 17:11). This is in a context declaring his full identification with the Father. Unity is not sameness; it is togetherness. We are not seeking to be like each other; we are just interested in liking each other.

Here Paul prays that the "God of steadfastness and encouragement grant you to live in harmony with one another." This text reminds one of Philippians 2:12: "Work out your own salvation with fear and trembling; for it is God who is at work in you, enabling you both to will and to work for his good pleasure." That is, we work out in life's expression what God is working into our experience. So in this text we are told to endure, as God works in us the strength to endure. We do not accomplish this in isolation from others, but in the unity of the community as we together follow Christ. As each disciple seeks to be like his master (Luke 6:40), we are united with each other. Unity is a gift of God.

The unity of God's people is a glory to God before the world. This is his purpose, to create a people for his name, not a worldly people, but a special people who herald the name. The glory of God is not acclaimed by word only, but by living as his people, following his will. G. K. Chesterton said, "If the world grows too worldly, it can be rebuked by the church, but if the church grows too worldly, it cannot be adequately rebuked for worldliness by the world." We are called to live faithfully in the world.

In the world, but not of the world—
this is our walk as strangers and pilgrims,
living as friends of God.

November 27

Accept One Another

Welcome one another, therefore, just as Christ has welcomed you, for the glory of God. For I tell you that Christ has become a servant of the circumcised on behalf of the truth of God in order that he might confirm the promises given to the patriarchs. Romans 15:7-8

We welcome one another in love, even with our faults and problems. The advice of this text is to accept one another, just as Christ accepted you. He accepts us with our faults into a covenant of love that places relationship ahead of perfection. Consequently, we enjoy a special relationship with him and with each other.

In early November of 1987 we traveled to Ranchi in Bihar, India, for a pastor's conference. Our trip included time with Esther's brother Paul and his wife, Esther. They are veteran missionaries, having been in India for forty-five years. We had a wonderful time of sharing in the conference at Chandwa with a hundred pastors from five denominations of Mennonite and related groups in India. It was an inspiration to see their fellowship with one another in Christ. I spoke on "A Spirituality of Discipleship" from 2 Corinthians, with the help of a translator into the Hindi language.

Testimonies given by various pastors were a wonderful expression of this text. In spite of our past, we accepted one another as Christ accepts us. Among the group were several pastors from a tribal group in North India, animists, among whom the Brethren in Christ church is at work. This particular group now has six hundred members in their local churches. One of the pastors had formerly been involved in witchcraft, carrying out a program of fear in which he had caused at least three deaths. Today he is a new man, a brother in Christ, a minister of love and of the new life in Christ. He was one of the persons who served the emblems in our sharing the Lord's Supper. His participation was evidence that "Christ has become a servant." God calls us to live as servants.

But of service, someone has quipped, "The only trouble with being a servant is that people will begin to treat you in that way." Service is first attitudinal and then action, and we are each called to live in this servile spirit. As Paul writes:

> *If we live by the Spirit,*
> *let us also be guided by the Spirit. (Gal. 5:25)*

Rejoice, O Gentiles

And in order that the Gentiles might glorify God for his mercy. As it is written, "Therefore I will confess you among the Gentiles, and sing praises to your name"; and again he says, "Rejoice O Gentiles, with his people"; and again, "Praise the Lord, all you Gentiles, and let all the peoples praise him." Romans 15:9-11

On this day every year, Esther and I celebrate our wedding anniversary. In 2000 it was fifty years! We have found love to be a growing, enriching relationship—not perfect, but increasingly satisfying as we share our lives together. Basic to marriage is the understanding of love as primarily covenant, and essential in this covenant is the recognition that each of us alike is created in the image of God.

The words in our text express joy in God's grace to the Gentiles. During our time in India we observed the contrast between the joyous Indian Christians and the majority of people around them who, as Hindus, did not express this freedom. Once a person knows Christ and enjoys the freedom of his fellowship, the whole of life changes for that person. Many of these Christians are still poor, limited in the opportunities of life which we have in the West, but their joy is inspiring.

The text moves from having shown Christ as a servant to the Jews, to here presenting Christ as leading the Gentiles in praise to God. This mystery is spoken of in Ephesians. God's work in Israel was not an end in itself but is offering salvation to all. Adding one quote to another, Paul emphasizes that all Gentiles, all peoples, join in singing God's praise. God is gathering a people for his name from all tribes, races, and cultures. Walls come down to make us one new humanity. The church is an open circle; as expressed by Yale professor Miroslav Volf, it is not one of exclusion, but of embrace.

"Let the whole world hear"—
but not as though competing religions.
Rather, the good news that God cares for all,
that above being religious, is the greater call;
a call to open our lives to God,
to respond to him, and
to experience his grace and love.

November 29

The Gentiles Will Hope in Him

And again Isaiah says, "The root of Jesse shall come, the one who rises to rule the Gentiles; in him the Gentiles shall hope." Romans 15:12

Many Old Testament passages are regarded by New Testament writers as relating directly to Jesus. Our text is a messianic passage from Isaiah which promises the Christ from the root of Jesse, "descended from David according to the flesh" (Rom. 1:3). This promise was the hope of Israel through the centuries. But the Israelites seem to have missed its universal implications, that the Messiah is also the hope of the Gentiles. Here, in our text, we see that God intended the gospel for the nations, not just for Israel.

This is the good news for all people, for all races, in all cultures, in all lands. In Christ there is hope for all. Life is not meaningless; it has meaning. Humanity is not hopeless; we have a Savior. God is not unapproachable; he opened himself to us in Christ. God is not partial: he is not a respecter of persons, but "everyone who calls on the name of the Lord shall be saved" (Rom. 10:13).

One of my students at Union Biblical Seminary in India told me that four years ago he was a Hindu, empty of heart, without hope and freedom. He was introduced to Christ, and in the good news of God's forgiving love, he committed his life to Jesus as Lord. The transformation in his personal life, in his relationships, and in his marriage became evident to others. Consequently, his new friends urged him to study for ministry. His goal is now to share the hope of Christ, the reality of salvation, and the quality of the new life that many Hindus will come to hope in God. This is the vitality of the church universally.

> *Now then we are ambassadors for Christ. . . .*
> *We pray you, in Christ's stead,*
> *be reconciled to God.*
> *For he has made him who knew no sin*
> *to become a sin offering for us,*
> *that we may be made the righteousness*
> *of God in him.*
> *(cf. 2 Cor. 5:20-21, KJV; Rom. 8:3)*

Joy and Peace in Believing

May the God of hope fill you with all joy and peace in believing, so that you may abound in hope by the power of the Holy Spirit. Romans 15:13

The word *hope* in the New Testament is a dynamic word of assurance. In our verse today, something of a benedictory note, Paul addresses "the God of hope." This verse is a very beautiful pronouncement of blessing from God. It concludes with the prayer that we "may abound in hope by the power of the Holy Spirit." This hope is an invigorating reality that fills us daily with joy and peace as we walk with him.

Unfortunately, the word *hope* has come to mean *wishful thinking*. But hope really means assurance of the fulfillment of God's promise. In this hope, when the first missionary from America to the Far East, Adoniram Judson, was gravely ill and the Baptist Mission Board called him home, he decided to remain to die in Burma, saying, "The future is as bright as the promises of God!"

The combination of joy, peace, and hope, a slight variation from the familiar, "faith, hope, and love," are subjective benefits of our trust in God. But they correspond to Paul's other statements in his reference to the fruit of the Spirit, as in Galations 5. We are saved in hope (Rom. 8:24).

A young musician, congratulated on his performance, was asked, "Why were your eyes so often turned to the second balcony?" "My teacher was sitting up there," he replied, "and seeing the smile on his face, I knew that I was pleasing him." In a similar spirit Peter Bohler said to Charles Wesley, "If I had a thousand tongues, I'd praise Christ with all of them." Wesley then wrote the great hymn, "O for a Thousand Tongues to Sing."

> *The fruit of the Spirit is love:*
> Joy, *the celebration of love;*
> Peace, *the practice of love;*
> Patience, *the preservation of love;*
> Kindness, *the expression of love;*
> Goodness, *the action of love;*
> Faithfulness, *the loyalty of love;*
> Gentleness, *the attitude of love;*
> Self-control, *the restraint of love.*

Competent to Instruct

I myself feel confident about you, my brothers and sisters, that you yourselves are full of goodness, filled with all knowledge, and able to instruct one another. Nevertheless on some points I have written to you rather boldly by way of reminder, because of the grace given me by God. Romans 15:14-15

Too often we are quick to critique but slow to encourage. More positive things arise from encouragement than from criticism. As a young college student, I had very little public speaking experience, but I shall long remember the encouraging words from an older student after I had given a talk. He said simply, "You have a gift for public speaking, a pleasant expression, and an appealing tone of voice. Keep at it." I doubt that he would remember that passing comment, but I have, and I thank him.

Paul's words in our text are an affirmation of people with whom he had no relationship except for a few that he knew from previous association before they went to Rome. Yet he complements them that they are full of goodness, mature in knowledge, and competent to instruct one another. This last point is essential for the community of disciples to share in the hermeneutical task of interpreting the Word of God. In many churches there is a lack of this exercise. The laity are more spectators than participants.

In verse 15:15, Paul refers to his own letter, written in boldness, as his participation with them in the hermeneutical exercise of faith. What a letter! For the epistle to the Romans stands as one of the greater theological works of the New Testament. Karl Barth's commentary on Romans, first published in 1919, jarred the theological world and brought a change of perspective for many. His uniqueness was in placing Christology at the center of his interpretation of Romans as a challenge to his contemporaries in theology. The focus was on Christ, on the incarnation as the expression of true humanity, as well as on the true expression of God.

In a black shantytown near Johannesburg, South Africa, a primary school teacher, Desmond Mpilo Tutu, saw a white man respectfully tip his hat to a black woman. Tutu had never seen a white man make such a gesture, and it helped reshape his life. The woman was his mother; the white man was Rev. Trevor Huddleston, later an Anglican bishop. In a Christlike spirit, this priest befriended Tutu, including visiting him in his long illness. As we know, Tutu followed him into the ministry, becoming an Anglican bishop.

December 2

Priestly Duty

Because of the grace given to me by God to be a minister of Christ Jesus to the Gentiles in the priestly service of the gospel of God, so that the offering of the Gentiles may be acceptable, sanctified by the Holy Spirit. Romans 15:16

This verse speaks of our priestly service. One of the most basic principles of the Reformation was, and is, the priesthood of the believer. Each of us as a believer is a priest at our brother's and sister's elbow, having the privilege of ministering God's grace to them. The priesthood of believers is often thought of as the freedom for each believer to come to God directly through Christ. While this is true, the concept also means that one can be a priest for another. As a husband, I have often thought of this as my privilege to support Esther, and she has been this to me. Together we have this priestly role for our children.

In a general definition, a prophet speaks from God to others. A priest represents persons to God. The priests of the Old Testament ministered at the altar; they ministered holy things before the Lord. They represented men and women to God, but also needed to represent God and his expectations to men and women. Otherwise they were not acceptable to God.

In today's verse, Paul picks up this image in a rare description of his own ministry. His priestly duty is to first minister before the Lord in sharing the gospel with the Gentiles. Second, the offering he presents to the Lord is the Gentile believers themselves. Here he speaks of the Gentiles being an offering acceptable to God, set apart, and sanctified by the Holy Spirit. This includes most of us—Gentile believers who share in the body of Christ.

It is an inspiration to read this text of Paul's affirmation of priestly service in ministering the gospel, preparing a people as an offering to God. The image has special meaning as we recall his arguments in chapter 9 that God moved through Israel to reach out to the other nations of the world. Paul's ministry was given to him by God for this purpose, to share Jesus Christ with the Gentiles. This is our priestly duty as agents of his reconciling grace, as ambassadors for Christ.

Lord, help me to be a priest at my neighbor's elbow,
serving in this priestly ministry of the gospel,
helping each to be conscious of the presence of God.

December 3

Glorying in Christ Jesus

In Christ Jesus, then, I have reason to boast of my work for God. For I will not venture to speak of anything except what Christ has accomplished through me to win obedience from the Gentiles, by word and deed. Romans 15:17-18

Paul gloried in the privilege of serving Christ to reach the Gentiles. We can share this joy in knowing that Christ works through us. All achievements in sharing God's reconciling grace are in themselves the fruit of God's grace. If we think of success just by our talents, they are no more of grace, but of works. We do not serve for our own glory. I once read this statement: "God can bless the person with whom he has found that his glory is safe."

All of us are born with our lives centered in ourselves. We didn't have to learn to be selfish. Our depravity is in being self-centered. But God is there, standing at the circle of our lives, waiting for us to welcome him. Jesus says, "Listen! I am standing at the door, knocking; if you hear my voice and open the door, I will come in to you and eat with you, and you with me" (Rev. 3:20).

As Christians, we still have the tendency to be self-oriented. Someone has said that there are three temptations that beset Christian workers: "The temptations to shine, then to whine, and then to recline." Paul says, "I have reason to boast of my work for God." He emphasizes that he has no confidence in the flesh, because neither circumcision nor uncircumcision matters, but rather, being a new creature. Paul says that he has won obedience of the Gentiles to God "by word and deed." This is an important balance. The word *interprets* the commitment, but the deed *actualizes* the commitment. Faith means commitment: the same Greek word is translated "believe" and "commit."

The wonderful Swiss psychiatrist Paul Tournier said that to describe the life of the unregenerate, you draw a large circle with a small one in the center, then put the ego (the altered self) in the center and the capital *I* (the true self) out at the edge. To diagram the life of the regenerate person, draw the two circles, but put Christ in the center and the ego out at the edge. This is the change at the heart of one's life. But there is one question left: where is the capital *I*? It is back in the center with Christ! Now you can be a true self, as Paul says in Galations 2:20:

> It is no longer I who live,
> but it is Christ who lives in me.

December 4

Through the Power of the Spirit

**By the power of signs and wonders, by the power of the Spirit of God.
Romans 15:19a**

When unique things happen that honor Christ, they are expressions of the Spirit. These happenings become signs and wonders in testifying to the gospel. The new creation and liberty he brings into lives are signs, and so is the fruit of the Spirit. The gifts of the Spirit are his work, signs through us. The life of the disciple is a life in the Spirit. Paul said, "Anyone who does not have the Spirit of Christ does not belong to him" (8:9). The Spirit dwelling in us empowers us in God's work, thereby honoring God.

Thinking of the previous verse, we can say that evangelism consists of both what one says and what one does in the deeds of love. Word and deed belong together; each complements the other. The word interprets the deed, and the deed demonstrates the word. The word articulates the message; the deed authenticates the meaning. We share the word of Christ as we live by the example of Christ. To the Thessalonians, Paul wrote, "You know what kind of persons we proved to be among you for your sake" (1 Thess. 1:5), commenting that he had lived blamelessly among them. We experience holistic salvation. We do not present a partial gospel with only a vertical piety that lacks the horizontal dimensions.

Paul tells us that the presentation of the gospel of Christ is attended by signs and miracles, which are through the power of the Spirit. But we should note that these do not become the gospel. The good news is Christ. These signs "accompany those who believe" (Mark 16:17). The Spirit meets persons in every culture with the transforming, liberating power of Christ. In West Bengal we saw how many persons came to Christ when they witnessed God moving in answers to prayer.

I once read of an unusual occasion in John Wesley's ministry when a person was slain in the Spirit. Wesley usually prayed that God would prevent such happenings and safeguard the gospel, lest people see this phenomena rather than seeing Christ. I have followed his example, praying over a person some would have called slain in the Spirit, asking God to prevent this from altering the focus on Christ. Someone has said:

*I looked at Christ, and the dove of peace flew into my heart.
I looked at the dove of peace, and lo, it flew away.*

December 5

Fully Proclaiming the Gospel

So that from Jerusalem and as far around as Illyricum I have fully proclaimed the good news of Christ. Thus I make it my ambition to proclaim the good news, not where Christ has already been named, so that I do not build on someone else's foundation. Romans 15:19b-20

Martin Luther said that though we may have preached all of the gospel except the particular point needed in a given situation, we will not have preached the gospel! How easily we can adjust our presentation and avoid confronting a people with the liberating truth. Adjustment to be relevant or tactful is legitimate, but the Scriptures condemn preachers who have itching ears, who offer what people want to hear rather than God's Word. Our right to minister the gospel is that we live in the authority of the gospel.

Paul's states that in all of his missionary ministry, he has proclaimed fully the gospel of Christ. This should be heard as a key to how he experienced the power of the Spirit. According to Jesus's own words, the Spirit has come to glorify Christ (John 16:14). We can evaluate various ministries as to whether they glorify Jesus or the preacher. It is when Jesus is lifted up that people can feel God's drawing power.

In our day of an acculturated gospel, it is imperative that we examine our message to see whether we are presenting the Christ of the New Testament or another Christ (for this I recommend Lesslie Newbigin's book *Foolishness to the Greeks*). Some are preaching a Christ who has not risen, a Christ who is not Lord, but such is only a christic idea. This would be a Savior who doesn't transform sinners, who no longer calls us to take up the cross—a Master who serves us rather than one whom we serve in the sacrifice of praise.

We need to be more itinerant in mission if we are to share with the billions in our world who should know Christ. We must find new ways of being expatriates in another country, where we are not there to compete with their religion but to live and present Christ. We should develop the expertise they need, such as economics, engineering, technology, or education, to be welcomed by them, and in so doing be a presence for Christ.

December 6

Longing to Come to You

But as it is written, "Those who have never been told of him shall see, and those who have never heard of him shall understand." This is the reason that I have so often been hindered from coming to you. But now, with no further place for me in these regions, I desire, as I have for many years, to come to you. Romans 15:21-23

We recognize in Paul what can be called a vocational missionary. Such evangelism is not a sideline, but a central passion. Earlier Paul wrote of being a debtor, being ready to preach the gospel in Rome itself, for he was not ashamed of the gospel of Christ. In today's text he returns to this longing to go to Rome and share the gospel. This meant going to the nerve center of the world, to the capital. We need this conviction for urban mission, to go where the people are, to confront the thought-makers of our world.

The philosophy of mission expressed here is that of going to new territory rather than repeating a ministry where people have already heard. Again, I am reminded of the words of Oswald J. Smith, "No one has the right to hear the gospel twice until all of the world has heard it once." J. E. Connant asked, "If ten men are moving a log and nine are on one end and one on the other, to be of help, to which end should you go?" Ours is a world of six billion people, where at least three billion don't have the gospel of Christ.

The passion in the text is that those who have not heard may hear and understand. Paul saw this as reason to move from region to region, presenting Christ. In these verses there is recognition of divine providence, there is an acknowledgment that God's plan had as yet not led Paul to Rome. Yielded to the Spirit, we can trust him to lead us to his place of service in his time. Our challenge is to be availabile.

Someone asked General Booth of the Salvation Army for the secret of his success. He answered softly, "I determined that God would have all of me that there is."

Dear Lord,
Consciously I want to give you my all.
But subconsciously my inner self is so reserved.
Help me to understand that in giving to you,
I yet receive the freedom to be myself, a better self.

Sent, After Enjoying Your Company

I desire . . . to come to you when I go to Spain. For I do hope to see you on my journey and to be sent on by you, once I have enjoyed your company for a little while. Romans 15:24

John Wesley said, "The world is my parish." It seems that he must have gotten this from Paul. His vision was for the world in a day when he could not think of the global village as we do, nor would he have had the means of travel such as we have. His conviction was to present to all peoples the truth of Christ.

The plans Paul made were not happenstance. His projected trip to Spain would enable a long-standing desire of his to visit the believers in Rome. He evidently had a deep interest in the church there, evidenced by the quality and length of this letter, showing that he took considerable care to write them. He had numerous friends there with whom he had worked in the mission of sharing the gospel in Asia Minor. In our text, he adds the very personal note that he would go on to Spain later, "once I have enjoyed your company for a little while." Not a loner, he appreciated partners and enjoyed the company of the church.

The longer I live and enjoy the church, the more important the fellowship of believers becomes to me. When Esther and I were in Asia on a four-month leave from our congregation, their letters and prayer support were a true encouragement. Loving the people back home, we knew that we were loved by them, and we were eager to see them again. But we shared a mission to serve, to help others know fellowship with Christ, and wished to model this by serving.

Serving is highlighted by an important incident when Esther was working on the sculpture at the seminary in India. As usual, students were gathered, watching the process, when a Sikh gentleman walked up and stood observing. After a few moments he asked, "What is this?" A student explained, "This is a sculpture of Jesus washing a disciple's feet." "Oh," he said, "but you Christians believe that Jesus was God, and God would never wash a *man's* feet." The student said to Esther, "You'll need to answer." She told of God coming to be one among us in Jesus, and that he served humanity, even to the death. In this occasion of the foot washing, he demonstrated the importance of our serving each other. The man pondered, then shook his head in amazement and walked away, deeply perplexed.

December 8

Contribution to the Poor

At present, however, I am going to Jerusalem in a ministry to the saints; for Macedonia and Achaia have been pleased to share their resources with the poor among the saints at Jerusalem. Romans 15:25-26

One of the marks of the church is mutual aid. This was expressed in the formative stages of the church on the day of Pentecost: "[The believers] had all things in common" (Acts 2:44), meaning for us, as disciples, that what is mine is the church's if my brother is in need. When Paul first began preaching the gospel, he went to Jerusalem and talked with Peter and his associates to compare notes. Paul tells us that the leading apostles added nothing to the gospel that he had received from Christ. The one instruction the apostles gave him was that he should remember to care for the poor (Gal. 2:10).

Now the tables are turned and Paul reports that he has gathered monies from the young churches in Macedonia and Achaia for the poor in the church at Jerusalem. It is important to read other passages in which Paul shares information of how carefully he handled their gifts, accompanied by other brothers who would assure the integrity of his group in financial matters (see 2 Cor. 8–9). Paul's own care for the poor is shown in his traveling to Jerusalem with this contribution to relieve the suffering there. Only then would he consider his long interest in a trip to Rome.

Biblical teaching on caring for the poor is one of the more prominent social themes in the Scripture. Other such social themes include justice, peace, nonviolence, racial equity, and sanctity of life, but caring for the poor appears more frequently. Why? Because God's love is for all persons. The poor, being limited in accessing privileges of life, need to be liberated. In turn, there is a reciprocal blessing expanding the lives of those who recognize that persons take priority over things.

Seeing the suffering in South Africa through the years, Michael Cassidy, an evangelist, called prayer meetings with as many as 35,000 people meeting in the stadium in Pretoria, as well as speaking on the issue over the radio. The president of South Africa, P. W. Botha, called Michael to come to his office and threatened him, demanding that he cease and desist. Michael turned to his accompanying colleagues and said, "If anything happens to me, you will know the source," then left the hall. Apartheid was brought to its end, not only by political change, but by the moving of the Spirit in answer to prayer.

December 9

Sharing Material Blessings

They were pleased to do this, and indeed they owe it to them; for if the Gentiles have come to share in their spiritual blessings, they ought also to be of service to them in material things. So, when I have completed this, and have delivered to them what has been collected, I will set out by way of you to Spain. Romans 15:27-28

In Christian theology there is what we call an ethic of gratitude. It basically means that, having received fully of God's grace, we in turn express our gratitude by our obedience. An ethic of gratitude is basically attitude, which is good, but its limitation is that it has no content except praise or thanks. Moral content has to be supplied by the law or, as I believe, by the example of Christ. This depends on one's theological perspective.

In this expression of stewardship in sharing with the poor, Paul expresses a guiding principle. Stating that the Gentiles have shared in the Jew's spiritual blessings, they now owe it to the Jews to share with them material blessings. The reference to the Jews is recognition that the Jews have been the carriers of the knowledge of Jehovah and of his salvation history, through which Christ came as the Savior for the world. The Jerusalem church was comprised mostly of Jewish Christians, and the gospel had gone out from it. Now it was only fitting that the Gentiles should share their appreciation in this gift of love. I think of many persons through whom God has enriched my life. I am the debtor. I cannot give to everyone, but I can share by giving to God's mission, expressing his love.

In verse 28, Paul affirms again his very definite plans to go to Spain and to visit the Roman believers on the way. We know that his plans got altered at Jerusalem. We do not know that Paul ever got to Spain. Some have theorized that he was released from prison for a time and then imprisoned again, and that in this interim he did go to Spain. This is not a part of the biblical story, and I prefer not to speculate. We do see in Paul the faith that could trust God's sovereignty and grace. He did get to Rome, as the story is found in the book of Acts 28, but as a prisoner. Even so, God gave him remarkable freedom for some four years of ministry as people came and went from his quarters (Acts 24:27; 28:30). Our service is not always in the form of our choosing, but with adjustments to circumstances.

December 10

The Fullness of the Blessing

And I know that when I come to you, I will come in the fullness of the blessing of Christ. Romans 15:29

David Livingstone, missionary explorer in Africa, lost his wife to a disease for which he did not have adequate medicine. With his helpers he prepared her body for burial, built the coffin, and dug the grave. He read the Scripture as the group shared his sorrow, then helped to lower her body into the grave, and shovel the dirt onto the coffin. When the grave was mounded over, he opened his Bible to the last chapter of Matthew and read verses 18-20, closing with the words, "Lo, I am with you alway, even unto the end of the world" (KJV). Holding his Bible before him, he said, "Jesus is too much of a gentleman not to keep his word. Let us go on with the work."

Paul's confidence is repeated variously, but especially in these words: "For I know the one in whom I have put my trust, and I am sure that he is able to guard until that day what I have entrusted to him" (2 Tim. 1:12). "I can do all things through him who strengthens me" (Phil. 4:13). Here in our text is the assurance that when Paul comes, it will be in the fullness of the blessing of Christ. As disciples of Christ, we are actually extensions of the Master's arms! He is doing his work through us. This gospel shaped Paul's life, and to this gospel he sought to be true. He wanted to share in its completeness.

When Esther was constructing the sculpture on the Union Biblical Seminary campus in India, it seemed that her helpers had a problem taking directions from a woman. For several hours I deliberately took her instructions and quietly demonstrated that a man could follow her directions. I helped stretch the wire mesh over reinforcement rods, which she carefully shaped into a sculptural form. In that part of the work, she is the master; she has the artist's creative vision and design in her mind. I only served as an extension of what she visualized. Seeing this pattern of respect, the next day the men began to help.

So it is in our relation with Christ. Our work is an extension of his vision, an expression of his Spirit, a communication of his word. Our deeds make our faith visible.

By the Love of the Spirit

I appeal to you, brothers and sisters, by our Lord Jesus Christ and by the love of the Spirit, to join me in earnest prayer to God on my behalf, that I may be rescued from the unbelievers in Judea, and that my ministry to Jerusalem may be acceptable to the saints. Romans 15:30-31

Courage is not the absence of fear. It is daring to stand when you feel like running. It is evident in our text that Paul was aware of the dangers to him at Jerusalem. His trip was not being made without some fear of serious consequences. He well knew that while there were saints in the Jerusalem church, there were many unbelieving Jews who were his opponents. He asks for the prayers of the Roman Christians: first, that he be rescued from the unbelievers in Judea; and second, that his service in Jerusalem would be acceptable to the saints. From the book of Acts we know how Paul was treated, so we can read this text with awareness that he knew the risk taken in this service (Acts 21:17-36).

Luke's account tells us that Paul was warmly received by the brothers, but on the seventh day some Jews stirred up the crowd against Paul and he was arrested. God's answer to Paul's prayers was to keep him strong under persecution, saving his life by having the Roman guard rescue him from death in Jerusalem. Significantly, Paul's appeal for the prayers of the Roman Christians emphasizes prayer expressly to the triune God: "by our Lord Jesus Christ and by the love of the Spirit, . . . prayer to God on my behalf." We are not talking about three Gods, but the One God known in three Persons.

David Shenk, a gifted writer especially on Muslim and Christian conversation, was a missionary for a number of years in Kenya. He taught at Kenyatta University. One day a Muslim leader came to his home in a very angry spirit, telling David that he was causing a real problem in teaching his children that there are three Gods. "But," David responded, "you haven't heard me correctly. I am teaching that God is love." The man said, "I don't understand." David explained, "God is love in himself, and this love is so great and so unifying that he expresses himself as Father, as Son, and as Holy Spirit, but he is One in this multiple expression." The man said softly, "That is a beautiful thought. I must think on that further."

December 12

The God of Peace Be with You

So that by God's will I may come to you with joy and be refreshed in your company. The God of peace be with all of you. Amen. Romans 15:32-33

There is an old statement, "Man proposes, but God disposes." As a believer, one should always recognize the will of God above our own will and beyond our own insight. Our text recognizes this great truth. Paul made plans to take the offering to the saints at Jerusalem and then to journey to Spain via Rome, but those plans were subject to the will of God. In our plans, we are not guaranteed that events will follow the course we have visualized, but we have the security that he will be at work with us.

In the community of faith, we find a refreshing of our spirits when we meet together in the fellowship of Christ. Paul thought both of his contribution to and desire to receive something from the church in Rome. Esther and I, in our extensive travels, find the truth of this text, for in each country, with the cultural differences, we find persons who walk with Christ, and we are mutually refreshed.

Paul's conclusion in this chapter could close the book, except for the personal greetings in the next chapter as a wonderful affirmation of the dynamic of community. But this is a benedictory expression of blessing. He does not simply close with the traditional shalom, but sets peace in the context of the Author of peace: "The God of peace be with all of you." We are a people of God, and so we are a people of God's peace. This is one of the greater titles given to God as our Father: "The God of peace." We can hear the angels at the birth of Jesus, "On earth peace among those whom he favors" (Luke 2:14).

In 1979 in South Africa, 6,000 of us shared in a remarkable witness against apartheid at the South African Christian Leadership Assembly (SACLA), Pretoria. I preached on Sunday at Amisville to a black congregation, and my friend Samuel Hines, an African-American pastor from Washington, DC, preached in another church. I was well received, but he told a different story. As he preached from Jesus's words to love our enemies, calling for nonviolent approaches to change, a young man jumped up and shouted, "That's too soft! What we need is revolution!" Hines didn't back down: "You are a revolutionary; let me see if I understand. You say 'there is a problem out there and I'm going out to solve it, and if you get in my way, I will kill you.' Is that correct?" The young man replied, "That's right." Hines said, "Well, I'm also a revolutionary, and I also say there is a problem out there, and I'm going out to solve it, and if you get in my way, ... I'll lay down my life for you. Now which one of us is soft?"

December 13

I Commend Our Sister Phoebe

I commend to you our sister Phoebe, a deacon of the church at Cenchreae, so that you may welcome her in the Lord as is fitting for the saints, and help her in whatever she may require from you, for she has been a benefactor of many and of myself as well. Romans 16:1-2

This amazing chapter expresses both the importance of community and Paul's capacity for friendship. Of special significance is the fact that he mentions nine women in his personal comments, a testimony that in the body of Christ male and female persons work together as equals, which was not experienced in the general society of his time.

The chapter begins with Paul's commendation of Phoebe, "a deacon of the church in Cenchreae." We know nothing more about her than what is given us here. We learn from Acts 18 that Paul, with Priscilla and Aquila, left Corinth to sail for Syria and first stopped in Cenchreae, where he got a haircut. The church in this city may have developed through converts from nearby Corinth.

Our text identifies Phoebe as a deacon, a servant of this church. Her leadership role is further suggested in Paul's commendation of her to the church in Rome. This may be the first women to serve as a deacon in the Christian church, a practice among Gentile Christians (1 Tim. 5:9-10), but among Jewish Christians there is reference only to men as deacons (Acts 6:3-6). Women were accepted as prophets, as in the ministry of Philip's daughters, but he was a Hellenist (Acts 21:8-9). Paul urged the church in Rome to receive Phoebe and give her whatever help she needed as a leader from another church community. I believe the Holy Spirit included this for our understanding of the early church. It was a man's world (Acts 21:5), but Christ changed relationships to equity.

In the history of my Mennonite denomination, Elisabeth Dirks was converted to Christ as a young woman, and then was imprisoned for a year. However, she ingeniously escaped by trading outer clothing with the milkmaid who brought milk to the convent. She put the maid's yoke over her shoulders, left disguised as the milkmaid, and found her way to an Anabaptist home. In a few years she became a Bible teacher in the Anabaptist movement. She was commissioned as a deacon, the first woman deacon in the Mennonite church. She worked so prominently with Menno Simons that, when arrested, the authorities thought they had his wife. She died a martyr for her faith on May 27, 1549.

December 14

Priscilla and Aquila as Fellow Workers

Greet Prisca [Priscilla] and Aquila, who work with me in Christ Jesus, and who risked their necks for my life, to whom not only I give thanks, but also all the churches of the Gentiles. Greet also the church in their house. Romans 16:3-5a

One of our wonderful riches is in our friendships. Edgar Guest, the poet, was at a party and seated beside a millionaire. As people passed where the two were seated, many greeted the poet. The millionaire commented, "It seems that you have many friends and I have none." Guest said, "While you were busy making money, I was making friends."

Paul had many friends and enemies, but with many friends, one doesn't feel only the affects of the enemies and become disheartened. The second person in his list is a woman also. Priscilla and her husband Aquila are first mentioned as having fled Rome under Claudius. Paul met them at Corinth, visited them, and arranged to stay with them to join them in their work as tentmakers. Later he traveled with them to Ephesus, and the couple stayed there for some time.

When the Alexandrian Jew, Apollos, fluent and "mighty in the Scriptures" (KJV), came preaching about Jesus as the Messiah with understandings of only the witness of John the Baptist, Priscilla and Aquila took Apollos to their home and "explained to him the Way of God more adequately" (Acts 18:1-3, 18-19, 24-26). Various scholars think that Paul's unusual pattern of naming Priscilla before Aquila is evidence of her special strengths. She may have served as his amanuensis (writer) and may even have composed the book of Hebrews from his teachings and completed it after Paul was gone.

The couple had now returned to Rome and had a church in their house. Paul calls them his fellow workers in team ministry. He affirms their dedication, having even risked their lives for him. This was known, for he says that in addition to his gratitude, he conveys the gratitude of the churches of the Gentiles as well. In a congregational setting, a team can minister to the variety of people in better ways than a single pastor. As a man in ministry, I relate from a masculine perspective and often more directly to men. A woman on the team relates to the women with special freedom. It is also good for women to hear a man's presentation, and for men to hear and think with a woman. For the past twenty years I have found the team ministry effective in pastoral work rather than being a solo pastor.

The First Convert in Asia

Greet my beloved Epaenetus, who was the first convert in Asia for Christ.
Romans 16:5b

This verse shows Paul's continued association and informational contact with converts. This is a tribute to Epaenetus, but also reveals a special attribute of the apostle. It is persons in whom we are interested, not just numbers.

Thinking of Esther and my ministries and teaching in numerous countries of Africa, Latin America, Asia, and Eastern Europe, our privilege has been to help strengthen the church. The importance of this is evident in the great land of India, where Christians number only about 3 percent of the population. It is not an easy place for the church to work. When William Carey came to Calcutta in mission, he worked for twenty years before seeing his first convert. So it is no surprise to read the deep feelings of joy in the heart of the apostle Paul as he greeted Epaenetus, the first convert to Christ in the province of Asia.

Reading this short sentence, there are several things that impress me. First, Paul speaks of Epaenetus as "my beloved" or "great friend," showing that in leading the man to Christ, he must have spent time with him, led him in discipleship, and enjoyed a fellowship that grew into a deep, satisfying friendship. Second, Paul refers to him as the "first convert to Christ." He does not say *my* first convert, as though the man related to him, but Epaenetus is a disciple of Christ. Third, as the first convert in the province of Asia, it is implied that there are others. The church is a growing community.

Jesus spoke of the kingdom of heaven saying that its small beginning is like a grain of mustard seed (Matt. 13:31-32), or that it works like leaven in the dough to spread through the whole lump (13:33). Paul's vision in mission was that new disciples of Jesus would form the beginning of a community of faith in a city, and eventually impact the whole society.

As light cannot be hidden by darkness no matter how deep the darkness, so disciples of Christ cannot be hidden in society. Any society will be the better for the presence of genuine Christians enriching the thought and improving the level of moral behavior. This is our calling in whatever context we find ourselves.

December 16

Greet Mary

Greet Mary, who has worked very hard among you. Romans 16:6

Many of us have a Mary, a Janet, an Elizabeth, a Peggy, or a Miriam, who, in my case, have worked very hard for me. This is especially true in my sharing with Esther, my special love. My life has been richer through her, my work greater in quality, and our family especially has been enriched.

After fifteen years in the office of president of Eastern Mennonite College and Seminary, I left for other work. My first adjustment was that I felt as though my arms had been cut off. I had been enabled to do a lot of things through other people. I hope they always felt like my colleagues and didn't feel that they were being used by me. The safeguard in such relationships is mutual recognition of different gifts and responsibilities given to each by God. Some who are visionaries and entrepreneurs have their vision rounded out and expedited by persons gifted at the tasks of administering detail.

Paul says simply, "Greet Mary, who has worked very hard among you." We do not know what Mary did among them. Was she one of the women who had followed Jesus in his earthly life? Mary Magdalene? The sister of Martha? Was she one who had been in Rome and expelled like Priscilla and Aquila, and had worked for the church in some setting in Asia Minor? Or was she one of the faithful in Rome who, like Phoebe, was a servant of the church? Only God knows the answers to these questions. Paul included her in this list of special people in the first-century church.

While historians can name church fathers, Nicene and post-Nicene, persons like Mary would doubtless have gone unmentioned by those more patriarchal in the hierarchy of leadership. But she is recognized in history because Paul tells us of her diligent service.

I knew as a friend a person whom the larger church recognized as Brother Orie Miller. Miller was a mission statesman of the Mennonite Church for over half of the twentieth century. He was an enabler of missions while never serving as a missionary in a foreign context. I heard him say that he had done as much in each decade after he was forty years old, as he had done in his whole life previously, simply by knowing what to select and doing it by enabling others.

December 17

In Prison with Me

Greet Andronicus and Junia, my relatives who were in prison with me; they are prominent among the apostles, and they were in Christ before I was. Romans 16:7

Too often we think of Paul's conversion on the Damascus Road as a solo event. In Jesus's words to him, "It is hard for you to kick against the pricks" (Acts 26:14, KJV), we are made aware that he had relationships through which convictions of the Spirit had been getting to him. One was the stoning of Stephen, at which event Saul was present, consenting to his death but hearing his testimony. Another was the spirit and witness of Christians whom Saul persecuted and imprisoned. A third source of conviction must have been that he had relatives who were Christians before his conversion: Andronicus and Junia.

This couple—there is considerable evidence that Junia was a woman—had suffered imprisonment with Paul for their faith in Christ. This precedes Paul's imprisonment in Rome; the earlier imprisonment was no doubt at Caesarea where he had been in prison for two years.

Paul refers to them as "prominent among the apostles," identifying more persons in the apostolate than the twelve, including Matthias, who replaced Judas (Acts 1:26), and the addition of Paul himself (1 Cor. 15:8-9). An apostle is "a sent one," a spokesperson for the risen Christ, one who has seen the risen Lord. They must have been among the five hundred to whom Jesus appeared after the resurrection, many who were still living when Paul was writing (1 Cor. 15:6). Chrysostom, one of the church fathers, wrote, "Oh, how great is the devotion of this woman, that she should even be counted worthy of the appellation of apostle." An unknown writer confessed in a prayer:

> *I asked God for strength that I might achieve;*
> *I was made weak that I might learn to obey.*
> *I asked for help that I might do great things;*
> *I was given infirmity that I might do better things.*
> *I asked for riches that I might be happy;*
> *I was given poverty that I might be wise.*
> *I got nothing I asked for, but everything I hoped for;*
> *Almost despite myself, my deepest prayer was answered.*

December 18

Approved in Christ

Greet Ampliatus, my beloved in the Lord. Greet Urbanus, our co-worker in Christ, and my beloved Stachys. Greet Apelles, who is approved in Christ. Romans 16:8-10a

In the several verses of text chosen for this meditation, Paul greets four different men: Ampliatus, Urbanus, Stachys, and Apelles. The list continues, but these four are addressed singly before he addresses households. For each of these friends, Paul has an identifying word which expresses their relationship: "my beloved in the Lord," "our co-worker," "my beloved," and "approved in Christ." I am impressed with how much Paul says about these persons in so few words. I would have been glad to have had a relationship with Paul and bear the characteristics of any one of the four.

The searching phrase for me is the last of the four, "approved in Christ." There is security in that phrase. After ministering for Christ for over fifty years, it feels good to be able to say, "I've tested what I am sharing. I have nothing I am trying to prove. I'm just interested in sharing the Christ who has enriched my life."

On a short visit to Delhi in late 1987, we spent time with Bruce and Kathleen Nichols, a missionary couple from New Zealand. Bruce had been a professor of theology in India, but left to pastor a congregation associated with the Church of North India in Delhi. Kathleen had taught communication and drama in the seminary and authored a fine book, *Art and Christian Hope*. She and Esther talked about art, and Bruce and I talked of his insights on contextualizing the gospel. Our time was rich, for they were career missionaries, "approved in Christ," esteemed by many.

To contextualize is an exercise of faith,
of dependence upon the Spirit for wisdom.
We need to hear honestly in another culture,
and relate the gospel authentically.
Culture itself is neutral but tends to idolatry,
yet culture is ubiquitous, inescapable,
for we all live our lives in a skin.

December 21

Chosen in the Lord

Greet Rufus, chosen in the Lord; and greet his mother—a mother to me also. Romans 16:13

At a pastor's conference in Bihar, India, Esther told of her childhood in India when her parents served as missionaries. In her presentation she told the true story of Jugu, an Indian Christian in their congregation. On one occasion, Jugu with his family traveled by oxcart to Dhamtari for supplies for his small store. They made the forty-mile trip through the jungle, purchased supplies, and were returning in the late evening. As they traveled through the jungle, the trail would occasionally fork, and Jugu knew that he needed to be careful because at one fork, to take the wrong path would lead to an area where a man-eating tiger had recently made several kills. Confused at the fork, he stopped the cart, turned to his family, and they prayed together, asking God's guidance.

He then made his choice and started off. Suddenly he heard a voice: "Jugu." Frightened, he hurried on, thinking it was robbers. A second time he heard the voice calling "Jugu," and he again hurried the oxen's pace. Then heard, "Jugu, this way." And looking back to the other trail from where the voice was coming, he saw a bright light, brighter and more beautiful than anything he had ever seen. Now sure that it was an angel who was speaking, he turned back, took the other road, and arrived home safely.

After Esther told the story, a young pastor came to her and said, "I'm Jugu's grandson. My mother has often told me that story, as she was in the oxcart." God works in sovereign care of his children.

Paul greets Rufus and his mother, referring to Rufus as being chosen or elect, meaning a prominent person in the Christian community, and to Rufus's mother as one who had been a mother figure to Paul as well. Scholars think that Rufus is the man referred to by Mark (15:21), in writing his gospel from Rome, when he identified Simon of Cyrene for his readers as the father of Alexander and Rufus, persons they well knew. We met Simon of Cyrene first as the man who was compelled to carry Jesus's cross. Here we find his wife, probably a widow, and his son Rufus, who were active Christians in the church.

The personal greetings of this chapter bring the early church to us very realistically. Real people were walking with Christ as we do. We follow as disciples of the risen Christ, "Although you have not seen him, you love him; and even though you do not see him now, you believe in him and rejoice with an indescribable and glorious joy" (1 Pet. 1:8). Thomas cried, "My Lord and my God!" Jesus said, "Blessed are those who have not seen and yet have come to believe" (John 20:28-29).

All the Saints with Them

Greet Asyncritus, Phlegon, Hermes, Patrobas, Hermas, and the brothers and sisters who are with them. Greet Philologus, Julia, Nereus and his sister, and Olympas, and all the saints who are with them. Romans 16:14-15

Here believers are called saints. The term "Christian" appears only three times in the Bible: twice in Acts and once in the epistle of 1 Peter. The term "disciple" is frequently used as Christ's designation for us who believe. The term "saint" is used as God's designation for us, his children, and the terms "brothers" and "sisters" are used to refer to our common bond in the community of faith. In this text, the greeting is to five men with the phrase "and the brothers and sisters who are with them," with a second reference to five persons, of which two are women. We see here that Paul is gender inclusive.

Many of these names appear in inscriptions from the imperial household. John Lightfoot, the Scripture commentator of the seventeenth century, found that many were freedmen and freedwomen, while some were slaves and members of a particular household. Since Rome was 60 percent slaves, it is significant that in the Christian church these are fellow believers bearing no designation of a class distinction. The grouping in verse 14, with the phrase "and the brothers and sisters who are with them," implies that they were a small Christian community in themselves. The next group may well have been a family: Philologus and his wife, Julia, with their children, Nerias, his sister, and Olympas, whose relationship is uncertain.

This chapter, with its inclusiveness, throws some light on Paul's statement to Timothy: "Let a woman learn in silence with full submission . . . and [not] have authority over a man" (1 Tim. 2:11). However, Paul declares clearly that she is to learn And Priscilla is recognized as a teacher and deacon/minister (Acts 18:26; Rom. 16:1, NRSV note). This is a partnership that honors God's liberating grace, of women studying and teaching, as well as men, in the freedom of the new community (cf. Matt. 10:25; 13:52). I didn't grow up with this perspective, but the Spirit has prodded me in change through his Word.

The church is transcultural, transracial, transnational, and transgender. This is the unity of the church, as we have seen in the weeks of meetings we shared in countries around the world. There is "one Lord, one faith, one baptism, one God and Father of all, who is above all and through all and in all" (Eph. 4: 5-6).

December 23

With a Holy Kiss

Greet one another with a holy kiss. All the churches of Christ greet you.
Romans 16:16

This meditation comes during the Christmas season, and in it, I recognize the kiss of peace. The words of the angels to the shepherds on the Bethlehem hills will live forever: "Glory to God in the highest heaven, and on earth peace among those whom he favors!" (Luke 2:14). As Isaiah said, his name shall be called "Wonderful Counselor, Mighty God, Everlasting Father, Prince of Peace" (9:6). Just as Paul has spoken of the God of peace at the end of the previous chapter, so here he envisions a family of peace as children of God—"Greet one another with a holy kiss," a kiss of peace.

There are various cultures of the East where this kiss of greeting or parting has a deep meaning and shows full acceptance. Often it is expressed by kissing on both cheeks, each person doing so in turn. While in India, Esther and I spent a weekend in Madras, ministering at St. Georges Cathedral. We were hosted by Bishop Azariah, secretary of the Synod of the Church of South India. When we met, very deliberately and yet warmly, he kissed me, first on one cheek and then on the other, two times. This symbolism declared to all others who are around that I was fully accepted.

In the Old Testament we read, "Righteousness and peace will kiss each other" (Ps. 85:10). God in his redeeming grace has brought to us his peace. This fellowship binds the church together across national and cultural lines, into one body in Christ. As Paul tells the Roman Christians, so we say to one another, "All the churches of Christ send greetings."

The greeting of the "holy kiss" is an expression that the congregational community is a family. I grew up with this pattern in our congregation in Ohio. It is a holy kiss, not a passionate kiss, but a kiss on the cheek as a simple affirmation of love. In many instances in our modern society, with various implications of the kiss, this passage may be well interpreted as "warm embrace," not a literal holy kiss, but acknowledging its meaning. A warm embrace is an expression of the intimacy of belonging, and this extends beyond our primary family to the extended circle in the family of faith.

December 24

Beware of Those Causing Divisions

I urge you, brothers and sisters, to keep an eye on those who cause dissensions and offenses, in opposition to the teaching that you have learned; avoid them. For such people do not serve our Lord Christ but their own appetites, and by smooth talk and flattery they deceive the hearts of the simple-minded. Romans 16:17-18

This is Christmas Eve, a celebration of the incarnation, of "the Word [who] became flesh and lived among us" (John 1:14). The glory of the Christmas message is that God has come to us, that God cares for us, and that God has involved himself in our problems. In the babe of Bethlehem, God made himself vulnerable. In Christ, God has made himself clearly known, and Jesus is the cornerstone of our faith. John writes that we can test the spirits of our age by whether they correspond to the Jesus who came in the flesh (1 John 4:2-3). The Christ of Christmas is thus the center of our faith.

In our text, we can turn to a meditation for Christmas by recognizing the calling of faithfulness to the Christ. A strange text, but it is relevant, for in the midst of revelry, commercialism, materialism, and secularism, we too need to be called to faithfulness to Christ, to beware of those who only serve themselves. Paul says we should beware of voices leading us away from Christ, personalities that cause division in the church, persons who by smooth words lead the naive to follow them rather than to follow Christ. Celebrating the incarnation means coming to him, "for he will save his people from their sins" (Matt. 1:21).

It is always a joy, whenever possible, to be with our family for Christmas. In this season we recognize what family relationships mean to God as well: "He gave his only begotten Son," and again, "The Word became flesh and dwelt among us."

Through the disclosures in history
God told us a lot about himself;
but that is not a full revelation
unless he himself should come,
and this he did in Jesus the Christ!

I Am Full of Joy over You

For while your obedience is known to all, so that I rejoice over you, I want you to be wise in what is good and guileless in what is evil. Romans 16:19

"Joy to the world! the Lord is come; let earth receive her King" (Isaac Watts). Again, "You are to to name him Jesus, for he will save his people from their sins" (Matt. 1:21). This is a Christ-mass, for in the community of the redeemed, we worship as a new people, a new family of God.

Paul commends the church at Rome for their faithfulness. Everyone, he says, has heard of your obedience. Paul rejoices in this witness; he is filled with joy over them. These are wonderful words of encouragement—positive and upbeat. His preceding warning was therefore not a judgment of them, but a word of caution, a recognition that the church is not made up of perfect people, but of committed people.

The text expresses a pastor's joy in seeing his congregation walking in obedience to Christ. When one gives his life to teaching and shepherding a congregation, it is a satisfaction to see it walking with integrity as disciples of Christ. In fact, a congregation's life of faith becomes a demonstration of grace, enriching the pastor as well.

Paul expresses a unique wish for the Roman Christians to be wise about what is good and innocent concerning what is evil. One is not robbed of a full life by saying no to perversions. It has been said, "You don't have to eat a whole apple to know it is rotten." The more we share the good, the more it permeates our life and thought. The less we are involved in evil, the less we will be obsessed with thoughts and temptations that derive from the selfish appeal of evil itself. Evil is a perversion of life, the enemy of the good, and a parasite, living by misusing benefits of the good. In contrast, good is proactive. The engagement of wholesome things enriches other aspects of life.

As we sing, "Joy to the world! the Lord is come," we recognize that joy is a matter of spirit. Joy is a matter of relationships, the dynamic interfacing of fellowship. We enjoy one another as we share fellowship; similarly, we enjoy God, finding that the joy of the Lord is our strength. John, in his first epistle, speaks of fellowship "with the Father and with his Son Jesus Christ," adding, "We are writing these things so that our joy may be complete" (1 John 1:3-4).

The God of Peace

The God of peace will shortly crush Satan under your feet. The grace of our Lord Jesus Christ be with you. Romans 16:20

In his book *Christus Victor*, the Lutheran theologian, Gustaf Aulén, has presented the atonement as Christ's victory over Satan, over the evil of sin and death. While Satan is active in the world, he is defeated. In the cross, Jesus absorbed all that sin and the demonic could do against him, experiencing death as the ultimate evil, and in it all he was victorious. The satanic forces crushed his body but could not crush his spirit.

Having warned the Christians at Rome about the evil which Satan propagates, Paul adds this strong word of assurance: "The God of peace will shortly crush Satan under your feet." This vanquishing of evil in extending the victory of Christ is graphically presented in the book of Revelation, especially in chapters 10 through 18, culminating in the final chapters with a reign of peace. God's ultimate purpose is to bring us into his presence and peace. This is his work within us, to bring each aspect of our rebellion to its end and to share his shalom, his completeness with us.

Someone asked a theologian why God doesn't pardon the devil, to which the scholar replied, "Because the devil never asked him to." This is what makes the devil to be the devil—he stands against God. This is the nature of evil, excluding God from one's life and experience. Thinking of future judgment for the lost, just imagine what will happen when God takes us to himself and withdraws all the love, light, goodness, justice, peace, and joy of his nature and leaves only evil itself in the realm where Satan operates. The existence that will be left, if one can call it existence, is hell! God's common grace saves; evil can only self-destruct. All God needs to do to crush Satan is to leave him totally to himself. Evil left to itself is a bottomless pit.

For all of us who are children of faith, there is one sustaining power—the grace of Christ. We have no other security, no other assurance, no other power for victory. It is our solidarity with Christ that gives us assurance of eternal life.

December 27

My Colleagues Greet You

Timothy, my co-worker, greets you; so do Lucius and Jason and Sosipater, my relatives. I Tertius, the writer of this letter, greet you in the Lord. Romans 16:21-22

Just as Paul sent greetings to many friends in Rome, so also do his friends about him. They are support persons who enable an extension of ministry that otherwise would be limited to what Paul, as one man, could do. The picture is one of team ministry, of being partners in the mission of Christ. Some will no doubt accompany him to Jerusalem. His co-worker is Timothy, a fellow worker ever since joining Paul in Ephesus, serving with him in Macedonia and adding greetings to those of the apostle.

Along with Timothy, there are three Jewish brothers, Paul's kinsman: Lucius, Jason, and Sosipater, who may be persons mentioned as Paul's hosts and companions in areas of Asia Minor (see Acts 13:1; 17:5-9; 20:4). The reference to these persons helps us to understand Paul as a team leader rather than to see him as a lone individualist.

In verse 22 we discover that Paul had an amanuensis, Tertius. By adding this greeting, we learn of Tertius and his service to Paul. We may conclude from the nature of the greeting that he was not only a secretary, but that he also helped express the ideas as Paul shared them with him. We may also conclude that Paul trusted Tertius and gave him freedom in his writing, although Tetius says that he was simply "the writer of this letter."

Often we praise persons who have the lead roles in a project and overlook how many wonderful persons have been their enablers. As president of Eastern Mennonite College for fifteen years, my own work was enhanced and expanded by many highly qualified colleagues on the faculty and staff. The public gave me a lot of credit for what we together were doing. The same was true later in the congregation in Washington, DC, where we developed a team ministry with others in leadership roles. As president of the Coalition of Christian Colleges and Universities, I had a wonderful team of vice-presidents and staff. Much of God's work is accomplished by teams of people, doing in ordinary ways, extraordinary work. On God's team we share in complementary, not competing, roles. We are each the better because of others.

Gaius, Whose Hospitality We Enjoy

**Gaius, who is host to me and to the whole church, greets you. Erastus, the
city treasurer, and our brother Quartus, greet you. Romans 16:23**

Apparently Paul was writing from Corinth, for he adds greetings from Gaius, his host, who was from
Corinth (1 Cor. 1:14). Paul's comment, which accompanies the greeting from Gaius, affirms that not
only Paul, but all the church enjoyed the hospitality of his home. The congregation may have met in his
house.

Along with Gaius, there are two other brothers of Corinth who send their greetings: Erastus, the
city treasurer, an influential member of the community, and Quartus, whom Paul simply calls "our
brother." In Paul's second letter to the Corinthians, he refers to "the brother who is famous among all
the churches," who accompanied Titus in coming to collect the offering for Jerusalem (2 Cor. 8:16-24).
In his second letter to Timothy, Paul refers to Erastus having stayed at Corinth (2 Tim. 4:20). Perhaps
he is the unnamed brother who went with Titus as a trusted financial agent. This we do not know, as
the person is anonymous. However, one thing is clear, the apostle Paul was able to share his work and
to trust significant persons who enriched his life and ministry (see Acts 19:22).

The reference to hospitality is an important note, for enjoying others in fellowshiping is an
investment in people. It is sharing our privileges with others. Here he compliments their hospitality as
a grace in the church. It is a dynamic of mission. Evangelism for today may be by hospitality, which
becomes an effective setting for conversation.

The reference emphasizes Paul's ability to get along with people. God's work has sometimes
moved on, while some took time off to engage in petty quarrels. A friend of mine, James Herr, a
successful Christian businessman, tells of going to see an ice hockey game. He saw two opposing players
clash, and it was evident to him that they wanted to fight, but the game was going on. He said that he
could sense their struggle in the decision: to fight and be out of the real action, or to stay with the
game. Christian people have spent time and psychic energy in little squabbles while God's game goes
on.

December 29

To Him Who Alone Is Able

Now to God who is able to strengthen you according to my gospel and the proclamation of Jesus Christ, according to the revelation of the mystery that was kept secret for long ages. Romans 16:25

As we now come close to the conclusion of this remarkable epistle, Paul breaks out in a doxology of praise, couched in phrases that are, in essence, a summation of his whole letter. We learned in Romans 1:11 that Paul wanted to visit the Christians in Rome to "impart some spiritual gift" (KJV), and now in his conclusion he offers praise to "God who is able to strengthen you according to my gospel and the proclamation of Jesus Christ." He emphasizes again the "mystery that was kept secret for long ages but is now disclosed." God's plan is for all peoples, Jew and Gentile alike, to share in the universal extension of God's love.

In this declaration, Paul is careful to show that this mystery is disclosed "according to the command of the eternal God" (Rom. 16:26). It is God who is sovereign, God who has taken the initiative, and God who has come to us in grace. It is God who acted in Jesus to redeem us, God who transforms lives and creates a new people by his Spirit, and God who brings to fullness his eternal plan. But with all that we understand of God, there yet remains so much that is mystery, and we bow before him in worship without fully mastering his disclosure.

As we look back over our pilgrimage through the book of Romans, we also look back over its applications in a very eventful year. We have been thinking and praying through this book so that we might be better Christians, more consistent disciples, and more completely taken up in the joy and love of God.

For Esther and me, with all of our varied ministries, extensive travel, cross-cultural sharing, and wide variety of church fellowships, we experience the riches of God's love of which Paul writes so effectively. With you, we close this year in our home with our family and within our congregational fellowship, with abundant cause for doxology. Just as Paul longed to see his friends in Rome and many other places, so we long to see the family of God around the world. We are a part of a global family. No matter what our denominational identity, as believers we are bound together in his love!

December 30

So That All Nations Might Believe

But is now disclosed, and through the prophetic writings is made known to all the Gentiles, according to the command of the eternal God, to bring about the obedience of faith. Romans 16:26

"For God so loved the world that he gave his only Son" (John 3:16). God's love is to share himself with us. "For our sake he made him to be [a] sin [offering] who knew no sin, so that in him we might become the righteousness of God" (2 Cor. 5:21). No one group of people have an edge on the kingdom of God, he is calling a people out of every kindred and nation and tongue. Our mission in Christ changes our attitude toward all peoples. Our doctrinal systems interpret our faith in God and are helpful, but they are only a means to the end: the end is fellowship with God himself.

This year we have recognized, with Paul, how people can become Christians—Japanese, Indian, African, Israeli, and Palestinian. In Christ "there is no longer Greek and Jew, circumcised and uncircumcised, barbarian, Scythian, slave and free" (Col. 3:11). We are partakers of a new covenant. "The obedience of faith" is an expression of participation in this covenant with the integrity of faith.

Stanley Green, executive director of the Mennonite Mission Network, formerly from South Africa, tells an amazing story of God's grace. The scene is a courtroom at the end of apartheid. An elderly black woman listens as Mr. Van der Broek, former chief of police, is tried for atrocities he committed. Several years earlier, he had come and taken her son, shot him, then returned and took her husband, and after several years came and took her to a riverbank; she witnessed her husband stretched on a pyre alive for burning. The last words she heard her husband say as they lit the fire were, "Father, forgive them; they don't know what they are doing." Now as she listened, it was evident that Van der Broek was guilty.

Before sentencing, the judge asked her if she had anything to say. Slowly, this elderly woman got to her feet. "Yes, I have three requests. First, I'd like someone to take me to the riverbank where my husband was burned so that I can scoop up some ashes and give them a fitting burial. Second, I'd like you to sentence Mr. van der Broek to come to my house in the ghetto twice a month and let me pour out on him the love I would have given my son. And third, will someone take me by the arm and lead me over to Mr. Van der Broek so that I can put my arms around him and tell him that it is because of Jesus that I forgive him?" As she started across the hall, Van der Broek fainted. The audience in the courtroom began to sing, "Amazing grace! how sweet the sound."

364

December 31

Soli Deo Gloria

To the only wise God, through Jesus Christ, to whom be the glory forever! Amen. Romans 16:27

Our journey through this epistle has been an identification with the marvelous grace of God, his electing call, his sovereign purpose, and above all his transforming fellowship. We are participants in a new creation as the people of God. Paul describes us as the body of Christ, and just as the body gives visibility to one's personality, so the church is to give visibility to Christ in the world. This is our mission.

Some emphasize the visible and the invisible church. The *visible* is the organized church, and the *invisible* are those truly regenerate. Harold S. Bender wrote his inaugural address for the American Society of Church History in 1943, presenting what is known as the *Anabaptist Vision*, stressing the nature of the church as his central point. His interpretation of the Anabaptist perspective was: first, the rediscovery of Christian experience as discipleship; second, that the church is a voluntary fellowship of the reborn; and third, that love is a lifestyle. These three points in defining the believers church all serve to emphasize that the church is visible, a fellowship of a new humanity in society.

This vision follows Paul's theology in Romans. We are justified by a faith, which reconciles us to God, with whom we walk as disciples. We hear the words, "I appeal to you therefore, brothers and sisters, by the mercies of God, to present your bodies as a living sacrifice, holy and acceptable to God, which is your spiritual worship" (Rom. 12:1). Our text closes with Paul's words of praise, "To the only wise God, through Jesus Christ, to whom be the glory forever! Amen."

Holy, holy, holy,
is the Lord God the Almighty,
who was and is and is to come. (Rev. 4:8)

Worthy is the Lamb, that was slaughtered
to receive power and wealth and wisdom and might
and honor and glory and blessing!
To the one seated on the throne and to the Lamb
be blessing and honor and glory and might
forever and ever! ... Amen. (Rev. 5:12-14)

The Author

Myron S. Augsburger is widely known for his leadership as president of Eastern Mennonite University and Seminary and the Council of Christian Colleges and Universities. He has led many evangelistic, preaching, and teaching missions in countries around the world, as well as across North America. As a pastor, he planted and served a vibrant young church in Washington, DC, where many of these meditations had their early testing. The author of more than twenty books, his recent titles include *The Robe of God: Reconciliation, the Believers Church Essential.* He and his wife, Esther, live in Harrisonburg, Virginia.